# Candidates, Parties, and Campaigns

# Candidates, Parties, and Campaigns

## Electoral Politics in America

### SECOND EDITION

Barbara G. Salmore
*Drew University*

Stephen A. Salmore
*Eagleton Institute of Politics,
Rutgers University*

A Division of Congressional Quarterly Inc.
1414 22nd Street N.W., Washington, D.C. 20037

Library of Congress Cataloging-in-Publication Data

Salmore, Barbara G., 1942-
    Candidates, parties, and campaigns : electoral politics in America /
Barbara G. Salmore, Stephen A. Salmore—2nd ed.
    p.    cm.
    Bibliography: p.
    Includes index.
    ISBN 0-87187-484-9
    1. Electioneering—United States.    2. Campaign management—
United States.    I. Salmore, Stephen A., 1941    II. Title.
JK 1976.S25      1989
324.7'0973—dc19
                                                      88-38053
                                                         CIP

In memory of
Walter Salmore, M.D.
February 20, 1903—November 21, 1983
and for
Elizabeth Hiatt Salmore
Born February 20, 1976
who represent the past and future of American politics

# Contents

# Preface

It has never ceased to amaze us how few political scientists who write or teach about American electoral politics participate actively in political campaigns. This observation is a fitting way to begin this book, because the disjunction between politics and political science was both our greatest frustration and our greatest challenge when we began work on the first edition of *Candidates, Parties, and Campaigns* in the early 1980s.

Over the course of our own lives, we have witnessed remarkable changes in American political campaigns. When we were children, various of our relatives were workers in powerful urban political party machines. When we were young adults, we enthusiastically joined the marches and movements directed at least peripherally at replacing those machine politicians with more issue- and candidate-oriented activists. As we reached middle age, we became sometime professional participants in candidate-centered campaigns. With this experience we did not, as the saying goes, need a Ph.D. to see how much more important candidates and their campaign strategies now are to election outcomes than they were in the days of party-centered campaigns.

Our problem, however, was that we *did* have Ph.D.s—in political science—and much of what we read in the political science literature and dutifully taught our students about candidates, parties, and campaigns did not match what we were learning from experience. Surely the favored academic interpretations of election outcomes—distributions of party loyalty, levels of presidential popularity, the state of the economy, and previous incumbency—were powerful ones. But we knew that candidates and their campaign strategies were having an increasing independent effect—and one that was little studied and not well understood by most political scientists. We set out to write about these changes.

It was not easy to do the "academic" research to which we were accustomed. The political science literature was sparse, and data archives did not collect much that was relevant to studying campaign effects. Even the professional literature was meager; full-time campaign professionals for hire were mostly a phenomenon of the past decade. Much of our original conceptualizing and the data to support it, therefore, came from our own experiential learning and from the generous formal and informal interviews, provisions of campaign materials, and critiques of our ideas that campaign participants granted us.

As we complete our work on the second edition, we are astonished and delighted at how much things have changed in only a few years. Some of the same political scientists who were interested in but skeptical about our views on the roles of candidates, campaigns, and parties now inundate the academic journals with elegant empirical confirmations of many of our central arguments. Campaign journals that were struggling or just beginning are now fat and glossy publications, and the American Association of Political Consultants has taken on the shape of other professional organizations. Internal campaign polls and texts of political advertisements are now readily accessible by subscription to electronic data base services; the year's best political ads can also be purchased on videocassettes. Raw data from the major media polls are available from the standard social science data depositories. Campaign reportage in the print media has expanded and become more sophisticated.

There is thus a growing consensus on the changed role and importance of candidates and campaigns of interest to anyone who wants to understand elections and the subsequent behavior of officeholders. In this book we try to give the reader a framework for comprehending how and why these changes occurred. We identify the characteristics of successful and unsuccessful campaigns and examine the changing role of American political parties in elections. Every chapter in this second edition has been extensively revised and updated to take account of the wealth of new material, and some of the chapters are partly or entirely new.

Chapter 1 elaborates on how and why candidates and campaigns came to play a larger role in determining election outcomes and sets out the major elements that influence contemporary campaigns. Chapters 2 and 3 provide historical background. We begin with a description of the era of party-centered campaigns and end with an accounting of the post-World War II socioeconomic and technological changes that brought an end to party-centered campaigns.

The next six chapters look intensively at the current candidate-centered and technology-driven campaigns. We see campaigns as proceeding through three stages. In the first stage candidates assemble the information and personnel that will enable them to find out what voters think, to become known to those voters, and to plan their broad strategies. Incumbents and challengers face such different tasks in this stage that we treat them separately, in chapters 4 and 5, respectively.

In the second stage, when candidates attempt to set their campaigns' agendas, they must develop specific themes and persuasive arguments. Themes may turn on issues, candidate images and records, national trends, or some combination. They are also affected by the candidate's position as an incumbent or a challenger and by the office being sought. Chapter 6 elaborates on these points. Chapter 7 discusses the determinants that affect which "paid" media, or advertising, are used to disseminate themes and the relationship between campaigns and the press—the "free," or "earned," media. This chapter also contains a new extended discussion of negative campaigning.

In the third stage campaign organizations attempt to counter charges by their opponents and get enough voters to the polls on election day to ensure victory. These activities, and the elements affecting them, are the subject of chapter 8.

Chapter 9, new to this edition, is devoted to a series of case studies that illustrate the major points made in the previous five chapters; these cases show how campaign organizations "put it all together"—or why they fail to do so.

In the final two chapters, we return to the broader questions with which we begin the book. In chapter 10 we look at newly emerging strategies in candidate-centered campaigns and the current and future roles of their major players—professional consultants, political action committees, and the political parties. Recent developments we discuss in more detail or for the first time in this chapter include changing patterns of independent expenditures, high-tech campaigning in local races, and the growth of the legislative caucus as a campaign instrument in the states. Because political parties historically have been so central to American elections, the final chapter focuses on their changing role. We suggest that the American parties are now best understood not as independent social formations but as loose coalitions of officeholders running under the same label and held together by a mutual interest in winning as a means of advancing their individual careers and policy preferences.

Any work that depends as heavily on observation and interviews as this one does truly could not have been written without the help of many people. Our first and greatest debt is to those we spoke with formally and informally about the campaigns described in this book. Many are named in the text; those who requested anonymity know who they are and how grateful we are to them. Some of these people also read part or all of the manuscript and gave us helpful suggestions.

Academic colleagues also assisted us. C. Anthony Broh, Richard Fenno, Julius Mastro, Larry Sabato, and Susan Tolchin read and commented on various versions of the original manuscript. John Bibby and John Petrocik reviewed the first edition for CQ Press. John R. Wright critiqued the first edition as we began to think about revisions and also commented on proposed changes and additions to the present version. These colleagues' suggestions helped to strengthen and clarify our thinking, and we are genuinely grateful to all of them. Any errors that remain are ours. Many friends, students, and students who became friends acted as volunteer clipping services in many parts of the country. We acknowledge with special appreciation the contributions of Steve Brown, Bill Faber, Peggy Williamson, and especially Marc Scarduffa.

CQ Press convinced us early that we had chosen the right publisher. We cannot sufficiently praise the encouragement, cooperation, and close attention given to us and our work by various individuals at Congressional Quarterly. We especially thank CQ Press director Joanne Daniels, whose sense of which of her authors' enthusiasms should be encouraged and which restrained is uncanny, and our editor, Ann Davies, who never met a modifier she couldn't place correctly.

Our respective employers, Drew University and Rutgers University, made our work possible. The Drew faculty development program and the Rutgers faculty academic study program gave us each a year free of teaching and administrative responsibilities and funds to defray travel and clerical expenses when we wrote the original manuscript; the second edition benefited from awards of released time and administrative support from the same institutions. The Eagleton Institute of Politics at Rutgers University provides a climate that encourages the study of both academic and practical politics, and this book reflects in many ways the unique blend that makes Eagleton distinctive.

Because our work on this book is a joint enterprise, we plan to reverse the order of authorship for each new edition.

Finally, we take note of the two people to whom this book is dedicated. Walter Salmore was born during Theodore Roosevelt's presidency, was raised in a partisan family, and served as a precinct captain in Edward J. Flynn's powerful Bronx party organization. Elizabeth Salmore was born on her grandfather's birthday, near the time of the 1976 New Hampshire primary. She began watching politics on television at an early age, listened to impassioned political debates between her parents, and by the age of four was a self-proclaimed independent. Together, their political experiences are the story of this book.

# Candidates, Parties, and Campaigns

# Studying American Political Campaigns

1

*The behavior of the candidates during the campaign is one of the least influential factors in determining electoral outcomes.*

A noted political scientist, 1968[1]

*Candidate evaluations have been shown to be a primary determinant of the vote.... In the American system of elections, the choice is ultimately between competing candidates.*

A noted political scientist, 1979[2]

American political campaigns have often been the subject of anecdotal gossip and entertainment but rarely of serious analysis. Those who have studied politics almost always have attributed electoral outcomes to anything but the actual campaigns. Some combination of factors—party loyalty, presidential popularity, incumbency, the state of the economy, and, occasionally, foreign affairs—was widely accepted as the explanation for the results. The majority party usually won, and so did incumbents, except when faced with damaging domestic events or personal scandal. This was particularly true of nonpresidential candidates, whose fortunes were closely tied to their political parties and the popularity, or lack thereof, of their parties' presidential candidates.

This may have been true a generation ago, when the main ingredients of a successful campaign for any political office in the United States were support by leaders of the candidate's political party, effective command of the party's workers, and heavy use of shoe leather. Today, candidates more eagerly seek the support of pollsters and media advisers than of party bosses. Computer-generated letters and television advertisements replace the party canvassers. Candidates still take to the stump, but where they go is determined by what appearance will make the best "visual" for television news. This book is about the role of campaigns in American politics, the effect of the new campaign styles on American voters and their government, and the critical change from party-centered to candidate-centered campaigns.

This change is illustrated by the stories of two candidates. Each wanted to be elected governor of the largest state in the nation during a period of social and economic upheaval. Each made government's role in management of the economy the centerpiece of his campaign. Each advanced somewhat radical ideas in the context of contemporary politics, but ideas that provoked much popular attention and discussion. Each was a charismatic figure who attracted many people by the force of his personality. Each was successfully elected and then reelected governor and later president of the United States.

One of these candidates was Franklin Delano Roosevelt, elected governor of New York in 1928. The other was Ronald Reagan, elected governor of California in 1966. Almost forty years separate their gubernatorial campaigns, and thereby hangs the tale of this book. A brief look at their very different political careers tells why.[3]

Franklin Roosevelt made his career by climbing through the ranks of the Democratic party. In 1910 the local party organization in Dutchess County, New York, where he was born, urged him to run for the New York State Senate. They saw to it that he was nominated at the county convention. For his work at the 1912 Democratic national convention on behalf of Woodrow Wilson, he was rewarded with an appointment as assistant secretary of the Navy. During his eight years in that position, he carefully cultivated Democratic politicians nationally and was eventually chosen to be the party's vice-presidential nominee in 1920.

Retired by defeat that year and shortly thereafter stricken with polio, Roosevelt used his long period of recuperation to correspond with local and national Democrats. Party leaders asked him to make what became his famous "Happy Warrior" nomination speech for Alfred E. Smith at the 1928 national party convention. A few weeks later the New York State party urged him to be its 1928 gubernatorial nominee. Roosevelt, unsure of his feelings, would not campaign for the post, but the party drafted and nominated him by acclamation at its state convention. His campaign manager was the Democratic leader in the state assembly. Two of his chief lieutenants were James A. Farley, secretary of the Democratic State Committee, and Edward J. Flynn, Democratic boss of the Bronx. With the support of the party, he eked out a narrow victory in a big Republican year.

As a member of the party's progressive wing, Roosevelt was

embroiled in many disputes with the famous New York City Democratic machine, Tammany Hall. He characteristically sought compromise, however, and, when necessary, alliance with Tammany. His position as governor of the country's most populous state made him a contender for the presidency in 1932. His vigorous efforts to revitalize the moribund national party machinery, which had atrophied during long years of Republican dominance, further enhanced his prospects.

Roosevelt had entered party politics shortly after completing law school. In contrast, after graduating from college in Illinois, Ronald Reagan became a radio announcer for an Iowa station, specializing in recreating baseball games as they came over a telegraph wire. His skill won him a Hollywood screen test in 1937. A career in mostly B movies followed. During these years, Reagan became president of the Screen Actors Guild and, as a New Deal Democrat, he actively supported Harry Truman in 1948 as well as local Democratic candidates in California. In the mid-1950s his movie career faltered, and he spent the next decade in corporate public relations for General Electric and the U.S. Borax Company. He hosted programs they sponsored (first "G.E. Theater" and then "Death Valley Days") in television's early days as a national medium and represented the corporations in public and at their work-places. Family influences and close association with corporate executives helped shift his political thinking in a more conservative direction.

Although still a registered Democrat, Reagan began to involve himself in conservative Republican campaigns in California in 1962, and he served as co-chairman of the California Committee for Goldwater-Miller in 1964. A group of wealthy business executives who had supported Barry Goldwater urged Reagan to run for governor in 1966. Throughout 1965 Reagan, his financial backers, and his brother (vice president of a large advertising agency) held talks with Spencer-Roberts, a political public relations firm, which had worked for Nelson Rockefeller and against Goldwater in 1964. As soon as Spencer-Roberts was hired in late 1965, the company began a direct mail campaign to collect money and supporters for Reagan's candidacy, which was announced in a televised speech in January 1966. Spencer-Roberts directed and organized his successful primary and general election campaigns. Both campaigns relied heavily on the kind of informal, friendly television presentations that Reagan had perfected in his years as a performer. After two terms as governor, Reagan would become in 1981 the president the media called the "Great Communicator."

Franklin Roosevelt was elected governor with the personnel and machinery of a great political party, after years of service in that party. Ronald Reagan was elected governor with the personnel and techniques of contemporary public relations—and with only the label of a party he had joined four years earlier. The changes their careers typify have come about because of technology. Television and the computer in particular have made it possible for voters to get political information from nonparty sources and for candidates to reach voters and learn their concerns without the party apparatus. Successful candidates who have campaigned as individuals rather than as representatives of a party tailor their appeals to a carefully targeted constituency. Often they have few ties to other elected officials, even of the same party, and little incentive to consider broad-based national interests rather than those of the constituency that elected them—and that they hope will elect them again. Thus the effect of media-based and candidate-centered campaigns does not end when an election season is over.

The new style of campaigning has had its greatest effect on nonpresidential elections because the material the campaign disseminates is often almost the only information voters will have. Long before major presidential contenders run for office, the public has at least vague images of them because of intensive media coverage of the candidates' activities. Almost no other candidates—senators, representatives, governors, mayors, and members of the state legislatures—are covered by the media in any way that would penetrate the popular consciousness. Most voters learn about these candidates as their campaigns progress. The result is that within constraints imposed by their environments and by the resources available to them, nonpresidential candidates have a great deal of freedom to shape the information voters receive about them. In short, the quality of the nonpresidential campaign has the greatest potential to determine its outcome—victory or defeat.

Many excellent academic and popular treatments of presidential campaigns have been written.[4] Nonpresidential campaigns have received much less sustained attention.[5] They are the focus of this book.

## Campaigns and Their Role in Elections _____

For a long time students of politics, in contrast to candidates and campaigners, believed that campaigns only minimally influenced the outcome of elections. The view of campaign participants is easy to understand. They would be disheartened, if not paralyzed, if they felt their efforts made no difference. Vigorous campaign activity and the rise of the political consulting industry—devoted exclusively to the theory and practice of the way campaign activities can affect electoral outcomes—are testimony to what participants think campaigns can do. But why did academics fail to share this view, and why is it now beginning to change?

The first major academic studies of voting behavior were done in the late 1940s and 1950s when, for reasons we discuss later, campaigns were not very important. Consequently, the theories put forward to explain voting choices and the outcome of elections did not include campaigns, and the accompanying research designs made it difficult to detect their effects. Thus there was a closed circle. Campaigns were left out of academic investigation, and academic research was structured so that any effects they had were unlikely to be discovered.[6] In the remainder of this chapter, we explain why campaigns are now beginning to attract scholarly attention, what we have learned about their conduct and effects, and what the arguments and findings of this book—drawn both from academic research and from campaigners themselves—can contribute to our knowledge about them.

Until recently, political scientists contended that the outcome of most elections was explained primarily by the distribution of loyalties to the two major political parties. The vast majority of voters identified with one or the other of the parties, viewed politics through a partisan lens, and cast their votes accordingly. Party identification, which developed early in life (it was generally passed along from parents to children), became more intense through time and was extremely resistant to change. Voters' reactions to events were shaped by their sense of party affiliation.[7]

Party identification thus was the major consideration in voting choice, and party strength and competition the major determinant of electoral outcomes and their meaning. The campaign consisted primarily of party workers making sure the faithful came out to vote on election day. Only massive social upheaval, on the order of the Industrial Revolution of the late nineteenth century or the Great Depression of the early twentieth, could move sizable numbers of voters to consider abandoning their parties. The elections of 1896 and 1932, for instance, were "critical," or "realigning," elections, followed by a long period of party stability.[8] The effects of these two elections are examined in chapter 2; for the moment we will explore the traditional and the revised view of the role of campaigns in determining election day results.

## The Traditional View: Campaigns as a Minor Factor

The scholarly consensus on the overwhelming importance of party identification and the lack of importance of campaign activities derived from empirical observation and from the conceptual framework and resulting theories of the first studies of voting choice. As noted earlier, the methodology adopted to test these theories of electoral behavior served only to reinforce scholarly belief in the marginal importance of campaigns.

Before the 1950s there was no survey research available to tell us why individuals made voting choices, but analysis of election returns indicated that electoral competition declined sharply after 1896, and for nonpresidential office an increasing number of constituencies were safely one-party.[9] In the 1940s researchers began limited studies of individual voting behavior and, beginning with the 1952 election, had reliable pre- and post-election data from national samples. These early studies, conducted by the Survey Research Center at the University of Michigan and known throughout the political science community as the Michigan surveys, shaped the perception of a generation of political scientists. They revealed the significance of party identification in voting choice and generated the theories about its role.[10]

Unlike some who studied their work, the Michigan researchers recognized the time-bound nature of their data, cautioning that party identification was crucial "in the period of our studies." [11] This era, the late 1940s and the 1950s, followed closely upon the Roosevelt realignment, when party identification could be expected to be most deeply entrenched. Because of the political realities of the time, however, the studies dismissed the effect of campaigns, and their methodology made it difficult or impossible to find evidence to the contrary. With only one survey before an election and one after, it was not easy to determine the consequences of specific campaign strategies or events. Additionally, the surveys asked respondents very little about the campaign, because the theoretical constructs being tested gave them no weight. Finally, national samples of fewer than two thousand respondents, and based on counties, did not permit analysis of nonpresidential campaigns.

In the 1960s it became clear that the public consensus on which the New Deal realignment rested was beginning to decay. The Michigan studies showed that the number of self-identified partisans was declining, that partisans held their allegiance more weakly, and that voting decisions were made later and later in the election season. The amount of split-ticket voting rose dramatically.

It was also apparent that candidates for every office, who had previously depended on party organizations to conduct their campaigns, were responding to the electorate's volatility with major changes in campaign techniques. Some of the new developments were heavy use of the new medium of television, a new reliance on polling and voting data analysis, and greater participation by nonparty personnel—especially public relations and advertising agencies—in campaign planning and direction.[12]

These developments were accompanied by a withering of party organizational activity, as the new actors took over the party's former roles.[13] The changed or weakened party attachments in the 1890s and the 1930s had also led campaigns to use the mass media of the time—printed materials in the earlier period and radio in the later one—to issue persuasive appeals. What made the 1960s different, however, was that, previously, the party organizations had devised these appeals and arranged for their dissemination. From then on it was the organizations of individual candidates that performed these functions.

American party organizations had little left to do. Many unusual features of the American political system absent in most other Western democracies—federalism, separation of powers, staggered elections, and voting based on geographic constituencies rather than a national party list—had always made the American parties instruments for nominating and electing officeholders rather than instruments of governing. It was no wonder that they atrophied as these functions were taken over by others.

## A Revised View:
## Campaigns as a Major Factor

The importance of this electoral volatility and candidates' response to it was at first dismissed. The Michigan researchers acknowledged that "short-term forces" (that is, stimuli other than party identification) were significant in individual elections but contended that they were unlikely to disturb party stability for long: "In the lengthening period of our observation, vote shifts have not been accompanied by conversion but rather have been followed routinely by actual return to the party of original choice." The chances of a "deviating election"—one in which the minority party won the presidency—were estimated as "very much less than even." [14]

This prediction was made in 1966. Since then the minority Republicans have won five of the six presidential elections without reaching majority party status. Their presidential victories did not bring any consistent improvement in Republicans' fortunes in other electoral contests. At first it was suggested that the United States had become a two-tiered party system, in which Republican presidential candidates profited from rejection of a leftward drift among Democratic party activists, although most Democratic identifiers returned to their majority party home in voting for other races. Some researchers pointed out, however, that while national party swings in congressional elections were modest, the range in individual constituencies was five to six times as large.[15]

These puzzling data still did not lead many political scientists to study individual candidates and their campaigns. Instead, incumbency, perception of presidential performance, the state of the economy, the role of the media, and the effect of issues all became objects of attention. Studies in the 1970s documented the increasing power of incumbency. Sizable numbers of party identifiers were voting for congressional and senatorial incumbents of the other party because they were better known to an electorate more and more detached from party loyalties. National congressional vote swings in midterm elections were explained as being strongly related to the popularity of the incumbent president and to shifts in personal disposable income. The role of the media was explored, with much attention given to their greater effect on the more visible presidential contests than on other races and to the greater coverage given to incumbents than to challengers. Finally, voter attitudes about the most salient political issues were seen as strongly affecting both vote choice and party identification.[16]

As work in these new areas of inquiry proceeded, however, the relevance of candidate and campaign effects became apparent. Incumbency was not uniformly helpful; some congressional incumbents of both parties benefited from it more than others. Incumbency was generally more valuable to representatives than to senators and to some senators more than others. Attention was given to variations among challengers and to the factors that were more likely to produce successful challenges—chiefly, political experience and the ability to raise money. Any media advantage enjoyed by congressional incumbents disappeared when challengers had these resources. The apparent rise in issue voting was discovered to be partly because of differences in research methodology and to be confined to certain kinds of electoral contests.[17]

The connection between economic conditions, presidential evaluations, and the competitive stance of midterm congressional challengers also received new scrutiny. Although analysis of election returns showed a relationship among these variables, survey data did not confirm that individual voting choices depended on individual attitudes toward the president or on perceived changes in personal financial status.

By the 1980s the models based on presidential popularity and the state of the economy also grossly overestimated their effects on legislative swings. These models predicted that the Democrats would win about twice as many congressional seats in 1982 as they did. A similar model applied to the 1986 Senate elections estimated the Republicans' chances of maintaining control of the Senate as better than even. It predicted the Republicans would most likely lose two or three seats. The actual outcome was that they lost eight seats and control of the Senate.[18] Studies attempting to link voting choices to attitudes about the economic condition of the country or to groups the voter felt psychologically close to—a phenomenon known as "sociotropic voting"—showed only weak relationships.[19]

The combined impact of these findings directed political scientists to a more serious consideration of the effect on election outcomes of candidates and campaigns. A review of the literature on determinants of the congressional vote concluded: "It makes a difference who the candidates are and what they do. If our interest is in particular congressional races, we would do well to focus on factors related to the candidates themselves." A study of Senate election outcomes reached similar conclusions.[20]

At the same time political scientists also began to study the response of party organizations to the new electoral environment. There was general agreement that the party organizations, in attempting to compete with the purveyors of the new campaign technology, had turned themselves into centralized service bureaus based primarily in Washington, D.C., and in the state capitals. The party organizations now saw their role as being less costly providers of the same services delivered by political consultants for hire. There was, however, substantially less agreement about their success and the extent to which they could reassert themselves as the central players in campaigns.[21]

In 1984 researchers published the first major study devoted to the effect of campaigns on congressional races. It stressed the critical importance of the voters' knowledge of the candidates in determining how they would vote. It is this fact that must lead us to the study of campaigns, because campaigns provide voters with the information they have, primarily through their own paid messages and secondarily through their influence on the media. The authors ended their study with this observation: "Understanding the campaign process requires attention to the considerable diversity among races. . . . Researchers need to think about campaigns as part of a dynamic process—a series of events with both short- and long-term consequences for the character of governance in our system." [22]

We believe that more attention to candidates and campaigns is particularly important, because, unlike the periods following the 1896 and 1932 realignments, parties probably will not reassume their central role either in determining the vote or in spearheading campaigns. Party continues to be important in both areas, but it is no longer the central factor. If voters learn about candidates through campaigns, then what candidates do in their campaigns, we argue in the final chapter, affects not only electoral outcomes but public policy as well.

# A Framework for Studying Campaigns _____

The greater role candidate-centered campaigns now play in American politics and governance makes it necessary to examine how such organizations are structured, what influences their outcomes, and how they differ from traditional party-based campaigns. In this book we discuss the function of campaigns, basic campaign resources and strategies, important contextual considerations that shape campaigns, and the way these considerations operate during the stages through which campaigns pass. The basic arguments are summarized in this section.

## The Function of the Campaign

A political campaign is an attempt to get information to voters that will persuade them to elect a candidate or not to elect an opponent. The first problem a campaign faces is to learn what information will best serve this purpose and to acquire it. The next step is to decide how and when its own messages should be communicated. Obtaining useful and reliable data about the voters—and getting appropriate and persuasive information to them—is what a campaign is all about.

The methods for *acquiring* crucial information are polls and targeting data. Polls are now the major source of information about voters' preferences, attitudes, behavior, and beliefs. Polling has grown ever more sophisticated since it was introduced into politics in the 1930s, but its basic function—ascertaining what voters know, think, and do—has remained the same. Modern-day targeting techniques are merely a more sophisticated version of Abraham Lincoln's call to "find 'em and vote 'em." Past voting patterns, registration data, and turnout statistics are now grist for a computerized mill, as campaigns attempt to identify a winning coalition.

The major vehicles for *disseminating* information to voters are advertising and news coverage. Media messages under the control of the campaign embrace the various forms of paid advertising, including television, radio, and direct mail. News coverage is the journalistic reporting of campaigns in newspapers and magazines and on television and radio. A campaign can and will attempt to influence its coverage by the press but clearly is less able to control those messages than its own.

Information can also be obtained and disseminated through field organizations. Campaign workers who engage in door-to-door or telephone canvassing are conduits to and from the campaign. Like the media, field organizations operate under more or less control by the campaign. In addition to workers recruited and deployed through the campaign structure, favorably disposed outsiders such as interest groups, party organizations, and independent political action committees may disseminate information of their choice about the candidates.

## Campaign Resources

A campaign's ability to conduct its two-way exchange of information depends heavily on the resources it commands.

The three critical resources for any political campaign are money, organization, and the candidate. Money buys polls, targeting data, and advertising, while organization permits direct contact with voters. To some extent, the two are interchangeable resources. A campaign with limited money to purchase media can get its message across with an army of canvassers and supervise the way they bring the message to the voters. A campaign with enough money to buy a great deal of paid advertising can make up for organizational deficiencies, or it can buy the elements of a field operation such as paid telephone banks. The candidates themselves bring a variety of resources to the campaign, including experience, knowledge, contacts, and organizations built in past campaigns. An increasing number also bring a substantial amount of their own money to finance their campaigns.

## Campaign Strategies

Campaign strategies fall into three basic types, although any campaign will be a mix of the three. First, a party-centered strategy relies heavily on voters' partisan identification as well as on the party's organization to provide the resources necessary to wage the campaign. Second, candidates may follow an issue-oriented strategy and seek support from groups that feel strongly about various policies. Finally, a campaign may be shaped significantly by the candidate's image. The candidates hope to gain support because of their perceived personal qualities such as experience, leadership ability, integrity, independence, trustworthiness, and the like.

There is no such thing as *the* winning mix of strategies, for each campaign takes place within a different context. The context does much to define the appropriate strategy and helps determine whether it will be successful. It is possible, however, to identify the important elements that help determine strategy.

## The Context of Campaigns

Any campaign organization operates within a series of givens, which it must consider as it plans its strategy. These aspects of the campaign environment cannot be altered. They significantly affect not only strategy but the amount and kind of resources the campaign requires. The two most critical contextual considerations are which office the candidate is seeking and whether he or she is an incumbent. Less central but still important are partisan balance and strength in the candidate's constituency, its demographic and geographic nature, and national trends.

The office the candidate seeks affects voters' interest, their evaluation of the nominee, and turnout. More people vote for candidates for an executive office such as governor than for a legislative office such as senator, even though both are statewide positions. Voters also measure the qualifications for executive and legislative office differently. Interest in statewide races is higher than in local races. In addition, other races on the ballot in any given year have an effect. Turnout for congressional elections, for example, is higher in presidential election years than in off-years.

The candidates' positions greatly influence campaign strategy. In most campaigns one candidate is the incumbent, and other candidates are challengers who may or may not hold political office. Sometimes the contested office is open—that is, no incumbent is running. The strategies adopted by incumbents, challengers, and contestants for open seats are very different. Strategies will also be affected by the candidate's history of officeholding.

Although both the organizational strength of American political parties and their capacity to inspire psychological attachments have declined, party identification and activity are by no means unimportant to campaign strategists. In many areas party activists constitute the majority of those voting in low-turnout elections. In many areas most voters still identify with one party, and the strength of that identification remains the best predictor of both turnout and vote choice. This is not to say that the candidate of the minority party invariably loses, but that party balance and strength, like the other factors listed, will affect strategy and the use and amount of resources needed.

The most important characteristics of a constituency are its compactness and its homogeneity. Some congressional districts in large, sparsely populated states cover areas bigger than entire small, densely populated states. Some electoral constituencies have economically, ethnically, and racially homogeneous populations, while others are highly fragmented. A constituency may be entirely urban, suburban, or rural, or it may be a mixture. All these considerations also affect the choice of strategy and the need for different kinds and amounts of resources.

Although the most important contextual considerations pertain to the candidates themselves and to their constituencies, significant national trends may often have a substantial effect. Issues of compelling interest, such as Watergate in the 1970s and the state of the economy in the early 1980s, can influence electoral contests. Other candidates for office on the same ticket, even in these days of weaker party identification, can affect the fortunes of those running with them. Campaign strategy must take the possible consequences of these trends into account. Much of this book is devoted to analyzing the complex interconnections of context, strategy, and resources for various kinds of campaigns.

## The Stages of a Campaign

Campaigns can be studied from two interrelated but different perspectives. We can look either at how campaigns attempt to influence voters or at what the effects of those influences are. The first approach focuses on campaigns as organizations and on their behavior; the second examines the way their activities shape the voters' behavior. In this book we concentrate on the first perspective, while realizing that campaign activities are determined in large measure by the expected and actual response of the electorate to the organizations' messages.

During an election contest, voters' attitudes about candidates are formed in a three-phase process, which corresponds to the three components of attitudes that social scientists call *cognition, affect,* and *evaluation.*[23] These phases are sequential and hierarchical. In the cognition phase voters become aware that a candidate is running for office and associate the name with the race. Political consultants call this *raw recognition,* and without media coverage and vigorous campaign activity, it is surprisingly difficult to achieve. Once the candidates are recognized, the second, or affect, phase involves voters' developing opinions about the candidates. Basing their decisions on the candidates' attributes, voters decide whether they are positively or negatively disposed toward them. Finally, in the evaluation phase the voters decide whether to vote or not and for whom.

A campaign can influence each phase a voter goes through in deciding whom to vote for or whether to vote at all. Candidates must become known if they are to have any opportunity to influence voters' choices. Candidates who do not achieve recognition and favorable evaluations have effectively lost the race long before election day.

A successful campaign organization also passes through a three-step process. In the first stage of a campaign, it must create the conditions that will make it possible for its candidate to become known to the public—by building an organization to publicize the candidate, by acquiring the necessary information about the electorate, and by generating the resources to carry out these tasks. In the second stage it must determine the criteria by which both its candidate and the candidate's opponent are to be judged by the public. It attempts to get voters to use the campaign's criteria in evaluating the contenders, by disseminating the messages that set the campaign's agenda. In the third stage it tries to reinforce or alter the images of the contenders the public develops, to mobilize a winning coalition and to ensure that its supporters vote.

The first stage of this three-step process is usually invisible to the public—what we call in chapter 4 the *internal campaign*. It is only in the second and third stages—*the external campaign*—that the campaign organizations begin their public arguments. But the ability to make convincing arguments is strongly dependent upon successfully completing the tasks of the first stage.

Each stage demands different uses of what resources provide— polling results, targeting data, media messages, and voter contact. In addition, strategies in each stage will vary depending on the contextual considerations of the campaign. These stages of a campaign are also sequential and hierarchical. A candidate who never becomes known cannot set the agenda of the campaign, acquire a winning coalition of supporters, or get its supporters to the polls.

The discussion in this book is organized according to the stages campaigns pass through, but it also necessarily attends, as campaigners do, to their effects on voters. In the chapters that follow we elaborate on the major points in this chapter: the evolution of party-centered campaigns into candidate-centered ones, the conduct of modern campaigns, the path that campaigns are likely to take in the future, and their effects on other important aspects of American politics and governance. We begin that process in the next chapter by looking at the way American campaigns were conducted before a great watershed—the rise and spread of television.

## Notes

1. Charles O. Jones, "The Role of the Campaign," in *The Electoral Process*, ed. Kent Jennings and Harmon O. Ziegler (Englewood Cliffs, N.J.: Prentice-Hall, 1968), 4.
2. Gregory B. Markus and Philip E. Converse, "A Dynamic Simultaneous Model of Electoral Choice," *American Political Science Review* 70 (December 1979): 1068.
3. See James MacGregor Burns, *Roosevelt: The Lion and the Fox* (New York: Harcourt, Brace, 1956), and Lou Cannon, *Reagan* (New York: Putnam, 1982), for excellent descriptions of their early careers.
4. Every presidential election brings a spate of popular analyses. The finest are the individual volumes by Theodore H. White on the elections between 1960 and 1980, summarized in *America in Search of Itself* (New York: Harper, 1982).

Academic treatments include many studies of individual elections as well as more general treatments of the presidential campaign process. Among the latter, some of the most durable are Nelson W. Polsby and Aaron Wildavsky, *Presidential Elections*, 7th ed. (New York: Free Press, 1988); Herbert Asher, *Presidential Elections and American Politics*, 4th ed. (Chicago: Dorsey, 1988); John Kessel, *Presidential Campaign Politics*, 3d ed. (Chicago: Dorsey, 1988); and Stephen J. Wayne, *The Road to the White House*, 3d ed. (New York: St. Martin's, 1988).

5. This smaller literature includes Edie N. Goldenberg and Michael W. Traugott, *Campaigning for Congress* (Washington, D.C.: CQ Press, 1984); Marjorie Randon Hershey, *Running for Office* (Chatham, N.J.: Chatham House, 1984); Stuart Rothenberg, *Winners and Losers: Campaigns, Candidates and Congressional Elections* (Washington, D.C.: Free Congress Research and Education Foundation, 1983); Alan L. Clem, *The Making of Congressmen* (North Scituate, Mass.: Duxbury, 1976). Most of these works are studies of campaigns for particular offices rather than general analyses of nonpresidential campaigns.

6. See the similar analysis in Goldenberg and Traugott, *Campaigning for Congress*, chapter 1.

7. Angus Campbell, Philip E. Converse, Warren E. Miller, and Donald E. Stokes, *The American Voter* (New York: Wiley, 1960), 135.

8. See James L. Sundquist, *Dynamics of the Party System*, rev. ed. (Washington, D.C.: Brookings Institution, 1983); Walter Dean Burnham, *Critical Elections and the Mainsprings of American Politics* (New York: Norton, 1970).

9. See Burnham, *Critical Elections*; Joel H. Silbey, Allan G. Bogue, and William H. Flanigan, ed., *The History of American Electoral Behavior* (Princeton, N.J.: Princeton University Press, 1978).

10. Campbell et al., *American Voter*. The earlier important studies are Paul Lazarsfeld, Bernard R. Berelson, and Hazel Gaudet, *The People's Choice* (New York: Duell, Sloan, and Pierce, 1944); Bernard R. Berelson, Paul Lazarsfeld, and William N. McPhee, *Voting* (Chicago: University of Chicago Press, 1954); and Angus Campbell, Gerald Gurin, and Warren E. Miller, *The Voter Decides* (Evanston, Ill.: Row, Peterson, 1954).

11. Campbell et al., *American Voter*, 135.

12. Important early studies of the new campaign techniques include Stanley Kelley, Jr., *Professional Public Relations and Political Power* (Baltimore: Johns Hopkins University Press, 1956); Dan Nimmo, *The Political Persuaders* (Englewood Cliffs, N.J.: Prentice-Hall, 1970); and James M. Perry, *The New Politics* (New York: Clarkson N. Potter, 1968).

13. On these developments, see Alan Ware, *The Breakdown of Democratic Party Organization, 1940-80* (Oxford: Clarendon Press, 1985); Larry J. Sabato, *The Rise of Political Consultants* (New York: Basic Books, 1983).

14. Philip E. Converse, "The Concept of a Normal Vote," in *Elections and the Political Order*, ed. Angus Campbell et al. (New York: Wiley, 1966), 15; Donald E. Stokes, "Party Loyalty and the Likelihood of Deviating Elections," in Campbell, *Elections*, 133.

15. See Everett C. Ladd with Charles D. Hadley, *Transformations of the American Party System*, 2d ed. (New York: Norton, 1978), 262-272; Thomas E. Mann, *Unsafe at Any Margin* (Washington, D.C.: American Enterprise Institute, 1978), 14-16.

16. On the incumbency effect, see David Mayhew, *Congress: The Electoral*

*Connection* (New Haven, Conn.: Yale University Press, 1974). The role of presidential performance and the state of the economy is documented in Edward Tufte, "Determinants of the Outcome of Midterm Congressional Elections," *American Political Science Review* 69 (September 1975): 812-826. Important studies of the role of the media are Thomas E. Patterson, *The Mass Media Election: How Americans Choose Their President* (New York: Praeger, 1980); Thomas E. Patterson and Robert D. McClure, *The Unseeing Eye: The Myth of Television Power in National Politics* (New York: Putnam, 1976); and Michael J. Robinson, "Three Faces of Congressional Media," in *The New Congress,* ed. Thomas E. Mann and Norman Ornstein (Washington, D.C.: American Enterprise Institute, 1981). The role of issues is treated in Warren E. Miller and Teresa Levitan, *Leadership and Change* (Cambridge, Mass.: Winthrop, 1976); Norman H. Nie, Sidney Verba, and John R. Petrocik, *The Changing American Voter* (Cambridge, Mass.: Harvard University Press, 1976); and Gerald M. Pomper, "From Confusion to Clarity: Issues and American Voters 1952-1968," *American Political Science Review* 66 (June 1972): 1256-1268.

17. Reconsiderations of the role of incumbency and the effect of the particular office appear in Mann, *Unsafe at Any Margin;* Alan I. Abramowitz, "Name Familiarity, Reputation and the Incumbency Effect in a Congressional Election," *Western Political Quarterly* 27 (December 1975): 668-684; Abramowitz, "A Comparison of Voting for U.S. Senate and Representative in 1978," *American Political Science Review* 74 (September 1980): 633-640; Abramowitz, "Choices and Echoes in the 1978 U.S. Senate Elections: A Research Note," *American Journal of Political Science* 25 (February 1981): 112-118; Abramowitz, "Explaining Senate Election Outcomes," *American Political Science Review* 82 (June 1988): 385-403; Barbara Hinckley, "House Reelections and Senate Defeats," *British Journal of Political Science* 10 (October 1980): 441-460. The role of challengers is explored in Gary C. Jacobson and Samuel Kernell, *Strategy and Choice in Congressional Elections* (New Haven, Conn.: Yale University Press, 1981); Mark C. Westlye, "Competitiveness of Senate Seats and Voting Behavior in Senate Elections," *American Journal of Political Science* 27 (May 1983): 253-283; Lyn Ragsdale and Timothy E. Cook, "Representatives' Actions and Challengers' Reactions: Limits to Candidate Connections in the House," *American Journal of Political Science* 31 (February 1987): 45-81. The role of the media in congressional elections is investigated in Peter Clarke and Susan H. Evans, *Covering Campaigns: Journalism in Congressional Elections* (Stanford, Calif.: Stanford University Press, 1983). The research on the role of issues is summarized in Herbert B. Asher, *Presidential Elections and American Politics* (Chicago: Dorsey, 1988), chapter 4.

18. Alan I. Abramowitz and Jeffrey A. Segal, "Determinants of the Outcomes of U.S. Senate Elections," *Journal of Politics* 48 (May 1986): 433-439.

19. D. Roderick Kiewiet, *Macroeconomics and Micropolitics: The Electoral Effects of Economic Issues* (Chicago: University of Chicago Press, 1983); Gerald H. Kramer, "The Ecological Fallacy Revisited: Aggregate Versus Individual Level Findings on Economics and Elections and Sociotropic Voting," *American Political Science Review* 77 (March 1983): 92-111.

20. Richard G. Niemi and Herbert F. Weisberg, *Controversies in Voting Behavior,* 2d ed. (Washington, D.C.: CQ Press, 1984), 206; Gerald C. Wright, Jr., and Michael B. Berkman, "Candidates and Policy in United States Senate Elections," *American Political Science Review* 80 (June 1986): 584.

21. This subject is addressed at length in chapters 10 and 11 of this book. Major

works painting an optimistic picture of the party organizations' role include Xandra Kayden and Eddie Mayhe, *The Party Goes On* (New York: Basic Books, 1985); Cornelius P. Cotter et al., *Party Organizations in American Politics* (New York: Praeger, 1984); Joseph A. Schlesinger, "The New American Political Party," *American Political Science Review* 79 (December 1985): 1152-1169; Paul S. Herrnson, *Party Campaigning in the 1980s* (Cambridge, Mass.: Harvard University Press, 1988). More modest assessments of their success include Leon Epstein, *Political Parties in the American Mold* (Madison: University of Wisconsin Press, 1986); Bruce Cain, John Ferejohn, and Morris Fiorina, *The Personal Vote* (Cambridge, Mass.: Harvard University Press, 1987); and Gary C. Jacobson, *The Politics of Congressional Elections*, 2d ed. (Boston: Little, Brown, 1987). In *The Party's Just Begun* (Glenview, Ill.: Scott, Foresman, 1988), Larry J. Sabato argues that while party-centered campaigns are unlikely to supersede candidate-centered ones, nonetheless, party organizations can take new steps to increase their relative importance.
22. Goldenberg and Traugott, *Campaigning for Congress*, 187-188.
23. Ibid.

# American Political Campaigns Before Television

# 2

*One of the most remarkable peculiarities of the present time is that the principal leaders of the political parties are travelling about the country from state to state, and holding forth like Methodist preachers, hour after hour, to assembled multitudes, under the broad canopy of heaven.*

John Quincy Adams, 1827[1]

*The media have done to the campaign system what the invention of accurate artillery did to the feudal kingdom—destroyed the barons and shifted their power to the masses and the prince. A candidate now pays less attention to district leaders than to opinion polls.*

Stimson Bullitt, 1961[2]

A summary of recent trends in American political campaigning would begin like this: Since about 1950 American political campaigns have become increasingly candidate-centered. All aspects of a campaign—its organization, fund-raising techniques, polling, and media messages— exist for the sole purpose of electing a particular candidate to a particular office. Appeals to voters communicate an "image"—a combination of a candidate's personal characteristics and his or her issue positions. Campaigns are organized and directed by "hired guns"—people who have performed the same specialized tasks in other campaigns in the past. They know what information should be gathered in polls at various stages, what kinds of media messages are required at various points in the campaign, which sorts of direct mail lists will produce the most contributions, and so on. Organizational efforts are directed at identifying, and bringing to the polls, those voters who might favor the candidate.

This description will sound banal to anyone who came to political maturity in the television age. Yet for a century or more, as observed in chapter 1, American political campaigns were party-centered, not candidate-centered. The appeals of campaigns were to party identification and loyalty; the campaign organizations were party organizations. Party domination extended beyond campaigns; for a long period parties largely controlled the nomination and election processes as well. Throughout the nineteenth century, candidates were chosen in party caucuses and conventions rather than in primary elections, and voters cast their ballots on forms provided by the parties, not by nonpartisan election boards. Clearly, this was a very different kind of politics.

# Reasons for the Decline
# in Party-Centered Campaigns

Some of the most important reasons that party-centered campaigns declined and came to be replaced by candidate-centered ones can be sketched here. First was the enormous growth in the voting population because of natural increase and the gradual extension of the franchise to nonproperty owners, women, southern blacks, and, most recently, eighteen- to twenty-year-olds. Second was the rising tide of industrialization, the attendant movement of the population into heterogeneous urban centers, and the breakup of longstanding homogeneous rural communities. Third was the rise of the mass media and their role in personalizing and nationalizing issues, individuals, and culture. Finally, there was the altered role of government itself. As government, particularly the federal government, grew larger and assumed regulatory and social welfare functions, its relation to the public changed profoundly. American political parties, designed for face-to-face local campaigns to a limited electorate living in stable communities, were hard-pressed to cope with these disruptions in the social order.

American campaigns did not, of course, evolve from the party-centered to the candidate-centered mode overnight. Rather, the premodern campaign era can be divided into three stages: the period until about 1830 to 1840, from the 1840s until about 1890, and the years between 1890 and 1950. Before the third decade of the nineteenth century, limits on the franchise and the indirect election of the president made it necessary to aim campaign messages at only a small portion of the population. As the franchise expanded and members of the electoral college were selected by voters rather than by the state legislatures, mobilization of a mass voting population by political parties became critically important. Thus until about 1890 all campaigns were in fact party-centered—the party organization, not the candidates, was in charge.

The years from 1890 to 1950 were a transition period. Superficially, parties still dominated the nomination and campaign processes, but beneath the surface antiparty and nonparty elements were gaining strength. The Populists and Progressives of the late nineteenth and early twentieth centuries pushed for changes that weakened the parties—the direct primary, the direct election of senators, and the secret ballot. The development of mass media—national wire services in the late nineteenth century, radio in the first decades of the twentieth century, and television a few decades later—made it possible for voters to receive political information from sources other than the parties. The spread of the railroads and the mass production of the automobile permitted the mobility that is now characteristic of Americans and that weakened their ties to local party organizations. These innovations made possible the first insurgent candidacies—candidacies not championed or sanctioned by party organizations.

Traditional campaigning, centered on party identification and organization, was first modified in presidential campaigns; the new style of electioneering worked its way down to lower offices only gradually. Presidential candidates always had to face the most heterogeneous constituency. Because the White House was the biggest prize, especially as issues became nationalized and federal patronage grew, presidential campaigns commanded the greatest resources in terms of both money and organization. These resources, and the national constituency of presidential candidates, made it both possible and desirable to adopt nonparty modes of campaigning.

We have described campaigns as a process of communicating information to persuade voters to elect a candidate. As technology advanced, parties and candidates adopted each newly available means of communication but often long after it had been used for other purposes. Three particular situations prompt campaigners to look for new ways of reaching voters: periods of social and political upheaval, attempts by insurgents to challenge a party-backed nominee, and vigorous efforts by minority party candidates to challenge the entrenched majority party's candidates.

Because presidential candidates had more available resources and because mass communication was especially well suited to their far-flung constituencies, it was in the race for the White House that the new techniques were first used. These techniques were then copied by lower level campaigns.

# The Era of Party-Centered Campaigns: 1830-1890 _____

In this chapter we describe the pure party-centered campaigns that characterized most of the nineteenth century and the transition period in the first half of the twentieth century that saw the beginning of the movement away from the party-centered campaign.

## The Importance of Politics in Everyday Life

To comprehend the role of political campaigns in nineteenth-century America, we need to understand the role of politics in that era. We have to imagine a world without television, without radio, without films, without organized spectator sports. For the nineteenth-century American, the two chief diversions were religious observance and politics; often they reinforced each other. The mass followings of the major parties were rooted in ethnic and religious divisions, particularly between Protestants and Catholics and between evangelical and non-evangelical Protestants. Religious and political groups had structural similarities. Discussing his vision for local party organizations, a Whig politician in 1840 wrote:

> The model of my primary local association is the Christian Church. The officers, the exercises, the exhortations, the singing, the weekly meetings, the enrollment of members, the contributions, and all are to be on the primitive apostolic model as presented in the Congregational churches of New England. Then I want itinerant lecturers, political preachers going about in regular circuits, next spring and summer, on the Methodist plan.... Each of all the hundreds of thousands of members of these associations will also make a weekly contribution of one cent to the great cause of our "church militant."[3]

The American zeal for politics was readily apparent to European visitors. Alexis de Tocqueville, in a famous passage in *Democracy in America,* described the unique role politics played in American social life in the 1830s:

> The political activity that pervades the United States must be seen in order to be understood. No sooner do you set foot upon American ground than you are stunned by a kind of tumult; a confused clamor is heard on every side, and a thousand simultaneous voices demand the satisfaction of their social wants.... To take a hand in the regulation of society, and to discuss it, is his biggest concern and, so to speak, the only pleasure an American knows.[4]

Endless rounds of political gatherings were a feature of both urban and rural life. In the cities they resembled street carnivals. A nineteenth-century New Yorker described a Democratic rally in New York City in 1864: "Tricolored lanterns were strung over the streets, and boys carrying more lanterns circulated among the mob of people who strolled past the dozen speakers' platforms eating peaches and oranges." [5] In rural areas farmers came from miles around to listen to political oratory at a local picnic or fairground. Crowds reached as high as twenty-five thousand. When Stephen Douglas and Abraham Lincoln held their famous series of debates in the 1858 Illinois Senate race, throngs of people attended, even though Senate elections then took place in the state legislature, and ordinary citizens could not vote directly for either Douglas or Lincoln. A Chicago journalist wrote of one of their rural encounters:

> It was a glorious sight to see the long line of teams filled with men, women and children, extending down the prairie as far as the eye could reach, the flags gaily flying in the morning breeze, and the brass instruments of the numerous bands gleaming in the sun. At every house and every crossroad, the procession received accessions, until when entering Charleston, it was nearly two miles long. [6]

## A Reliance on Partisanship

The political parties were able to organize these massive rallies because of the fervent partisanship of their supporters, rooted in social and religious issues such as prohibition, antislavery, nativism, and Sunday observance. Careful studies of nineteenth-century partisanship in various regions of the country repeatedly confirm that "party loyalty was extraordinary and almost unshakable, and voting turnout amazingly high," particularly after the the cultural and sectional disputes of the 1830s and 1840s and the Civil War. [7]

Although partisanship was virtually unshakable during most of the nineteenth century, the two major parties (first the Whigs and the Democrats, later the Republicans and the Democrats) were nationally very close in strength through much of the period. It was essential that their easily identified supporters come out to vote on the numerous state and federal election days. Campaign appeals were aimed at rallying the faithful and were often vituperative and contemptuous of the opposition. The major campaign technique in this era has been aptly described as "military." Parties commonly organized paramilitary units of supporters whose job it was to get out their vote. In the 1860 four-candidate presidential election, for instance, these quasi-military uniformed units were Stephen Douglas's Little Giants, John Breckinridge's National Democratic Volunteers, Abraham Lincoln's Wide-Awakes, and John Bell's Bell Ringers.

Urban party machines also had their generals, troop commanders, and foot soldiers. The typical city machine was organized by wards. The head of each ward was represented on a citywide party council, presided over by a "boss." The ward leaders controlled the activities of the machine's foot soldiers, the precinct captains. It was the job of the leaders and the captains to turn out the mass vote. Much of this activity went on in the neighborhood bars. James Bryce described the typical ward politician of the 1880s: "A statesman of this type usually begins as a saloon or barkeeper, an occupation which enables him to form a large circle of acquaintants, especially among the 'loafer' class who have votes but no reason for using them one way more than another, and whose interest in political issues is as limited as their stock of political knowledge." He further reported, "of the 1,007 primaries and conventions of all parties held in New York preparatory to the elections of 1884, 633 took place in liquor saloons." [8]

## Party Control of the Ballot

Party control of the ballot made the task of turning out a reliable vote easier. In the nation's earliest days ballot casting was informal. Some states let voters create their own ballots or used items such as corn or beans to designate a vote. The new political parties saw the opportunity to take over the preparation of ballots. In 1829 the Massachusetts Supreme Court upheld the legality of party-prepared ballots, which became the national norm until almost the end of the nineteenth century.

Each party had ballots, called party strips, of a different color, size, and shape. In most states the names of the party's candidates for all offices appeared on the same ballot, although a few states at various times had party strips for each office. Party hawkers peddled ballots "to the voters in what resembled an auctioneering atmosphere in and around the polling station." [9] This system was obviously a powerful incentive for already partisan voters to cast a straight party ticket. Splitting one's ticket required either scratching out the names listed on the ballot or fastening several ballots together. Few voters bothered to do so. Ticket splitting in states with single party strips averaged only slightly more than 1 percent in the years from 1876 to 1908. [10]

## Election Fraud

Party control of the ballot, combined with lax election laws and even laxer enforcement, almost invited vote fraud, particularly in places where the parties were highly competitive and many elections were very close. An eyewitness describes the 1827 election for the New York State legislature, the body that would cast the state's votes for president in the following year: Two hundred voters "were marched to the polls by one of the Jackson candidates who walked at the head with a cocked pistol in each hand and then without leaving the polls they voted three times apiece for the Jackson ticket."[11]

Party workers frequently resorted to such "repeaters" and "floaters"—men brought in from other states. A Republican organizer intent on carrying a hotly contested 1888 race in Indiana instructed his local man on the scene: "Divide the floaters into blocks of five and put a trusted man with necessary funds in charge of these five and make him responsible that none get away and all vote our ticket."[12] In the cities newly arrived immigrants were particular targets for mobilization by the machines. In the three weeks before the 1868 elections, machine-appointed judges naturalized enough recent arrivals to swell the number of registered voters in New York City by 30 percent.[13] Generally, the attitude of the militaristically organized party organizations toward such sources of votes "was that of a regular army towards mercenaries: it was necessary to buy their services."[14]

## The Australian Ballot: A Reaction Against Corruption

As the nineteenth century wore on, citizens became more and more exasperated with the corruption surrounding elections. Exposure of the unsavory activities of the party machines outraged the public. For instance, the inner financial workings of New York City's Tammany Hall and its notorious Tweed Ring were revealed by the *New York Times* in 1871. Reform leaders placed a spy in the city controller's office. He passed on to the newspaper irrefutable evidence that those doing business with the city were told to add increasingly larger percentages to their bills for kickbacks to the machine.[15] In Chicago a survey of the delegates to the 1897 Cook County party convention revealed that among the 727 delegates, 17 had been tried for murder, 36 for burglary, and 265 were saloon keepers.[16]

The aura of corruption led reformers in many states to press for the secret, or Australian, ballot, which had been introduced in that country in midcentury. In 1888 Massachusetts became the first state to adopt a ballot prepared by nonpartisan election authorities and cast in secret; within eight years 90 percent of the states—almost all of those outside the South—had adopted the system. The secret ballot was, as we shall see shortly, one of the changes that contributed to the gradual weakening of party organizations in the first half of the twentieth century.

## Reaching the Voter

Through most of the nineteenth century, parties communicated with voters principally through rallies and speeches by traveling orators. Direct contact with voters first became necessary when the franchise expanded to almost all adult white males in the Jackson era. Candidates did some of the traveling and speaking; for instance, during their 1858 debates Lincoln and Douglas traveled more than five thousand miles by train, carriage, and riverboat. State and local party organizations coordinated these speaking trips.

It was impossible, however, for presidential aspirants to undertake much personal travel. Without a transcontinental railroad, visiting the far corners of their national constituency was unthinkable. The presidential candidate's time was "spent chopping wood, planting crops, and dispensing folk wisdom." [17] He waited at home for a delegation from the party convention to notify him of his nomination and later issued a detailed letter of acceptance setting forth his views.

The presidential campaign itself—on which the fortunes of so many other candidates depended—was fought not by the candidates but by surrogate party speakers. The national party committees were formed in the middle of the nineteenth century to coordinate the surrogates' trips and to raise funds to support speakers on the road during presidential campaigns.

Highly partisan newspapers carried the presidential acceptance letters, the words of the orators, and other political communication to the public. The struggling and impoverished press was tied very early to the parties when the government authorized the establishment of up to three "by authority" newspapers in each state to publish the content of federal legislation. The papers were selected at the discretion of the secretary of state; this was one of the first instances of political patronage. Andrew Jackson cemented the alliance by awarding friendly publishers postmasterships, positions in the Customs Service, and other appointments. At least fifty-nine journalists received such patronage jobs from the Jackson administration.[18]

The printed word—the only form of mass communication available to campaign strategists in the nineteenth century—was almost totally controlled by the parties. It became the standard practice of nineteenth-century politicians to buy—or buy off—the small weekly newspapers, and later the dailies, that served most of the population. Henry Clay and Daniel Webster raised money to pay off newspapers sympathetic to the Whigs, and Abraham Lincoln bought a German language newspaper to advance Republican doctrine and his own congressional and senatorial campaigns. Wealthy party activists also bought newspapers. August

Belmont, chairman of the Democratic National Committee from 1860 to 1872, purchased the *New York Morning Star* in 1851 to promote the candidacy of James Buchanan and tried to buy the *New York Times* in 1860 so that he could turn it into an organ for Stephen Douglas. Newspapers thus served as "important parts of the party organization themselves." [19] As printing presses and paper gradually became less expensive, other forms of party-prepared campaign literature—broadsides, handbills, candidate biographies, and the like—supplemented the newspaper.

## The Role of Money in Nineteenth-Century Politics

Campaigns dependent primarily on oratory and organization were not expensive affairs. Money was needed principally for speakers' travels and get-out-the-vote expenses on election day. Although political fat cats such as the Democrats' Belmont were already important for raising funds, during most of the nineteenth century almost all the money needed for campaigns could be collected by assessing holders of political patronage jobs from 1 to 3 percent of their salaries; these included postmasters, school principals, and state and municipal employees. Richard Jensen has estimated that during this period there was one patronage position for every hundred voters and that 2 to 5 percent of the adult male population was involved in ten to fifteen hours of active political work weekly. Even the well-to-do avidly sought patronage jobs. The postmastership of a small city paid five times the average factory wage and was worth more than most lawyers or doctors earned. As Jensen observes, "American politics in the nineteenth century was publicly financed in effect, though not by law." [20]

During the latter part of that century, large amounts of political money were intended not for campaign coffers but as payoffs to officeholders for favors or protection. The Tweed Ring, which bought votes to gain control of city or state governments, was archetypical. Once in control, politicians could sell the goods at their disposal—government contracts or favorable regulation, licences, jobs, or protection—to the highest bidders. The political machine has been described as a "business organization in a particular field of business—getting votes and winning elections" [21] Other businesses bought the services available fom the machine's bosses and candidates. As Jay Gould of the Erie Railroad testified to a committee of the New York state assembly in 1873: "In a Republican district I was a Republican; in a Democratic district a Democrat; in a doubtful district I was doubtful, but I was always for Erie." [22]

## An Appraisal of the Period

The picture of American campaigns in the nineteenth century that emerges is of political parties preeminently in control. In their caucuses and conventions parties nominated candidates for every office. Their workers and sympathizers militaristically drilled strong partisans to the polls, where they voted with ballots provided by the party. Their organizations raised and spent the necessary campaign funds, coordinated the travels of stump speakers to party rallies, subsidized a strongly partisan press, and printed and distributed campaign literature.

Some have seen this as a golden age of American politics, in which the vast majority of the population was highly aware of political issues and in which almost everyone voted, often several times a year in various elections.[23] Others perceive the era, particularly its latter part, as a sinkhole of political corruption, in which votes were manufactured and bought, elections were stolen, and political machines and their elected representatives did the bidding of the new big-business class for mutual financial gain.[24] But however elected officials behaved, everyone agrees that the organized political parties were solely responsible for their being in office.

Yet as the nineteenth century came to an end, there were already signs that the sway of the parties over campaigns was beginning to weaken. The social and economic upheaval that swept the United States in the latter part of the century had profound effects on its politics, effects that would broaden and deepen through the first half of the twentieth century.

# The Era of Transition: 1890-1950 ⸻

The nineteenth century was an era of strong and enduring partisanship, but as it was ending, industrialization and the appearance of powerful corporations, or trusts, disrupted this stability. These economic changes began to erode party control of campaigns.

## The Populists and the Progressives

The first threat to party stability and hegemony came from the Populist movement, centered in the South and the West, two areas often described as "colonies" of the Midwest and Northeast in the latter part of the nineteenth century. In the South small farmers saw themselves as captives of the northern manufacturers to whom they sold their raw goods, of a local merchant class that charged them increasingly exorbitant interest on loans, and of the railroads, which were the only way of conveying goods to market. Additionally, a gold-based currency exacerbated the plight of southern and western farmers, who desired "cheap money," embodied by their growing demands for a silver-backed currency.

Through the 1880s rural America sank deeper into agricultural depression. Farmers began to organize politically in regional Farmers' Alliances, and in 1892 they held a national convention to found the People's, or Populist, party. The Populists called for unlimited coinage of silver, a graduated income tax, government ownership of the railroads, direct election of senators, the secret ballot, and limits on immigration. Their presidential nominee received more than a million votes in that year's election. Populist politicians in the South succeeded in taking over the Democratic party in several states and electing their leaders to governorships and the U.S. Senate. State legislatures in the South and West fell under their control.

While the Democratic party was split on the issues of the tariff, bimetalism, and immigration, the Republican party was being torn apart by the Progressive movement, which followed Populism a few years later. Although the Progressives did not share the Populists' positions on nationalization of industry and easy money, they joined them in their antipathy to the trusts and their support of political reform measures. The most important of these reforms was the direct primary, which spread widely in the early twentieth century. The primary was critical because it took away from the party organizations their most significant source of power—monopoly over the selection of the candidates who eventually became officeholders.

Progressives could be found in both parties, as exemplified by Republican Theodore Roosevelt and Democrat Woodrow Wilson, but they were predominantly Republican. Progressive Republicans were able to win the vice-presidential nomination in 1900 for their Spanish-American War hero, Teddy Roosevelt, who became an accidental president with the assassination of President William McKinley less than a year later. Roosevelt later abandoned the conservative-dominated Republican party to run as the Progressives' presidential candidate in 1912. He received four million votes, came in second, and split the Republican vote to give the election to Woodrow Wilson, the Progressive-leaning Democratic governor of New Jersey. In the Midwest, Republican Progressives, disenchanted with the conservative economic policies of their state parties, sporadically mounted state Progressive campaigns. Their most notable leader was Robert La Follette, who received almost five million votes in the 1924 presidential election.

The Populist and Progressive movements had a major impact on party organizations and their campaign strategies. Populists and Progressives succeeded at the polls because the social and economic unrest that brought them into being tore large numbers of voters loose from their accustomed party moorings. A new note of uncertainty was introduced into campaigns beginning in the early 1890s. Helped by the advent of the Australian, or secret, ballot and an increasingly less partisan press, Populists began to win elections and dealt the Republicans a severe defeat in the congressional elections of 1890.[25]

The Panic of 1893, the worst depression in the nation's history, struck shortly after the inauguration of the conservative "gold Democrat" Grover Cleveland, leading many to believe the Populists had a real chance of becoming one of the two major parties. In the 1894 midterm elections Democrats lost control of the House and Senate. In a move that essentially amalgamated the Populist and Democratic parties, the 1896 Democratic National Convention nominated the Populist hero, Nebraskan William Jennings Bryan, after being overwhelmed by the famous speech in which he declared, "You shall not crucify mankind upon a cross of gold." The country was in turmoil, and both parties saw that agitated voters could not be summoned to their party homes in the old ways: "Instead of a campaign carried on in a few dubious states, the field of action was enlarged to include half the country." [26] Uncertainty and political instability produced significant changes in political campaign styles, which were seen for the first time in the 1896 presidential campaign.

## The Watershed Campaign of 1896

In the Democratic campaign Bryan broke precedent by conducting what amounted to the first candidate-centered campaign. Blessed with extraordinary oratorical gifts and embodying a highly emotional cause—the silver issue—Bryan was the first presidential candidate to take his case directly to the people. Between July and November of 1896 he made five hundred speeches, personally addressing thirty to forty million people as far west as Nebraska, as far south as Tennessee, and as far north as Boston, traveling eighteen thousand miles in four swings around the country.[27] To a nation accustomed to presidential candidates who were neither seen nor heard, it was an astounding performance, one that convinced many in the opposition camp that Bryan was leading in the race.

The Republican campaign, under the direction of candidate McKinley's patron, Mark Hanna, realized it would also have to take dramatic action to counter the appeal of the "Boy Orator from the Platte." The departure from electioneering as usual saw the advent of another innovation. As Hanna's biographer tells it, the Republicans "decided to oppose Mr. Bryan's personal appeal with an exhaustive and systematic educational canvass of the country."[28] A later, more dispassionate historian describes it this way:

> Hanna conducted the first modern advertising campaign, selling his candidate like soap to the American people. Cartoons, posters, inscriptions, were turned out by the carloads. Hanna set up twin headquarters in Chicago and New York, dispatched an army of 1,400 trained speakers, sent out over 120 million campaign documents.[29]

Unlike the Bryan campaign, the Republicans' effort did not feature new campaign tactics. The party organized the traditional surrogate orators and production of campaign literature. What made McKinley's campaign different was its deliberate orchestration: the careful attention to finding and targeting likely Republican voters and then winning them to the Republican side through a series of persuasive negative messages about the Democratic candidate and program as well as positive messages about the Republicans' own. One of their tactics was painstaking canvasses of doubtful areas. When a house-to-house canvass of Iowa in September showed Bryan leading, in "the next six weeks, speakers and campaign documents were poured into every town and village."[30] A second canvass in late October showed the state safe for McKinley.

The flood of almost three hundred different campaign documents was carefully tailored for target groups and for different stages in the campaign. To reach immigrant workers who had been strongly Democratic, literature was printed in French, German, Italian, Spanish, Yiddish, and other languages. The early phases of the campaign dealt mostly with the silver issue, detailing the Republican view that silver-backed currency was a quick fix that would benefit only a minority sectional and class interest. Later, the silver issue seemed to lose appeal, and campaign literature switched to other issues such as protectionism.

Running such a campaign cost a great deal of money. The uncertainty that had already crept into politics had started to drive campaign costs up, a condition that generally benefited the Republicans. The new captains of industry had unbelievable amounts of capital at their disposal and a willingness to spend it to protect themselves from the Populist threat.

The outlays in 1896, however, were unprecedented. Bryan's war chest of $675,000, provided primarily by silver interests, was very large for the period but paled to insignificance compared with the $3.5 million the Republicans reported spending. The money was raised by a canvass of business as thorough as the canvass of voters:

Inasmuch as the security of business and the credit system of the country were involved by the issues of the campaign, appeals were made to banks and businessmen, irrespective of party affiliations. . . . Responsible men were appointed to act as local agents in all fruitful neighborhoods for the purpose of both soliciting and receiving contributions.[31]

Thus the campaign of 1896 made significant departures from campaigns as usual—particularly in Bryan's personalization of his candidacy, in the Republicans' targeting of voters and marketing of their message, and in the liberal use of money not for bribery of officials or voters but for legitimate and ordinary campaign purposes. Additionally, Bryan ran the first successful insurgent campaign, in which a presidential candidate took over a party convention through the force of his personality, ideas, and personal following. These phenomena were to have an important impact in the next fifty years, a period that marked the transition from party- to candidate-centered campaigns.

## The Return to Politics as Usual

What we see clearly now was not as evident at the time. Although in 1896 the Republican party employed a new strategy, the fundamental tactics remained the same, and the campaign effort was a *party* effort. As the electorate settled into a heavily Republican voting pattern after 1896, the Republicans actually spent less in every presidential election from 1900 to 1916, when they saw a chance to recapture the prize Theodore Roosevelt had "stolen" from them as a third-party spoiler in 1912. The volatility of the congressional vote, which reached its apogee in the 1890s, ended. (The Democrats, who had held 61 percent of the seats in the House of Representatives after their great victory in 1892, saw themselves reduced to slightly more than 29 percent of the seats in 1894.) Voters who had switched to a new party in 1896 stayed with it, voting the party and not the candidate. Even in 1896 split-ticket voting remained under 5 percent in the Australian ballot states and was generally lower thereafter.

In nonpresidential races the route to electoral success in most of the country continued to be through service in the locally dominant party organization, traditional campaigns mounted by the parties, and relatively low campaign expenditures. Warren G. Harding, running for senator from Ohio in 1914, relied on the Republican organization and spent $6,000. Even as late as 1940, Harry Truman had to raise less than $9,000 for his Senate reelection campaign, despite the fact that he had two serious opponents: he put his faith in the St. Louis Democratic organization. Examining data from several states in the late 1920s and early 1930s, Louise Overacker reported in an exhaustive study of campaign finance, "One is forced to conclude that in the great majority of cases campaigning for a seat in the House of Representatives is not an expensive business." [32] Academic analysts and practicing politicians agreed that in the early 1940s, $5,000 was more than enough to run a very well financed congressional campaign. Lyndon B. Johnson, who in 1940 was able to draw on a campaign fund provided by Texas oilmen and contractors, saved close to a hundred Democratic members of Congress that year by strategically placing contributions of $100 to $1,000.[33]

Moreover, the party machines, which were expected to wilt under the onslaught of the secret ballot, the institution of the federal civil service, the direct primary, and the voter registration systems that took hold in most states between 1910 and 1920, remained as strong as ever for most of the first half of the twentieth century. "With a few exceptions, the bosses found ways to either deflect or to use the new reforms that were meant to unseat them."[34] The way the machines operated under the new system is captured in an account of an election in Hudson County, New Jersey, where the Hague machine reigned for most of the first half of the twentieth century. Describing the Hudson County results in the 1925 New Jersey gubernatorial election, a latter-day Hudson County politician commented:

> This was the time of paper ballots. It was relatively easy for [Frank] Hague's people manning the polls to erase ballots, change ballots, destroy ballots, miscount ballots—while Hague-controlled policemen looked the other way or pressured inspection officials to stand aside. . . . Election superintendent John Ferguson [said] "we know it is futile to arrest anyone belonging to the Democrat organization in Hudson County on Election Day. The accuser usually finds himself in jail as the arrested party by the time he gets to the station house . . . the only way to have an honest election in Hudson County is with a militia, and if the present conditions are to continue, it is futile and ridiculous for us to attempt to hold further elections." [35]

## The Direct Primary and the First Nonpresidential Insurgent Campaigns

The major effects of the weakened party loyalty brought on by the Populist and Progressive movements and the personalized and marketing candidacies of 1896 were seen in the two regions where they had had the greatest impact—the West and the South. Strong party organizations did not have nineteenth-century roots in these areas. As a result of the Civil War and Reconstruction, the southern states were virtually one-party systems, with factions of the Democratic party vying for ascendancy. In the thinly populated western states, party organizations were often creatures of the hated mining companies and railroads, whose local agents served as organizers and fund raisers.[36]

Because of the absence of party machines in these areas, the direct primary was the most significant of the Progressive reforms from the perspective of campaigns. The direct primary gave insurgents—candidates not championed by party organizations—a chance to appeal successfully to the majority of voters, who had weak ties to parties. Once nominated, however, insurgents took over whatever organizational machinery and patronage there was. Of the leading Progressive and crusader for the direct primary, Robert La Follette, V. O. Key observes, "La Follette and the voters who followed him perhaps wanted to go to heaven but they insisted on traveling under Republican auspices." [37]

Still, Populism and Progressivism introduced a fluidity into southern and western politics that made it possible to mount campaigns outside the party apparatus in a way that was still not possible elsewhere. In the South politicians such as Louisiana's legendary Huey Long were able to use Populist appeals to defeat the conservative courthouse gangs that dominated Democratic politics in much of the old Confederacy. Using his own newspaper and the technological innovations of radio and sound truck, Long won the Democratic nominations (tantamount to election) for governor and then senator. He was preparing to mount a challenge to President Franklin Roosevelt when he was assassinated in 1935.[38]

The most important progenitor of the candidate-centered campaign, however, may have been the California gubernatorial contest of 1934, a race notable for two developments. It was the first time a neophyte attempted to launch a political career at the statewide level with the help of a personal organization and the first time that business interests, usually dependent on party machines, struck back with their own nonparty-based effort. The real contest was between the EPIC movement of Democratic candidate and political amateur Upton Sinclair and Whitaker and Baxter, a public relations firm that later would become the first independent political consultants for hire.

EPIC (End Poverty in California) was the organizational creation of Sinclair, a muckraking socialist reporter, novelist, and scriptwriter, who decided to run in the 1934 Democratic gubernatorial primary. California, like the rest of the nation, was still in the grip of the Great Depression, with more than a million citizens receiving public relief. The EPIC platform called for steeply graduated inheritance and income taxes and pensions for dependent widows and children. It also proposed a rather vague plan for state purchase of fallow farmland and idle factories to make work for the unemployed, a plan Sinclair's alarmed opponents described as socialism. Sinclair was entering the primary of the distinctly minority party. As he wrote, "The Republican Party has named the governors of California for more than forty years, and during that period the Democratic Party has been a small and feeble minority . . . split among themselves, living in the memory of old-time factional fights." [39]

Stepping into this Democratic vacuum, Sinclair formed about two thousand neighborhood EPIC clubs and began the *EPIC News,* which achieved a circulation of almost two million by the end of the campaign. The candidate also bought what radio time he could afford for speeches and wrote a best-selling book, *I, Governor of California.* EPIC precinct captains were present in virtually every district of the state; "tireless and dedicated, they were Sinclair's greatest source of political strength, and far more productive of results than the official party machinery." [40] Sinclair won the Democratic primary by better than two to one.

The California Republican party also had a history of factionalism, based on the old conservative-Progressive split in the party. Hiram Johnson, elected governor in 1910, and later senator, was a leading Progressive. Johnson, who made a career of fighting the Southern Pacific Railroad, pushed through all of the Progressive political agenda—direct primaries and initiative, referendum, and recall elections. At the time Sinclair ran for governor, however, the conservatives had the upper hand in the Republican party. The state committee chairman was Louis B. Mayer, president of Metro-Goldwyn-Mayer studios. California's major industries were among the first to hire public relations and advertising firms, and by the time of Sinclair's race they had employed them to wage publicity campaigns against referenda questions considered detrimental to business; however, they had never been used for or against a candidate in an election. Sinclair's economic program was seen as so threatening that the film industry and other corporations decided that such a campaign was necessary and provided the Republican party with the financial backing to carry it out.

Whitaker and Baxter, the public relations firm hired by the Republicans, produced enormous numbers of pamphlets, circulars, and newspaper advertisements with alarming themes. One handout resembled a piece of American currency, emblazoned ONE SINCLIAR DOLLAR at the top and ENDURE POVERTY IN CALIFORNIA at the bottom. "Good only in California or Russia," it proclaimed. Other literature accused Sinclair of being opposed to organized religion and in favor of "free love." With little money and no organization capable of penetrating the frightened Republican middle class, Sinclair lost the general election by more than two hundred thousand votes.

The Sinclair campaign, as well as Huey Long's, demonstrated how insurgent candidates with charismatic personalities and strong issues could run independently of weakened party organizations and wage campaigns through the mass media of the time. Reliance on newspapers was traditional, but a new medium was entering the political arena.

Radio was first widely used in the presidential campaign of 1928. By the early 1930s it had spread to state-level campaigns. Gubernatorial and senatorial candidates in New Jersey and Massachusetts in 1930 reported that a fifth to a third of their total campaign expenditures went for radio broadcasts. Radio was regarded as a way to make stump speeches to a large audience. A 1940 Democratic handbook for precinct leaders advised them to encourage supporters to tune in when important party leaders made broadcast addresses. "Radio is the streamlined way of reaching voters in a streamlined age," it concluded.

Air time was typically bought in chunks of fifteen minutes to an hour, for traditional political oratory by candidates or surrogate speakers. Some of radio's most accomplished users employed it less for campaigning than for maintaining a political base once they were elected. Franklin Roosevelt delivered his famous fireside chats by radio. During a protracted newspaper strike, New York's Mayor Fiorello LaGuardia read the funnies over the air on Sunday mornings. Gov. Lee "Pappy" O'Daniel of Texas, a political neophyte who had the state's most widely listened-to radio program before his election, continued it from the governor's mansion. O'Daniel may have been the first politician whose career was entirely the creation of the media.[41]

## An Overview of the Era of Transition

As the twentieth century reached its midpoint, campaigns in much of the country continued to be party-centered affairs. In response to the loosening of party identification that occurred at the turn of the century, organizational efforts to get sure party voters to the polls were supplemented but not supplanted by merchandising techniques. Insurgent candidacies became commonplace in those regions most affected by the Populist and Progressive movements, as candidates espousing their ideas moved into the Democratic and Republican parties, respectively, and challenged the traditional organizations through the direct primary. Candidates of the local minority party could sometimes win in times of strong national tides, but for the most part traditional majority party candidates reigned supreme.

The California public relations campaign against Upton Sinclair, however, was a straw in the wind. As the second half of the century began, these techniques were adopted first at the presidential level; in the next twenty years they filtered down to statewide campaigns and then even lower. By the 1980s California, once again leading the way, would see a million-dollar media race for a seat in the state assembly. The beginnings of that process are described in the next chapter.

## Notes

1. Quoted in Alexander Heard, *The Costs of Democracy: Financing American Political Campaigns* (Garden City, N.Y.: Doubleday, 1962), 352.
2. Stimson Bullitt, *To Be a Politician* (Garden City, N.Y.: Doubleday, 1961), 65.
3. Jasper P. Shannon, *Money and Politics* (New York: Random House, 1959), 1920.
4. Alexis de Tocqueville, *Democracy in America* (New York: Knopf, 1945), vol. 1, 259-260.
5. David Black, *The King of Fifth Avenue: The Fortunes of August Belmont* (New York: Dial, 1981), 254.
6. *Chicago Times*, September 21, 1858, quoted in Paul M. Angle, *Created Equal? The Complete Lincoln-Douglas Debates* (Chicago: University of Chicago Press, 1958), 232-233.
7. Joel H. Silbey and Samuel T. McSeveney, ed., *Voters, Parties and Elections: Quantitative Essays in the History of American Popular Voting Behavior* (Lexington, Mass.: Xerox College Publishers, 1972), 2. See particularly the essays by V. O. Key, Jr., and Frank Munger; Samuel T. McSeveney; and Paul Kleppner.
8. James Bryce, *The American Commonwealth*, ed. Louis Hacker (1888; reprint, New York: Putnam, 1959), vol. 1, 166, 205.
9. Jerrold G. Rusk, "The Effect of the Australian Ballot on Split-Ticket Voting, 1876-1908," *American Political Science Review* 64 (December 1970): 1221. The description here draws heavily from Rusk.
10. Ibid., 1227.
11. Daniel Boorstin, *The Americans: The Democratic Experience* (New York: Random House, 1973), 257.
12. George H. Mayer, *The Republican Party: 1854-1964* (New York: Oxford University Press, 1964), 219.
13. Martin Shefter, "New York City's Fiscal Crisis: The Politics of Inflation and Retrenchment," *Public Interest* 4 (1977): 102-103.
14. Richard J. Jensen, *Grass Roots Politics: Parties, Issues and Voters, 1854-1883* (Westport, Conn.: Greenwood Press, 1983), 31.
15. See Samuel P. Orth, *The Boss and the Machine* (New Haven, Conn.: Yale University Press, 1919), 71-80.
16. *Review of Reviews* 16 (1897): 322.
17. Mayer, *Republican Party*, 12.
18. See Richard Rubin, *Press, Party and Presidency* (New York: Norton, 1981), 2038 and *passim*, for an extensive discussion of the relationship between the press and the political parties.
19. Ibid., 52.
20. Jensen, *Grass Roots Politics*, 31. See also William Goodman, *The Two-Party System in the United States*, 2d ed. (Princeton, N.J.: Van Nostrand, 1960), 103.
21. Edward C. Banfield and James Q. Wilson, *City Politics* (Cambridge, Mass.: Harvard University Press, 1963), 115-116.
22. Louise Overacker, *Money in Elections* (New York: Macmillan, 1932), 177.
23. See Mayer, *Republican Party*; Walter Dean Burnham, "The Changing Shape of

the American Political Universe," *American Political Science Review* 59 (March 1965): 7-28; Burnham, "Theory and Voting Research: Some Reflections on Converse's 'Change in the American Electorate,'" *American Political Science Review* 68 (September 1974): 1002-1023.

24. See Philip Converse, "Change in the American Electorate," in Angus Campbell and P. E. Converse, *The Human Meaning of Social Change* (New York: Russell Sage, 1972); Jerrold Rusk, "The American Electoral Universe: Speculation and Evidence," *American Political Science Review* 68 (September 1974): 1028-1049; and the interesting fictional treatment by Gore Vidal, *1876* (New York: Random House, 1976).

25. Among the most important reasons that the press became less partisan toward the end of the nineteenth century were the rise of the news wire services, with clients in both parties; the growth in advertising revenue that accompanied increasing population and readership, making newspapers financially independent of the parties; and the rise of mass-circulation muckraking magazines with Progressive attitudes.

26. Herbert J. Croly, *Marcus Alonzo Hanna: His Life and Work* (New York: Macmillan, 1912), 212-213.

27. Wayne C. Williams, *William Jennings Bryan* (New York: Putnam, 1936), 162.

28. Croly, *Marcus Alonzo Hanna*, 212.

29. Francis T. Russell, *The Shadow of Blooming Grove* (New York: McGraw-Hill, 1968), 125.

30. Croly, *Marcus Alonzo Hanna*, 217.

31. Ibid., 220.

32. Overacker, *Money in Elections*, 60.

33. See Robert A. Caro, *The Years of Lyndon Johnson: The Path to Power* (New York: Knopf, 1982), chapters 31-32.

34. Richard Hofstadter, *The Age of Reform* (New York: Vintage, 1960), 258. See also Richard L. McCormick, "The Party Period and Public Policy: An Exploratory Hypothesis," *Journal of American History* 66 (September 1979): 279-298.

35. Thomas F. X. Smith, *The Poweriticians* (Secaucus, N.J.: Lyle Stuart, 1982), 75-76.

36. Excellent analyses of politics in the West and South in this era include V. O. Key, *Southern Politics* (New York: Knopf, 1949); David Mayhew, *Placing Parties in American Politics* (Princeton, N.J.: Princeton University Press, 1986), chapter 1; and Martin Shefter, "Regional Receptivity to Reform: The Legacy of the Progressive Era," *Political Science Quarterly* 98 (Fall 1983): 459-483.

37. V. O. Key, *American State Politics* (New York: Knopf, 1956), 93.

38. See Key, *Southern Politics*, and T. Harry Williams, *Huey Long* (New York: Bantam, 1970).

39. Upton Sinclair, *I, Governor of California* (Los Angeles, published by the author, 1935), 41-42.

40. Walt Anderson, *Campaigns: Cases in Political Conflict* (Pacific Palisades, Calif.: Goodyear, 1970), 117.

41. Caro, *Years of Lyndon Johnson*, 698-702.

# The Rise of the Candidate-Centered Campaign

3

*[John Kennedy] was only nominally a Democrat. He was a Kennedy, which was more than a political affiliation. It quickly developed into an entire political party, with its own people, its own apparatus and its own strategies.*

Tip O'Neill on Kennedy's 1946 congressional campaign[1]

We have shown how, in the nineteenth century, parties regulated the flow of political information by dominating the press. They controlled the nomination of most candidates through caucuses and conventions. Their organizations financed campaigns and distributed ballots. But by the early part of the twentieth century, the daily press was becoming independent. Parties had already lost control of the ballot. The direct primary began to threaten party control of nominations, and the combined onslaught of the Populists and the Progressives made some insurgent candidacies possible.

In the middle decades of the twentieth century, however, another series of developments occurred that would affect politics, and thus campaigns, even more profoundly. Among them were the aftermath of the Great Depression of 1929, suburbanization, further technological advances (particularly television and the computer), the civil rights movement, the Vietnam War, and Watergate. The political fluidity induced by these events made the 1890s pale in comparison, and the effect on campaign techniques was profound. With the advantage of hindsight, one can see that most campaigns of even the 1950s were more similar to those of the 1880s than of the 1980s. The decades after the 1950s would see the eclipse of local party organizations as a factor in most campaigns and the rise of the candidate-centered campaign run by professional consultants—a style of campaigning that demanded much greater amounts of money to purchase expensive technology. These developments were first evident in presidential campaigns; only gradually did they move to lower level races.

# The Changing Historical Background

Although the political outcome was different, the presidential election of 1932 was as much a watershed as the race in 1896. The Republicans fought and won the 1896 campaign with the argument that their platform held the key to economic prosperity, and indeed it seemed to be so. The United States prospered for decades thereafter, and Republicans enjoyed great political favor. With the exception of Wilson's two terms, Republicans occupied the White House continually from 1896 to 1932. For almost three-quarters of that period, they had a majority in both houses of Congress and controlled most governorships and state legislative seats. Their long tenure ended with the Great Depression, the election of Franklin Roosevelt to four consecutive terms, and the implementation of the New Deal. The Democrats would hold both houses of Congress for forty of the forty-eight years between 1932 and 1980 and the presidency for two-thirds of that period. Thus the 1932 election brought a realignment similar to that of 1896, and both elections were conducted in the same party-based way.

Events, however, were eroding the organizational strength of both parties and the psychological ties that bound the electorate to them. Party machines were buffeted by the changing role of government, by the increased size and mobility of the population, and by the presence of television in most living rooms. Beginning with Roosevelt's New Deal and extended by Lyndon Johnson's Great Society, the federal government's greater role in social welfare programs and in regulating business prompted those in need of assistance to look to Washington rather than to local government, to the bureaucrat rather than to the precinct captain: "To the voter who in case of need could now turn to a professional social worker and receive as a matter of course unemployment compensation, aid to dependent children, old-age assistance and all the rest, the precinct worker's hod of coal was a joke." [2]

Population growth in the first half of the century was restrained by stiffer immigration laws, the depression, and the two world wars. After World War II the population exploded. In addition, the franchise was gradually extended to southern blacks and to those between eighteen and twenty years old; women, granted the vote in 1920, participated in growing numbers. Almost 50 million people voted in the 1952 presidential election; sixteen years later, 73 million. Stimson Bullitt described the changes graphically: "In 1956, Eisenhower was given more votes in New York and Ohio alone than Wilson received from the entire nation in 1912. . . . In losing a race for Congress I received 10,000 more votes than John Quincy Adams did when he was elected President." [3]

Party organizations designed for campaigning to a limited electorate on a personal basis were not an efficient means of reaching this vastly growing pool of voters. Moreover, organizational strength had depended on tightly knit, stable neighborhoods. With postwar prosperity, the spread of the automobile, and new highway construction, Americans' mobility expanded enormously. Approximately a fifth of the population changed addresses every year. Many went to new and sparsely populated suburbs, leaving behind family and friends—and the neighborhood political organizations.

Television, too, affected voters' behavior. Among its other dramatic roles, it claimed more of the leisure time Americans had devoted to other forms of recreation, including political activity: "The precinct captain who visits in the evening interrupts a television program and must either stay and watch in silence or else excuse himself quickly and move on." [4] Having lost the patronage jobs they depended upon to the civil service and much of their rank and file to the suburbs, most party machines subsided into impotence.

Still, the party could count for a while on the psychological pull that kept voters in the fold. Although this factor is important even today, its strength has diminished. Just as the Panic of 1893, industrialization, and urbanization had produced social turmoil, the events of the 1960s and 1970s also caused great upheaval. The breakdown of racial and sexual codes, the apparent change in America's place in the world, and the political cynicism engendered by Vietnam and Watergate made core groups in both parties reconsider their affiliations.

George Wallace's third-party presidential candidacy in 1968 and John Anderson's race in 1980 echoed the minority party candidacies of the earlier period of dislocation. From the 1950s to the 1980s, the number of people calling themselves strong partisans declined 10 percent, while the number styling themselves political independents rose about 15 percent. Most worrisome to campaign strategists was the number of split-ticket voters. From the 1970s onward, in various elections, between two-thirds and three-quarters of independents and Democrats and one-half of Republicans divided their ballots between the parties. [5] Split-ticket voting, in other words, became the norm. Party was fading both as an organizational device and as a psychological voting cue.

At roughly the same time, however, technology provided campaign strategists with new ways to determine what voters were thinking and with new methods to send out the desired messages. For the first task the chief tool was data-processing equipment; for the second the medium was television. The most important applications of these technological developments for campaign strategies were polling, voter targeting, and political advertising.

Scientific polls became possible in the 1930s, with the perfection of probability sampling techniques. The first known scientific poll was taken for a Democratic candidate for secretary of state in Iowa in 1932. The lucky beneficiary, who won her race, was George Gallup's mother-in-law. Gallup began his series of public polls on presidential races in 1936, and Republican candidates Thomas E. Dewey and Wendell Willkie hired private campaign pollsters during the 1940s. Polling did not become a major element in presidential campaigns, however, until the 1960 Kennedy-Nixon election, when analyst Louis Harris became a senior adviser to the Kennedy campaign. Theodore White's classic account of this race gives what now seems an amusingly quaint picture of Lou Harris bent over a slide rule.[6] The party also commissioned a computer simulation of demographic groups in the electorate and their likely responses to various aspects of the Kennedy campaign—a project fictionalized in a best-selling novel named for the number of demographic groups in the model—*The 480*.[7]

Polls became necessary to presidential campaigns for two reasons. First, the decline of party organizations removed the chief source of information about political opinions and voting inclinations at the grass roots. Second, the Eisenhower landslides of the 1950s showed that an appealing presidential candidate could draw large numbers of voters from the opposition party. Campaigns needed to know from which groups wavering voters might come and how they would respond to various candidates and issues. As computers became more widespread, it was possible to target potential supporters, requesting both money and votes. Polling and targeting came later to races for lower offices because in state and local contests voters were less ready to desert their parties. An important reason for this was that television paid much more attention to presidential campaigns than to other races, giving otherwise partisan voters information on which to base defecting votes.

## Campaigns in the Television Age

In 1946 there were only seven thousand television sets in American households. By 1952 there were nineteen million, and by 1960 the number of homes with sets had reached forty-five million. During much of the 1950s ten thousand people were buying TV sets every day.[8] Seldom had a technology with such potential spread so rapidly. In November 1951 the coaxial cable linking all the nation's television sets was completed, thus making possible the first nationwide broadcasts. In 1963 the national networks expanded their evening news broadcasts from fifteen minutes to half an hour, and in the same year, for the first time, pollsters reported that more people had come to rely on television than on newspapers for their information about public affairs. Television would make "image" campaigns possible in a way that had never been possible before. Viewers could see candidates in the flesh with no mediating influences—not through the lenses of party workers or those of a partisan press.

## Presidential Candidates

The age of television campaigns began with the presidential election of 1952, in which Republican Dwight Eisenhower ran against Democrat Adlai Stevenson. In 1952 the Democrats had been in power for twenty years. They still depended on their declining but not yet dead party organizations and on interest groups, particularly the labor unions that had profited so enormously from New Deal legislation. The party paid scant attention to communications technology, thinking little about the power of television, which had been almost nonexistent only four years earlier.

The Republicans, in the minority and closer to business, which had already discovered the impact of television advertising, thought about TV a great deal. Republican partisans might be in relatively short supply, but money and public relations skills were not. Soon after their 1952 convention the Republicans set up a strategy board for the presidential campaign. To this group Robert Humphreys, public relations director of the Republican National Committee, presented a formal "Campaign Plan." It was the first time such a detailed marketing strategy was drawn up for a presidential campaign:

> Prepared in standard advertising agency format, the plan outlined basic strategy, organization, appeals, types of speeches, literature, advertising, television and radio programs, the relative weight to be given to the various media, the kinds, places and times of campaign trips and rallies, and the areas in which efforts were to be concentrated.[9]

The Democratic campaign for Stevenson was considerably less centralized and much less professional in a public relations sense. The director of the campaign worked out of Springfield, Illinois, the state capital and Stevenson's base of operations as governor. His handpicked choice for national committee chairman had headquarters in Washington, D.C., while the head of the volunteer organization was based in Chicago. Rather than coming from the world of advertising and public relations, as did Humphreys and his subordinates, the propagandists of the Democratic campaign came directly from journalism or from jobs as government information officers. There was "little evidence that the Democratic publicity professionals exercised important influence on the strategy decisions made by Stevenson and his principal advisors. They served more as tacticians than as strategists . . . and were therefore not well integrated into any over-all campaign plan." [10]

The differing backgrounds and philosophies of the campaign organizations were evident in the way they approached advertising on the new medium of television. The Democrats regarded television as both parties had previously regarded radio—as an extension of the stump speech. Fully 96 percent of the Democrats' television time was devoted to traditional speeches. For instance, they bought eighteen half-hour blocks of time on a national hookup for Stevenson. The Republicans bought similar time blocks for speeches, but the heart of their television campaign was a heavy purchase of spot announcements to present the first political commercials. These spots were carefully targeted to forty-nine counties in twelve critical states and to the Deep South, where the Republicans correctly sensed a chance for breakthroughs. The party spent about $1.5 million on the spot ads during the last three weeks of the campaign. The advertising executive who devised the plan called it "an unheard of saturation campaign in the TV-radio field" for a "national advertiser." [11] The spots were the staged interviews with which we are now so familiar:

ANNOUNCER:  Eisenhower answers the nation!
VOICE:  Mr. Eisenhower, what about the high cost of living?
EISENHOWER:  My wife, Mamie, worries about the same thing. I tell her it's our job to change that on November 4.

The Republicans made forty-nine different spots for television and twenty-nine for radio. The Democrats attempted to retaliate but had only $77,000 to spend. The high echelons of the Stevenson campaign did not yet understand the new medium as a vehicle for marketing messages rather than as another forum for making speeches. The Republicans did. As early as May 1952 they had televised a program, devised by Humphreys, called "The Case for a Republican Congress," which put the Democratic party on trial by Republican congressional leaders and professional actors. The Republican efforts were aimed at getting away from formal speeches; they presented the Republican political message as a show.

Although the Republican media campaign concentrated on the GOP's very attractive "nonpartisan" war hero candidate—a most appropriate strategy for the minority party—it was still the party machinery that ran the campaign, an employee of the party who devised it, and the party national committee that hired B.B.D. and O. and Ted Bates, the advertising agencies that created and placed the spot ads. This approach changed in succeeding years, however. Insurgent Barry Goldwater captured the Republican nomination in 1964 with a campaign team from outside the party. Richard Nixon, although a more mainstream party candidate, also established a candidate-centered organization in 1968; rather than hiring an outside advertising agency, he created a short-lived one, the November Group, whose only client was his campaign.

Television gradually became the focus of presidential campaign advertising. In 1952 advertising expenditures were split almost evenly between television and radio, and both media could make a major impact. The two most important paid media events were Richard Nixon's famous "Checkers" speech, in which he defended himself against charges of having profited from a political slush fund, and Eisenhower's speech announcing, "I will go to Korea." The first was televised, but the second was carried only on radio. In 1956 and 1960, however, spending for television in presidential campaigns outpaced radio by better than two to one, and by 1980 the ratio was approximately eight to one.[12]

At the same time that presidential campaigns were devising ways to send their commercial messages to the public, the contests were coming under increasing scrutiny by print and television journalists. In 1960 Theodore White began his series of books about presidential campaigns, with an unprecedented reliance on insider accounts of the politics of nominations and elections. In the same year the first televised presidential debates were widely credited with giving Kennedy his narrow victory. In 1968 a journalist insinuated himself into the Nixon entourage and published an account of the way Nixon stage-managed his appearances and shaped his media coverage.[13]

With the development of more mobile equipment, television journalists were able to cover national conventions from the floor, seeking out interesting stories rather than being forced to follow the proceedings from the rostrum. The most striking images of the 1968 Democratic Convention were not of the speech making at the podium but of the delegates themselves watching the televised clashes between antiwar demonstrators and the Chicago police outside the convention hall. "Investigative" and "advocacy" journalism became the hallmark of both print and television coverage. American presidential elections were now a spectator sport. The players in the game were the candidates, with their teams of pollsters and media consultants, and a vigilant press corps, which not only described but explained and judged what the candidates were doing. The role of the national news programs was now to *"act as the shadow cabinet."* [14]

The new style of presidential campaigning, which relied not on party workers and political machines but on highly paid professional consultants and expensive broadcast media, drove up costs enormously. Through the 1950s costs had been mounting, but this was almost entirely because of the expansion of the electorate. Between 1912 and 1956 presidential campaigns fairly consistently cost 19 to 20 cents for each vote cast. This figure rose to 29 cents in 1960, 35 cents in 1964, 60 cents in 1968, and $1.31 in 1972, the last presidential election before the advent of public financing and controls on spending. Inflation accounted for only a small part of the increase. In the period from 1960 to 1972, the cost of living went up 41 percent, but the cost per vote in presidential elections more than quadrupled. [15]

The rapid increase in the number of contested primaries also drove up the cost of campaigns. In the 1960 election sixteen states held presidential primaries, of which only about half were seriously contested. The number shot way up in the 1970s, and the 1980 presidential campaign saw thirty-seven primaries. As late as 1968 only 40 percent of the delegates to presidential conventions were selected in primaries; the others were chosen in state party caucuses and conventions. By 1988 more than 75 percent of the delegates were selected in thirty-eight primaries, most of them bound to support particular candidates.

Although some delegates were still chosen in caucuses, these meetings did not resemble the party gatherings of old. Spurred by candidates' television and radio advertising in caucus states, pursued by direct mail, and encouraged to attend by occupational or cause groups to which they belonged, political activists of all stripes outnumbered party organization regulars. Aside from procedure, in fact, there was little to distinguish the Iowa caucuses, for instance, from the New Hampshire primary; they had both become media- and candidate-centered events. Before the late 1960s candidates had little need to engage in advertising during the preconvention phase; they could use the much less expensive strategy of courting potential caucus and convention delegates from the party. After that period effective campaigns in all states required an expensive advertising campaign to reach potential caucus participants and primary voters, along with the attendant research and "get-out-the-vote" expenses.

Thus, in the last third of the twentieth century, American presidential elections have become almost entirely candidate- and media-centered events. Candidates make their way through a complex maze of state primaries and caucuses. The television networks present special programs each Tuesday night during the primary season, but the party nominating conventions have become so insignificant that the networks have abandoned the traditional gavel-to-gavel coverage. Weekly public opinion polls chart the candidates' progress at least two years before the election, before any of them have even formally announced they are running. Throughout, the candidates are followed by a huge entourage from the press, which reports on their every move. What has happened to nonpresidential candidates as these events have unfolded?

## Nonpresidential Candidates

Most candidates for nonpresidential office were affected later than their presidential counterparts by the new developments in electronic campaigning. One of the first systematic studies of the activities of professional political consultants concluded that the "California syndrome," which saw Whitaker and Baxter (directors of the anti-EPIC campaign—see chapter 2) and then other public relations firms enter state politics in the 1930s, was slow to spread. Despite a steady expansion of activities in the 1950s, "in 1960, professional campaign managers were working in fewer than ten states on a regular basis." [16] Television provided viewers with little information about nonpresidential candidates, and the electorate tended to rely on party identification and incumbency as voting cues.

Although many state and local governments still controlled enough patronage to keep machines viable for gubernatorial and mayoral campaigns, congressional candidates, with little patronage at their disposal, could depend less on party organizations and had to construct more personal followings. A report in 1959 concluded, "The feeling is strong that local, state and national party organizations are indifferent and/or ineffective in lending support" to congressional campaigns. One House member observed:

> I don't think there is any element of the party that is particularly interested in or concerned with the election of members of Congress. The National Committee is preoccupied with the White House. The state committee has its eyes on the state house and the county committee is interested only in the court house. The congressman is just sort of a fifth wheel on the whole wagon.[17]

Instead, representatives turned to organized groups in their constituencies—unions, small businesses, civic associations—in which many had been active before they were elected to the House. Those who later entered the Senate tried to expand these networks. Almost 80 percent of the senators serving between 1947 and 1957 had been in public office at least five years before their election to the upper house. Almost two-thirds had served as representatives, governors, or state legislators immediately before their election.[18]

However, as party organizations continued to weaken through the 1960s and split-ticket voting increased, candidates for nonpresidential office found it necessary to employ the research and media professionals who had already ensconced themselves at the presidential level. The number of campaigns using such services advanced in a direct relationship with the increase in split-ticket voting. In 1962, 168 campaigns involved professional consultants; two years later the number was 280. Four years after that, in 1968, the number had jumped to 658.[19]

At first most of the candidates purchasing the services of consultants were nonincumbents and Republicans.[20] As with all campaign innovations, this one was first heavily employed by the out-party. More Democrats benefited from the advantages of incumbency and from outside help from favorably inclined constituency groups, particularly labor unions. The Republicans, with fewer shock troops but more money, struck back by buying assistance.

The candidate-centered campaign took root first and most widely in Senate contests. Unlike governors and mayors, senators did not have the services of state and local party organizations, nor was it as easy for them to practice at the statewide level the "friends and neighbors" politics of the representative. Senators were most vulnerable to the charge that they had lost touch with their states. The return rate of Senate incumbents in the 1960s and 1970s averaged only about two-thirds, as opposed to the 90 percent or so for House incumbents. Consequently, a survey of the sixty-seven Senate candidates in contested races in 1970 found that sixty-two employed advertising firms, twenty-four engaged national polling firms, and twenty had entrusted total management of their campaigns to consultants. A similar picture emerged in 1972. An earlier study, comparing the periods 1952-1957 and 1964-1969, found that the number of Senate campaigns employing consultants increased about 400 percent in primary elections and 500 percent in general elections.[21]

Additionally, the Senate, more than the House, attracted wealthy political amateurs willing to spend their own funds to finance a professional campaign. Among the hundred senators elected or re-elected between 1966 and 1970, only twelve, evenly divided between Democrats and Republicans, had held no previous public office. About half of these had been practicing attorneys, the traditional route to political office; only two were in business. The group elected between 1976 and 1982, however, was significantly different. The number holding no previous elective or appointive office more than doubled.

Only about a fifth of these were attorneys; twice as many were in business; and about two-thirds were Republicans. Although the House of Representatives remained the leading incubator for prospective senators, the number who came to the Senate from the state legislatures was halved. This latter group, which came up through the party ranks, was replaced not only by business executives but by former astronauts, a Vietnam POW, a professional athlete, and a television news director.

Although, as statewide officials, senators are more visible than representatives (but much less so than presidential candidates), it is more difficult for them to develop personal organizations in their larger constituencies. Television provided an answer to this problem, because senatorial constituencies tend to coincide better with television's media markets. (In most instances, a representative who bought TV time would be wasting resources, because advertisements would reach a large audience outside the representative's district.) Other statewide officials gradually succumbed to the lures of the media-based and professionally run campaign as party organizations and loyalties continued to weaken. From the 1950s to the 1960s, the proportionate use of consultants by candidates for these offices rose only about 150 percent in primaries and a little more than 200 percent in general elections, less than half the rate for Senate candidates.[22] The real breakthrough came in the early 1970s. In the 1972-1973 election cycle candidates employing at least one professional consultant numbered thirty-eight of forty-two gubernatorial candidates, thirty of thirty-seven aspirants for state attorney general, twenty of the thirty-two candidates for state treasurer, and nineteen of the thirty-one running for secretary of state.[23]

A typical early practitioner of the new candidate-centered campaign for an obscure statewide office was John Danforth, who was elected state attorney general in Missouri in 1968 (and later U.S. senator). Danforth was the first Missouri Republican to win a statewide election in twenty-two years and the first to go to the state capitol in twenty-eight years. At the age of thirty-two, he had spent his entire adult life outside Missouri until two years before his election. At least half of his campaign budget was spent on media, primarily television. His menu of television ads consisted of eighteen different spots, which were played 376 times in the last two weeks of the campaign. Extrapolating this rate of saturation on a national and yearly basis, his chief consultant compared it to the advertising expenditures of General Motors or Procter & Gamble, then the country's two largest advertisers.[24]

Representatives, as noted, tended to bypass the new style of campaigning. The various reasons for this reinforced each other. First, because their constituencies were smaller and hard to reach by television on a cost-effective basis, they were better insulated from well-financed challengers seeking instant recognition through television. Second, they were relatively free from press scrutiny. The information constituents received about them was almost entirely self-generated— through newsletters, questionnaires, and the like, or in press releases about pork barrel projects for the district. Through the 1960s and 1970s representatives also enlarged their local district offices and staff, which helped constituents cut through the red tape of the federal bureaucracy. Third, having to run for reelection every two years, rather than every four or six years like statewide and other federal officials, turned the nursing of their constituencies into what amounted to a permanent campaign. A constant presence in the district maintained the strength of the representative's electoral coalition and tended to discourage challengers. Fourth, the less glamorous life of the representative did not appeal to the kind of wealthy business executive who, tiring of life as the chief executive officer of a large corporation, found the possibility of being chief executive of a state or a member of the world's most exclusive club, the Senate, attractive.

Most of all, the weakening of the parties worked to the benefit of incumbent representatives. In the polling booth voters more or less divorced from party might be swayed to go with a gubernatorial or senatorial candidate who said something they agreed with or looked attractive on a television commercial. When the same voters came to the congressional column, though, they would be likely to press the lever for the only candidate they had ever heard of—the incumbent.

Thus a survey of 1980 voters found that 92 percent recognized the name of their congressional incumbents, but only 54 percent could identify the challengers. More than 90 percent said they had had some contact with the incumbent, either in person or through the media, compared to 44 percent who remembered some contact with the challenger. On the other hand, the figures were more nearly equal for Senate incumbents and challengers.

While representatives could generally ward off a challenger, senators faced with strong campaigns by well-known opponents had good reason to feel threatened. The propensity of voters to split tickets in Senate and House races was about the same. In 1956 only 9 percent of voters defected from the party in their congressional vote, but this figure had risen to 23 percent in 1980. The figure for Senate votes was similar: 12 percent in 1956 and 21 percent in 1980. As time went on, party defectors in House races increasingly opted for the incumbent. In the off-year elections of 1958, for instance, defectors chose the incumbent by about a two-to-one ratio; twenty years later this preference escalated to ten to one. In the Senate the story was different. Although no figures are available for the earlier year, defectors in 1978 favored

Senate incumbents by a margin of only three to one. Their more visible, better-financed, and professionally managed challengers had an easier time surmounting the advantages of incumbency.[25]

# The Restructuring
# of Campaign Finance

Candidates found that running campaigns in the increasingly partyless atmosphere of the 1970s was becoming more and more expensive. Statewide candidates had to lay out huge sums for polling, broadcast media, and voter targeting and contact. Members of Congress and state legislators who did not use television still had to pay for radio time, direct mail lists, production and postage costs, and telephone banks. The ability of challengers to mount expensive candidate-centered campaigns made even the most secure incumbents begin to feel shaky.

Adjusting for inflation, in 1986 constant dollars the average campaign war chests of House candidates rose from about $117,000 in 1974 to $260,000 in 1986, while the comparable Senate figures went from about $962,000 to more than $2.5 million. In the twelve years between 1974 and 1986, House campaign expenditures went up 487 percent in actual dollars, while the general cost of living rose only 220 percent. Senate campaign spending was up more than 60 percent in actual dollars in only the four years between 1982 and 1986.[26] These figures, of course, mask broad variations. Seventeen House candidates spent more than a million dollars in 1986, and Senate races exceeding $5 million were not uncommon.

The pressure to reach the expanding and volatile electorate through expensive technological means was the chief reason for the escalation in campaign costs. The Watergate scandal of 1972-1974 symbolized the dangers of the new campaign style. The unfolding saga, with its revelations of massive illegal contributions to Richard Nixon's 1972 presidential campaign, demonstrated the need for more fundamental campaign finance reforms than modest congressional legislation in 1971, which dealt primarily with public disclosure of contributions. Amendments to the 1971 legislation and court cases dealing with various aspects of the finance laws reshaped the financing of federal campaigns.

These campaign finance reforms reflected several themes: the need to limit the contributions of wealthy individuals and business interests, the corresponding need to increase small individual contributions, and the increasing nationalization of American politics. Although complex in detail, the major provisions of the new regulations, as they affected senators and representatives, may be summarized in four major points:

1. Individuals may not contribute more than $1,000 to any single candidate in each election, primary or general.
2. Groups, such as business, labor, or cause organizations, may not contribute more than $5,000 to any single candidate in each election, primary or general. The vehicle for such contributions is the political action committee.
3. The direct monetary contributions of political parties to campaigns are severely limited, but their ability to contribute indirectly, through provision of "in-kind" services, can be substantial.
4. Neither individuals, political action committees, nor parties are limited in the amount they can spend on "uncoordinated," or independent, expenditures (outlays for any form of political communication that are separate from a particular candidate's campaign). Nor are candidates limited in what they can spend on their own campaigns.

These provisions led to important changes in the environment of federal campaigns.[27] The next two sections examine the effects of the new regulations.

## The Effects on Individual and Group Contributions

The need to raise small amounts of money from large numbers of individuals put a premium on direct mail solicitation—and on efforts to obtain contributions from people who lived outside the candidates' constituencies but shared their policy views. Past campaign contributors grew accustomed to a deluge of mail from out-of-state candidates urging them to "elect a progressive Democrat to the Senate" or "help the Republicans regain our Senate majority." Like-minded candidates shared the names of contributors who had, in the Washington lingo, "maxed out"—contributed the maximum amount permissible to one candidate—but who might be willing to contribute to other candidates with similar policy stands. The proportionate contribution of out-of-district individual givers and political action committees rose steadily. By 1982 nonconstituent donors accounted for more than half of all contributions greater than $100.[28]

The second provision, which channeled group contributions through political action committees, changed campaign financing dramatically. Political action committees, or PACs, were first able to contribute significantly in 1974, and their expansion in both numbers and absolute levels of giving has been enormous. The number of PACs registered with the Federal Election Commission grew from 608 in 1974 to 4,211 in 1987; their contributions to House and Senate candidates jumped from $55 million in 1980 to $139 million in 1986. PAC outlays in 1986 comprised one-third of all funds contributed to congressional candidates. Incumbents collected 42 percent of all their campaign funds from PACs in 1986, a figure that grew to 45 percent in 1988.[29]

Political action committees fall into four basic categories: corporate, labor, trade, and "nonconnected." The first three types donate more than four out of five PAC dollars. Congressional legislation and the federal regulatory activity that Congress oversees have major effects on business and labor groups—producing a powerful incentive for them to contribute to legislative campaigns. Oil companies, for instance, are interested in deregulation and tax policy affecting their companies. Trade associations such as milk producers, automobile dealers, and real estate agents have a stake in issues such as dairy price supports, quotas on foreign car imports, and mortgage rates. Labor unions have wider interests but are specifically concerned about legislation affecting wages, workplace safety, and job and income security. Nonconnected PACs, which include environmental, right-to-life, feminist, and various other ideological groups on both the left and the right, also understand that legislation affects their interests. In addition, political figures, especially presidential aspirants and those holding or seeking congressional leadership positions, are forming their own PACs.[30]

In general, business and labor PACs are much more likely to contribute to incumbent officeholders, while nonconnected PACs give relatively more often to challengers. Business PACs are also more likely to donate to Republicans; their contributions to Democrats are almost exclusively confined to incumbent officeholders serving on congressional committees that regulate their industries. Although labor PACs give a small amount to incumbent Republicans, more than 90 percent of their donations go to Democrats. The Democrats' narrow advantage in PAC money has been attributable to their monopoly on donations from labor groups and their larger number of incumbent officeholders.

Independent expenditures by political action committees—specific campaign-related activities undertaken directly by PACs as opposed to general-purpose campaign contributions to candidates—have grown in recent years, increasing to $9.4 million in 1986 from $5.7 million in 1982. Their character and purpose has also changed. In the late 1970s and early 1980s conservative "cause" groups such as the National Conservative Political Action Committee (NCPAC) were responsible for most independent spending. NCPAC, which specialized in airing early negative television advertising against liberal senators up for reelection, was responsible for 58 percent of all independent expenditures in 1982.

In the 1984 election such groups still dominated independent spending efforts but switched to mostly positive messages about conservative heroes involved in close races—for instance, Texas senator Phil Gramm and North Carolina senator Jesse Helms. By 1986, however, vulnerable liberals seemed in short supply, and many of the conservative PACs were experiencing fund-raising problems.

Less ideological groups interested in preserving economic advantages were the largest independent spenders in 1986. Six PACs that each made more than $400,000 in independent expenditures were responsible for 86 percent of the total independent spending that year. NCPAC, the National Rifle Association, and the National Right to Life Committee (an antiabortion group) spent about $2 million among them, but this amount was outdistanced by the more than $5 million spent by the American Medical Association's AMPAC, the real estate interests' RPAC, and the National Committee to Preserve Social Security. The dominance of the less ideological independent spenders was even more pronounced in 1988, when the cause groups switched their attention to the presidential race.[31]

## The Effects on Party Contributions

**Republicans.**   Another major infusion of funds into campaigns, beginning in the 1970s, came from the Republican party's national committees based in Washington. State and local Republican parties were more active than their Democratic counterparts, but few of the organizations below the national level in either party played a substantial role in congressional or senatorial races. Between the 1960s and the 1980s there was some organizational strengthening of the state parties, as they became more likely to have permanent headquarters and staff and to undertake activities such as campaign schools for legislative hopefuls and registration drives. Nevertheless, the state parties through this period recruited candidates for fewer offices, contributed less money directly to campaigns, and raised funds at a rate that did not match inflation.[32] The most important party activity, in other words, was at the national level and affected federal candidates.

Behind the Republicans' national fund-raising drive was a well-orchestrated campaign to engineer a comeback. Until 1980 the Republicans, except for a brief period during the Eisenhower presidency, had been in a decided minority in both houses of Congress for fifty years. They had barely recovered from their severe defeat in the 1964 Goldwater debacle when they suffered an equally devastating loss in the 1974 elections as a result of Watergate. The Republicans therefore determined that only a massive and well-financed effort by the national party to build up its grass roots could make their candidates competitive.

Aware of the premium the new campaign finance laws placed on small contributions, the Republicans used the technological developments of the 1970s to embark on a spectacularly successful direct mail campaign, which by the 1980s had raised enormous sums from a donor base of more than two million names. Between 1976 and 1986 all Republican committees together increased their receipts more than five times, from about $46 million to $252 million. Their receipts outstripped the Democrats roughly two and a half to one in 1976; this figure escalated to better than five to one in 1982 and was still more than four to one in 1986.

Further revisions in the campaign finance laws made the overflowing coffers of the national Republican party increasingly valuable to its congressional and senatorial candidates. New legislation permitted the Washington-based party committees to make further expenditures as "agents" for state and local parties, which could pay for in-kind services such as polling and media production costs. The upshot was that by 1986 national party committees could give a maximum of almost $73,000 to each House campaign. Much more was available to Senate candidates, whose permissible party contributions were governed by the size of the state's population. Senate candidates could receive as much as $1.7 million.

By the elections of the 1980s, the Republicans could afford, if they chose, to contribute to the legal maximum in every federal campaign. In fact, they targeted their expenditures to marginal House contests, giving little either to safe incumbents or to seemingly hopeless challengers. With fewer Senate seats being contested in any given election, almost all Republican Senate candidates received the maximum permissible amount.

In 1984 the Republicans devised another method to expand the limits on party-generated contributions to Senate campaigns. The National Republican Senatorial Committee (NRSC) solicited contributions to several closely contested races from individuals and forwarded them to candidate campaign committees as individual contributions, a practice known as "bundling." By 1986 its bundled contributions to tight Senate races exceeded $4 million.

In addition, the Republican party used its money for institutional activities that benefited all of its candidates and that were not connected to particular campaigns. It spent millions on polls to identify vulnerable Democrats and their weaknesses, devised elaborate targeting programs for selected districts, offered training schools to congressional candidates it recruited, and deployed field representatives to advise campaigns. The party's media center produced generic national television advertising, telling voters in 1980 to "vote Republican for a change," to "stay the course" in 1982, that "America is back" in 1984, and that the prosperity small children had known all their lives could be maintained by Republican victories in 1988. More diffuse party messages in 1986 were aimed at young voters and southern Christian fundamentalists. The party media center also produced advertising for individual House candidates. In 1984 twenty-five candidates got "full-service" National Republican Congressional Committee (NRCC) assistance, which included writing advertising copy, sending NRCC film crews to the candidate's district, and editing the film.

In the late 1970s the Republicans turned their attention to the state legislatures, hoping to get control of more of them by 1980 and thus give Republicans a greater role in shaping the congressional redistricting that followed the 1980 census. GOPAC, a unit of the Republican National Committee (RNC), contributed a half-million dollars, ran 120 campaign seminars, and deployed fourteen field personnel in 1978 and 1980. This effort met with little success, and by 1988 the number of state legislative houses controlled by the Republicans had dropped to twenty-nine, down from the thirty-five of 1980, or less than one-third of the total. Consequently, the RNC planned to spend $15 million on state legislative races by 1990, with the hope of being more effective in the next reapportionment period.[33]

Finally, the Republican party cooperated closely with a number of friendly political action committees, meeting weekly with interested Washington-based PACs to inform them about targeted races. A coordinator of this activity boasted, "We're making sure that everyone gets from 150 to 400 grand extra, and that's a big wallop out there in a congressional district."[34]

**Democrats.** The opportunities to contribute to federal campaigns were of course theoretically open to the Democratic party as well, but early in the period particularly, it had substantially less money to offer its candidates. The Democrats' average donation was only a fourth of the Republicans' in Senate races and only a tenth in House races. There were three factors behind the paucity of Democratic money. First, the Democrats were in a sense the victims of their own success. With large majorities for so many years in both houses of Congress, they did not have the same need to raise money in pursuit of electoral success, nor as compelling a message to send to would-be givers. Second, because of the party's heterogeneity, whatever message the Democrats transmitted would be rejected by either its conservative or liberal wing. A consultant close to the national committees observed, "It's so broad, as soon as they ran an institutional ad for half the party, the other half would scream and holler and you can't do it. The only thing they can be is against something." Third, much of their support was among the economically disadvantaged. As a staffer at a Democratic national committee said:

> Our inability to raise the money probably has something to do with not knowing which buttons to push, but it has something to do with our constituency. If the Democratic party is the party that represents minorities and poor people, those are the very people who cannot contribute to us. How many middle class people do you know that became wealthy as a result of Democratic policies and then became Republicans? Republicans are wealthy people. Are we Democrats not motivating them, or are they not out there?

Nevertheless, the loss of the presidency and the Senate in 1980 mobilized the Democrats to emulate the Republicans' direct mail fundraising efforts, and they met with some success. By 1986 the Democratic Senatorial and Congressional Campaign committees (DSCC and DCCC) could make the maximum party contribution in most of the closest races. Their success at fund raising permitted them to open a state-of-the-art media center in 1984 and begin generic advertising. They were able to expand their field staff, polling activities, and communication with PACs; they could assist candidates and state parties and perform most of the other endeavors previously monopolized by the Republicans.[35]

The Democrats also had other resources. One party staffer observed: "Republicans pay for things Democrats don't pay for. People volunteer to work on Democratic campaigns." The volunteers were frequently labor union activists or members of other groups associated with the Democratic party. A Republican consultant who earlier had worked with Democrats remembered the constituency groups and union activists who flocked to Democratic campaigns: "They had the capability; it was expected that they would do it. The only thing you had to do, when they had their local dinner—the congressman had to show up, stroke the leaders, and buy a table. Republicans don't have it." Additionally, the Democrats' domination of entry-level positions in the state legislatures gave them a larger pool of candidates who had developed their own resources: "Without a strong contingent of state legislators, a party's talent pool is severely restricted."[36] One of the reasons the Republicans had to raise money and recruit candidates was that there were fewer potential candidates engaged in self-recruitment.

**An Appraisal of the Role of Parties.** The dramatic success of the Republicans at raising money and strengthening their national organizations and the Democrats' gains would seem to argue against a thesis of party decline. However, if one reviews the ostensible major functions of parties—to structure the nomination process and provide alternative policy agendas—it is questionable whether the parties have in fact arrested the move to candidate-centered politics. Although we will discuss this issue in detail in chapter 11, it can be persuasively argued that current party activity merely subsidizes candidate-centered campaigns. By concentrating on aiding candidates who are "electable," usually staying out of primary races and not demanding programmatic commitments from the candidates it supports, parties may be viewed simply as giant, well-financed PACs that can make larger contributions than other PACs.[37]

## The Nationalization of Politics

The provisions of the new campaign finance laws contributed to the nationalization and homogenization of politics. Candidates who in the past had run modestly financed campaigns, depending upon party workers and local party financial support, found themselves seeking funds from individuals nationwide who shared their positions and from the national party apparatus (a shell until the late 1970s) rather than from the frequently enfeebled state and local organizations. Many PACs also took an essentially national rather than local view. Although some PACs based their giving on local considerations (such as whether they had plants or offices located in a particular constituency), the major rationales for supporting candidates were their positions on national issues and their ability to influence federal legislation of interest to the PAC.[38] The consultants candidates hired often did not have local roots, either, but roamed the country; they were recommended by candidates who had used them in earlier races. Their specialization might be moderate Republicans or populist Democrats, but it made no difference to them whether the candidate was in New Jersey or in Arizona. The techniques, and often the message, were the same.

Thus, by the 1980s, the candidate- and media-centered campaign had penetrated to every level of American politics. The local party bosses were all but gone, and media consultants, pollsters, direct mail specialists, and professional organizers had come to the fore. How did these new specialists approach campaigns? What considerations made for the success or failure of given campaigns? These are the questions we address in the next six chapters. We begin at the beginning—the first stage of candidate-centered campaigns.

# Notes

1. Tip O'Neill with William Novak, *Man of the House: The Life and Political Times of Speaker Tip O'Neill* (New York: Random House, 1987), 76.
2. Edward C. Banfield and James Q. Wilson, *City Politics* (Cambridge, Mass.: Harvard University Press, 1963), 121.
3. Stimson Bullitt, *To Be a Politician* (Garden City, N.Y.: Doubleday, 1961), 68.
4. Banfield and Wilson, *City Politics,* 122.
5. See William J. Crotty, *American Parties in Decline,* 2d ed. (Boston: Little, Brown, 1984), 34-36, for a discussion of the growth in split-ticket voting.
6. Theodore H. White, *The Making of the President, 1960* (New York: Harper and Row, 1961), 23.
7. Eugene Burdick, *The 480* (New York: McGraw-Hill, 1964). The actual project is described in Ithiel de Sola Poole, Robert B. Abelson, and Samuel Popkin, *Candidates, Issues and Strategies: A Computer Simulation of the 1960 and 1964 Elections,* rev. ed. (Cambridge, Mass.: MIT Press, 1965).
8. Theodore H. White, *America in Search of Itself: The Making of the President, 1956-1980* (New York: Harper and Row, 1982), 165. The number of TV stations also grew from 108 in 1952 to 661 in 1964. Frank J. Sorauf, *Money in American Elections* (Glenview, Ill.: Scott, Foresman, 1988), 25.
9. Stanley Kelley, Jr., *Professional Public Relations and Political Power* (Baltimore: Johns Hopkins University Press, 1956), 1. For details of the plan, see Harold L. Lavine, ed., *Smoke-Filled Rooms: The Confidential Papers of Robert Humphreys* (Englewood Cliffs, N.J.: Prentice-Hall, 1970).
10. Kelley, *Professional Public Relations,* 160.
11. Ibid., 188. The Eisenhower-Stevenson television campaigns are also discussed in detail in Edwin Diamond and Stephen Bates, *The Spot: The Rise of Political Advertising* (Cambridge, Mass.: MIT Press, 1984), chapter 3.
12. Herbert E. Alexander, "Broadcasting and Politics," in *Elections and the Political Order,* ed. Kent Jennings and Harmon Ziegler (Englewood Cliffs, N.J.: Prentice-Hall, 1966), 86; Herbert E. Alexander, *Financing Politics: Money, Elections and Political Reform,* 3d ed. (Washington, D.C.: CQ Press, 1984), 127.
13. Joe McGinniss, *The Selling of the President, 1968* (New York: Trident Press, 1969).
14. Michael J. Robinson, "Television and American Politics," *Public Interest* 48 (Summer 1977): 21.
15. See the data in David Adamany, "Financing National Politics," in *The New Style in Election Campaigns,* ed. Robert Agranoff, 2d ed. (Boston: Holbrook Press, 1976), 381-384, and Herbert E. Alexander and Brian A. Haggerty, *Financing the 1984 Election* (Lexington, Mass.: Lexington Books, 1987), 84. In constant dollars the presidential elections of the public finance era have cost only slightly more than was spent in 1964.
16. David Rosenbloom, *The Election Men* (New York: Quadrangle, 1973), 50-51.
17. Charles L. Clapp, *The Congressman: His Work as He Sees It* (New York: Anchor, 1964), 397, 398.
18. Donald R. Matthews, *U.S. Senators and Their World* (Chapel Hill: University of North Carolina Press, 1960), 53, 55.
19. Rosenbloom, *Election Men,* 53.
20. See *Congressional Quarterly Weekly Report,* April 5, 1968.
21. Data from *National Journal,* September 26, 1970, 2084-2085; Agranoff, *New Style in Election Campaigns,* 8; Rosenbloom, *Election Men,* 51.

22. Rosenbloom, *Election Men*, 51.
23. Agranoff, *New Style in Election Campaigns*, 8. The absolute numbers for the three latter offices are smaller because not all states elect these officials.
24. Harry N. D. Fisher, "How the 'I Dare You!' Candidate Won," in Agranoff, *New Style in Election Campaigns*, 79-86.
25. The data in these paragraphs appear in Thomas E. Mann and Raymond Wolfinger, "Candidates and Parties in Congressional Elections," *American Political Science Review* 74 (September 1980): 617-632. Some methodological questions about the validity of the recognition data are raised by David John Gow and Robert B. Eubank, "The Pro-Incumbent Bias in the 1982 National Election Study," *American Journal of Political Science* 28 (February 1984): 224-229, and Robert Eubank and David John Gow, "The Pro-Incumbent Bias in the 1978 and 1980 National Election Studies," *American Journal of Political Science* 27 (February 1983): 122-139.
26. Data constructed from tables 3-1, 3-4, and 5-9 in Norman J. Ornstein, Thomas E. Mann, and Michael J. Malbin, *Vital Statistics on Congress, 1987-1988* (Washington, D.C.: Congressional Quarterly, 1987), 72-73, 77-78, 150.
27. The campaign reform ethos also had some effect on the states. Approximately half the states have enacted contribution limits for state elections, and about a fifth have passed spending limits. Generally, however, the restrictions are much less stringent than federal legislation. See Alexander, *Financing Politics*, chapter 7; Sorauf, *Money in American Elections*, chapter 9.
28. Janet Grenzke, "Campaign Financing Practices and the Nature of Representation," paper presented at the annual meeting of the American Political Science Association, Washington, D.C., August 30-September 2, 1984, 6.
29. Data in this paragraph are from Sorauf, *Money in American Elections*, chapter 4, and *Congressional Quarterly Weekly Report*, November 12, 1988, 3271.
30. For discussions of these member PACs, see Sorauf, *Money in American Elections*, 174-181; *Congressional Quarterly Weekly Report*, August 2, 1986, 1751-1754.
31. Some good recent discussions of independent expenditures include Sorauf, *Money in American Elections*, 110-117; Thomas R. Berglund and Peter Lauer, "Political Prescriptions: AMPAC and Independent Expenditures," *Election Politics* 3 (Fall 1986): 18-20; *Congressional Quarterly Weekly Report*, November 5, 1988, 3185-3187.
32. See David A. Leuthold, *Electioneering in a Democracy* (New York: Wiley, 1968), chapter 3; Cornelius P. Cotter, James L. Gibson, John F. Bibby, and Robert J. Huckshorn, *Party Organizations in American Politics*, (New York: Praeger, 1984); Advisory Commission on Intergovernmental Relations, *The Transformation of American Politics* (Washington, D.C.: Advisory Commission on Intergovernmental Relations, 1986), chapter 3. Assessments of the Cotter et al. findings appear in David E. Price, *Bringing Back the Parties* (Washington, D.C.: CQ Press, 1984), 34-36, and Advisory Commission on Intergovernmental Relations, *Transformation of American Politics*, chapter 3.
33. See *Congressional Quarterly Weekly Report*, October 25, 1980, 3188-3192; March 9, 1985, 459; and November 12, 1988, 3299-3300; *Public Opinion*, December-January 1985, 27.
34. Elizabeth Drew, "Politics and Money, I," *New Yorker*, December 6, 1982, 54ff.
35. Among the numerous accounts of party campaign activities, see Xandra Kayden and Eddie Mahe, *The Party Goes On* (New York: Basic Books, 1985); Larry J. Sabato, *The Party's Just Begun* (Glenview, Ill.: Scott, Foresman, 1988);

Sorauf, *Money in American Elections*, chapter 5; Dan S. Nimmo, "Teleparty Politics," *Campaigns and Elections* 6 (Winter 1986): 75-78; Paul S. Herrnson, *Party Campaigning in the 1980s* (Cambridge, Mass.: Harvard University Press, 1988).

36. John Bibby, "State House Elections at Midterm," in Thomas E. Mann and Norman J. Ornstein, *American Elections of 1982* (Washington, D.C.: American Enterprise Institute, 1983), 127.

37. An argument suggested in F. Christopher Arterton, "Political Money and Party Strength," in *The Future of American Political Parties*, ed. Joel L. Fleishman (Englewood Cliffs, N.J.: Prentice-Hall, 1982), 101-139.

38. On PAC decision making, see Diana Owen, "The Information Environment for PAC Decision-Making," paper presented at the annual meeting of the American Political Science Association, Washington, D.C., August 28-31, 1986; John R. Wright, "PACs, Contributions and Roll Calls," *American Political Science Review* 79 (June 1985): 400-414; Theodore J. Eismeier and Philip H. Pollock, "Strategy and Choice in Congressional Elections: The Role of Political Action Committees," in *American Journal of Political Science* 30 (February 1986): 197-213; Eismeier and Pollock, "The Political Geography of Political Action Committees: National Cash and the Local Connection in Congressional Elections," paper presented at the annual meeting of the American Political Science Association, Washington, D.C., September 1-4, 1988.

# Creating a Credible Campaign: Incumbents   4

> *Look at the incumbo-phobia in New York. They have a conservative Republican senator they can't find an opponent for and a governor who is the last unreconstructed Democratic liberal, and they can't find an opponent for him. That tells you something about the power of incumbency.*
>
> Politician's comment on the 1986 New York elections[1]

There is an old saying that American political campaigns do not begin until after the World Series, when Americans shift their attention from one great spectator sport to another. With the lengthening of both the baseball and campaign seasons, this axiom no longer holds true. The seeds of most campaigns have taken root many months—sometimes several years—before the autumn of election year. By early fall they have developed in significant ways that determine whether the candidate has any real chance of winning. Some may already have made decisions that will almost certainly lead to failure. Others have made important strides toward success.

In understanding why this is so, it is helpful to distinguish between the internal campaign and the external campaign. The external campaign is the visible one directed to voters; the internal campaign is the activity going on within the apparatus set up to conduct the race. By early fall serious candidates for any public office, from a seat in the state legislature to a race for the governorship or the U.S. Senate, must have formulated a successful strategy and must be in a position to carry it out.

Formulating a strategy requires information about the electorate, gathered from polling and analysis of other data, primarily past voting patterns. A campaign organization must be in place to determine what information is needed, to commission its collection, to analyze it, to devise the strategy, and to direct its implementation. Collecting the information and sustaining the organization require money. These processes must begin long before the contest enters the consciousness of the public, and they are the job of the internal campaign.

By September the internal campaign must have completed these tasks, although the external campaign—to the general public—may have barely begun. Even if candidates have not yet publicly laid out their major appeals, they must have achieved some recognition and acceptance from prospective voters. With the decline of party as a voting cue, the candidate becomes the most important cue. A candidate who is unknown, or known and disliked, does not have much time to rectify a blank or negative image. Therefore, the first stage of a successful external campaign is becoming known and becoming liked.

Although all credible campaigns must meet these requirements, many considerations, as noted in chapter 1, affect the way this stage of the campaign is played out. Foremost is whether an incumbent is in the race. Incumbents have tremendous advantages; no matter what the office, they begin their campaigns with a much better than even chance of winning reelection. Other factors shape a campaign's early activities. Among them are the office for which the candidate is running, the relative strength of the political parties in the constituency and its geography and demography, and prevailing national trends. In this chapter we discuss how incumbents plan their campaigns and how strategy decisions are affected by the context in which the campaign operates. The following chapter does the same for challengers.

## Assets of Incumbency

As we have noted, the incumbent in any race usually begins with formidable advantages, the most important of which are recognition, money, and time. Widespread positive recognition goes a long way toward satisfying the requirements of the early external campaign. Money and time are necessary ingredients for the internal campaign. Incumbency also has possible disadvantages, though, and two in particular can sometimes defeat an incumbent: negative recognition (the perception that the incumbent has not done a good job) and complacency. In this section we look at the way successful candidates use the advantages of incumbency and cope with some of its disadvantages during the internal campaign. The liabilities of running as an office-holder are discussed in a later section.

# Recognition

Because of their previous campaigns and their activities in office, incumbents usually are much better known than their opponents. How well informed voters are likely to be about an incumbent depends in part on the office the candidate is seeking. Knowledge is greater when (1) the constituency is broader (representatives are better known than state legislators; senators are better known than representatives), (2) the office is executive rather than legislative (governors have greater recognition than senators), and (3) the office is more widely covered by the media (both print and broadcast media give more attention to the activities of governors than those of senators). The more exposure voters have to a candidate, the easier it is for them to make a positive or negative judgment. Within this framework incumbents must plan how to exploit the recognition that incumbency gives them.

**House Members.**  It is always to the candidates' advantage to be able to shape the information voters have about them. The office of U.S. representative provides a good example. Most members of Congress receive little media coverage and even less critical scrutiny from the press, but they have substantial resources for direct communication with their constituents.

Except for the handful in the House leadership or the unhappy few involved in scandal, representatives generate media coverage primarily through their own press releases: "Most newspapers in the country simply have no congressional coverage they can call their own. This is fine with most congressmen. Among the various high crimes and misdemeanors with which they charge the press, noncoverage is not one of them."[2] A thoughtful reporter describes the relationship between representatives and the press:

> Between the big story and the local sewer grant lies a vast unreported landscape ... which is almost never seen in the daily paper, let alone on local television. In this wasteland, a symbiotic relationship flourishes between congressman and correspondent, a relationship based on mutual need and sometimes mutual laziness. This relationship permits the typical invisible congressman to become visible in a highly selective way in his home district.[3]

Even if the will were there, it would be difficult for the media to cover most representatives. Large urban areas elect too many for metropolitan newspapers or television stations to report on them in any reasonable fashion. Within the New York City television market, for instance, thirty-five congressional districts span three states: twenty-three in New York State, ten in New Jersey, and two in Connecticut. The nineteen districts in the Chicago market also cross three states: Illinois,

Indiana, and Wisconsin. Television stations faced with covering this number of representatives, all but one of whom will be of little or no interest to most of their viewers, generally cover none. In less densely populated areas a representative's district may stretch across several media markets, none of which considers the official to be "its" representative. It is the rare member of the House whose district is small enough to dominate a TV market and offer the officeholder some expectation of regular coverage. Wichita, Kansas, and Little Rock, Arkansas, are two such rare cases.[4]

Evidence exists that the office itself affects the media coverage. In Wyoming in 1982, for instance, there were races covering exactly the same constituencies for governor, for senator, and for the one at-large (statewide) congressional seat. Both the Senate and gubernatorial races received extensive front-page attention in the three newspapers in Casper and Cheyenne. The House race got one front-page story late in the campaign. The headline was telling: "Who vs. What's His Name: Wyoming's Other Campaign." Asserting that the senatorial and gubernatorial races "are both household conversation topics and certainly issues for debate in social circles," the reporter observed of the House race, "But what about Ted Hommel vs. Dick Cheney? Discussion about that contest is almost as hush-hush as hemorrhoids."[5]

Representatives, as we noted, are ready to fill the void created by the lack of media attention. Their major resources for communication, in addition to news releases, are the congressional frank (free mailing privileges to all "postal patrons"—all households in their districts) and district offices and staff. Since representatives face another contest less than twenty-one months after each Congress convenes in January of odd-numbered years, it is not surprising that these resources almost immediately become tools for reelection. Nearly anything short of a campaign brochure appears to fall within the rubric of "official business," the legal limitation on the use of the frank. Questionnaires, newsletters, and invitations to town meetings pour out of congressional offices, increasing dramatically as election time draws closer. The volume of postal patron mailings in September of election years, compared with the same month in nonelection years, is more than double. In advance of the 1988 elections, House members spent more than $5 million on 58 million mail pieces. The average of eight staff members now assigned to district offices is more than twice the number in 1974.[6]

Newsletters inform citizens about legislation or other government matters, and questionnaires and town meetings help representatives elicit the views of their constituents and carry out the functions of the office. But another clear effect is to bring the House member recognition—and positive recognition. One top aide in a congressional office has commented:

> The thing that makes you the concerned congressman is the town meeting. It's immaterial how many people show up; it's the fact that I mailed two hundred thousand postcards that we're having it. We don't care if six people show up, as long as we got the extra mail out.

Similarly, district offices, which aid individual constituents in cutting red tape at the Social Security Administration, the Immigration and Naturalization Service, or the Veterans Administration, or help local governments deal with federal agencies, garner much favorable feeling for incumbent members of Congress. Activities that assist constituents are known as casework. A manual for congressional caseworkers distributed by the National Republican Congressional Committee (NRCC) advises its readers:

> A CONSTITUENT is the LIFEBLOOD of this and every other congressional office. Let your constituents know that you are willing to serve. This can be accomplished by coordinating with your press aide by inserting articles in the Member's newsletters advising of the Congressman's willingness to help or by sending out postcard mailings with the same message. Make it impossible for the constituents not to know that the Congressman is accessible and anxious to help.

A 1985 franked mailing from Arizona Republican representative John McCain, elected senator in 1986, shows how officeholders take this advice. Accompanying an eight-page pamphlet explaining the benefits available from the Social Security program, a "Dear Friend" letter explained: "This material will help you determine what services are available to meet your specific needs. If there are any questions . . . please call my office. . . . My staff and I will make every effort to help you." It concluded with the telephone numbers for his two district offices. The mailing also notified McCain's constituents of the eight town meetings and two cable TV call-in programs he had planned during a three-day period that month.

Although constituency service has become prominent in virtually every congressional office, it is particularly important to junior members seeking to strengthen their positions in the district and to members of the minority party who do not have the additional resources that come from committee or subcommittee chairmanships. A head staffer in a first-term representative's office explained, "As a freshman, constituency service is more important than legislation because he has no power and he needs to get re-elected."[7] Arizona Republican representative Jim Kolbe was convinced that the fourteen-point increase in his victory margin between his first and second elections was attributable to dedicated constituency service:

We've solidified our position despite a six to eight point margin against us in voter registrations. . . . We've done it because we worked hard at it. We said we'd do 100 town meetings and we did. We opened up constituency service offices in the rural counties.[8]

Systematic evidence confirms that constituency service has become more noticeable to constituents and that it is having the desired effect. Between 1958 and 1978 the number of voters who recalled an instance of constituency service by their representative more than tripled to almost one in five. The number citing attentiveness to constituents as the prime reason for evaluating their representative positively rose from a tenth to a quarter. At the same time the corresponding figures for those citing the member's party affiliation, experience, and record declined.[9]

In addition to the benefits stemming from the resources of the office, incumbent House members often run in districts deliberately drawn to advantage them. State legislatures shape congressional districts every ten years after the results of the decennial U.S. census are known. In the past their propensity to draw districts that were as safe as possible for one party, a strategy known as gerrymandering, was notorious. In recent years, however, court decisions striking down the most blatant attempts at partisan gerrymandering and the growing importance of incumbency rather than party as a voting cue have shifted the focus of those who shape congressional districts.

Where possible, those who control redistricting now think in terms of advantaging their party's incumbents and breaking up the strength of the other party's incumbents. Where court-imposed decisions make that impossible, their impulse is to protect all incumbents.[10] The redistricting that occurred in 1980 gave rise to oddly shaped districts that journalists and pols dubbed with names such as the "fish hook" and the "swan." Outraged Republicans in one state with a Democratic dominated legislature complained that a coastal district with a perenially shaky Democratic incumbent was "only contiguous at low tide." Members affected by redistricting have time to deal with its effects, too, because they know their new district lines about a year before the next election. Since 1973 incumbents have been permitted to use the postal frank and other official resources to communicate with the new areas of their districts as soon as the lines are set.

It is not surprising, then, that on average more than 90 percent of incumbent members of Congress who run for reelection are successful. In 1988 incumbents set historic records for success: more than 98 percent were reelected (three-quarters with more than 60 percent of the vote), and eighty had no major party opposition. Commenting on the outlook for 1988 eight months before the election, *Congressional Quarterly Weekly Report* observed that "the lack of competition this year is beyond the ordinary," strongly suggesting "that the expense and effort required to oust an incumbent is increasingly prohibitive in many parts of the country."[11]

**Senators.** Incumbent senators face a different situation. Voters know their senators in a different, more impersonal way than they know their representatives in the House. Senators, who represent entire states, come up for election only once every six years, and have more limited use of the postal patron frank, cannot maintain the same close ties with their constituents. Although they have about the same amount of contact with their constituents as representatives do, the nature of the contact is different. Constituents are much more likely to say they have met their representatives, seen them at meetings, or talked to their staffs. Conversely, they are more likely to say they have seen their senators on television or heard them on the radio.[12] A study of reporting by Washington-based journalists found that television covered activities in the Senate twice as often as events in the House of Representatives, and mention of the names of particular senators occurred three times more frequently than those of individual representatives.[13]

Senators try to use official resources in much the same way that representatives do. Although only about a third of all Senate staff is based in district offices, compared to two-fifths of all House staff, the Senate figure has almost tripled since 1972. Senate use of the frank has also risen dramatically, with the heaviest users concentrated among those facing difficult reelection contests. Nebraska senator David Karnes, for example, sent out more than a million pieces of mail in 1988, including eight targeted newsletters on subjects ranging from Alzheimer's disease to agriculture. When Karnes's mail account was depleted, two of his Republican colleagues not up for reelection that year transferred $73,000 from their accounts to that of their beleaguered and ultimately unsuccessful associate.[14]

Taking advantage of their better access, however, senators look increasingly to the media to maintain favorable recognition. Only thirty-one of the hundred senators had press secretaries in 1960; ninety-eight did by 1984.[15] Any important domestic or foreign policy event finds senators heading for the Senate television studios, local news programs, and the Sunday morning talk shows. Newspapers routinely call them for their reactions to such events. But this coverage is uncritical and unanalytical, permitting senators to frame a response in whatever they regard as the best possible light. Their task is made easier by the nature of the statewide press corps, which is usually based in the state capital and engaged most of the time in covering state politics, particularly the activities of the governor. A political reporter has observed: "It's less important to find out what a senator thinks of an issue than a governor. The senator is not going to be guiding the policy of the country the way a governor guides the state." A good Senate staff can take advantage of this relative lack of scrutiny by shaping the early media coverage of the candidate in a favorable way. A Senate press secretary described the process:

> We have an operation that runs on a campaign footing. We have a very active press and mail outreach, even though our next election is four years off. For example, we recently did something manufactured for TV. We went to a house mentioned in a HUD scandal and we packaged the whole event. When we went to the site, we had every TV station in the city. We had a live shot from the house at noon go back to the number-one-rated station. Everything was made simple. They got us making the charges. They got the HUD people on the right answering them, the aggrieved residents on the left. They got the lock being broken, the visuals. Even though we're not campaigning, that's the quintessential campaign "hit."

A top staffer in the same office gave the rationale for planning such events: "His name ID hasn't gone up since he was elected. It's like nothing has happened in a year. It isn't good enough. It's only two or three years until the Republicans decide if they're going to target that seat." As a result of such efforts, 73 percent of Senate incumbents retained their seats in the six elections between 1974 and 1986.

**Governors.**   Other than the president, governors are the officials of whom the public gains the clearest view from mass media sources. Even more than senators, governors become known to voters because they are seen on television.[16] In one of the nation's largest states, a former governor, out of office for four years, was debating whether to run against an incumbent senator who was serving his fourth term and was chairman of a major Senate committee. A poll commissioned by the former governor to explore his chances a year before the election found that the senator's recognition level among voters was 67 percent, while the ex-governor's rating was 72 percent. The pollster commented, "What a graphic illustration of news coverage that four years after a governor has left office he is better known than a senator who has been in office for better than two decades!"

Covered on an almost daily basis by the print media—whose bureaus are based in the statehouses—governors, as initiators of controversial policy proposals, are constantly in the limelight. Any slip they make, no matter how minor, can result in negative appraisals of their official behavior. The media's frequent attention, and substantive and critical scrutiny, leads to more negative public perceptions of governors than of legislators.[17] Consultant Vincent Breglio describes the susceptibility of a governor to a bad press:

A governor's record is far more crucial than a senator's record. Governors have their hands on the throttle of all the things that directly influence people in a state. A race for governor is a microcosm of the presidential race. They see in that chair all the power to make good things happen or bad things happen. That's not true with senators or representatives. For a governor, it's meat and potatoes—what's his or her record? If the farmers haven't had rain, the governor's going to get blamed.

The location of the state capital is important in determining the public's evaluation of a governor. A consultant who has worked on many gubernatorial races explained:

It's very critical what proportion of the state is served by the media market the state capital is in. In Mississippi, say, 50 percent of the people are in the Jackson media market, and they all know about state government. It's the same with Denver and Colorado. New York State is very well covered by TV, but state politics isn't because Albany is a jerkwater town. In a state like West Virginia, only about a quarter of the population lives in that media market. An incumbent has the opportunity to tell people what his record is during a campaign, whereas in other states they already know.

The 1985 gubernatorial race in New Jersey, whose state capital, Trenton, is hardly the center of the media universe, provides a graphic example of the consultant's last point. New Jersey has no network TV station of its own, and the capital lies within the Philadelphia market, which serves a much smaller part of New Jersey's population than does the New York City market to the north. Reassuring polls throughout the second half of incumbent Thomas Kean's term showed him well liked by the public and well ahead of his largely unknown Democratic opponents. These same polls indicated, however, that while the public regarded their governor very favorably, most of them could not cite anything specific he had done in office. His campaign consultants therefore advertised his record in heavy media buys during the 1983 legislative midterm elections, two years before he had to face the voters. Although he was unopposed in the spring 1985 primary, his campaign launched another major advertising effort on New York television to remind voters of his accomplishments. His principal strategist, Roger Stone, explained that the ads were intended to "flesh out Kean. People knew him, but nothing about him."

Traditionally, the high visibility of governors and their association with often unpopular legislation such as tax increases made them more vulnerable to defeat than senators or representatives, but in recent years a governor's prospects for reelection have improved. Between 1900 and 1930 the percentage of governors (who were legally able to do so) seeking reelection ranged from under one-half to less than two-thirds;

in the 1960s the average rose to more than three-quarters. And those who sought to stay in office were more successful than their predecessors. Whereas a third suffered defeat through the 1960s, 76 percent were successful in 1982, and 89 percent in 1986.[18] Each of the nine governors who won victories of more than 60 percent of the vote in 1986 was an incumbent, and more than half of the incumbents running that year achieved victories of that magnitude. Governors on average now enjoy greater job security than do senators, the reverse of the situation before the 1970s.

Stronger institutional resources and thus greater ability to dominate state government and media coverage have made it likely that a gubernatorial incumbent will win another term. Changes in state constitutional provisions for gubernatorial elections have significantly strengthened the office. Not long ago many governors were up for election in presidential years, when they ran the risk of being buried in landslides by the opposition party's candidate. Many were limited to two-year terms or were not permitted to run for reelection. The trend is now strongly against all these provisions. Between 1948 and 1988 the number of governors elected in nonpresidential years rose from sixteen to thirty-seven. Those limited to two-year terms decreased from twenty-one to three, and those denied the chance to run for reelection went from eleven to three. Most of the changes occurred after the mid-1960s, when extensive ticket splitting began.[19]

Governors have also taken to using official resources for electoral purposes. A common technique is to use state "institutional" advertising, conspicuously featuring the governor and paid for by state government. In 1985 New Jersey state government bought and paid for a major tourism advertising campaign on New York and Philadelphia television, prominently showcasing Governor Kean. It ran throughout the campaign season. In 1987 visitors to state historical commission sites in Pennsylvania found a lavish exhibit favorably detailing the political history of newly elected governor Robert Casey, described in an accompanying glossy brochure as "an ongoing effort to record the Commonwealth's history and collect artifacts illustrating our past."

Perhaps the most frequent and direct use of parallel state government "public service" advertising and gubernatorial campaign advertising occurred in the 1986 Illinois contest. Late that summer incumbent James Thompson ran paid commercials showing the governor signing legislation committing state lottery profits to education. (The ads of course did not mention that he had previously twice vetoed the same measure.) Beginning October 1 the Illinois Lottery Commission spent $288,000 for a statewide TV advertising buy on the same topic. Additionally, the state's Department of Commerce and Community Affairs bought $73,000 worth of radio advertising on the Chicago Bears' radio network during the football (and election) season for messages promoting Illinois's standing as the nation's third-ranking state for high-tech industry, another Thompson campaign theme. Thompson's outraged opponent complained: "The governor is trying to brainwash people with their own money. . . . This commercial is nothing more than a gift to Thompson's campaign from the taxpayers." Governor Thompson, acknowledging the parallel advertising themes in the "state" and "campaign" commercials responded: "That's true. Well, I'm the governor, and part of a governor's campaign talks about what's going on in the state under his administration." [20]

For many governors, then, institutional resources can be used effectively for electoral purposes, and the advantages of constant attention from the media outweigh the risks. A reporter explained the process from the media's point of view:

> Symbolically, it's appropriate that in the statehouse reporters are summoned by a bell. There's a bell in all their offices and whenever there's an event, it's a Pavlovian response; the bell rings, and everybody just gets up and takes their pencils and goes into the governor's office. That bell was rung on a lot of bullshit. It was not a case where you declined to answer the bell. If you spend thirty minutes in the governor's office, minutes with other competing reporters there, you're bound to write something, and they know that.

Even though reporters are aware of this manipulation, they are still likely, when campaign time rolls around, to give a reasonably competent governor the benefit of the doubt. This same journalist added: "The press that covers the candidates is basically the statehouse press. Despite the political guys they throw in, the statehouse regulars are still the cutting edge of the press. They've had four years of working with this guy. There's a built-in institutional bias." So while governors can suffer from mistakes made under media scrutiny, a state chief executive who uses the media well can also create an image that will be relatively impervious to charges made in the campaign season—unlike senators, who have not established the kind of working relationship that governors have with the media. A consultant who works in both senatorial and gubernatorial campaigns has said:

> No advertising is likely to significantly alter a governor's image. So much has been said about him over so many years that voters are relatively immunized to negative information about him. When senators' images are similar to governors', it must be regarded as their peak, whereas for a governor, it is probably a floor below which he cannot sink and above which he will probably be able to rise.

We can see that incumbents, from representatives on up the scale, enjoy substantial advantages in recognition, not merely because they have previously campaigned and garnered some notice but because they use the resources associated with incumbency to build positive recognition during their terms of office. For the most part they can shape the publicity they receive to ensure that, as they enter the campaign season, the voters' views of them will be favorable.

## Money

Incumbents also enjoy a significant advantage when it comes to raising money, particularly early money. A healthy bank balance at the beginning of a campaign permits a candidate to do the polling and other research necessary to develop an effective strategy. It also enables the candidate to hire other consultants such as media and direct mail specialists. Direct mail solicitation has become an important source of campaign funds, but candidates must have a lot of ready cash to pay for the production of the appeals and the cost of mailings.[21]

By June 1987 Senate incumbents running for reelection in November 1988 had already raised more than $20 million, twice the amount raised by their counterparts in the 1984 election at the same point in the cycle. By February 1988 Sen. Alfonse D'Amato of New York, known among exasperated but admiring colleagues as "the vacuum cleaner," had already raised more than a million dollars for a reelection contest in 1992, more than four years away.[22]

For all officials, but particularly for House and Senate members, a major source of early money is the political action committee, or PAC (see chapter 3). Of the $20 million raised for 1988 races by Senate incumbents as early as June 1987, 35 percent was contributed by PACs.[23] Even when PACs prefer a challenger, they are aware that most incumbents are reelected and that they are likely to have to continue to deal with them.

Incumbents do not have to travel far to obtain substantial PAC funds; much of the early fund raising takes place at Washington receptions. Democratic senator Donald Riegle of Michigan, up for reelection in 1988, issued invitations for his first PAC fund raiser in the capital three days after the 1986 election. In July 1987 five representatives had invitations out for fund raisers, with ticket prices ranging from $300 to $1,000.[24]

Fund raisers are by no means limited to the House members up every election cycle or to the Senate class closest to reelection. The brand-new Senate incumbents, who a few months previously were successful challengers, are particularly active early fund raisers. In the first six months of 1987, the thirteen new senators elected the previous November raised $3.1 million, more than half of it from PACs. The combined million-dollar debt of the nine freshmen who ended their campaigns in the red was by June converted into a $364,000 surplus.

All this early fund raising, and the ability of many incumbents to raise much more than they need to spend, results in large amounts of "cash on hand," money held in campaign accounts throughout the interelection period that may never be needed for campaign expenditures. After the 1986 elections the Federal Election Commission reported that twenty senators, including twelve who would not face the voters until 1990 or 1992, each had more than $400,000 in cash on hand. An equal number of House members, all of whom had received more than two-thirds of the vote in their most recent contests, also had at least that much. Cash on hand totaled more than 13 percent of all House incumbents' 1986 receipts, more than double the percentage in 1978.[25]

Incumbents use these funds in various ways. More than forty have established their own PACs and contribute in their own names or in the names of their PACs to other federal candidates in close contests or to candidates in their states (particularly state legislators who can influence redistricting decisions). Some incumbents find ways to spend the money to entertain their constituents. The late Tennessee Republican representative John Duncan held a barbeque every two years in the Knoxville coliseum for thirty-six thousand people at a cost of $50,000, feeding about as many people as the total vote for any of his Democratic opponents. A Texas Democrat sponsors an annual domino tournament; the winners receive a trip to Washington. Most commonly, candidates use the money for purposes such as leasing an automobile for travel while in the district or maintaining a "political office" (separate from the taxpayer-financed district offices) that can perform overtly political tasks and oversee the permanent fund-raising operation. Finally, any incumbent sworn in before January 1980 may legally convert unspent campaign contributions to personal use upon retirement from Congress.

Incumbents at the state level also have an edge over their challengers. Almost all incumbents in races for governorships or for the state legislatures benefit from those who do business with the state, who are regulated by the state, or who are employed by the state. Attorneys, contractors, real estate developers, the financial community, health interests, and unions figure heavily in every state, and agricultural interests are important in many. Residents of other states who were employed by bond-writing brokerage houses such as Kidder, Peabody and Bear, Stearns were big contributors to gubernatorial incumbents in Ohio and California in 1986. Ohio incumbent Richard Celeste even traveled to New York to hold a Wall Street fund raiser. Nevada governor Richard Bryan was impressively supported by the state's hotel and casino interests, and he amassed a treasury ten times larger than that of his opponent. For the most part, such contributors are pragmatic, ignoring ideology and partisan preferences to support the likely winner (usually the incumbent) or even playing both sides in close contests.

## Time

The third major advantage of the incumbent is time to organize. Incumbents begin to plan for reelection often two years in advance. Their first task is to build a campaign organization and appoint a campaign manager (or director, as these persons are increasingly called) to head it. Good campaign managers are in notoriously short supply. As one has commented: "It's the biggest problem there is. Anyone who's done it once or twice is either too old or too smart to do it again." Moreover, managers must either have no other job or hold a position they can abandon for several months such as in a law firm or on an incumbent's staff. Managers have traditionally been drawn from among the candidate's closest friends, from a group of perennial managers in the various states, or from the incumbent's office staff, but a cadre of professional managers for hire has begun to emerge. For instance, James Carville, New Jersey senator Frank Lautenberg's 1988 manager, assumed his post after successfully directing the winning 1987 campaign of Kentucky governor Wallace Wilkinson. Carville went to Kentucky after guiding Pennsylvania governor Robert Casey to victory in 1986. His opposite number, challenger Pete Dawkins's manager Doug Goodyear, had played the same role in the 1986 Colorado Senate campaign of the unsuccessful Republican challenger and had also served as executive director of the Colorado Republican party.

Reporting to the manager are those in charge of field organization, campaign administration (which maintains the payroll, Federal Election Commission reports, and so on), fund raising, press relations, issue and opponent research, and candidate scheduling. These last three functions—press, research, and scheduling—often fall under the aegis of a communications director, who coordinates all nonadvertising aspects of the candidate's message. Outside this formal staff, which runs the campaign from day to day, are consultants hired to do polling, media advertising, fund raising, and voter contact. Finally, many campaigns have a "kitchen cabinet"—an informal advisory group of old friends and supporters, important party figures, and volunteer fund raisers.

The candidates themselves are both the most and the least important members of a good organization: "He or she may play a large role in the selection of the campaign staff and be the final arbiter in struggles among the staff, but a candidate is not so much a member as an object of the organization." [26] The old adage about doctors who treat themselves applies to campaigns as well: "A candidate who directs his or her own campaign has a fool for a manager." One experienced manager noted:

> Ultimately, every campaign reflects the candidate, and the campaign flows from that. But a campaign the candidate wants to manage doesn't have a manager at all. A manager's authority is constantly undermined by the candidate intervening in decisions that aren't properly his. A candidate can't be his own manager because of scheduling requirements and because so much of a winning campaign is dependent on the candidate being out talking to voters. The three major resources of a campaign are money—which is focused on too much—the candidate's time, and staff time. All those things have to be budgeted. If you have an interventionist candidate, he's squandering a valuable resource—his time.

Most incumbents have already learned this and are comfortable leaving the details of the campaign to the staff. Their managers have often run their previous campaigns or have at least worked with or known the candidate well in another capacity. They have proven their loyalty and reliability and earned the candidate's trust. A congressional staffer who alternates between running campaigns and serving as Washington office chief describes his boss's campaign activities:

> I would say he was pretty well directed. He was like an actor on a movie set. He had a couple of directors who knew him very well. It wasn't like we were telling a robot what to do; we just told him what he would do anyway. He had a lot of trust in us. In many cases I would pick him up at the airport and tell him where we were going.

Having the important members of the staff in place long before the beginning of the external campaign can be tremendously useful to an incumbent, as the challenger to California senator Alan Cranston discovered in 1986. Republicans had great hopes of finally defeating the three-term Democrat. The seventy-two-year-old Cranston this time faced a young, attractive moderate Republican, Rep. Ed Zschau of the Silicon Valley, who occupied the ideological center Cranston's previous conservative opponents had disdained. The Senate veteran had also earned the hostility of many California moderates for embarking on a short-lived presidential campaign in 1984, "which seemed to be pitched to the most single-minded feminists and nuclear freeze enthusiasts," and during which, mortified constituents noticed, "he had dyed his hair a ridiculous shade of orange." A presidential preference poll of California Democrats shortly before Cranston dropped out of the contest showed him thirty-two points behind Walter Mondale. Moreover, fund raising for the 1986 Senate contest was complicated by a $300,000 debt left from the 1984 presidential campaign.[27]

Cranston, however, had the advantage of being able to assemble a Senate campaign team as soon as he withdrew from his presidential attempt. While his opponent began later and was tied up until early summmer in a high cost, bitter, and closely fought primary, Cranston's team had the time to plot strategy. The day after the primary, the exhausted Zschau found himself the object of a surprise attack—a massive negative advertising campaign that disrupted the Republican's strategy.

As California's leading political journal observed, the incumbent "had plenty of time to prepare for the attack. He had the money and the resources and his goal was to rock Zschau back on his heels and keep him there." [28] Many credit Cranston's razor-thin victory margin to the early strategic ploy only an incumbent could have had the time to plan and the money to execute. The lesson was not lost on California's other incumbent senator. Republican Pete Wilson, who won reelection in 1988, began a negative advertising barrage against his challenger, Democratic lieutenant governor Leo McCarthy, several months before the June primary. Having raised more than any other incumbent up to that time ($5 million by March 1988), he could afford to do so.

# The Role of Consultants

The number of consultants in a campaign is determined both by the candidate's tenure in office and by the position sought. Incumbents have experienced staffs and a record to defend. Compared to challenger campaigns, there are more ground rules for consultants and a greater sense among the staff about what messages they want to convey in the campaign. Some staff members and consultants may have worked together in the candidate's previous races. Although rancor and disagreements are rarely totally absent from any campaign, the staff and consultants, all with prior political experience, are more likely to respect each other professionally and understand their roles better than those in challenger campaigns.

## House Members

Generally speaking, representatives have less need for consultants than do candidates running in statewide races—especially senators and governors. Congressional constituencies are smaller and more homogeneous and, for incumbents particularly, are less likely to require extensive polling programs or heavy broadcast media planning. Because elections occur every two years, much of a representative's previous campaign team remains intact, providing an experienced core strategy group for the next race. Many representatives develop in-house expertise and have staffers capable of devising mail and radio messages and analyzing polling data. Moreover, many do not face serious competition. A manager for a Republican incumbent who regularly rolls up pluralities exceeding two-thirds of the vote said a year before his boss's most recent race:

> We have it all laid out until next December what next year's mail program will be—deadlines, print. We'll probably do an issues pacification program, which is a circle around all of the pro-ERA, NOW women, and we'll mail the hell out of them the first three months of the year on favorable issues. We won't do anything very involved—no phone banks.

House incumbents who do fear a tough race have the time to mobilize for it and the money to hire outside professionals. Consider Florida representative Sam Gibbons, who has represented his Tampa district since it was created in 1962. Gibbons traditionally conducted low-key campaigns, winning with large margins or running unopposed. In 1982 he spent under $100,000 to collect 74 percent of the vote. Two years later, however, a little-known ex-judge mounted a negative advertising campaign against Gibbons that forced him to spend almost three times as much and brought his vote below 60 percent. After this election the worried Gibbons hired Democratic media superstar Robert Squier in 1985 to begin advertising production for the 1986 race. He commissioned $18,000 worth of surveys of the district in the same year, raised $900,000 in the 1985-1986 election cycle, and made judicious contributions from this cash on hand to local and state officeholders. His reward was no Republican opponent in 1986 or 1988.[29]

## Senators and Governors

For those in statewide office who have four-year or six-year terms, although reelection thoughts are never absent, formal campaign planning—often including the appointment of consultants—begins at least a year and a half before the election. The 1984 campaign organization of Minnesota incumbent senator Rudy Boschwitz is a good example. Boschwitz's campaign manager, who began work in the spring of 1983, was a native of the state and had previously worked on the National Republican Senatorial and Congressional Campaign committees (NRSC and NRCC). He oversaw the campaign's finance, communications, and organizational divisions. Four consultants—for conceptual and organizational strategy, polling, and media—worked with the manager. A kitchen cabinet, composed of trusted Minnesota advisers and headed by Boschwitz's 1978 manager and former Washington office chief (now practicing law in Minnesota), met every three weeks to review the general campaign operation. By the end of March, the campaign had raised more than $3 million through efforts that began with the appointment of a full-time fund raiser in 1981. A major source of funds was Boschwitz's "Washington club," 850 contributors, primarily from Minnesota, who pledged $250 a year to the campaign through 1984. Another source was PACs, mostly out of state, which by March had contributed almost $400,000.[30]

The heavy involvement of professional political consultants in Boschwitz's early campaign is typical of such races, not only because of the need for expertise in reaching a large and diverse constituency through the media but because of the paucity of in-house campaign veterans. As Mitch Daniels, a former executive director of the NRSC, said of Senate incumbents:

> Most of them don't have any organization at all. Senators are very ill prepared for their races. As they get to the election cycle, all the combat marines on their staffs are gone. A lot of the staff has drifted in since the last election. People in House offices are far better politicians because they're at it all the time. Senators have less of a standing organization, but they're self-sufficient financially so they sort of assemble one that is partly mercenary and partly political organization.

## Liabilities of Incumbency

Despite its many advantages, incumbency is a mixed blessing. Being in an official position may carry with it a number of potential difficulties, principally complacency and negative recognition.

### Complacency

Successful candidates "run scared." In the previous section, we considered the case of Sam Gibbons, who took strong preemptive action after what is still usually considered a landslide victory of 59 percent. House members may not be familiar with the academic research demonstrating that incumbents must achieve a much greater victory to expect the same probability of job security in the next election that much smaller victories brought them two decades ago.[31] But many know this intuitively. For instance, another representative, who regularly wins overwhelmingly, was worried some months before the election about his most recent opponent—at the time not a credible challenger:

> He's a retired war hero military guy—not too bright or good on the issues, but he looks good. If someone dumped $400,000 in his lap and put him on TV in his uniform, he could be formidable. I am convinced that there is no district that is unwinnable these days.

This representative held his Republican opponent to a quarter of the vote but felt compelled to outspend him five to one to do so—and to ensure that no one in the future would think it worthwhile to "dump $400,000" in an opponent's lap.

Complacency no doubt contributed to the unexpected defeat of John Y. Brown in the 1987 Kentucky gubernatorial election. The Kentucky Fried Chicken magnate and husband of television personality Phyllis George served as governor from 1979 to 1983. It is likely that he was not elected governor in 1983 only because Kentucky is one of the three states that still prohibit two consecutive gubernatorial terms.

When Brown entered the May 1987 Democratic primary (tantamount to election in recent Kentucky history), most February and March polls showed him ahead of the leader among three credible opponents by two to one. Yet when the race heated up and Brown suffered telling attacks from his opponents, he still practically refused to acknowledge their existence. Mandy Grunwald, media consultant to primary winner Wallace Wilkinson, described Brown's attitude: "I was a great governor. I'm back. Aren't you lucky." Brown's own chief consultant and architect of his 1979 victory, Robert Squier, basically agreed with Grunwald's description: "John's problem in the campaign was that he really didn't believe he could lose. . . . We were for John being in the dialogue; John was not. John's feeling was that he could ride above the fray." [32]

Yet as their win-loss records demonstrate, few incumbents these days fall victim to complacency; if they did, many fewer would remain incumbents.

## Negative Recognition

Much more troublesome for incumbents is the danger of negative recognition. It can take a number of forms, producing varying degrees of difficulty for a campaign. Incumbents may acquire negative reputations if they (1) are involved in personal scandal, (2) are thought to have handled salient issues incorrectly or incompetently, or (3) are on the wrong side of the trends of the times. [33] An incumbent who does no advance planning to militate against these dangers is an officeholder at risk.

**Scandal.** History is replete with examples of incumbents who could not survive personal scandal. The fondness of the media for drama and the warts-and-all style of the "new journalism" make it certain that scandalous behavior from officeholders will receive wide publicity and destroy most incumbents' favorable press.

Not every kind of scandal is equally injurious. Over time, voters have become more tolerant of personal peccadilloes, if they do not affect an incumbent's conduct in office or fly in the face of a candidate's public image. In 1983 one of the most conservative electorates in the nation elevated to the Mississippi governorship a man who had been accused of (but who had denied) homosexual acts with black transvestites. Massachusetts representatives Barney Frank and Gerry Studds suffered no electoral retribution for their admissions of homosexuality. The 1987 revelations that a Supreme Court nominee had occasionally used marijuana in his youth brought a parade of officeholders admitting that they, too, had experimented with recreational drugs in the past; the headlines quickly faded and had no political effect. Even the highly publicized personal flaws that drove Democrats Gary Hart and Joe Biden from the 1988 presidential race had less to do with their actions than that the actions belied their public personas. Hart's early denials negated his image of integrity and truthfulness; Biden's plagiarism challenged his reputation as an effective rhetorician and orator.

An almost sure route out of office, however, is to be convincingly accused of financial irregularities, particularly involving public funds. When the Arizona state legislature impeached and convicted Gov. Evan Mecham in 1988 on several charges of malfeasance, Mecham's use of public funds to bail out his faltering automobile dealership was the impeachment count that drew the most votes. New York representative Mario Biaggi chose not to seek reelection after a bribe-taking conviction in the 1988 Wedtech scandal. Of the six House incumbents defeated in 1988, four—Democrats Fernand St Germain of Rhode Island and Bill Chappell of Florida and Republicans Joseph DioGuardi of New York and Pat Swindall of Georgia—faced significant charges of financial misdealings. When charges of official corruption can be substantiated, politicians may as well start packing up their offices; there is rarely a way to surmount such accusations.

**Dangerous Issues.** Charges that an officeholder has handled issues inappropriately or incompetently are another matter. Dealt with properly by an incumbent, these charges may be survived, even if they are true. The kind of charge that is effective often depends on the office being contested. Incumbents in executive offices—presidents, governors, mayors—are most subject to charges of incompetence, since, to paraphrase the famous sign on Harry Truman's desk, the buck stops there. It is no accident that public polls regularly measure the "job performance" of presidents and governors but rarely ask such questions about legislators. Legislators are less likely to be accused of incompetence because most participate in major policy decisions only collectively; they cannot single-handedly make policy the way executives do (or seem to do).

Voters unhappy with government policy are likely to attach their hostility to executives or legislative institutions, not to individual legislators. Legislators' use of constituent communications for credit taking and for self-advertising gives some insight into the question, "If, as Ralph Nader says, Congress is the 'broken branch,' how come we love our congressmen so much?" [34] However, legislators are subject to other criticisms about the way they handle their jobs. Frequently heard complaints are that their voting is "out of sync" with the district or, particularly in the case of senior legislators, that they have become more interested in big-picture issues of importance in the state and national capitals than in the parochial concerns of their own constituencies—that they have lost touch with the district.

The Senate election massacres of Democrats in 1980 and of Republicans in 1986 provide examples. Although there were other considerations, the twelve Democrats who were defeated in primaries or in the 1980 general election included many—Birch Bayh, Frank Church, Herman Talmadge, George McGovern, Warren Magnuson, Gaylord Nelson—who were powerful committee chairmen with national interests. They were accused, at least in part, of forgetting the folks back home. Some of the 1986 Republican victims such as Jeremiah Denton of Alabama and Mack Mattingly of Georgia were neophyte politicians without deep political roots in their states. Swept in on President Reagan's coattails, they could not survive the charge of being "Reagan robots," more interested in the "Reagan Revolution" than in local concerns.

A similar pattern emerged in the 1980 House elections, when powerful Democratic representatives in the House leadership—such as former majority whip John Brademas of Indiana and Ways and Means Committee chairman Al Ullman of Oregon—were defeated, and Agricultural Committee and Democratic Caucus chairman (later majority leader) Tom Foley of Washington State came close to defeat. They faced the dilemma one representative expressed:

> I'm beginning to be a little concerned about my political future. I can feel myself getting into what I guess is a natural and inevitable condition—the gradual erosion of my local orientation. I'm not as enthused about tending my constituency relations as I used to be and I'm not paying them the attention I should be. . . . I'm getting into some heady things in Washington, and I want to make an input into the government. But I'm beginning to feel that I could be defeated before long. And I'm not going to change. I don't want the status. I want to contribute to government.[35]

**Trends of the Times.** Legislative officeholders have learned that assiduous attention to their constituents' needs is a necessary insurance policy to permit them to pursue wider interests or to survive locally unpopular votes. Incumbents face the most difficulty, however, when charges against them combine with strong national or state tides flowing away from the stance represented by the particular officeholder. Fortunately for incumbents, particularly in the House, these tides are rarely strong enough to outweigh the many advantages incumbents possess, if only they use them properly.

Let us look more closely at the 1980 election, which would seem to belie these arguments. After all, the Democrats lost the presidency, twelve Senate seats, and thirty-four seats in the House. Certainly, many losing Democratic candidates attributed their defeats to the tides running in the Republican direction. As Bayh strategist Eve Lubalin put it:

> He had huge leads from May till the poll we took a week after the Republican presidential convention, at which point it was a dead heat. The simple truth about the campaign that we knew one and a half years in advance was that the presidential race was going to be absolutely decisive. How you did something about it given that overwhelming trend in the state was maddening. The voters didn't even know his opponent. He lost his lead to a total stranger.

The "total stranger," Republican Dan Quayle, went on to win a landslide reelection in 1986 and his party's vice-presidential nomination in 1988. Lubalin's explanation of the 1980 Democratic rout was echoed by many commentators; however, "no explanation of House elections relying on national forces is very helpful when we find that no fewer than 73 of the 185 Democratic House incumbents who faced Republican opposition in both 1978 and 1980 actually improved on their 1978 vote." [36] Despite the substantial losses in the House, 89 percent of all Democratic incumbents were reelected.

Senators, more in the glare of the media and with closer ties to the issues represented by national trends, had greater difficulty in 1980 than House members. But even in the Senate, where only ten of the twenty-two incumbent Democrats running managed to hold on to their jobs, four got a larger share of the vote than they had received in their previous election in 1974 (an excellent Democratic year), and one was not even opposed by a Republican. Governors can also get caught in national trends. Voters in midterm elections, when the majority of state chief executives are judged by the electorate, usually blame the president more than the governor for economic conditions, but they still take their feelings out on the only executive they can vote for at the time.[37] Governors, however, have more resources with which to withstand national trends than do senators. Pollster Bill Hamilton has commented:

> There are things senators have less control over because they're part of a body that does certain things and has an image, as opposed to a

governor that usually has a little more control over what he does, or at least can separate himself from a cantankerous legislature. With a governor you feel you have more control over your own destiny.

National trends have some effect, but the extent of the effect depends on the office, the constituency, the candidates, the quality of their campaigns, and the opposition; rarely do tides run strong enough, in themselves, to threaten a large number of incumbents.

## Coping with Liabilities

What does an incumbent do in the face of the dangers we have discussed? In the words of a consultant, "the most important thing you do as an incumbent is negative research on yourself. You anticipate negatives and preempt them." Discovering one's own weaknesses is a critical early task for incumbents; it is done primarily through early polling. One strategist for an incumbent representative facing a potentially tough primary in a newly drawn district (which he eventually won easily) described their early surveys:

> Who was ahead was the last number we looked at. I don't think the candidate batted an eyelash when he saw himself fifteen points down in the first poll. We checked poll results for ad content and strategy, gauging the theme. We played the devil's advocate, giving our worst case.

The appropriate strategic response to the information gained from early polling depends on the severity of the incumbent's problems. Incumbents who find themselves far ahead six or eight months before the election, with no strong challengers in view, can take prudent steps to buttress their positions. The key to popular incumbents' "damage control" in the earliest stages of a campaign has been to campaign without campaigning—to retain the aura of officeholder and use the resources of the office before openly entering the fray. Republican strategist Vince Breglio said:

> One of the problems incumbents have, if they're doing a good job, is starting political activity too soon. Some of our incumbents had commercials on the air as early as April, the standard stuff you'd put on to vote for the incumbent again. The result of that is to politicize your image, making that person a candidate, not a senator. Once you put candidate instead of senator in front of someone's name, all of a sudden the perceptual screen of the electorate seems to change. It's now okay to challenge his views, take this guy on.

But Breglio agrees with Democratic strategist Bill Hamilton: "That doesn't mean it's okay to wait." Instead of a full-blown media effort that signals "campaign," the well-regarded incumbent must act in an official role in a manner calculated to gain further approval from supportive constituencies and perhaps make discreet contact with the groups that need shoring up. Breglio explained:

> How do you start without provoking that candidate image? You do it by going to direct mail and you do it with rifle shotting particular messages to particular groups of people with as much accuracy as you can muster. Targeting in that sense has clearly exceeded the value of the broadcast media for incumbents. You can do it right up to September without showing a broad-brush flag that says, "Hey, I'm a politician." Yet you've been able to take your political message to those who need it most with a very personal appeal.

What of incumbents who are not widely perceived as doing a good job and risk being opposed by challengers who are as well known and perhaps more popular than they are? The officeholders most susceptible to this unusual incumbent problem are senators. Senators do not have representatives' close personal ties to their constituents or governors' daily media attention. Voting for them only every six years, many constituents may forget who their senators are or may not even have lived in the state when they were previously elected.[38]

Without protection from a strong party base in the electorate, a few senators have simply thrown in the towel early. After barely surviving two tough races in a state that tends to be Republican in federal elections, Colorado's Gary Hart chose not to run again in 1986. When Virginia's Paul Trible, who barely won a majority in 1982, learned that his 1988 opponent would be Charles Robb, the popular ex-governor who was constitutionally barred from a second term in the statehouse, Trible resigned and thought about running for governor in 1989.

The larger number of incumbents who want to keep their jobs are beginning their public external campaigns earlier and earlier, feeling they have nothing to lose. If their deficiencies are widely known, it is better to fight back long before election day, in the hope of depriving opponents of fresh ammunition closer to election time. By April 1988 none of the twelve incumbent senators judged solid favorites for the November election by publications in the political community had purchased any political advertising.[39] Conversely, of the sixteen judged in shakier positions, nine were already on the air in the winter and early spring, including all those considered in a toss-up position or worse.

The senators airing early advertising had two motives. One group, including California's Pete Wilson, Ohio's Howard Metzenbaum, and Nevada's Chic Hecht, had won very close races in 1982 and faced experienced and potentially imposing 1988 opponents—respectively, the California lieutenant governor, the popular mayor of Cleveland, and the governor of Nevada. With early polls showing them trailing or barely leading, rather than enjoying the thirty-point leads typical for incumbents at this stage of campaigns, these officeholders could not afford months of unanswered speculation about their weaknesses. Wilson and Metzenbaum went on to solid victories, and Hecht, who trailed badly early in the race, lost very narrowly.

A second group did enjoy fairly wide leads in poll trial heats but had softer support than their "solid" colleagues. These included New York's Daniel Patrick Moynihan, New Mexico's Jeff Bingaman, and North Dakota's Quentin Burdick. These senators advertised early to bolster their support, to remind their constituents of their records, and most of all to deter strong challengers who were considering a race but had not yet decided. All three were successful in their aims. After New York U.S. district attorney Rudolph Giuliani, famed for prosecutions of major political corruption and organized crime cases, declined to run, New York Republicans were hard-pressed to find a credible opponent for Moynihan. Bingaman drew a "second-tier" field of challengers after all of New Mexico's Republican representatives refused to oppose the first-term Democrat. The seventy-nine-year-old Burdick persuaded the state's popular Democratic at-large representative, Byron Dorgan, who had been well ahead of Burdick in the polls, to continue waiting for his turn at a Senate seat. Moynihan, Bingaman, and Burdick all won their races easily.

This survey of the advantages and disadvantages of incumbent officeholders in the early stages of their campaigns is not encouraging for those who challenge them. It would seem that no challenger should run and expect to win unless the country is on the brink of upheaval and the incumbent is about to be indicted. Often this advice is not far from the mark; however, there are relatively frequent occasions when no incumbent is in the race, and in every election year some incumbents are beaten. So let us next consider, in chapter 5, what a successful challenger must accomplish in the early stage of the campaign to remain in contention.

## Notes

1. Peter Shapiro, 1985 Democratic gubernatorial candidate, in a speech at the 1986 annual meeting of the New Jersey Political Science Association, Kean College, Union, New Jersey, April 12, 1986.
2. Peter Clarke and Susan H. Evans, *Covering Campaigns: Journalism in Congressional Elections* (Stanford, Calif.: Stanford University Press, 1983), 16.
3. Lou Cannon, *Reporting: An Inside View* (Sacramento: California Journal Press, 1977), 181-182.
4. *Congressional Quarterly Weekly Report*, July 18, 1987, 1554.
5. *Wyoming Eagle*, October 13, 1982, 1.

6. *Congressional Quarterly Weekly Report*, August 16, 1980, 2387; *Washington Post National Weekly Edition*, September 26-October 2, 1988, 32. Legislation currently prohibits postal patron mailings within sixty days of general elections; thus early September is the last permitted mailing time in congressional election years.
7. Bruce Cain, John Ferejohn, and Morris Fiorina, *The Personal Vote* (Cambridge, Mass.: Harvard University Press, 1987), 79.
8. *Tucson Citizen*, November 5, 1986.
9. Cain, Ferejohn, and Fiorina, *Personal Vote*, 103-106.
10. Richard Born, "Partisan Intentions and Election Day Realities in the Congressional Redistricting Process," *American Political Science Review* 79 (June 1985): 305-317; Bruce E. Cain, "Assessing the Partisan Effects of Redistricting," *American Political Science Review* 79 (June 1985): 320-331.
11. *Congressional Quarterly Weekly Report*, February 27, 1988, 391.
12. Thomas E. Mann and Raymond Wolfinger, "Candidates and Parties in Congressional Elections," *American Political Science Review* 74 (September 1980): 617-632.
13. Stephen Hess, *The Washington Reporters* (Washington, D.C.: Brookings Institution, 1981), 101-102.
14. *Washington Post National Weekly Edition*, September 26-October 2, 1988, 32. On the increased use of the frank and district staff, see Norman J. Ornstein, Thomas E. Mann, and Michael J. Malbin, *Vital Statistics on Congress, 1987-1988* (Washington, D.C.: Congressional Quarterly, 1987), chapter 5.
15. Stephen Hess, *The Ultimate Insiders* (Washington, D.C.: Brookings Institution, 1987), 78.
16. See the data reported in Malcolm E. Jewell, *Parties and Primaries: Nominating State Governors* (New York: Praeger, 1984), 262-263; James Clotfelter and William R. Hamilton, "Electing a Governor in the Seventies," in *The American Governor in Behavioral Perspective*, ed. Thad Beyle and J. Oliver Williams (New York: Harper and Row, 1972), 32-38.
17. See the data in Clotfelter and Hamilton, "Electing a Governor in the Seventies," 32, and Charles M. Tidmarch, Lisa J. Hyman, and Jill E. Sorkin, "Press Issue Agendas in the 1982 Congressional and Gubernatorial Election Campaigns," *Journal of Politics* 46 (November 1984): 1227-1242.
18. See the articles by Jim Seroka, "Incumbents and Reelection: Governors and Senators," *State Government* 53 (Summer 1980): 160-165, and William H. Flanigan and Nancy J. Zingale, "Ticket-Splitting and the Vote for Governor," in *State Government* 53 (Summer 1980): 157-160; Thad L. Beyle, "Incumbency and Money in Gubernatorial Elections," *Election Politics* 5 (Fall 1988): 18-23.
19. See Andrew McNitt, "The Impact of State Legislation on Political Campaigns," *State Government* 53 (Summer 1980): 135-139; Larry Sabato, *Goodbye to Good-time Charlie: The American Governorship Transformed*, 2d ed. (Washington, D.C.: CQ Press, 1983), chapter 2.
20. *Chicago Tribune*, October 27, 1986, 3.
21. For a discussion of the "up-front" costs of direct mail, see Larry J. Sabato, *The Rise of Political Consultants: New Ways of Winning Elections* (New York: Basic Books, 1981), chapter 4.
22. *New York Times*, August 8, 1983, A11; *National Journal*, September 5, 1987, 2214; *New York Times*, February 17, 1984, B3.
23. Ibid., *National Journal*.
24. Kristine E. Heine and Richard F. Mann, "Wheedle a Fortune," *Campaigns and*

*Elections* 7 (March-April 1987): 52-54; *Roll Call,* July 19, 1987, 30.

25. Frank J. Sorauf, *Money in American Elections* (Glenview, Ill.: Scott, Foresman, 1988), 157.
26. Xandra Kayden, *Campaign Organization* (Lexington, Mass.: Heath, 1978), 3.
27. Gary C. Jacobson and Raymond E. Wolfinger, "Context and Choice in Two Senate Elections," paper presented at the annual meeting of the American Political Science Association, Chicago, Illinois, September 3-6, 1987, 10-12; quotation at 10.
28. *California Journal,* October 1986, 486.
29. *Congressional Quarterly Weekly Report,* September 12, 1987, 2186; Michael Barone and Grant Ujifusa, *The Almanac of American Politics 1988* (Washington, D.C.: National Journal, 1987), 254-256.
30. Richard E. Cohen, "Boschwitz Hopes Incumbency Can Work to Senate Republicans' Advantage," *National Journal,* June 23, 1984, 1217-1222. For another study of how Senate candidates assemble experienced staffs, see the discussion of the 1986 Missouri Senate race in Stephen Lilienthal and Carin Dessauer, *Running to Win: An In Depth Look at Two Senate Races* (Washington, D.C.: Free Congress Foundation, 1988), 31-38.
31. Gary Jacobson, *The Politics of Congressional Elections,* 2d ed. (Boston: Little, Brown, 1987), 30-33.
32. David Beiler, "White Knights, Dark Horses," *Campaigns and Elections* 7 (September-October 1987): 47.
33. The relevance of these factors in House races is analyzed in Lyn Ragsdale and Timothy E. Cook, "Representatives' Actions and Challengers' Reactions: Limits to Candidate Connections in the House," *American Journal of Political Science* 31 (1987): 45-81. Their effect in Senate races is examined in Alan I. Abramowitz, "Explaining Senate Election Outcomes," *American Political Science Review* 82 (June 1988): 385-403.
34. Richard Fenno, Jr., "If, as Ralph Nader Says, Congress Is the Broken Branch, How Come We Love Our Congressmen So Much?" in *Congress in Change,* ed. Norman J. Ornstein (New York: Praeger, 1975), 277-287.
35. Richard Fenno, Jr., *Home Style: House Members in Their Districts* (Boston: Little, Brown, 1978), 216.
36. Gary C. Jacobson and Samuel Kernell, *Strategy and Choice in Congressional Elections* (New Haven, Conn.: Yale University Press, 1981), 74.
37. John E. Chubb, "Institutions, the Economy, and the Dynamics of State Elections," *American Political Science Review* 82 (March 1988): 133-154.
38. For instance, Jacobson and Wolfinger, "Context and Choice," 17, were surprised to find that less was known about three-term senator Alan Cranston by the California electorate in 1986 than was known about the typical House member.
39. Among the most widely respected newsletters are the *Cook Political Report,* published by the Government Research Corporation; the *Political Report,* published by the "New Right"-connected Free Congress Foundation but generally accepted as nonpartisan and accurate; and the *American Political Report,* published by columnist Kevin Phillips. More general publications, *Roll Call* and *Congressional Quarterly Weekly Report,* also publish frequent estimates of candidates' strength. The twelve senators widely regarded as unbeatable were Democrats Bentsen (Texas), Byrd (W. Va.), DeConcini (Ariz.), Kennedy (Mass.), Matsunaga (Hawaii), Mitchell (Maine), Riegle (Mich.), Sarbanes (Md.), and Sasser (Tenn.) and Republicans Hatch (Utah), Heinz (Pa.), and Lugar (Ind.). All won with more than 60 percent of the vote.

# The Challenger: Running While Not Campaigning 5

*We have two kids in private school. You have no job and we are opening our lives to public scrutiny. Do I have this correct?*

A Senate challenger's spouse, reflecting on the effects of a first bid for office[1]

The challenger's problem is simply summarized: he or she is not the incumbent. Most challengers, especially strong ones, wait for a "target of opportunity," and it rarely presents itself far in advance. With few exceptions challengers do not initially have the recognition or the organizational and financial resources available to almost all incumbents. Those who cannot acquire them quickly are doomed to almost certain failure.

This chapter considers challengers and their problems. First, we analyze their backgrounds—who they are and where they come from. Second, we consider how they become credible contestants—by building recognition, raising money, and organizing.

## Who Are the Challengers?

Challengers' backgrounds vary most notably by office, by party, and by size of state. Some positions—such as governor or senator—are more likely to be the goal of challengers who have already served in government. Party plays a role because, in many cases, Republican party organizations are more active in candidate recruitment than Democrats.

The size of the state also helps determine the number of officeholders likely to be considered serious contestants for higher positions. This section expands on these points.

## The Challenger's Prior Service in Government

Experience in state government is virtually a requirement for candidates seeking the governorship. Most of the governors serving in 1988 came to office from other positions in state government such as lieutenant governor, state attorney general, or member of the state legislature. Of the eight who had been business executives just before becoming governor, five had previously held positions in state government. A few others had been mayors of large cities. U.S. senators rarely run for governor, although there is some traffic in the other direction.

Members of Congress run for governor infrequently; only five of the governors elected between 1984 and 1988 were former representatives.[2] Representatives are more likely to run for senator than for governor. This finding is ascribed to the longer length of the Senate term, the similarity of the legislative functions, and the traditional (but disappearing) lower likelihood of an incumbent's defeat in the Senate.[3]

Representatives grow tired of the incessant campaigning during their two-year terms and may yearn for the relative peace and stability of the six-year Senate term. As one newly elected senator said: "I set a certain standard of expectation when I was in the House, going home every weekend, but I'm not going to do that now. One of the reasons I ran for the Senate was so that I wouldn't have to go home every weekend."[4]

Most often representatives who succeed to the Senate are from relatively small states, and their congressional districts comprise a significant part of the state. They have already achieved substantial recognition over a wide area when they first run for election as Senate challengers. Current examples include both senators from Hawaii, Idaho, Maryland, and South Dakota. The next largest contingent of senators are former governors, who also tend to come from small- to medium-size states—for instance, both senators from South Carolina and Arkansas. They also began their races as challengers with wide recognition.

Most senators without previous electoral records are from the largest states. This group includes a number of business executives, a scattering of academics, and a few "celebrities" (professional athletes, astronauts, and the like) who represent states such as New York, New Jersey, Texas, Ohio, and Minnesota. California, the most populous state, now has two senators with previous political experience, but among their recent predecessors are a professional actor and an academic. The cost of gaining recognition through advertising in these states is so high that successful contestants must either have wide public recognition when they first run (for example, former UN ambassador Daniel Patrick Moynihan of New York or professional athlete Bill Bradley of New Jersey) or be wealthy enough to buy saturation advertising (for example, businessman Rudy Boschwitz of Minnesota).

## The Challenger's Resources

Other factors determining the credibility of challengers are the resources, contacts, and organization that candidates bring to a race. Members of the state legislature who run for governor have often built up resources that can be used for another run within the state but are not as readily available for a Washington-based office. A consultant points to a former state senate majority leader who ran for both the governorship and the House of Representatives: "Any bill in the state Senate had to go across his desk. Everybody had to ante up when he ran for governor. Look at the contributor list—they all gave to the legal limit. As a congressional candidate, he couldn't raise it like he did for the governorship." A local reporter observed of the same candidate, "Inside the walls of that statehouse, he was given twenty points more than when he walked outside the statehouse or left the county."

Those who have served in other elected offices are usually in a better position to seek federal office. Massachusetts senator John Kerry, chair of the Democratic Senatorial Campaign Committee, observed of the hopefuls he deals with: "Generally, someone who has been a successful governor or member of Congress comes with an underlying strength. That brings a knowledge of the issues and an ability to raise money." Another not insignificant factor is how the candidate feels about fund raising; many candidates detest asking people for money, an activity that is estimated to consume at least half their time in a campaign. Kerry noted that 1988 Democratic Rhode Island challenger Frank Licht, the only challenger to have outraised an incumbent by the summer of 1988, was able to do so because he positively enjoyed the fund-raising challenge: "He has been outstanding at marketing his own race." [5]

## The Challenger's Party Affiliation

The final consideration affecting legislative recruitment is the candidate's party banner. In chapter 3 we detailed the strong role the

Republican party plays in recruiting efforts, noting the relative paucity of Republican officeholders at lower levels available and willing to move to higher office and the great financial and organizational support the Republican party can offer its candidates. The result is that, particularly at the congressional level, successful Republican challengers are more likely to be amateurs with less of a record of service than their Democratic counterparts.

As noted earlier, political experience exercises a powerful effect on the likelihood that a congressional challenger will be successful. Between 1972 and 1984 about 23 percent of the experienced challengers who ran against incumbents defeated them; only 5 percent of those with no political experience were victorious. This relationship held for both parties. Strong challengers (defined as those with political experience) are more likely to run when they perceive the trends as propitious for victory. Thus experienced challengers who ran in the same time period, in the "best bet" open seats with no incumbents, were successful 54 percent of the time.[6]

In every year since 1974 fewer Republican than Democratic challengers have held previous office. Even successful Republican challengers in the most recent elections have been notably less experienced than their Democratic counterparts. In 1988, 94 percent of the seventeen new Democratic representatives had previously held office, compared to 63 percent of the sixteen new Republicans. Republican amateurs who could mount a credible campaign in promising districts were assured of full funding from their party; Democrats were more likely to be on their own. This often meant that only Democrats with a track record could run and expect to win.

A final reason that it is more difficult for Republicans to recruit experienced House challengers is the disinclination of those in other responsible positions to enter a legislative body where, for all but a few years in the past half-century, their party has been the minority. For example, it is hard to persuade a Republican leader in a state legislature to give up that power and become a freshman member of a seemingly permanent minority.

Democrats have a somewhat similar problem in recruiting House incumbents in prestigious positions to run against strong Republican senators. One such candidate, urged to run in 1986 with the argument that enough Senate victories would return the Democrats to the Senate majority they had lost in 1980, observed that this was "not a motivating factor. I can only afford the micro view." [7] The Democratic "farm team" is so much larger and deeper, however, that despite some strong candidates' decisions not to run, there were enough others to produce a strong crop of Senate challengers in both 1986 and 1988.

# Overcoming the Disadvantages
# of the Challenger _____

In our discussion of incumbents, we pointed to three of their chief advantages: recognition, money, and time. To become credible, a challenger for any office must negate these advantages. He or she must also have achieved a substantial level of recognition or acquire it quickly; must turn the incumbent's recognition into a negative rather than a positive factor; must raise sufficient early money for information gathering and advertising; and must begin early enough to be able to build an organization and formulate a strategy for the external campaign. A challenger who by early fall has not achieved substantial recognition, has not increased the public's negative perceptions of the opponent, has not acquired sufficient money, and is not in a positive or at least neutral position in relation to national trends has probably already lost the election, even if the public is barely aware that a campaign is going on.

## The Pressures on the Challenger

For the challenger, recognition, money, and time are closely linked. Incumbents win recognition through their activities in office and their ability to publicize them. Most challengers, even if they are serving in some other office, do not receive the same kind of publicity the incumbent gets. It is usually necessary for challengers to buy coverage— in the form of paid advertising—through television, radio, and direct mail. Further, the money that challengers can raise affects to a great extent the amount of free media coverage they receive. Raising and spending money is what makes a challenger credible to the press. "High-resource" challengers—those with publicity expenditures above the median for all candidates—are able to match or exceed incumbents in their newspaper coverage.[8]

A few challengers determine years in advance when they are going to make a race. For instance, former North Carolina governor Jim Hunt, who lost the most expensive Senate race in history to Sen. Jesse Helms in 1984, began raising funds in 1988 for a 1990 rematch. New Jersey representative Jim Courter, who decided in 1987 to run for governor in 1989, spent $500,000 during the fall of 1988 on television commercials extolling his leadership abilities. It was unlikely that Courter would have resorted to such a strategy simply to hold a congressional seat he had won four times by landslides and which represented a minuscule part of the viewing audience. The expensive television buy was clearly intended to build his name recognition for a tough open seat gubernatorial contest, in which his primary opponents were likely to include the state's assembly speaker and sitting attorney general.

But most challengers decide, begin to raise funds and organize, and announce their candidacies perhaps nine months before the general election. To run effectively against an incumbent who typically has been planning the race for a year or more, a challenger must be able to compress time, creating an instant organization by hiring experienced consultants. This, of course, also costs money.

Ideally, a challenger's professional staff is similar to the incumbent's, which we described in chapter 4. The difference is that challengers do not have the perquisites of incumbents. They do not have an existing staff with appropriate campaign experience, and they are less likely to be attractive to the national consultants who specialize in statewide races. In most races challengers are assumed to be the underdogs, and consultants' reputations depend on their "win and loss" records. As one consultant described the problem of taking on a tough challenger contest, the candidate could "lose by one point and you've done absolutely nothing to help yourself get new clients the next cycle." Masterminding successful challenger races, however, is the way consultants move up in reputation. One example is Democratic media consultant Frank Greer. Greer took on underdog Senate races in Georgia, South Dakota, and Washington State in 1986 and won all of them. He was much in demand in 1988. As one of his colleagues put it, Greer "hit the quinella." [9]

Raising the money to pay consultants is, as we have already noted, a major problem. Most challengers making the rounds of funding sources encounter skepticism. PACs and party organizations want some demonstration that their funds will be well spent and ask to see polls and targeting data before they invest. But where is the challenger to get the funds to pay for them? A PAC director has observed: "Before you're off the ground, you're already spending $25,000. It isn't a situation where you can pay $10 to find out your chances." [10]

At the same time, challengers need the consultants more than incumbents do, both for their experience and for the credibility their presence bestows. The challenger's need for hired guns, and the difficulties in retaining the well-known ones who are most likely to be both competent and credible, becomes a vicious circle.

Mario Cuomo, first elected governor of New York in 1982, after a surprise victory in a primary against Mayor Edward Koch of New York City, recorded in his campaign diaries the frustrations of finding a campaign manager and consultants to do his polling and media work. His first choice for a campaign director, the well-known consultant David Garth, opted to go with Koch. His second choice declined because he was involved with a Senate campaign in the same state. In a diary entry seven months before the primary, Cuomo wrote:

> We're caught in a circular problem. . . . many of the money people are reluctant to commit to me. They are waiting for signs of organization and potential success before they "invest," but they are almost indispensable ingredients in forming up the effort in the first place. I must get a "name" campaign manager and a headquarters as soon as possible.[11]

Two days later Cuomo commented further on the price exacted by the failure to get the staff he needed: "The value of a Garth is clear from the way our campaign is shaping up—or rather, isn't. It has no form. It is not being driven by anyone along any particular path." [12] The Cuomo campaign muddled through with a neophyte staff, helped by Koch's errors and Cuomo's own savvy and experience. As late as July, Cuomo was writing most of his own television commercials; he prepared his afternoon speech for the state party nominating convention at 5:30 a.m. that very day.

When and if challengers finally hire the consultants they need, their organizations are particularly prone to conflict and struggles for turf. Such conflict is never absent in a campaign but is more likely in a challenger's efforts, where the participants have not worked together before and consultants may discount the abilities of the day-to-day staff. The deputy manager of a gubernatorial campaign described the hostility between the staff and the polling and media consultants:

> The campaign manager talked to them, but I would have to say there was nobody in the campaign that was their boss; they basically did what they wanted to. A flunky worked with us. He would issue orders. This underling would call and say, "We're coming to shoot commercials and I want this, this, and this," and I'd say, "Did you think of—" and he'd say, "I didn't ask you for your thoughts; this is what we want."

The field director in another gubernatorial campaign had similar recollections:

> I was press secretary and field director, running the daily operation, doing the press, working with all the local organizations, and moving the mail. I was working sixteen hours a day, six days a week, and here's this consultant who comes in one day a week and is getting paid five grand a month. There's natural resentment, there's suspicion, there is jealousy, and there is competitiveness.

## Races Below the Statewide Level

Challengers for the state legislature or the House of Representatives find recognition extremely difficult to come by. The media generally do not give much coverage to these candidates. Moreover, legislative districts at the state and federal levels are often drawn to the advantage of one party. Challengers, almost always from the other party and running in low-turnout elections in which party activists are predominant, begin with two strikes against them. The legislative or congressional challenger who seeks to buy media advertising finds that television, which is most effective at building quick, widespread recognition, is not only very expensive but usually not well tailored to the district.

The time-honored method of gaining recognition at the local level is shoe leather, and the attempt to reach personally as many voters as possible remains a leading stratagem for the legislative or congressional candidate. Legislative districts and many congressional districts are still small enough for door-to-door campaigning. Interviews with more than two hundred state legislators in nine states revealed that "many of them won their first election by door-to-door campaigning, and they are convinced that this is the most effective way to maintain contacts and visibility." [13] Reflecting on his first races for both the state legislature and the House of Representatives, Jim Florio of New Jersey said: "You have to go strategically around the district. Breaking in is a very physical thing. There is no substitute for physical work." [14] The theme is echoed by Larry Pressler, now senator from South Dakota, in describing his first congressional race:

> I tried to shake 500 hands a day. That is where you really take their hand and look at them and talk to them a little bit. I succeeded in doing that seven days a week. I put in a lot of twelve hour days starting at a quarter to six in the morning at some plant.... You would not believe the physical and mental effort this requires. [15]

These days, however, the doors on which a challenger knocks are not selected randomly. Analysis of swing precincts directs the candidate to particular locations, and the friendly or at least neutral voter who answers the door is likely to receive a computer-generated letter in the next few days, addressing the voter by name and favorably recalling a small child, the attractive landscaping, and so on. [16] Such letters, a technique known as direct mail, are increasingly important in campaigns for the state legislatures and the House. Although most analysts who have written about direct mail concentrate on its use as a fundraising tool, [17] campaign professionals regard it as an important method of informing and persuading voters, especially in lower level races where television is very expensive and not cost efficient. [18]

In addition to opportunities to meet and greet the voters and to send out direct mail solicitations, a key asset for a local level challenger seeking recognition is early support from politically active groups willing to serve as surrogates for the candidate in canvassing or fund raising. These include the remnants of the party organizations, labor unions, civic associations, and special-interest groups such as environmentalists and feminists. They serve as an organizational base for the challenger and as a counterweight to the existing organizations of most incumbents. Organized support is especially important in primary elections, which many challengers have to negotiate successfully before moving on to the general election; it is vital to the challenger who has held no previous office. For instance, Rep. Chris Smith was part-time executive director of New Jersey Right-to-Life when he first gained the Republican nomination in his district. A salesperson in a family sporting-goods business, he had no political record aside from his antiabortion activities.

Candidates without existing group ties can often create them. Consultant Hank Parkinson described a two-year program he designed to elect an unknown optometrist to the Kansas state legislature:

> We arranged for him to join a group of eye doctors in Mexico fitting indigents for eyeglasses.... Through direct mail we made sure that all Lions Club members in the southeast corner of Kansas were made aware of Dr. Whittaker's work—important because our man was active in the organization, which has sight-saving as a major service project.
> Included with the direct mailings were return cards with which Lions Club program directors could indicate if they wanted Dr. Whittaker as a speaker. The response was gratifyingly heavy. Each speech appearance was publicized without fail.... In about four months, Dr. Whittaker was a pretty well-known figure in that part of Kansas.[19]

Dr. Robert Whittaker served one term in the state legislature before winning the Republican congressional primary as a dark horse and an easy general election victory in Kansas's Fifth District.[20]

Candidates who have previously held local office are more apt to turn to what remains of the local party organizations, which still recruit candidates for the state legislature. Not uncommonly, such candidates have been active in local parties or have held county office, where many party activists still subsist in what may be the last patronage-rich environments. Pete Curtin, a Democratic campaign consultant who works with legislative and congressional campaigns, described an early primary campaign for a congressional race, in which the candidate had previously held county office:

> Whatever is there of the party organization, you work it to the highest level possible. Hook the candidate up close with the county committee members. A lot of that is personal contact on the part of the candidate, but we sent out thirty-five hundred pieces of direct mail in connection with his announcement—every county committee member, every elec-

tion board member, every party official, the leaders of every constituent group identified with the Democratic party. It was a "Dear Joe," not a "Dear Democrat," letter and included in it was a copy of his announcement.

This candidate embodied both the old and the new techniques of high touch and high tech. In addition to personal campaigning, he reached out, in Curtin's words, "to the traditional Democratic family," with computerized direct mail. He won his primary easily.

Although both Democratic and Republican challengers use all of these strategies, Democratic candidates below the statewide level are more likely to depend on personal organizations deriving from past officeholding or interest-group contacts, while Republicans rely more on paid mail and telephone. These different strategies reflect the strengths and weaknesses of each of the parties.

**Democrats.** The Democrats have enjoyed a numerical advantage among psychological party identifiers for half a century. Party affiliation is still important in most elections below the statewide level. In explaining the continuing dominance of Democrats in the state legislatures, Republican consultant Dave Murray said: "On the grand scale of elections, the further you go down the ladder, the more people have a tendency to vote party line as opposed to issues and personality, because there's a dearth of information. People don't want the information; it's not that important." Thus, in the majority of legislative and congressional districts in which Democrats are the "natural" majority, they need only reinforce an existing base—always a simpler job than persuading independents. The Republicans' task is to convert the opposition's partisans. Additionally, the Democrats are a party of constituencies. Democratic candidates start out with a road map; they know they can probably find support among such groups as union members, minorities, public employees, and feminists—or, in the words of Democratic strategist Tim Ridley, "Democrats know where the mother lode is."

Democratic challengers at the legislative and congressional levels therefore are more likely to have run lower level races, to have strong interest-group ties, and to represent districts where their partisans are in the majority. In our earlier discussion of recruitment at the congressional level, we noted these differences.

**Republicans.** Faced with minority party status since the Great Depression, Republicans have traditionally been bereft of substantial interest-group support. Religious fundamentalists have played an important role in some Republican campaigns in recent years, but some groups are limited in their activities if they wish to retain tax-exempt status. By the mid-1960s many observers believed that the Republicans would cease to be one of the two major parties. As late as 1978 a distinguished political scientist could convincingly write, "The United States lacks a competitive two-party system at present because of the exceptional weakness of the Republican party." Almost as an aside, he added in a footnote, "The Republican weakness to which we refer here, is, of course, primarily that of 'the party in the electorate,' rather than of party organization." [21]

As we have seen in chapter 3, however, it was in fact the national Republican party organization, beginning in the mid-1970s, that was in large measure responsible for a steady increase in the Republican share of the House vote after the low ebb of Watergate and for the election of many Republican challengers. Assurance that the party would back them to the hilt persuaded strong Republican candidates to run even in "bad" years.

Candidates who accept Republican party assistance lose some freedom in running their campaigns, but the loss is less ideological than procedural. They remain free to adjust their issue appeals to their constituencies. One congressional candidate from Texas said: "I let the NRCC [National Republican Congressional Committee] know my positions on the issues at the first. They did not encourage us to take any particular theme." Another from Illinois added: "They wanted to talk about national issues and I wanted to talk about local issues. It was a long discussion, and I disagreed with them, but they gave me money anyway." [22]

What the national committees do require of candidates is that their money be used for purposes the party considers worthwhile. As much as possible, contributions are made in kind—as payments for polls, phone banks, direct mail, media production, and the like, frequently provided by committee-approved vendors. The committees can thus shape the campaigns professionally. Major effort is put into voter contact—early identification and persuasion of independents and even Democrats to vote Republican. Not every Republican House challenger can expect a large infusion of party funds. Republican strategists concede many seats with heavily Democratic populations or effective Democratic incumbents.

The experience of the 1988 Republican challengers to Democratic House incumbents Thomas Downey and Robert Mrazek in New York's strongly Republican Suffolk County is typical. By September neither hopeful had been able to raise even a tenth of the half-million-dollar average campaign treasury of successful House challengers. Dismayed at the lack of moral and financial support from their party's congressional campaign committee, one of the Republican aspirants said of the NRCC, "they have not been much help," while the other called their backing "less than I was hoping for." Sources at the committee, who refused to be identified, pointed to their many unsuccessful and expensive past attempts to unseat the two Democrats as a major reason for their reluctance to invest heavily again.[23]

**Party Similarities.**    Only challengers in potentially winnable districts are the beneficiaries of national party largesse. The more modestly financed Democratic Congressional Campaign Committee (DCCC) follows the same strategy as the NRCC. A DCCC staffer commented: "There are 435 races, but you're probably looking at under a hundred that are really contests. Those don't change very much, and every year you take a look at those same races."

Further, as campaigning costs escalate, particularly for hotly contested races, challengers in both parties need to look far beyond their parties for money. The five Democrats and one Republican who managed to defeat House incumbents in 1986 raised an average of $532,000. The maximum permissible party contribution is less than a seventh of that figure. PACs are increasingly disinclined to back any challenger; between 1976 and 1986 challengers' share of all PAC contributions fell from 19 percent to 11 percent. Even those contesting open seats saw their share drop from 21 percent to 13 percent in the same period. The 1988 election cycle saw the trend intensify. By June all the challengers to the more than four hundred House incumbents had received only 6 percent of the $57 million already committed by PACs; the smaller number of open seat contestants collected only 5 percent of the total.[24]

Thus more new candidates in both parties will need to dig deep into their own pockets. Less than 9 percent of all candidate spending in 1984 came from personal funds, but this amount rose to 23 percent among contestants for open seats. Four of five 1984 House challengers who received at least 40 percent of the vote contributed to their own campaigns, with an average investment of $20,000. These personal contributions were an important source of early "seed money."[25] Of the fifty new House winners in 1986, fifteen personally had invested more than $75,000 in their own races.

**Summary.**    A review of the circumstances facing congressional challengers in the past decade reveals both continuity and change. Throughout the period the chances for challenger victory have been much less than even, but over time the odds have become even longer. In 1988 House incumbents set a record when more than 98 percent of them defeated their challengers, and about 80 percent either won landslide victories of more than 60 percent or faced no opposition at all. The number of House seats considered marginal—that is, with any realistic possibility of the incumbent being defeated—dropped in 1988 to half the number of 1984.[26]

In broad comparative terms Democratic challengers still are more likely to have past experience, need to spend less on their campaigns to win, and get less party assistance than their Republican counterparts; however, the shrinking number of genuinely competitive contests and the growing costs of campaigns diminished party differences as the eighties progressed.

Fewer promising opportunities for challengers meant that Democratic campaign committees could offer significant amounts of help in most contested races. High campaign costs made the maximum permissible Republican assistance worth proportionately less than it had been in the past. The "experience gap" between successful Democratic and Republican candidates narrowed. With the number of marginal contests dropping and party financial assistance in those contests becoming more equal, the advantages of elective experience—a personal organizational and financial base—became almost as important to Republicans as to Democrats who won.

## Statewide Races:
## Senators and Governors

Challengers for the offices of senator and governor encounter a different set of problems from those of legislative and congressional challengers. This section discusses the special problems of these challengers and their differences from lower level office.

**Senate Races.** Senate campaigns differ in two ways from contests for the House. They are more likely to be competitive, and the media play a larger role. Both of these differences can significantly affect the activities of statewide challengers.

As for competition, the figures speak for themselves. About a fourth of the challengers running against Senate incumbents were successful between 1976 and 1988, compared to less than a tenth of House challengers. Successful Senate incumbents also had closer races. In the same period about seven in ten House incumbents won reelection with at least 60 percent of the two-party vote; only about four in ten Senate incumbents did as well. These data paint a considerably brighter picture for Senate challengers than for House challengers.

We noted in chapter 4 that statewide candidates receive much greater media attention during their campaigns than do congressional office seekers. Although this observation generally holds true, some Senate campaigns resemble House campaigns in which a hopeless challenger runs. They are neither competitive nor well covered by the media. Mark Westlye points out that "a substantial proportion of Senate races are low-key affairs that attract scant notice: media coverage is limited, spending by the challenger is relatively low, and the outcome is often a foregone conclusion." [27]

Westlye studied the 122 Senate races between 1972 and 1980 in which incumbents figured. They were divided almost evenly between hard-fought and low-key campaigns. The challengers in low-key races, as in most congressional races, were much less well known than the incumbents, with their recognition rates averaging 60 percent, as opposed to 92 percent for challengers in hard-fought contests. In hard-fought races voter defections—votes by partisans for the Senate candidate of the other party—were moderately high and in both directions, whereas in low-key races defections were strongly in the direction of the incumbent. When a race for the Senate does not have the excitement of competitiveness, the media tend to treat the contest as they do the typical House election, and the absence of coverage reinforces the voters' lack of interest.

What makes a Senate race hard-fought or low-key is not entirely clear, although there are clues. Lightly populated states are more likely to have less competitive races when incumbents are involved. Between 1968 and 1980 two-thirds of the Senate races in the twelve most populous states were decided by fewer than ten percentage points, whereas the same proportion in the twelve least populous states was decided by more than ten percentage points. Researchers speculate that less densely populated Senate constituencies are like congressional districts—more homogeneous and more strongly one-party: "For incumbent legislators, the more constituents there are, the more difficult they are to please." [28]

Population density is not the entire explanation for competition levels, however. States with large populations such as Illinois, Massachusetts, and Michigan currently have two senators of the same party elected by widely varying margins. The explanation must also lie in the quality of various senatorial candidates' campaigns, their attractiveness as candidates, and the strength of their challengers. Like representatives, senators whose votes approach or exceed two-thirds of the total count devise strategies to make themselves appear so invulnerable that strong challengers decline to run against them, even though they stand a better chance of winning than do their House counterparts. The weak challengers who do run are less able to raise money, have no previous experience that would give them widespread recognition, are thus not taken seriously by the media, and do not receive the free media coverage they need to acquire recognition.

Most media organizations make their election coverage plans in the summer during the internal campaign period. One political reporter observed the winter before a federal election, "We basically decide we're going to cover the elections that will be in doubt." Comparing the Senate race that would take place in his state that fall with the contest for the other Senate seat two years earlier, he was already practically dismissing the fall contest: "There probably will have been a lot more stories two years ago than this year mainly because it's not perceived as a close race." In fact, no challenger to the incumbent had even emerged definitively at that point. Like the reporter, potentially strong challengers presumably had read the polls giving the incumbent the highest favorability rating of any politician in the state and knew about his $4 million war chest.

Another factor influencing the competitiveness of Senate contests is whether a challenger must face an incumbent or simply another challenger. Open seats almost always attract two strong candidates. Half the incumbent races Westlye studied were low-key, but fewer than a fifth of the races for open seats were. Whereas only about one of three open House seats is hard-fought, four of five open Senate seats are. The higher media profile of Senate contests and the greater heterogeneity of most Senate constituencies mean that party identification and prior recognition are less crucial than in House contests, and either candidate has a reasonable chance to win.

The greater chance of winning a Senate race, compared with a House race, also makes it easier in many cases for candidates to raise campaign funds. Almost all Republican Senate challengers can expect to receive more party money and support than their Democratic counterparts can count on, although the proportionate advantage in races perceived as close is quickly declining. The major difference is that the Republican party, unlike the Democrats, can afford to give every Senate challenger the maximum permitted by law, and in most cases it does. Mitch Daniels, former executive director of the National Republican Senatorial Committee said:

> I just feel very strongly that this committee is uniquely positioned to recruit candidates and therefore has a party responsibility to do so, and to be effective in the long haul, has to keep its commitments. We'll fulfill every commitment we made even though we know some of them will never come close.

Because there are only 33 or 34 Senate races in each two-year election cycle, as opposed to 435 House races, and they are more likely to be competitive, both candidates in a promising Senate race stand a chance of raising sizable amounts of PAC money. For instance, in the 1986 open seat race in Missouri between former Republican governor

Christopher Bond and Democratic lieutenant governor Harriet Woods, both candidates were able to raise about 20 percent of their war chests from PACs.[29]

Wealthy individuals finance their own early campaigns for the Senate as well. Although political amateurs are still less common in the Senate than in the House, the decline of party-based voting and the growing importance of paid media advertising in Senate campaigns have attracted a growing number of affluent political novices to Senate races. Enough money to ensure high recognition levels is crucial to Senate challengers' success. In Senate races between 1974 and 1986, the level of challenger spending was by far the most important variable affecting the outcome.[30] In 1984 seventeen Senate candidates each spent more than $200,000 of their own money. Such candidates were especially prevalent in states with expensive media markets.

The Senate has always had its share of members who amassed power and wealth in nonpolitical spheres, but in earlier days would-be senators—men like Mark Hanna, for instance—would first have had to pay their party dues. In recent years, as the parties' role in campaigns has diminished, wealthy individuals such as Dave Durenberger and Rudy Boschwitz of Minnesota, Howard Metzenbaum and John Glenn of Ohio, and Bill Bradley and Frank Lautenberg of New Jersey have been able to effect lateral entry into the Senate.

**Gubernatorial Races.**   Gubernatorial challengers must also deal with a deficit of recognition, money, and time. As in some Senate contests, there is a class of gubernatorial races in which these deficits are never overcome; they attract only weak challengers, and the outcome of the election is a foregone conclusion. In 1986, of fifteen incumbent governors who ran for reelection, nine won easily (with 60 percent or more of the vote), five had a relatively close contest (getting less than 60 percent), and two lost. Among the nine challengers who lost badly, only two had ever held or previously run for a statewide position.

As with Senate races, there is a strong and positive correlation between the quality of the challengers, the statewide recognition levels they begin with, and their likelihood of success. Inexperienced or unknown gubernatorial challengers also find it difficult to get the early financial resources and free media attention that permit them to run a credible race. Consultant Vince Breglio described most challengers' early problems:

> The package for a challenger is really different because their up-front money is always, always thin. A statewide survey, for example—you're looking at $35,000. That's a potful of money for a challenger to come up with. In all the challenger statewide races I'm working on right now [in March of the election year], we have yet to do any full-blown surveys.

Maybe they're in a position to get a good piece of research by late August, early September. But it comes very late. They just don't have the dough to do it before.

Gubernatorial hopefuls who seek to make up for a lack of resources with free media attention also find themselves up against the attitude of reporters such as the one who observed of gubernatorial candidates: "Coverage is post-filing day. They are just average citizens until they file for office. You don't plan your coverage until the gun goes off." Even though coverage may increase after the race formally begins, it is usually too late for an unknown challenger to profit sufficiently from free media.

Because of these problems, successful novice challengers are often wealthy individuals who can personally finance the requirements of the early internal campaign; like similar Senate challengers, they often run in large, competitive states with expensive media markets they can afford to dominate. Nelson Rockefeller of New York and Milton Shapp of Pennsylvania are examples of rich amateurs who pioneered this type of campaign in the 1960s; Texan William Clements was successful in 1978 and 1986; and businessman Wallace Wilkinson triumphed in Kentucky in 1987.

Although disclosure provisions in the states vary widely and are rarely as stringent as the federal rules, credible gubernatorial challengers appear to raise their money from the same sources as incumbents. Their war chests also bulge with the contributions of recipients of official state patronage. Bond-writing brokerage houses were heavy contributors in the 1986 open seat gubernatorial races in Kansas and Florida. Both candidates in Kansas's close race received contributions from interests hoping the new governor would support the legalization of greyhound racing.

The involvement of the national party committees in gubernatorial races traditionally has been limited or nonexistent. The Republican Governors Association, however, was particularly active in 1986, when it placed many Reagan campaign veterans on its staff. The party picked up eight governorships that year.[31] Although the Republicans are expanding their commitments to governors' races somewhat, the emphasis remains on Washington. The Democratic committees can afford only minimal involvement in such races.

Finally, in a few states, gubernatorial campaigns receive substantial public funding, as presidential candidates have since 1976. In the two with the most generous public financing—New Jersey and Michigan—a challenger has yet to be successful when running against an incumbent on a level financial playing field. Public financing, however, has made campaigns easier for the contestants in the one open seat race each state has had since public financing was instituted in the late 1970s.

# The Challenger: A Summary _____

Most challengers must overcome serious deficits of time, money, organization, and recognition. If they do not make up these deficits quickly, they have probably lost their contests long before election day. Although not enough by itself, money is usually the key to solving the other problems. If challengers do not have the kind of track record that will convince PACs, party organizations, and large individual contributors that their races are good investments, heavy personal spending is probably the only alternative. As we saw in the previous chapter, the national trends that lifted many challengers to victory in the party-centered era are of greatly diminished assistance, making money more important than ever. The challengers who surmount these hurdles can then go on to the next stage of electoral contests—the need to set the agenda of the campaign and seize control of its dialogue. We examine that phase of a campaign in the next chapter.

## Notes

1. Judi Dawkins, wife of New Jersey Senate candidate Pete Dawkins, quoted in *National Journal*, March 19, 1988, 735.
2. See the discussion of career paths in Larry Sabato, *Goodbye to Good-time Charlie: The American Governorship Transformed*, 2d ed. (Washington, D.C.: CQ Press, 1983), 33-45.
3. David Rohde, "Risk-Bearing and Progressive Ambition: The Case of Members of the U.S. House of Representatives," *American Journal of Political Science* 23 (February 1979): 1-26.
4. Richard F. Fenno, Jr., *The United States Senate: A Bicameral Perspective* (Washington, D.C.: American Enterprise Institute, 1982), 43.
5. *National Journal*, March 18, 1988, 737, 738.
6. Gary C. Jacobson, *The Politics of Congressional Elections*, 2d ed. (Boston: Little, Brown, 1987). See also Jacobson and Samuel Kernell, *Strategy and Choice in Congressional Elections* (New Haven, Conn.: Yale University Press, 1981); Robert J. Huckshorn and Robert C. Spencer, *The Politics of Defeat: Campaigning for Congress* (Amherst: University of Massachusetts Press, 1971).
7. *National Journal*, November 16, 1985, 2626.
8. Peter Clarke and Susan H. Evans, *Covering Campaigns: Journalism in Congressional Elections* (Stanford, Calif.: Stanford University Press, 1983), 32.
9. *Congressional Quarterly Weekly Report*, December 19, 1987, 3143, 3144.
10. *Congressional Quarterly Weekly Report*, October 3, 1987, 2381.
11. Cuomo, *Diaries*, 153.
12. Ibid., 153-154.
13. Malcolm L. Jewell, *Representation in State Legislatures* (Lexington: University Press of Kentucky, 1982), 29.
14. In a presentation at the Eagleton Institute of Politics, Rutgers University, New Brunswick, New Jersey, September 20, 1982.
15. Quoted in Alan Clem, *The Making of Congressmen: Seven Campaigns of 1974* (North Scituate, Mass.: Duxbury Press, 1976), 140.

16. See Lorene Hanley Duquin, "Door to Door Campaigning: How to Get the Most Out of Your Pedometer," *Campaigns and Elections* 3 (Spring 1982): 15-24.

17. For instance, Larry J. Sabato, *The Rise of Political Consultants: New Ways of Winning Elections* (New York: Basic Books, 1981), chapter 4.

18. "C&E Direct Mail Fundraising Roundtable: The Pros Speak," *Campaigns and Elections* 1 (Fall 1980). See chapter 8 for further discussion of this point.

19. Hank Parkinson, "How to Get Elected to Your State Legislature," *Campaigns and Elections* 1 (Summer 1980): 50.

20. Michael Barone and Grant Ujifusa, *Almanac of American Politics 1984* (Washington, D.C.: National Journal, 1983), 446.

21. Everett C. Ladd with Charles D. Hadley, *Transformations of the American Party System*, 2d ed. (New York: Norton, 1978), 377, 377n.

22. *Congressional Quarterly Weekly Report*, July 2, 1983, 1351.

23. Richard E. Cohen, "Incumbent Goliaths," *National Journal*, October 8, 1988, 2533.

24. Frank J. Sorauf, *Money in American Elections* (Glenview, Ill.: Scott, Foresman, 1988), 99; *National Journal*, October 8, 1988, 2532; *New York Times*, October 20, 1988, B10.

25. Sorauf, *Money in American Elections*, 68; Clyde Wilcox, "I Owe It All to Me: Candidates' Investments in Their Own Campaigns," *American Political Quarterly* 16 (July 1988): 266-279.

26. *National Journal*, March 5, 1988, 636; *National Committee for an Effective Congress, Election Update* (Washington, D.C.: National Committee for an Effective Congress), April 1988.

27. Mark C. Westlye, "Competitiveness of Senate Seats and Voting Behavior in Senate Elections," *American Journal of Political Science* 27 (May 1983): 253. Low-key races were defined as those in which the challenger trailed at least two to one in fund raising and which the preelection issue of *Congressional Quarterly Weekly Report* judged as noncompetitive.

28. John R. Hibbing and Sara L. Brandes, "State Population and the Electoral Success of U.S. Senators," *American Journal of Political Science* 27 (November 1983): 817.

29. *St. Louis Post Dispatch*, November 3, 1986, 6A.

30. Alan I. Abramowitz, "Explaining Senate Election Outcomes," *American Political Science Review* 82 (June 1988): 396-397.

31. *National Journal*, April 13, 1985, 818; December 7, 1985, 2828.

# Setting the Agenda: Campaign Themes  6

*In a democracy, campaigns are adversarial. People understand that. . . . They want you to draw a distinction between yourself and the field. . . . Whoever gets to define the race will generally win it.*

James Carville, campaign manager[1]

When campaigns go public and enter their external phase, the key task for them is to communicate a message that will persuade a majority of the electorate to vote for one candidate rather than another. To be successful, a candidate must set the agenda of the campaign. Setting the agenda means advancing a set of themes or issues that the electorate will find more convincing than those of the opponent. Jeff Greenfield, who used to work in campaigns and now writes and broadcasts about them, described it this way:

> We are talking about what the undergraduates at Princeton once labeled "megacepts," essential themes which knit the entire campaign, from speeches to advertising to slogan to press interviews, together. . . . The choice of such a theme is extremely difficult, because it depends on a specific mix of the candidate and the political atmosphere. The same megacept which crashes on takeoff in one election year can take a candidate to victory in the next.[2]

Agenda setting in a campaign is pursued through all the means of mass communication—those controlled entirely by the candidate (all forms of advertising including direct mail) and those over which less influence can be exercised (the news media, partly controlled by print and broadcast journalists). Political consultants refer to these communication channels as *paid media* and *free media;* they are discussed in detail in chapter 7. In this chapter we analyze the themes candidates put forward and consider what influences their choices and what contributes to the selection of a persuasive theme.

# The Choice of the Campaign Theme

Choosing a thematic emphasis is the most fundamental decision candidates and their organizations make. As Greenfield writes: "Your first task in mapping out a campaign is to put aside all thought of alliances, marketing strategy, and makeup artists and figure out *what your campaign is all about. What is the premise on which you run for office?"* [3] Setting out these basic assumptions, or themes, is the foundation of a campaign's grand strategy. Without a theme a campaign is likely to founder. It is no wonder, then, that most successful campaigns have clear and convincing themes.

## Selecting the Theme: The Role of Issues

It is important to understand how campaign themes are related to issues. The classic model of democratic elections assumes that candidates advance a set of detailed issue positions that give voters clear alternatives, that voters understand the alternatives being offered to them, and that they make their choices on that basis. Scholars discovered long ago that this situation never holds true. Even in the present information-rich environment, two out of five voters cannot correctly identify the issue positions of both presidential candidates, and four out of five cannot do the same for congressional candidates.[4]

This does not mean that issues are irrelevant. In the era of strong party identification, the candidate's party banner served as a shorthand for a set of issue positions, although "Democrat" signified very different concepts to voters in the rural South and the urban North, as "Republican" did in the urban East and the rural Midwest. Today issues play a role in cuing voters but not in the sense posited by democratic theorists. Although a candidate may have detailed position papers on a whole range of issues, campaigns cannot be waged on all of them. Voters have neither the time nor the interest to weigh every issue carefully. Moreover, they are likely to agree with a given candidate on some issues and not on others. Campaigns have taken on the role of substantially determining *which* issues voters think about when they make their party choices.

Candidates use issues not just to appeal to voters who agree with them on policy but to convey messages about their personal qualities. Candidates cannot simply say to voters that they are competent, compassionate, or trustworthy, but they can suggest these qualities through the way they talk about issues. As a Republican consultant told a group of hopeful challengers at a party candidate training school, "Issues are a vehicle to build images." [5] Campaigns emphasize a limited range of issues with which they hope to identify a candidate to his or her benefit: "Issues are like chips that get moved around a board, the means but not the ends of political life." [6]

When a campaign organization surveys the issue context of an election, there are many possibilities from which to choose. All issues fall into two basic types, however. First is the substantive, positional issue. Where does the candidate stand on tax reform, national defense, foreign policy, or domestic programs? The other type focuses on personal qualities. Does the candidate convey leadership, compassion, empathy, integrity, trustworthiness?

Almost all personal themes are based on what political scientists call "valence" issues, or, in common speech, "motherhood and apple pie" issues: Everyone is for and not against qualities such as trustworthiness or leadership. When elections revolve around valence issues, the campaign agenda becomes, "Which candidate is more effective in demonstrating the desirable qualities?" Some substantive questions may appear to be positional but, depending on how they are presented, can also be valence issues. If candidates treat a substantive issue as one they are better equipped to handle than their rivals because of personal qualities rather than because of programmatic solutions, then positional issues become valence issues. Democratic media consultant Tony Schwartz says of a substantive issue often treated in this fashion: "I don't think inflation is an issue. Who's for it? . . . The real issue is which of the two candidates would best be able to deal with [it]." [7]

Genuine positional issues, in contrast, have two sides, and the candidates are perceived as taking opposing views. The challenge for campaigns is to select the positional issues that capture public imagination and win public approval. If the issue is strong enough, it may come to be what Democratic pollster Bill Hamilton calls a "referendum issue." In other words, the agenda of the campaign becomes a yes-or-no vote on candidates based on their positions on the issue.

## Selecting the Theme:
## The Role of Polls and Pollsters

The substance of campaign themes varies widely, but to be persuasive, they must be carefully tailored to the candidate, to his or her opponent, to the constituency, and to the current political environment.

To use a marketing analogy, the choice of a theme can be likened to "product positioning" and the identification of a "comparative advantage." Comparative advantages are "the unique characteristics that differentiate a candidate from his competitors, which give his supporters a reason to prefer him over the competition." [8] A candidate cannot pick a seemingly attractive theme out of the air and expect it to work. The theme must be credible coming from that candidate; it must fit the constituency, and it must be more convincing than the opponent's theme. The information that strategists need to determine appropriate campaign themes now comes from polls.

The most certain indicator of a state-of-the-art campaign is the presence of technologically sophisticated consultants—pollsters and media advisers. The two work together closely, for the pollster's findings determine the message media consultants design. Their functions have always been a part of American campaigns. The media adviser who produces elaborate television commercials is the direct descendant of the nineteenth-century writer of partisan newspaper articles and political tracts. Although the modern campaign's forebears did not have scientific sampling techniques or elaborate data analysis routines, the straw poll has a lineage that stretches back to the early 1800s.[9] What distinguishes the modern consultants is their autonomy of action, the technology available to them, and, in the most recent years, the growing role of pollsters in shaping the message that media consultants convey. We will elaborate on each of these developments.

In the days of party-line voting and party-directed campaigns, party leaders shaped the media message and directed the canvassing activities. It was Mark Hanna's party minions who produced the McKinley pamphlets that poured out of Republican headquarters in 1896 and the public relations director of the Republican National Committee who worked with his former colleagues in the advertising agencies that produced the first campaign television commercials for Eisenhower in 1952. Similarly, parties directed the canvassing operations that predated polls. In the early twentieth century workers in New York's Tammany Hall machine would fan out to critical locations across the city, asking people their voting choices: "Thus, Tammany had what it regarded as a reliable day-to-day reading of the election situation during the campaign period." [10]

As the party organizations declined, campaigns turned to media consultants—first in advertising agencies and then in the political firms that sprang up—to devise thematic messages. Scientific polling began as an arcane specialty with a few practitioners. It had to await the spread of the computer and the growth in the number of specialists before it became a staple of campaigns below the presidential level. These occurred in the late 1960s and early 1970s, fortuitously conterminous with the rise in the number of independent and ticket-splitting voters. Then the pollster was ready to step into the shoes of the party organization. Democratic pollster Bill Hamilton observed: "As political bosses trail off, it's natural that the pollster delivers where the campaign is going. The bosses, opinion leaders, and labor people used to suggest how to get their people. Now the pollsters do. They have the data."

Some media consultants responded to the increased importance of polling by creating their own polling organizations. More commonly, however, media consultants interact with, and even take direction from, independent pollsters. Republican consultant Vince Breglio, who began as a pollster, described the changes in the relationship:

> The media person's role has changed. It used to be that campaigns would go to their media person and ask for strategy. Now they ask their pollster. The pollster translates those numbers into the strategic recommendations that identify who your voter should be, what is of greatest concern to those who should be voting for you, and how you can best influence those groups. The media person becomes more of a technician . . . more of an implementor who gets marching orders from the pollster: "Now come back with several scripts so we can determine if you're on target or not."

**The Polling Package.** Pollsters have developed a fairly standard package for statewide races, consisting of benchmark, trend, and tracking polls and focus groups.[11] Ideally, the polling program for campaigns below the statewide level should follow the same format. Most of them, however, cannot afford such an elaborate undertaking.

A *benchmark poll* gives a campaign information about the voting preferences and issue concerns of various groups in the electorate and a detailed reading of the images voters have of the candidates in the race—information that dictates a campaign's allocation of resources in several important ways. It tells the campaign how and where to schedule the candidate, what issues to stress, and how to convey them. It suggests the theme and content of broadcast advertising and where it should be placed. Usually, a benchmark poll is done no later than the winter of the election year. Incumbent Senate candidates often commission benchmarks as much as eighteen to twenty months before the election and then repeat them in late summer or early fall when their opponents are definitively known.[12]

The benchmark is followed by several fairly detailed *trend polls* to determine the success of the campaigns in altering candidate images and voting preferences. By early October a campaign begins its *tracking polls*, conducting short nightly interviews with a small number of respondents, keyed to the variables that have assumed importance. Combining a few nights of tracking polls into *rolling averages* furnishes a larger, more reliable sample for general strategic assessment.[13] For reasons of cost, speed, and efficiency almost all political surveys are conducted by telephone rather than in face-to-face interviews.

Unlike surveys—which consist of structured questions on a large number of topics, are asked in identical fashion to large numbers of people chosen by scientific sampling procedures, and rarely exceed twenty minutes—*focus groups* consist of perhaps twenty people who informally discuss narrow topics for as long as two hours. The participants, chosen to represent particular target groups the campaign wants to reinforce or persuade, are led in their discussion by persons trained in small-group dynamics. The purpose of the focus group, which is further described below, is to give some texture and depth to the findings that emerge from the more standard survey instruments.[14]

A typical benchmark poll for a statewide candidate begins with screening questions, which ask respondents whether they are registered, whether they have voted in the past, and whether they are likely to vote in the coming election. Interviews with those deemed unlikely to vote are terminated. Because in most statewide elections half or fewer of the eligible adults actually vote, effective screening questions to assess who those voters will be are crucial.

The survey goes on to ask respondents whether they recall or recognize the names of all the potential candidates in the race and whether they have an opinion of them ("favorable, unfavorable, or one of the best"). Respondents are then asked to rate each candidate on characteristics such as credibility and compassion ("doesn't care about people like me" versus "cares about people like me," for example) and to rate each candidate's past performance ("he's done a lot to hold down taxes," or "he's grown a lot in office"). Then come a large number of questions about issues—both the respondents' view of them and their perceptions of the candidates' views. These questions are followed by several head-to-head voting choices.

At the time that most benchmark polls are done, before state primaries, there may be many possible candidates, and different combinations of candidates usually produce different possible electoral outcomes. For instance, in a conjectured match a year before the 1988 election, Missouri senatorial incumbent John Danforth led his eventual opponent, Jay Nixon, 59 to 21 percent, but he trailed Rep. Dick Gephardt (then still running for president) 40 to 43 percent. Incumbents who dip below 50 percent in such match-ups are considered to be at least vulnerable to defeat.

Another frequently used measure of a candidate's underlying

strength is the "reelect" question: Voters are asked whether they generally believe an incumbent should be reelected, as opposed to being "replaced" or "giving a new person" a chance. Incumbents whose "reelect numbers" hover at or fall below 40 percent are considered vulnerable. Reelect numbers vary widely, as can be seen in 1987 soundings for senators who would face voters in 1988. The numbers ranged from 64 percent achieved by Massachusetts's Edward Kennedy to 54 percent by New Mexico's Jeff Bingaman, 47 percent by Michigan's Donald Riegle, and 40 percent by Wyoming's Malcolm Wallop. All four of these incumbents eventually won, and the rank order of their reelect numbers was the same as the rank order of their actual victory margins.

Surveys may also include questions in which a candidate is matched against a hypothetical rival who the campaign assumes would give their candidate the toughest race—a form of "worst case" analysis. Thus, although Wallop easily defeated all the announced or likely 1988 contenders for his job in 1987 polls, a description of a "perfect" opponent found him trailing 29 to 52 percent. Wallop went on to defeat challenger John Vinich by fewer than two thousand votes, the closest Senate race in 1988. If a candidate can defeat a perfect opponent, he or she can defeat anyone. Conversely, if a perfect opponent can win, it is the campaign's job to ensure that the real opponent is not seen as that perfect contender.[16]

If a candidate has any personal or political weaknesses that could become an issue in the campaign, respondents may be asked how such shortcomings—including brushes with the law, marital problems, and real or rumored scandals—would affect their choice. Polls also often test the credibility of possible explanations or rationalizations of the candidate's difficulties.

Surveys then test a variety of themes that the campaign is considering. Such themes, dealing with both the candidate and an opponent, are presented to the respondent as "scenarios" or "editorials." In a survey for an experienced challenger, the "best-case scenario" read like this:

> X was a great governor. He held down government spending, kept taxes low, and ran the state like a business. He never turned his back on basic human needs. He fought for money for highways, fought for money for education, and he did a lot to help poor people. He would be a great senator.

In contrast, the "worst-case scenario" argued:

> X was a governor who put the needs of business ahead of the needs of people. He turned his back on the needs of poor people. He put the needs of business ahead of the need to protect the environment. He did a very poor job of running the state. He would not make a good United States senator.

After each scenario is presented, respondents are asked to give their overall reaction to the statement, to indicate whether they think the assertions are true, and to weigh the strength of their agreement or disagreement with each charge in the statements. Similar scenarios are presented for the candidate's opponent, and corresponding assessments are done. When "scenario" probes are taken, respondents are often asked the head-to-head questions again to see whether the information provided has changed their voting choices, on the assumption that this is the dialogue that will take place during the campaign.

The focus group is another way to test possible campaign themes, and this is its main purpose. A few "typical" members of important groups in the electorate are asked to react at length to themes the campaign is considering or to comment on the persuasiveness of commercials advancing particular themes—both by the campaign's candidate and the opponent. Although the focus group is no substitute for systematic mass surveys, it is the campaign's only chance to try out its messages before they are aired publicly. Pollster Paul Maslin has commented: "The crux of most campaigns comes down to perhaps a handful of TV spots. If you're going to spend millions of dollars and have a whole career depend on a couple of commercials, you better know they work." [16]

Such fine-grained examination of the effect of various campaign themes is the greatest difference between private campaign polls and public polls done by newspapers, television stations, and academic researchers. Public polls are retrospective; they try to find explanations of why the public holds its particular opinions at a particular moment. Campaign polls have a prospective orientation; they examine how the public will react to different messages and themes. As Republican pollster Richard Wirthlin puts it: "The kinds of questions we use are very different from those in a media poll. The media's polling is informative; ours is strategic. Theirs measures what is; ours attempts to give us an idea of what can be." [17]

Prospective information can be of great value. At the beginning of a poll done by Democrats in September 1987, 36 percent of Washington State voters said they would vote to reelect Republican senator Dan Evans, 47 percent said they would consider another candidate, and 17 percent were ready to replace Evans. After the voters were presented with various credible charges against the incumbent, Evans's reelect number dropped thirteen points, and those willing to consider an opponent rose ten points. These discouraging figures and other considerations prompted Evans not to run for reelection. Similarly, a spring 1987 media poll on the 1988 Connecticut senatorial race found incumbent Lowell Weicker with a comfortable lead over challenger Joseph

Lieberman. A poll for Lieberman showed them in a dead heat after voters were apprised of negative factors about Weicker.[18] Lieberman defeated Weicker in a close contest.

Unfavorable poll results, of course, do not mean that an incumbent is a sure loser, but they do give both candidates a realistic idea of possible outcomes. In some cases it is unrelieved bad news. Unsuccessful 1978 Maine congressional challenger Sandy Maisel has recounted his pollster's summary of the benchmark results: His incumbent opponent had the highest positive evaluation the firm had ever recorded among voters in the opposition party. "No strategy for a November election appears feasible." [19] Other candidates get new hope, however. The manager of a successful Senate challenger said of the campaign's benchmark data: "We knew what information, which strategies would work and which ones wouldn't. The benchmark gave us some precision in terms of where we were going."

The final components of a typical questionnaire concern the wider political environment in which the campaign takes place. The questions range from such topics as the job rating and performance of the president to voter demographics, including party identification, age, occupation, education, marital status, religion, ethnicity, and race. Questions may also be asked about respondents' media habits; their responses assist campaigns in determining where to place print and broadcast messages.

A good pollster is careful to tailor a survey to each candidate and to make the campaign staff feel that whatever the pollster's other commitments, he or she is sensitive to the race at hand. Surveys that ask the same questions whatever the race—known as "canned," or "packaged," polls—miss the idiosyncracies peculiar to an individual contest. The issues director for an experienced Senate incumbent explains why that campaign chose one national pollster over another:

> X had a feel for the region, and Y was too intellectual, too set. He had a campaign and poll strategy that he ran in every campaign, that was not tailored, or not sensitive, to specific factors in the campaign. He also would have too many candidates and not enough time to devote to us— that was a major concern of the senator.

**Interpreting Polls.** A mark of the good pollster, in addition to sensitivity to the particular circumstances of a given campaign, is the ability to read what practitioners call the *internals* of polling results. Experienced pollsters know that an early strong or weak showing is often more apparent than real. It is the pollster's job to go beneath the numbers and tell the candidate what they really mean. This sometimes means telling an apparently strong leader that he or she has serious problems. As one national pollster has said:

There are lots of cases where an incumbent has a high job rating, but with a little higher than normal negatives, with the wrong words being said about him. We sort of know that a year later, with the right campaign against him, that guy is really in trouble.

Both the greatest satisfaction and the greatest frustration can come to pollsters when they can see the promise in overtly discouraging results. A candidate who sees the potential in the internals of a poll and is willing and able to commit resources to a "hopeless" race is the pollster's joy—and is not the rare exception. But the needlessly cowardly candidate is ubiquitous as well. Bill Hamilton has explained it:

> As much as the pollster says, "Your opponent's vote is soft . . . because they generally like you, as this segment makes up its mind, they are going to move in your direction," you have candidates start thinking about getting out of the race. The pollster's got to be strong enough to make them understand a more sophisticated analysis than they can make of the data.
> I've had a candidate get out of the race. The poll showed him thirteen down but also that the incumbent's support was very soft. I fought, and he still got out. His administrative assistant decided to run using that poll—never did any more polling—and he became a United States senator. Candidates get it in their heads about where they want to be when you do a poll, and if they're not there, they're not sophisticated enough to look underneath.

Some examples demonstrate the kinds of advice that pollsters can give to shore up a seemingly invincible candidate with feet of clay or an apparently hopeless case who has genuine potential. One gubernatorial incumbent running for reelection received an extremely high job rating in his benchmark poll and easily defeated his likely opponents in head-to-head questions. His benchmark showed, however, that half of the electorate had specific issue-related complaints about him and that he garnered only a bare 50 percent in a head-to-head question against a hypothetical strong opponent. His pollster recommended a summer media initiative aimed directly at responding to the troublesome issues. The trend polls conducted later showed increasing strength and fewer complaints; the incumbent went on to win two to one.

On the other hand, Edward King of Massachusetts was not discouraged when his February 1978 benchmark showed him with 11 percent of the Democratic primary vote for governor, in contrast to the 64 percent who favored his incumbent opponent, Michael Dukakis. The survey's internals showed that large numbers of Democratic primary voters said that "under no circumstances" would they support a candidate who opposed minimum jail sentences for violent crimes, opposed the death penalty, or favored abortion—all positions taken by Dukakis. King's campaign manager said of these findings, "That's when we discovered we could get significant defections from Dukakis if we could let people know where he stood and where we stood on the issues." [20] After a primary campaign highlighting Dukakis's stand on these social issues, King defeated the incumbent by a 9 percent margin. The King campaign was a preview of some of the themes George Bush would employ successfully against Dukakis in the 1988 presidential race.

Thus good benchmark and trend polling help campaigns to identify possible themes. Successful campaigns are those that choose the most effective themes, based in part on their judgment of what the theme and responses of the opposition campaign will be. These vary with each contest.

## Some Winning and Losing Campaign Themes

We next look at several campaign themes, to capture their variations and to extract the few general rules that apply to all campaigns in selecting a theme.

**Valence Issue as Theme.**  Sometimes a major issue is judged by both sides to be so compelling that the two candidates will choose essentially the same theme. The campaign debate then revolves around which candidate can deal better with the overriding problem—what we earlier described as a valence issue. Such was the case in the 1986 Florida Senate race, pitting incumbent Paula Hawkins against popular outgoing governor Bob Graham. The issue was which candidate would be tougher in combating the use of illegal drugs and the crime drugs generated.

The candidates' advertising messages and official actions played heavily into this theme. Hawkins, styling herself "the Senate's general in the War on Drugs," persuaded the Republican Senate leadership to let her manage a major drug bill on the Senate floor, while a TV ad charged that Graham permitted convicted drug pushers easy parole from prison. Graham retaliated by arguing in his advertising that Hawkins had voted to cut the Coast Guard budget, voted against funds for drug education, and lied about a purported discussion with China's political leader on stopping the flow of drugs from Asia.

In the end Hawkins lost the debate about who would be tougher and more effective on this issue because of the images both candidates had acquired among Florida voters over time. Some of Hawkins's previous activities had raised questions about her credibility and reliability. Graham, on the other hand, because of such measures as his strict and repeated enforcement of the state's death penalty, was perceived as genuinely tough. Hawkins's charges against Graham contradicted his latent image, while Graham's charges against Hawkins reinforced what many voters already believed about the incumbent.

**Issue and Image Themes.** Not every political race is like the Florida contest, in which both candidates fought to attain the high ground on the same valence issue. In some races the competitors stress different themes, hoping their choice will prove more convincing than those of their opponents. Candidates may highlight different issues, they may present contrasting personal images of themselves and their opponents, or one candidate may emphasize a specific issue while the other contender bases the campaign on personal images.

Three hotly contested campaigns of the 1980s illustrate each of these cases. The 1986 Texas gubernatorial campaign was fought on opposing issues. Incumbent Democrat Mark White stressed his popular educational reforms. In a typical commercial portraying a small child having trouble with the alphabet, White told voters that challenger Bill Clements, whom White had defeated in 1982, would move the state backward: "If Clements wants to run for governor to get even, that's his business. But if he takes it out on education, that's your business." Clements, in contrast, stressed Texas's economic and crime problems. A Clements advertisement, featuring a picture of a smiling White and the newspaper headline "Rapist serving 123 years gets parole after seven years," questioned: "Why was the criminal freed? Ask Governor Mark White."

On the other hand, the 1986 California Senate race between seventy-two-year-old Democratic incumbent Alan Cranston and his much younger opponent, Republican representative Ed Zschau, depended heavily on contrasting images. Zschau, who had been a principal in a major Silicon Valley high-tech firm, painted himself as the exemplar of traditional values and California's future and his opponent as the worn-out symbol of a discredited liberal past. Zschau's advertising made extensive use of space-age graphics and featured him and his young family engaged in such activities as riding river rapids. Cranston, in contrast, pointed to his decades of public service to California, his record of consistent positions, and his strong identification with the state. One Cranston advertising spot showed magnificent jagged California mountains dissolving into Cranston's craggy features with the tag line "Alan Cranston. California in the Senate."

At the same time, Cranston eroded Zschau's image by raising questions about the challenger's ideological "flip-flops" during his political career. One of the incumbent's most clever and devastating attack messages was aimed squarely at the "high-tech baby boomers" Zschau particularly attempted to cultivate. The ad was modeled after local, late night TV commercials for cheap record albums. As the text scrolled "Ed Zschau's greatest hits," including such "titles" as "The Sanctions Shuffle," "Who Cares About the Environment Anyway," "I

Agree With Both Sides Now," and "I'm All Over the Map," an announcer intoned:

> This is Jackman Wolf with the greatest hits of that great song and dance man, Ed Zschau. Zschau will tell you anything—you remember his classic about toxic waste:
> [Song] Caught in a dump about picking it up, because I took too much money, baby. . . .
> Or what about:
> [Song] How many times can a man change his mind. . . .
> And who can ever forget:
> [Song] Do the Zschau bop flip-flop. . . .
> But wait: We'll give you additional Zschau flip-flops for free, like that never been previously released in the U.S. international hit:
> [Song] I sent the bucks to Nicaragua. . . .
> And never in one place at one time, so many great flip-flops. And it's available for a limited time only, because on election day, November the fourth, the Zschau song and dance comes to an end. Alan Cranston. Senator.

Finally, the Senate race in South Dakota the same year featured a contrast between the principally image-based strategy of low-key incumbent Republican Jim Abdnor and the issue-based campaign of the attractive young challenger, Democrat Tom Daschle. Abdnor, a quiet and retiring long-term officeholder, sat on his South Dakota doorstep and shyly told viewers:

> Once I realized I didn't have the talent to make it as a baseball player, the only thing I dreamed about as a kid was to serve my state and my country. Now I know that may sound corny, but it's true. God didn't make me a flashy speaker, that's for sure. But we've got a lot of flashy speakers in Congress, and if speeches solved problems, we wouldn't have any problems. So I'm not a great speaker. Heck, I'm not a great dancer either. But I'm a great fighter for South Dakota.

An announcer then concluded, "Jim Abdnor—he's more than a senator; he's a South Dakota institution of integrity."

Daschle, on the other hand, ran issue-based ads attacking the Reagan administration's unpopular farm program and tied Abdnor to it. A Daschle ad on agriculture, farm subsidies, and international trade policy began with speech footage of his opponent talking to a farm audience. It continued with Daschle addressing the same audience:

> ABDNOR: Maybe we have to sell below cost for a while, but I think until we regain that market that's the way we're going to have to go.
> DASCHLE: I think it's a big, big mistake. By the time we have that export market, half the people in this audience won't be there any longer. That to me is the difference. We've got to have a price. We've got to have income.
> ANNOUNCER: Abdnor. Daschle. The issue is price.

All three of these races were close contests, but Clements, Cranston, and Daschle eventually won because the themes they chose were the most persuasive to voters.

## Themes and Credibility

Whatever theme a candidate chooses, it is critical that it meet an important precept: *"Do not offend reality."* [21] Offending reality means depicting a candidate in a way that is not persuasive to voters or depicting the opponent in a negative way that is also not convincing to them. In Florida Paula Hawkins found it impossible to convince voters that she would be a strong and decisive leader. In South Dakota the diffident incumbent Abdnor had a difficult time convincing the state's many farmers that he could best deal with the rural economy.

Attacks on opponents also fail when the electorate does not find them credible. Although "attack themes" vary widely, depending upon the candidates and the constituency, two that are frequently used and frequently found unconvincing are assertions that an opponent is inexperienced or unqualified or that a wealthy opponent is trying to "buy the election." In 1982 Mario Cuomo of New York combined these attacks in his first gubernatorial campaign against a free-spending challenger. Using the slogan "Lieutenant Governor Mario Cuomo for governor—Experience money can't buy," Cuomo got 51 percent of the vote, a much narrower margin than had been expected given his commanding early lead in the polls in what was a good year for Democrats.

The problem with the experience strategy is that it can often be easily deflected. The presumed value of political experience is that it makes an officeholder more competent to do the job. But if the candidate being attacked can demonstrate competence, the experience factor loses its punch. Democratic strategist Tim Ridley commented, "I would never run a candidate on an experience stand, because all the other candidate has to do is stand up and appear competent, and the experience qualification doesn't catch." The experience factor works only if the candidate being attacked is widely perceived as wavering and ineffectual. It can even have a jujitsu effect if the opponent manages not only to deflect the charge but also to poke holes in the "experienced" candidate's record.

North Carolina Democrat Terry Sanford provided a powerful example of political jujitsu in his successful 1986 Senate race against incumbent Jim Broyhill. Broyhill, billing himself as "the conservative choice," ran as the Republican archetype who stood for low taxes and a strong defense policy. He contrasted his stands with Sanford's decision as governor twenty years earlier to extend the state sales tax to food in order to finance educational programs, and he implied that Sanford shared a national Democratic reluctance to use American military power. Sanford, a veteran paratrooper at the Battle of the Bulge, turned the charges on Broyhill by asking why the incumbent had not served in the military and why he had voted for a 1982 Republican-sponsored tax increase of $153 billion. In one instance the sixty-eight-year-old Sanford even parachuted into a campaign appearance. The tag line on Sanford's advertising encapsulated the issues: "Terry Sanford for the U.S. Senate. Because you can't lead without courage."

Similarly, charges that an otherwise qualified wealthy opponent is buying an election with his or her own money usually fall on deaf ears. As we saw in chapter 4, financial chicanery is often enough to cause a candidate to be rejected at the polls. But the legal, above-board use of a candidate's own money rarely is an effective campaign issue. At various times between 1960 and 1980, voters in New York, Arkansas, and West Virginia elected Nelson, Winthrop, and Jay Rockefeller to the governorships of their respective states despite charges in every election that they were "buying the election" with the family fortune.

Two 1988 Senate races also demonstrated the unpersuasiveness of such charges. In New Jersey mid-October polls showed some movement toward Republican challenger Pete Dawkins until Dawkins ran an ad accusing the Democratic multimillionaire incumbent, Frank Lautenberg, of voting for a Senate pay raise and government contracts for companies in which he held stock. The ad concluded that Lautenberg would "do anything to get elected as long as he can make some money on the side." The state's press and even its Republican governor made it known that they considered the charge preposterous. A similar charge by Susan Engeleiter, Republican candidate for Wisconsin's open seat, that her opponent, wealthy Democratic businessman Herbert Kohl, had profited unreasonably from government contracts was also greeted with disbelief. Wisconsin voters apparently were more impressed that Kohl had refused to accept PAC money and accepted the claim of his slogan, "Nobody's senator but yours." Voters seem to believe that if politicians are independently wealthy there is at least some assurance that they will not become beholden to nefarious interests.

In short, the dominant themes that candidates use must fit the context and the participants in a particular contest, and they must be believable. There are no all-purpose themes that will work in any situation, although some common ones such as inexperience and election buying are often ineffective. Certain factors do influence the general tenor of particular candidates' themes, however, and we consider them in the next section.

# What Shapes Campaign Themes? _____

Three elements are important in shaping campaign themes. First is the candidate's status as a challenger or incumbent; second is the office for which the candidate is running; and third is the role of broad national trends. We analyze each of these in turn.

## Candidate Status and the Theme

In most contests one candidate is the incumbent and the other is a challenger. In such races the organizing construct for both campaigns is the incumbent's record. The incumbent advances that record as the principal reason he or she should be reelected, while the challenger attempts to frame it as the reason to replace the current officeholder. This organizing principle often holds true even in races where there is no incumbent. Open seats are likely to attract ambitious politicians seeking to move to higher office. One or both candidates are thus likely to have political experience that becomes the major theme. Even challengers without political experience promote or defend their previous records if their activities have brought them public recognition.

**Incumbents.** Typically, incumbents must trumpet the positive aspects of their records to reinforce the electoral base that brought them victory in the past. But more important, as we discussed in chapter 4, wise incumbents will do a painstaking job of "negative research" on themselves, preparing to confront possible weaknesses early by inoculating voters against charges that are sure to be made by the challenger. James Blanchard, first elected governor of Michigan in 1982, did this with unusual openness when he described his opponent as "a guy who is willing to give fetuses rights in the U.S. Constitution that he is not willing to give women." He explained to a reporter "that he had to bring these social issues into the open to avoid a last minute 'Pearl Harbor' by right-to-life and Moral Majority groups. He noted 'that way the abortion issue will come out a wash, and, on the ERA issue, I end up a winner.' " [22]

Incumbents can neutralize an attack in a variety of ways. One positive way is to incorporate a potential weakness into the basic theme of the campaign, communicating to voters almost subliminally. Florida senator Paula Hawkins, possessor of a well-known quirky personality, ran on the slogan "unique and irreplaceable." New Jersey senator Frank Lautenberg suffered from regular and frequent comparisons with his state's much better known and more charismatic officeholders, Sen. Bill Bradley and Gov. Tom Kean. His 1988 opponent, Pete Dawkins, seemed cut from the Bradley mold. Dawkins was, among other things, a former Heisman Trophy winner for his football prowess at West Point, a Vietnam War hero, and, at the time of his promotion, the youngest brigadier general in the army. Lautenberg's 1988 reelection announcement therefore featured endorsements not by well-known or glamorous political figures but by numerous "ordinary" New Jersey constituents whom Lautenberg had helped with problems.

A closely related method of dealing with a potential liability is to turn a negative into a positive. California senator Pete Wilson provides one illustration. Early polls for his 1988 campaign indicated that Wilson, like Lautenberg in New Jersey, was not well known by California voters. His first television advertisement advanced a persuasive explanation for his lack of visibility:

> Wonder why you don't get those self-serving newsletters from Sen. Pete Wilson? Because he wants the $100 million Congress spends on them to go to Alzheimer's research. And he didn't take that pay raise Congress voted either. He gave his to fight AIDS and other diseases. Spending tax money for self-promotion may be okay for the other guy, but not Pete Wilson. He knows what's important. And he's there for California.

Texas senator Phil Gramm provides another example. Gramm, a conservative Democrat, was discovered to have been passing on sensitive information about the Democrats' budget strategy to the Reagan White House. Gramm was stripped of his seniority and removed from the Budget Committee. In retaliation, he resigned from the House, ran as a Republican in the special election called to fill his seat, and won handily. In his first statewide race for senator in 1984, however, it was clear that his opponent would call his integrity and reliability into question. Gramm's advertising framed the issue in a positive way:

> ANNOUNCER: When was the last time you witnessed an act of political courage? Congressman Phil Gramm became a Republican when liberal Democratic leaders removed him from the Budget Committee for leading the fight for President Reagan's tax and spending cuts.
> GRAMM: That I should be punished for representing the people who sent me to Washington is intolerable. That they should be disenfranchised in an effort to silence my voice on the number one issue in America—the budget—is intolerable.
> ANNOUNCER: Phil Gramm had the courage to let the people choose.
> GRAMM: The only honorable course of action is to resign my seat in Congress and seek reelection as a Republican.
> ANNOUNCER: Gramm took his message to the people.
> GRAMM: I had to decide between y'all and Tip O'Neill, and I decided to represent y'all.
> ANNOUNCER: And the people overwhelmingly reelected him. President Reagan called Phil Gramm a man...

REAGAN:  ... that has courage, that has principle.
ANNOUNCER:  Phil Gramm for the United States Senate. Common sense.
Uncommon courage.

A third strategy is to educate voters about the validity of an apparently unpopular policy. Sen. William Cohen of Maine took on the nuclear freeze issue in his 1984 reelection contest. Cohen opposed the popular freeze, instead supporting the Reagan administration's "build-down" proposal. Discussing the problem, Cohen's media strategist explained:

> Bill Cohen is a member of the Senate Armed Services Committee and supported most of President Reagan's military initiatives. Anyone who would run against him would try to capitalize on the profreeze sentiment in Maine and paint him as a militarist. We'll respond by educating the people whose tendency is to support the freeze, to show them that it's not in the best interests of the United States to have a unilateral freeze. And your senator, Bill Cohen, has taken the leadership in coming up with a responsible arms control proposal that has bipartisan support.

In an extensive advertising campaign Cohen coupled his argument of responsible leadership on arms control with a reminder that he also had a strong record of constituency service, exemplified in his campaign slogan, "A senator for Maine and America."

Republican consultant Dave Murray summarized the case for early inoculation: "I don't think you skirt an issue. If it's there, it'll come back and haunt you, no matter what." Thus for a candidate with a record to defend, most often the incumbent, it is not enough merely to make the positive case. Weaknesses, inconsistencies, and liabilities in the incumbent's record must be faced honestly and responded to forcefully if there is any sign that the charges are getting through to the voters.

**Challengers.**  Challengers face a different situation. Most challengers must simultaneously erode the favorable reputation of the incumbent and build a positive case for themselves. As one consultant observed:

> In order to defeat an incumbent, you have to give people a compelling reason to vote that incumbent out. Half of the reason is the positive things about your candidate, but another dimension is where the incumbent is lacking. What has that incumbent done that's wrong? You've got to give people that compelling reason to oust the incumbent, or they're going to take the attitude, "If it ain't broke, don't fix it."

Challengers whose campaign themes portray only a negative picture of their opponents or only a positive picture of themselves will probably lose. In the 1984 Maine Senate race, unsuccessful Democratic challenger Libby Mitchell unrelentingly attacked William Cohen for his support of nuclear weapons programs and opposition to the nuclear freeze, but she never gave voters a reason to choose her as a replacement for the affable and popular incumbent. A Maine publicity specialist observed of Mitchell's advertisements: "Negative campaigns like this almost never work. I can't think of an example of a challenger winning with a negative campaign." A colleague added, "She raises questions about Cohen, but we don't ever find out what she is for besides the freeze." [23]

Challengers who don't make the case against their opponents and present only the positive argument for themselves are not likely to fare any better, however; they give voters no reason to remove the "known-quantity" incumbent. Indiana Democratic challenger Jill Long, running against incumbent senator Dan Quayle in 1986, resisted making attacks on her opponent: "I think it is inappropriate. . . . I think voters benefit considerably more when candidates talk about the issues rather than talk about what the other candidate is doing incorrectly." [24] Quayle outspent Long twenty to one, used his almost $2 million war chest to tout his legislative accomplishments and Indiana's economic recovery, and crushed Long in a 61 to 38 percent victory.

The themes employed by successful incumbents and challengers are mirror images. Successful incumbents run proudly on a record, taking care to preempt negative charges the opposition may raise. Successful challengers must make a compelling case against the incumbent, at the same time giving voters reasons to prefer the challenger. Ed Zschau could not convince the voters of California that Alan Cranston was out of date or out of step and that Zschau was a credible representative of the future. But Tom Daschle did convince South Dakotans that Jim Abdnor was not effective against his state's agricultural problems and that Daschle advocated preferable agricultural policies and could be more effective.

## The Office Sought and the Theme

Another influence on the choice of a theme is the office sought. Most notable is the difference in themes between candidates for executive positions and those for legislative positions. Candidates for executive office—such as governors—pick themes that stress leadership and competence and focus on issues that emphasize these qualities. Candidates for legislative office—such as senators and representatives— stress their command of national policy, particularly as it relates to their constituents. Senators, especially those with national reputations, are inclined to emphasize thoughtful consideration of "big issues"—for instance, the economy or foreign policy. Representatives, who have a more parochial orientation, usually concentrate on the hard work they do for constituents and on their success in using legislation to "bring home the bacon."

We return again to the need for incumbents to defend their records and for challengers to be on the attack, because both affirmative and attack themes are strongly influenced by the office sought. We elaborate on this below.

**Affirmative Themes.**   The range of thematic issues for executive candidates is rather narrow. Most gubernatorial campaigns are waged over who can better manage the state's economy—a valence issue of leadership. This translates into discussions about taxes, spending, and the programs on which state money is spent—highways, education, social welfare, and crime. Incumbent governors seek to make the case that their stewardship of the state has demonstrated leadership and has been good for its economy, as in this 1986 message from Rhode Island's Edward DiPrete:

> In 1984 Rhode Islanders demanded a change, and we elected Ed DiPrete. With his strong leadership Governor DiPrete has brought economic recovery and a new direction to Rhode Island's future. People are earning more money. There are more jobs, more construction. And state income taxes have been cut. The result? A new beginning is taking hold, providing greater opportunity for all of us in Rhode Island. Let's keep Rhode Island working. Reelect Governor DiPrete.

In contrast to executive officeholders' emphases on leadership and competence, senators emphasize their comprehension and command of national policy. But because of a growing need to defend against charges from challengers that they are distant and out of touch, incumbent senators are adopting a thematic style that also stresses the more parochial concerns that usually characterize congressional campaigns. A message for Wisconsin senator Robert Kasten combined these national and local concerns:

> Bob Kasten—he's fighting to protect shoe and textile workers from the flood of cheap foreign imports. His votes helped save over two hundred billion taxpayer dollars by cutting wasteful federal spending. He wrote the law to protect our children by speeding up recalls of unsafe toys. He won the fight against a federal plan to withhold 10 percent of the interest earned on every savings account in Wisconsin. He led the fight to set aside twenty-four thousand new wilderness acres for Wisconsin. Sen. Bob Kasten—working and winning for Wisconsin.

As we noted, this ad has some similarities to the thematic appeals that incumbent representatives make. These officeholders concentrate almost exclusively on the favors they have done for their constituents, either in bringing federal help to their districts or in cutting government red tape. A ten-second spot for Idaho representative Richard Stallings made the case succinctly:

> Congressman Richard Stallings. Lower interest rates for farmers. Expanding foreign markets. Protecting our sugar beet industry. Keep Richard Stallings working on the Agriculture Committee.

The closeness of representatives to their districts and their hard work are also emphasized. These typical themes are present in advertising for Rep. Leon Panetta of California. Panetta's district includes the cosmopolitan and liberal-leaning coastal communities of Santa Cruz and Monterey, but its inland portions are agricultural and more conservative. The rather liberal representative often stresses his roots in this part of the district, as in the following spot, which showed him attired in overalls and wrestling some recalcitrant farm animals onto the back of a pickup truck:

> When Leon Panetta grew up on this farm, he didn't just learn about programs, he learned about helping others. He learned about trust, about patience. . . . And he learned about what it means to deliver—day in and day out, working under pressure. He learned about these things because it isn't just a farm, it's a family. Panetta. A friend we can count on.

**Attack Themes.** Candidates who challenge incumbents, as we have discussed, must make a negative portrayal of the incumbent an important part of their theme. The nature of the attack is also conditioned by the office the challenger seeks. A consultant who works for gubernatorial and senatorial candidates in both parties summarized the differences between executive and legislative races that affect the criticisms their challengers can make:

> It is my view that voters are well informed about the bad news concerning a governor. Since he is in the newspaper every day, people follow his activities intimately over the years. By contrast, most voters know little about the performance of their senators or congressmen. Since voting records are hardly reported at all by the local press, a senator or congressman can have an image removed from the reality of his performance in Washington. Since there is not always a clear voting record as governor, it is hard to target specific positives or negatives.
>
> With senators and congressmen, a great deal of new information can be introduced, since they each cast thousands of votes, adding up to a portrait that can be very carefully sketched to suit needs as an election progresses. I have always found that when voters find out important new facts about a candidate when they thought they knew the candidate, they tend to blame the candidate for lying to them, which then impugns his credibility as well as his popularity.

The result of these differences is that criticism of gubernatorial incumbents frequently takes the form of generalized attacks on their leadership ability or competence—often tied to their management of the state's economy. Ads for Michigan auto executive Richard Chrysler made this argument in his ultimately unsuccessful 1986 gubernatorial primary campaign for the Republican nomination:

> Can we really trust Jim Blanchard not to raise our taxes again? In 1982 Blanchard said raising taxes was not the answer. But once elected, Blanchard flip-flopped and raised our taxes a whopping 38 percent. Now this election year he's trying to take credit for a Republican-sponsored tax rollback. How clever. Dick Chrysler is committed to more jobs with no new taxes. On August 5 vote against a tax increase. Vote for Dick Chrysler.

Attacking the leadership of legislative incumbents is more difficult since individual lawmakers can rarely be held responsible for state or federal programs. The few exceptions are congressional committee chairmen who become closely identified with unpopular national policies under the purview of their committees. One example is Illinois Democratic challenger Paul Simon's successful 1984 campaign against Sen. Charles Percy, then chairman of the Senate Foreign Relations Committee. Percy campaigned with the slogan "The Illinois Advantage," arguing that Illinois's extensive foreign trade profited from his chairmanship. Simon took another tack, charging in his commercials that Percy voted for tax breaks to American corporations that "take our jobs overseas." With a picture of the Eiffel Tower in the background, an announcer says, "Illinois may be hurting, but somewhere in the world Charles Percy has made someone very happy." Another announcer, speaking in French, adds, "Merci, Monsieur Percy."

Much more common in legislative contests than competence themes is the characterization of the incumbent as distant from the problems of constituents. The Simon attack on Percy contains elements of this theme. This kind of charge is accompanied by a procedure known as "vote shopping," in which the challenger's staff sifts through the hundreds or thousands of votes cast by the incumbent to find some calculated to surprise and enrage constituents. Often these votes can be rationally explained by setting them in the context in which they were cast, but the necessarily complicated explanations, often involving arcane points of parliamentary procedure, put their victims on the defensive.

Similar to the vote-shopping strategy is an attack on incumbents involving their attendance records. A challenger will charge, for instance, that the incumbent missed a large percentage of votes on a critical issue such as Social Security or failed to attend several committee meetings. The fact that many of these votes are irrelevant to the final outcome of the issue or that senators serve on so many committees and subcommittees that regular attendance at all of them is impossible of course is not mentioned.

Criticisms of Kentucky senator Walter "Dee" Huddleston's attendance record were almost entirely responsible for the only defeat of an incumbent Democratic senator in 1984. After months of positive advertising touting his own record as executive officer of the state's most populous county, Huddleston's challenger, Mitch McConnell, still trailed Huddleston 22 to 68 percent. In August, McConnell's media consultant recalled: "We had to take some points off Huddleston very quickly. We kept racking our brains looking for the home run. We brought 'Bloodhounds' out, and it was like lighting a match on a pool of gasoline. It simply exploded." [25] The "Bloodhounds" TV spot showed a pack of dogs searching for Senator Huddleston in Washington and chasing a Huddleston lookalike through various scenic vacation locales while an excited announcer reported:

> Our job is to find Dee Huddleston and get him back to work. Dee Huddleston's been missing big votes on Social Security, defense, even agriculture. Huddleston was skipping votes but making an extra $50,000 giving speeches. I just missed him! When Dee skipped votes for his $1,000 in Los Angeles I was close—and Dee's $2,000 in Puerto Rico. I can't find Dee, but we're gonna let him make speeches and switch to Mitch for senator!

A related tactic is to paint the incumbent as ideologically out of tune with constituents. The "ideologically out of step" theme is considered particularly effective against representatives and senators who, in the view of their challengers, have built up positive reputations in their districts through constituency service and pork barrel legislation but who vote the "wrong" way on less locally visible issues. It can often assist the challenger if some outside, disinterested party will make the case against the opponent, leaving the candidate free to take the positive high road. Beginning in 1978 the National Conservative Political Action Committee pioneered widespread media advertising critical of liberal senators. A NCPAC staffer described the way the political action committee saw its function:

> There was no one playing NCPAC's role of attacking the incumbent. The candidate challenging an entrenched incumbent has to work to build up his own name recognition, his own issues, his own image. NCPAC gets into a race to say: "Your senator is duping you. He does one thing in Washington and talks another way back home."

In 1980 NCPAC claimed a lion's share of the credit for the defeat of four of five of the senators it targeted, but between 1982 and 1986 its negative campaigns were not as successful. Among the reasons that NCPAC's theme was less convincing after 1980 was that voters, reacting to uncertainty about the economy, were less responsive to Republican conservative arguments, particularly in the states that had liberal incumbents up for reelection. After 1986 NCPAC, along with several other conservative PACs, was virtually bankrupt and no longer a major player in campaigns. These observations bring us to a third consideration that may shore up or overwhelm a given campaign theme—the trends of the time.

## The Effect of National Trends

National trends, even when they are very strong, have a major impact on only a limited number of incumbents. State-level officeholders such as governors can insulate themselves from national trends as long as they have their statehouses in order. Representatives, who build electoral coalitions based on trust, constituency service, and attention to their districts, are also not easily dislodged by national swings. Those who regularly win two-thirds or more of the vote can afford the few points' difference that a national swing in the vote may produce in their own districts. The representatives at risk when national tides are running are the relatively few first-termers from marginal districts who, in the previous election, were swept in narrowly on the coattails of a popular issue or well-liked presidential candidate. They have only a short time to consolidate their bases before the next election, when the trends may not be in their favor.[26]

Incumbent senators are the most vulnerable to national trends. Their office makes them more closely identified with major issues. They are more likely than representatives to face well-financed challengers who can "educate" the voters about their records on significant legislation through paid mass media advertisements, particularly on television. National trends alone, however, are not enough to defeat most senators. Other factors that make senators vulnerable must also be present before a challenger can defeat an incumbent. One is marginality—a history of close elections—which can play a role even when no major policy questions are at stake. Another is advancing age or tenure. Senate incumbents who lose are disproportionately in their late sixties or older or are vying for their fourth term.[27] Finally, the incumbent's opponent must represent a clearly different ideological and issue stance—and one that is more in tune with the times. It is only in such situations that voters tend to opt strongly for the candidates riding these trends.[28]

Most of the nine Democratic senators defeated in 1980 and the seven Republicans who were bested in 1986 suffered from one or more of these conditions, while their successful colleagues did not. In 1980, for instance, Indiana's Birch Bayh was seeking his fourth term after three close races in a state that had never elected a senator to a fourth term. Herman Talmadge of Georgia was involved in a financial scandal.

Warren Magnuson of Washington State was in his late seventies. In 1986 Republican first-termers Jeremiah Denton of Alabama, Paula Hawkins of Florida, and Mack Mattingly of Georgia were among those who had achieved only razor-thin victories in 1980. These liabilities combined with their being on the wrong side of national trends brought them defeat.

On the other hand, eleven of the twelve Democratic senatorial incumbents running in the Republican landslide presidential election year of 1984 were victorious, and seven of them won by greater margins than Ronald Reagan did in their states. All but one were first elected in 1972 or 1978, both difficult years for Democratic candidates. Few were identified with the left wing of their party. Victors such as Bill Bradley of New Jersey and Joseph Biden of Delaware were well known "neoliberals"; Georgia senator Sam Nunn was a leading proponent of a strong military; David Boren of Oklahoma, J. J. Exon of Nebraska, and Howell Heflin of Alabama, among others, were some of the most conservative members of their party in the Senate.

The success of the 1984 Senate Democrats in the second Reagan landslide shows the generally diminishing effects of presidential coat-tails and national trends. There is no doubt, however, that national trends do affect campaigns to some degree. Presidential and midterm elections present different contexts for federal candidates, particularly for senators. Challengers from the presidential "out-party" do better in midterm elections than in presidential years. During the Reagan era Democratic challengers did better than Republican ones during the 1982 and 1986 midterms; Republican challengers did better during the 1980 and, to a lesser extent, 1984 presidential contests.

A major reason for this pattern is the flood of casual, usually independent, voters who come out for presidential elections but not for the midterm contests, which have a lower turnout.[29] These voters, after casting their votes for Reagan, supported Republican challengers in 1980 and protected Republican incumbents in 1984. The president's appeals to, in effect, vote for him one more time in 1986 fell on deaf ears. Voter turnout plummeted and public opinion moved somewhat in the Democrats' direction. George Bush, a less charismatic candidate than his predecessor, was notably without coattails in 1988, when his party lost seats in both the House and the Senate.

Thus the status and record of the candidates, the office they seek, and to a lesser extent the trends of the times all influence the choice of a campaign's themes and its chance of success. We now consider more fully how these themes are communicated to voters through the mass media.

## Notes

1. Quoted in David Beiler, "White Knights and Dark Horses," *Campaigns and Elections* 8 (September-October 1987): 47.
2. Jeff Greenfield, *Running to Win* (New York: Simon and Schuster, 1980), 75.
3. Ibid., 74-75.
4. Paul R. Abramson, John H. Aldrich, and David W. Rohde, *Continuity and Change in the 1980 Elections* (Washington, D.C.: CQ Press, 1982), 129, 215.
5. "Bill Moyers' Journal, Campaign Report 4," WNET transcript, October 3, 1980, 17.
6. Xandra Kayden, *Campaign Organization* (Lexington, Mass.: Heath, 1978), 158.
7. "Tony Schwartz: Radio's Responsive Chord—A *C&E* Interview," *Campaigns and Elections* 2 (Spring 1981): 23.
8. Gary A. Mauser, *Political Marketing: An Approach to Campaign Strategy* (New York: Praeger, 1983), 12. See also Philip Kotler and Neil Kotler, "Business Marketing for Political Candidates," *Campaigns and Elections* 2 (Summer 1981): 24-33.
9. See Charles W. Roll and Albert H. Cantril, *Polls: Their Use and Misuse in Politics* (Cabin John, Md.: Seven Locks Press, 1980), chapter 1.
10. Ibid., 9.
11. A good description of the typical polling package is Jerry Hagstrom and Robert Guskind, "Calling the Races," *National Journal*, July 30, 1988, 1972-1976.
12. As we discussed in chapter 4, incumbents increasingly conduct trend polling throughout their terms. Their benchmark polls thus explore problems and opportunities identified in the earlier trend polling during their terms in office.
13. A rolling average comprises the results of a few consecutive nights of tracking polls (usually three), to decrease the margin of error in the smaller daily tracking samples.
14. For a discussion of focus groups, see Joshua D. Libresco, "Focus Groups: Madison Avenue Meets Public Policy," *Public Opinion*, August-September 1983, 51-53.
15. Data from Mason-Dixon Opinion Research poll of 831 registered voters in Missouri, December 1987; *Boston Herald* poll of 501 adults in Massachusetts, January 1988; NRSC poll of 800 registered Michigan voters, September 1987; Hamilton, Frederick, and Schneiders poll of 500 likely New Mexico voters, April-May 1987; DSCC poll of 501 Wyoming registered voters, July 1987.
16. Hagstrom and Guskind, "Calling the Races," 1975.
17. "*C&E* Interview: Richard Wirthlin, Harrison Hickman," *Campaigns and Elections* 8 (September-October 1987): 27.
18. Poll of 600 Washington likely voters by Cooper and Secrest for the DSCC, August 1987; *Hartford Courant* poll of 516 Conecticut registered voters, April 1988; Analysis Group poll for Lieberman of 900 likely voters, April 1988.
19. Louis Sandy Maisel, *From Obscurity to Oblivion: Running in the Congressional Primary* (Knoxville: University of Tennessee Press, 1982), 50.
20. John K. White, "All in the Family: The 1978 Gubernatorial Primary in Massachusetts," *Polity* 14 (Summer 1982): 648.
21. Greenfield, *Running to Win*, 191.
22. *Detroit Free Press*, September 23, 1982.
23. Quoted in the *Portland Press-Herald*, October 25, 1984, 8.

24. *Indianapolis Star,* October 23, 1986, C1.
25. Larry McCarthy, quoted in *Congressional Quarterly Weekly Report,* December 7, 1985, 2561.
26. See the discussion of the roles of issues, marginality, and seniority in John L. Sullivan and Eric M. Uslaner, "Congressional Behavior and Electoral Marginality," *American Journal of Political Science* 22 (August 1978): 536-553; also John R. Hibbing and John R. Alford, "The Electoral Impact of Economic Conditions: Who Is Held Responsible," *American Journal of Political Science* 25 (August 1981): 423-439; Alan I. Abramowitz, "National Issues, Strategic Politicians, and Voting Behavior in the 1980 and 1982 Congressional Elections," *American Journal of Political Science* 28 (November 1984): 710-721.
27. Warren Kostroski, "The Effect of Number of Terms on the Reelection of Senators, 1920-1970," *Journal of Politics* 40 (May 1978): 497; Peter Tuckel, "Length of Incumbency and the Re-election Chances of U.S. Senators," *Legislative Studies Quarterly* 8 (May 1983): 283-287.
28. Alan I. Abramowitz, "Choices and Echoes in the 1978 U.S. Senate Elections: A Research Note," *American Journal of Political Science* 25 (February 1981): 112-118; Gerald C. Wright, Jr., and Michael B. Berkman, "Candidates and Policy in United States Senate Elections," *American Political Science Review* 80 (June 1986): 584.
29. James E. Campbell, "The Revised Theory of Surge and Decline," *American Journal of Political Science* 31 (November 1987): 965-979. See also Gary Jacobson,"Enough Is Too Much: Money and Competition in House Elections," *Elections in America,* ed. Kay Lehman Schlozman (Boston: Allen and Unwin, 1987), 173-195.

# Mass Media in Campaigns

# 7

*It is in my best interest to get my face on TV as often as possible. . . .
I am never too busy to talk to local TV. Period. Exclamation point.*

Rep. Dan Glickman[1]

*If you're not on television, you don't exist.*

Gubernatorial candidate

The information the electorate receives about campaigns comes from
both paid media and free media. *Paid media* are the advertising messages
controlled by campaigns; they are disseminated on television and radio
and in print advertising and direct mail. The scope and content of these
messages are limited only by libel laws, ethics and taste, and the money
available to pay for them. *Free media* are news stories, analyses, editorial
comment, interviews, and debates. Campaign organizations obviously
have considerably less influence over unpaid media; nonetheless, they
seek to shape news content as well.

A campaign's themes must be transmitted effectively if a candidate
is to set the agenda. A good media program advances the themes clearly
and repetitiously. It should have the effect one strategist credited to an
opponent's advertising: "When I looked at his billboards, I heard his
television ads." Additionally, the candidate's activities, as reported in
the free media, should complement what he or she is saying through the
paid media. In this chapter we consider what determines which media a
campaign will select and how a campaign transmits its themes through
paid and free media.

# Which Paid Media Are Used _____

Broadcast advertising and direct mail are the primary forms of paid media. Although many candidates use print advertising, fewer people read newspapers than watch television or listen to radio, and print ads are easier to ignore. Several considerations affect which media are preferred for political advertising: Among them are the audience sought; the office sought; the size, cost, and number of media markets in the candidate's constituency; and the amount of money available. We now examine how candidates facing different conditions decide which paid media to use.

## Statewide Contests

Television is the most effective way to generate quick recognition, and it is now virtually impossible for a candidate to run an effective statewide campaign without heavy reliance on television commercials. On average, television advertising absorbs about two-thirds of the budget of a statewide campaign. Because of the differences in media markets, however, the cost of the same amount of television advertising for the same office varies enormously from state to state.

Television forces campaigns to think of their constituencies not simply in terms of geography but in terms of what the television rating services, Arbitron and Nielsen, call, respectively, *areas of dominant influence (ADIs)* and *designated marketing areas (DMAs)*. In many areas these media market boundaries cross metropolitan and state lines.

The cost of TV advertising depends on the size of the population to be reached, the number of media markets that cover them, and the degree of penetration desired. Advertising charges are based on the cost per thousand viewers. The measure of penetration is calculated in *gross rating points (GRPs)*, the probability, given the ratings of particular programs, that a certain proportion of the state TV audience will see a commercial. The conventional assumption is that purchasing a hundred GRPs will ensure that the entire viewing audience will see a message once. It is also generally assumed that the average viewer needs three to five exposures (that is, three to five hundred GRPs) for a message to "sink in" and be internalized.[2]

Thus the important determinants in estimating the costs of a statewide media campaign are the number of markets in which a candidate must advertise and the population of those markets (the population determines the cost of advertising in any single one of them). Some examples show how these elements interact. A candidate purchasing a thirty-second spot on the highly rated "Bill Cosby Show" in 1986 would have paid $450 in Sioux Falls, South Dakota; $1,000 in Fargo, North Dakota; $6,500 in Tampa, Florida; $9,000 in Cleveland; $30,000 in Los Angeles; and $35,000 in Chicago. The differences in the size of the audience in each market account for the cost differences.

From a candidate's point of view, New Jersey has the country's worst media environment. New Jersey has no network stations of its own (and until 1984 it had no commercial VHF stations at all), and it is served primarily by the New York City and Philadelphia markets, two of the most expensive in the country. Two-thirds of the viewers who see New Jersey political advertising purchased on New York and Philadelphia stations live outside the state, in Connecticut, New York State, or Pennsylvania. When 1988 New Jersey Senate challenger Pete Dawkins purchased a two-week spring buy on New York and Philadelphia stations to introduce himself, it cost him about $1 million and left him unrecognized by half of New Jersey's voters because half a million dollars a week buys only modest penetration in these markets.[3]

Dawkins's difficulty in getting his message out on television, despite a record $8 million campaign budget, was in some part responsible for his loss to incumbent Frank Lautenberg. Lautenberg spent about the same amount as Dawkins but conserved his funds for massive advertising buys in the last few weeks of the campaign. Although Dawkins began to close the gap between the candidates near the end of the race, his financial situation was so desperate that he had to go off the air entirely for a few days. At the same time, Lautenberg was increasing his planned thousand-point weekly New York buy to fifteen hundred GRPs, at a cost of well over a million dollars.

In contrast, statewide candidates can saturate the Montana airwaves for about $65,000 a week. When successful Republican Senate challenger Conrad Burns began to gain decisively on Montana incumbent John Melcher at the end of their 1988 race, Burns could advertise heavily in all Montana markets for an entire week for about the same cost as only two prime-time spots, played once each, in the New York market.

Since television advertising can be so expensive and accounts for such a large share of a campaign's budget, more attention is being given to the art of "time buying"—targeting audiences as precisely as possible. The major rating services can provide media buyers with information on radio and television audiences for particular programs broken down by fifty demographic categories.

In Florida, for instance, when strategists in the 1986 Paula Hawkins-Bob Graham race were deciding where to place Social Security spots, they could learn that the size of the over-fifty-five audience of the three nightly network news programs in Miami ranged from 69,000 persons to

201,000 and that a "roadblock" purchase (buying all three programs simultaneously) would reach 80 percent of Miami's senior citizens. They could also determine that the purchase of forty-seven radio spots on certain Tampa stations meant that the ads would be heard four times by 60 percent of the total Tampa population, ages eighteen to twenty-four, at a cost of $7,760—much less expensive than a comparable television purchase. Demographic analysis also suggested that Social Security spots should be placed on programs such as "Murder, She Wrote" and on game shows, while drug spots aimed at young white males should run on "Monday Night Football" and "Miami Vice." [4]

Taking full advantage of such precise information raises costs, however. Federal law requires that stations sell political candidates time at their lowest unit rate (LUR) for forty-five days before a primary election and sixty days before a general election. But if a station can sell out a program to regular advertisers at the going rate, they are permitted to move LUR political ads to any available slot. Stations can also set quotas for how much time they will sell in a desirable period at LUR rates. In the 1986 Texas gubernatorial contest, for instance, stations limited each candidate to 180 seconds per week on ABC's sought-after "Good Morning America." To "lock in" a particular program or advertise outside the specified calendar period, candidates must pay the same rates as commercial customers.

Thus for all these reasons the cost of ads in various media markets is important both in planning campaign strategy and in accounting for variations in campaign expenditures for the same office in different states.

## House Contests

In most congressional campaigns television is less important than in statewide campaigns, although the use of it varies. A study of congressional primary campaigns found broad regional differences associated with the media markets in the various candidates' districts. In the Southwest television is relatively inexpensive, and markets frequently correspond closely to constituencies. In that region almost three-quarters of the candidates bought television advertising, in contrast to a quarter of the candidates on the West Coast and fewer than a fifth of those in the Middle Atlantic region. Studies of general election races yield similar findings. Fewer than half of all House candidates use television advertising. The cost efficiency (the certainty of reaching only viewers in the candidate's district) and the market potential (the number of reachable households divided by the cost of an average advertisement) are much greater in rural districts than in urban districts and in midwestern, southern, and border states than in New England and the West.[5]

Vulnerable congressional incumbents, contestants for open seats, and serious challengers all see personal contact, radio, and direct mail as more important than television.[6] These communication channels are preferred because they are easily adaptable to district audience targeting. Although radio is the least targeted of the three, it is cheaper than television. Some radio stations do have fairly well defined geographic and demographic audiences such as particular minority groups or age groups. Morning "drive time" can target commuters, and various formats—talk shows, all-news programs, particular kinds of music programs, and so on—also permit some demographic targeting. Direct mail's major virtue is its great ability to target, by mailing only to voters in the candidate's district and by sending specific messages to specific groups. Direct mail is especially important in urban congressional districts, where no other mass media are as cost-efficient. John Simms, a Washington, D.C., direct mail consultant who works on many congressional campaigns, explained:

> In the expensive media markets, they don't have an opportunity to put much on the tube. They may do some radio. There's a lot of political advertising on all the media at that time; it's hard for them to be heard. So they spend a lot more money on list development and direct mail and voter contact.

In accord with Simms's comments, use of direct mail is especially heavy in California. In federal election years California voters must often make choices in statewide, congressional, and legislative contests and must also decide on judgeships and vote on large numbers of public questions. The California state government maintains excellent voter lists with some merged demographic information; candidates can purchase these lists at reasonable cost. Rep. Nancy Pelosi spent a million dollars on her first primary and general election contests in a San Francisco district. Pelosi's campaign produced seventy-five thousand pieces each of twenty-seven different mailings; the average unit cost was forty cents, or more than $800,000.[7]

For many candidates, particularly little-known congressional challengers, campaign strategists see direct mail and even radio and television as adjuncts to intensive personal voter contact—preferably by the candidate but by surrogates if necessary. In Arizona, for instance, John McCain won his first election in the state's solidly Republican First Congressional District in 1982 by defeating three other candidates in the all-important primary. McCain had moved to the district only a year before and embarked on his primary campaign with virtually no recognition. He spent almost $600,000 on his primary and general election races, much of it devoted to television. McCain's district, encompassing only the city of Phoenix, was appropriate for a television campaign, which made him known quickly. The television advertising was accompanied by heavy door-to-door campaigning. His media adviser, Jay Smith, described this combination of tactics:

> He wound up knocking on fifteen thousand Republican household doors in Arizona, where the summer temperature is about 115 degrees in the shade. I remember distinctly being out there when the first TV ads hit, and he came back and said it was night and day in terms of the response on the street. It was a combination. He couldn't have done it with just the TV advertising.

On the other hand, when New Jersey Republican representative Jim Courter was redistricted into a new, heavily Republican constituency and faced a difficult primary, he used no television at all. Messages in the New York City market would have been extraordinarily expensive and would have been beamed to an audience of which his constituents made up less than 5 percent. Courter instead relied on several waves of direct mail to likely primary voters. Because his exurban and rural district was ill-suited to heavy door-to-door campaigning, the candidate took to the telephone. An aide recalled: "Courter would call five hundred people a day. We'd have five phones going at once. They'd keypunch the addresses [of the people he spoke to] that night, and a letter would go out the next day."

It is in the area of direct mail and personal contact that statewide races, except in the smallest states, differ from congressional contests. Consultant Vince Breglio discussed the reelection campaign of Sen. Orrin Hatch of Utah:

> When Orrin would come into the state, we'd put him in front of a five-button phone and have five people calling into a neighborhood. They would call and say, "Senator Hatch is here and wants to say hello." By preidentification we would know if they supported him. In twenty seconds he'd give them a little spiel. The word of mouth was incredible.

Breglio added that this technique is less effective in larger states:

> When you're in a state with big numbers, personal contact and direct mail can help if you can identify a reasonably small subgroup, but for some reason direct mail loses its impact with four million pieces. It's a tool that works best with forty to fifty thousand households. If you're talking New York or California or even New Jersey or Florida, you have a much heavier dependence on electronic media.

In general, statewide campaigns usually rely more on broadcast advertising, while candidates for lesser office turn to direct voter contact—both in person and by mail and telephone.

# Types of Paid Messages

The messages that candidates transmit in their paid media fall into four general categories: positive messages about themselves, negative messages about their opponents, comparisons of the candidates, and responses to charges by opponents. The kind of message a candidate sends is affected by the stage of the campaign, the status of the candidate, and the competitiveness of the race. Most candidates begin their campaigns with positive messages that present their experience, credentials, and accomplishments. Negative or comparative messages, if used, generally come later in the race. Voters react to negative advertising with hostility unless candidates first draw a positive picture of themselves to which criticism of an opponent can be compared.

Campaign strategists used to believe that only challengers should use negative messages in their efforts to paint incumbents as unworthy of reelection. A well-known incumbent was thought to be giving an opponent free publicity by mentioning his or her name, even in an attack. The thinking now is that only incumbents who face weak challengers whose charges never penetrate (either because the challenger lacks the money to publicize them or because they are unconvincing) can afford to take the high road—sticking to a positive campaign and ignoring the challenger. A strong challenger, on the other hand, cannot be ignored. This new approach has produced much more negative advertising.

In this section we analyze positive messages, negative messages, comparative messages, and response messages to see how each is used. Since there is much controversy about the rise in negative advertising and its presumed undesirable effect on the tone of American politics, we end the chapter with an examination of the reasons for its sharp increase and its apparent effects.

## Positive Messages

In a statewide campaign early television messages are usually positive and biographical, stressing the high points of a candidate's career; for instance, an ad for California governor George Deukmejian opens with a picture of a radio playing and the graphic subtitle "Remember back? 1982?"

> [Radio sound] No sunshine in California today. Unemployment's over 11 percent. The state is near bankruptcy. Experts call for a tax increase. Student test scores are down.
> [Switch to picture of Deukmejian striding to work and announcer voiceover] Then George Deukmejian became governor, and in three

short years unemployment was cut nearly in half, and a million new jobs were created. Deukmejian cut excessive spending. He increased school funding to the highest levels in twenty years. And he did it all without a general tax increase. Great state, great governor. Deukmejian.

A challenger who lacks such experience in government of course must take a different approach. Because Herbert Kohl, who in 1988 won the Senate race for Wisconsin's open seat, had no record of elective service, his biographical ads discussed his accomplishments and success in other spheres and suggested their relevance to his Senate bid. In one spot Kohl told viewers: "I spent my life running a business, not running for office. I've created jobs, balanced budgets, and learned how to cut waste."

Another common theme in early positive messages is identification of the candidate with the state's history and values. Recent election advertisements have featured candidates striding across a typical area landscape while a musical soundtrack invokes such lyrics as "Idaho so beautiful, so rugged, wild, and free...." Alternatively, the candidate discusses the state's culture, against appropriate backdrops. In 1984 in New Hampshire, which prides itself on still having no state taxes and whose motto is "Live free or die," Republican senator Gordon Humphrey, accompanied by members of his family, told viewers:

> More government means less freedom, and New Hampshire people know that. They're independent, proud, self-reliant. Patti and I share these values. We really appreciate the New Hampshire way of life. When we're home, we love to go down to the pond. I don't know if it attracts more frogs or kids, but it's a refreshing thing to me to just enjoy innocent life. And I think the New Hampshire philosophy ought to be extended to the national government as well.

In the same year in Montana, viewers saw a video of Democratic senator Max Baucus, attired in jeans and a down vest, walking a spectacular mountain trail and fishing in mountain streams. That state's residents are perennially disturbed by development pressures and the federal government's extensive ownership of Montana land. The images of Baucus were accompanied by a voiceover telling watchers:

> It's about two thousand miles from here to there—from Montana to Washington. We're not like them, we don't dress like they do, and they don't understand our problems or even care. So the person we send there to represent us, our senator, had better be effective. Ours is Max Baucus, and he's made a difference. Max has roots that are generations deep in the soil of Montana....

Senator Baucus then addresses an unseen listener:

> I think a lot of people want to take advantage of Montana. They want to take advantage of our resources, they want to take advantage of our

way of life, they want it for themselves, and we're not gonna let that happen. We're going to stand up to them. We know we've got the best state. . . .

Positive advertising also highlights the issues or images candidates want to stress. As we noted in chapter 6, some candidates use issues to transmit the central messages they want to convey about themselves. In an important sense the issue is not the key message but, rather, what the issue suggests about the candidate. Other candidates focus on a generalized image that gives voters a sense of what their approach would be to a particular issue. The contrast between "issue as image" and "image as issue" was drawn strongly in the 1986 senatorial contest in Alabama between Republican incumbent Jeremiah Denton and Democrat Richard Shelby. Shelby focused on a specific issue, contrasting his and Denton's votes on Social Security. The challenger's media adviser argued that Denton had "a record that makes him extremely vulnerable" on the issue and that he was a man "who deep down views it as a welfare program." Denton, on the other hand, offered viewers a picture of himself as a Vietnam War hero, who had spent many years as a POW. His media consultant observed: "I think he reflects the basic patriotism of the state. . . . He reflects where Alabama is politically, its concern for family values, for religious values." [8]

These positive message ads show how candidates use their appearances in front of the camera to make a particular statement about themselves. Once candidates have established a positive image, they may find it necessary to go on the attack. This is essential for the challenger running against a favorably regarded incumbent and for the incumbent whose challenger is gaining ground. Negative, or attack, advertising comes in two varieties—pure negatives and comparisons.

## Negative Messages

The purely negative message concentrates entirely on the opponent, reminding the voter of the alternative at the very end or not mentioning the sponsor of the ad at all. For example, in 1986 a negative ad run in the ranching state of South Dakota by Sen. Jim Abdnor against his ultimately successful challenger, Rep. Tom Daschle, had the following text:

Jane Fonda's been identified with radical causes including warning people against eating red meat. So which "expert" did Tom Daschle invite to testify before the Democratic Task Force on Agriculture? [Picture of Fonda wearing long diamond earrings] That's right. And last December 4 when the House Agriculture Committee voted on emergency farm credit, Tom Daschle missed that crucial vote. Where was

Tom? In Miami, Florida, raising money for his campaign. Tom Daschle talks a big story for farmers, but when the chips are down, Tom's in Florida.

Consultants agree that the most effective negative ads are those that, like the Abdnor ad, distance the targeted candidate from the needs and feelings of the electorate. These messages are the "flip side" of positive advertising, which links candidates to the values of their constituents.

## Comparative Messages

Increasingly, campaigns are moving away from purely negative attack ads to "comparatives," which consultants believe are more convincing and less distasteful to voters than pure negatives. Comparatives examine the record of the two candidates, to the benefit of one of them. In the 1988 New Jersey Senate race an early ad for Democratic incumbent Frank Lautenberg sought to contrast the senator's lifelong residence in the state and his legislative focus on its problems with his challenger's arrival in New Jersey only a few months before his announcement of Senate candidacy. The ad opened with a short clip of challenger Pete Dawkins explaining he had moved to New Jersey because, "I never found a single place that had as good people or as much promise as I've found right here in our Garden State." An announcer then continued in a skeptical tone:

> Why did Pete Dawkins *really* move to New Jersey? Because he likes us so much? Then why did a national magazine say polls were taken in four other states? Or why did he say just two years ago, "I'm a Michigan boy"? Or tell Texans, "I come from New York"? Frank Lautenberg has been fighting for New Jersey all his life: raising the drinking age, a national leader on the environment. Pete Dawkins: Does he care about New Jersey? Or are we just a political pit stop?

Lautenberg's 1988 victory owed much to his ability to convince New Jersey voters that this comparison was a valid one.

## Response Messages

The fourth kind of message candidates transmit in their paid media is the response—answers to an opponent's attacks. When campaigns react to each other in this way, they become "electronic debates," with candidates commenting on the validity of each other's themes and arguments. We will enlarge on this final stage of a campaign in the next chapter. Before going on to the debate stage of campaigns, however, let us consider the role of the unpaid, or free, media in the earlier stage of campaigns, when candidates attempt to set their themes and seize control of the agenda. Understanding the role of the free media in campaigns will also help explain the increase in negative advertising and the increase of advertising in response to negative charges, our final topic in this chapter.

# The Role of Free Media

To understand the role of journalism in political campaigns and the way campaigns relate to the free media, it is necessary to keep in mind several characteristics of the journalists who are assigned to campaigns and of the press coverage that candidates receive during campaigns. These traits include (1) the preference of journalists for covering politics rather than policy, (2) the greater coverage given to incumbent or better-known candidates, and (3) the differences between print and electronic journalism. There are also important differences in the coverage of nonpresidential and presidential campaigns.

## Political Journalists and Journalism

The central finding of every study about political journalists and campaign reporting is that the press treats campaigns as "horse races" (who is ahead and who is behind?) and as strategic exercises rather than as debates about issues.[9] There are three interrelated reasons for this: the reporters' definition of what is news, their stress on objectivity, and the backgrounds of political reporters.

News, to reporters, is something that *happens*. Michael Robinson and Margaret Sheehan explain the significance of this apparently trite observation:

> "Horse races" happen; "horse races" are themselves filled with specific actions. Policy issues, on the other hand, do not happen; they merely exist. Substance has no events; issues generally remain static.[10]

Once a candidate's position on the issues is reported, it is not news unless it changes. On the other hand, candidate appearances, charges against other candidates—whatever their merits—new poll results, discord within the campaign organization, and the like, are all events that merit being reported as news. They will thus get more coverage than discussion about issues.

Second, reporters' adherence to the canon of objectivity means they do not regard evaluating policy positions as part of their job, except in rare investigative pieces or analysis columns. A well-thought-out position on a complicated issue implies an ideological or philosophical construct, a certain way of looking at the world. The news reporters do not consider it the job of an objective press to make value judgments about the validity of a candidate's philosophy. Reporters know that the quantitative horse-race aspects of the campaign—the crowds that candidates draw, their standings in polls, the amount of money they raise, the endorsements they garner—can be measured, whereas issue positions cannot be so easily reduced to statistics. Reporters' interest in issues thus has a strategic quality. One reporter described the attitude of campaign organizations toward distributing position papers: "Everybody knows they're bullshit. But if you don't do it, you'll get criticized for having a vacuous campaign. If you do do it, they won't get written about, but you won't be criticized."

Issues become important to political reporters when they take on a dynamic quality that can be written about as events. Two common examples are candidates' inconsistencies and gaffes or factual errors. If a candidate makes the slightest alteration in a position without a convincing rationale or commits the smallest error in fact, reporters are likely to pounce. Such slips are seen as illustrative of candidate incompetence or of conflict within a campaign about what strategic positions to take. And they are factual, colorful, and interesting—in short, news.

Finally, most reporters working on major campaigns are specialists in covering politics. Their own interests and skills direct them away from issues and toward evaluation of campaign strategy and its success:

> Political reporters tend to be fascinated by the process, the mechanics of politics. They are not particularly interested in, or knowledgeable about, policy issues. Issues tend to be covered by other reporters—specialists on economics or foreign policy or what have you—in the relatively large news organizations where full-time political reporters work.[11]

## Coverage of Incumbents

Second only to campaign journalists' preference for covering politics rather than policy is their tendency to cover incumbents rather than challengers. One study of congressional races found that the average incumbent received more than 50 percent greater coverage than the challenger in the last six weeks of the campaign. Even in the final week names of incumbents were mentioned in 88 percent of the campaign stories, whereas challengers' names were mentioned only 52 percent of the time. Another study, which confirmed these findings, also demonstrated that incumbents were frequently mentioned in stories predominantly about challengers, but the reverse was not the case.[12]

Incumbents get more attention from the press simply because they are easier to cover. Their official activities would be reported anyway, and they have an established relationship with the press. Reporters "want to simplify and regularize their work load. Given a choice they stick to the most accessible ways to gather news. . . . Like other occupations, newspaper work is more habitual than innovative. Habits favor the status quo—incumbents more than challengers." [13] Greater coverage of incumbents is also a function of the reporter's assumption, usually correct, that the incumbent is the front runner and the likely winner. Thus the attitude about candidates is that "unless or until they exceed public expectations at the polls or in the polls, hopeless cases get hopeless coverage." [14]

## Differences Between Print and Electronic Journalism

Another important consideration for campaigns is the differences between print and electronic journalism. First, a political story on the network news receives between thirty seconds and two minutes of coverage. The written text of all the news presented on an evening network broadcast would not fill the front page of the *New York Times.* Thus, even if television reporters want to present an in-depth story on a candidate, time constraints make it virtually impossible. Second, to hold viewers' attention, a TV news story must have an interesting visual background. The way the story looks is as important as how it sounds. If a campaign event is not graphically appealing, it will probably be ignored.

Radio, the stepchild of electronic journalism, presents a different situation. The news departments at music or talk stations are starved for funds and attention. Many are "rip and read" operations, tearing copy off a wire service machine and presenting it as the news. Radio stations are much more likely than major-market television stations to use political press releases exactly as they are written by a campaign staff or to feature "actualities," comments taped by candidates on issues of their own choosing and offered to stations for free play. (The sophisticated media production facilities of both national party organizations have made it possible for them to offer video actualities by satellite to local TV stations as well.) Candidates consider actualities to be particularly desirable because they sound or look like news stories rather than commercials, and they are indeed blended into news programs. Because of the difficulty many candidates for office below the statewide level have in getting TV and newspaper attention, alert campaign staffers may take advantage of the availability of radio air time.

## Coverage of Nonpresidential Campaigns

Beyond these general precepts about campaign reporting, there are significant differences in the coverage of nonpresidential and presidential campaigns. The two most important ones are the volume of coverage and the extent to which candidates are subjected to critical analysis.

Presidential campaign coverage begins as much as two years before the election and by January of the election year is the subject of daily reporting. The state caucuses and primaries become a "handle" for the coverage. In contrast, one reporter estimated that daily newspaper coverage of gubernatorial races does not begin until Labor Day and that Senate races are not covered extensively until Columbus Day—less than a month before the election. Another reporter said:

> There used to be a tradition that you'd write a story on Labor Day kicking off the campaign. We do that later and later now. Even though in some respects the candidates are getting ready earlier than they ever did, I don't think the public awareness is; we have to wait a little bit to grab them.

Furthermore, nonpresidential candidates receive less critical scrutiny than do presidential candidates. Even in many news stories, as opposed to commentary or editorials, network television reporting of presidential campaigns is analytical, thematic, and critical. As Bill Wheatley, executive producer of "NBC Nightly News," said of the network's 1988 presidential coverage: "We don't want here-they-come, there-they-go coverage. Our airtime is limited and very valuable, and we feel every piece has to count." [15] Television reporting on the presidential race is also somewhat more likely than print reporting to be thematic and critical because, in addition to television's greater time and space constraints, the print media by their nature have to report what the candidates said and did. The aural and visual medium of TV permits candidates to do this themselves, leaving commentary on the film as the principal job of the correspondent.

This is much less true of television coverage of nonpresidential candidates. Network news essentially does not report on nonpresidential candidates. In the ten weeks between Labor Day and election day in 1984, NBC ran a total of fourteen minutes of news on nonpresidential candidates.[16] What media coverage such candidates do receive is on local television and in local newspapers, and it is rarely critical or analytical, particularly of candidates for federal rather than state office.

The differences in the amount and kind of press attention occur for three reasons. First, unlike presidential candidates, most senatorial and congressional contestants do not travel with a press entourage; they have no campaign bus or plane. When candidates come to a local media market, reporters who have not otherwise been following them are assigned to cover their appearances. With only a remote idea of the details of a story they may not cover again for weeks, if ever, they are unlikely to subject the candidate to a searching analysis.

Second, local reporters who do have political beats are usually based at the statehouse. A Senate campaign manager explained, "You have a state press corps that is highly conversant with state issues, knows them intimately, can get in a dialogue, and suddenly they're covering a federal campaign." Statehouse reporters attach less priority to federal races. One commented:

> Gubernatorial elections are inherently more interesting and important than Senate elections, and you have to go with that. The set of issues they deal with is different. One person is being asked how they would run the state and the other how they'd vote in the Senate. They're not equivalent.

Third, small papers without several full-time political reporters use wire service coverage of campaigns extensively. The diverse clients of wire services make them tend to "stick to the facts" and avoid making analytical judgments about the events they report.

Even statewide candidates can find it difficult to get as much coverage as they would like. Discussing Senate races in Texas, a reporter observed:

> [Candidates] avoid the big cities because it's difficult to get in the paper and almost impossible to be on local TV unless you're caught doing something illegal. So they go to the secondary markets where the local press is flattered. They get on local TV news, which is the main thing, and they get a spot in the local paper, which is a bonus.[17]

Strategist Charles Black gave a similar rationale for North Carolina senator James Broyhill's whistle-stop tour through small communities, which attracted small crowds: "Even if a lot of people weren't there, their newspaper or radio station was."[18]

Below the statewide level the ability of candidates to get free media coverage is so limited that relations with the press are almost an afterthought. The director of a Republican campaign to gain control of the New Jersey state legislature stressed the almost total reliance on radio advertising, direct mail, and phone banks, saying, "We were assuming we would get no free media." A New Jersey political reporter for one of the state's most respected papers confirmed the correctness of this view: "We cover seven legislative districts, which means forty-two candidates for the assembly and senate, so no one of them is going to get a whole lot of play."

House campaigns, particularly those of incumbents, also stress their paid messages and voter contact activities and take the same view of the press. They do not expect television coverage and assign little importance to newspaper coverage. A ranking aide to an entrenched incumbent described the print coverage as minimal: "We didn't go out of our way to cultivate it. We weren't out there to do media events. There was very little coverage that wasn't our press releases. They played our releases." A staffer for another incumbent first recalled that the campaign did not have a press secretary, then remembered: "Oh, actually it was the candidate's brother, who hung around. He also did the print ads and the bumper stickers. The campaign manager didn't care."

In summary, free media coverage can help challengers below the statewide level build recognition; however, they are unlikely to get whatever meager coverage there is unless they have raised enough money to establish a presence with their paid advertising. Reporters, along with the rest of the political community, share the view of the consultant who said, "Money is a reflection of your political support." Generally, though, free media are a more basic concern of candidates for statewide positions—senators and governors—and for the latter more than the former.

# Campaign Interaction with the News Media

Although nonpresidential candidates may find the news media's casual attitude toward their campaigns frustrating, there can be an advantage to this lackluster and tardy attention. Nonpresidential campaigns can establish their themes before the press takes an interest and devise events that reinforce the messages presented in their paid advertising. This is the reverse of the situation in presidential campaigns, where, media strategists agree, "The messages each candidate communicates to viewers in the nightly news shows are far more important than the messages they convey in their ads." [19] In the following sections we examine how campaigns respond to the challenges and opportunities offered by the news media.

## Media Events: Meshing the Advertising and Press Messages

Senatorial and gubernatorial candidates want press coverage that reflects the themes they are purveying in their paid media. If the campaign is not successful in meshing the advertising and press messages, voters are unlikely to internalize the campaign's theme or understand exactly what message the candidate wants to send. Media consultant Robert Squier describes such disjunctions between free and paid media messages as "sending out static" that is indecipherable to voters.[20]

In reporting on statewide candidates, the press concentrates on candidate appearances, known in the trade as "media events." The task of a good campaign staff is to coordinate speaking engagements and other events covered by the press with the paid commercials for the candidate. In the Florida Senate race between Paula Hawkins and Bob Graham, advertising and media events often became almost indistinguishable. A Hawkins press release accusing then-governor Graham of approving an oil pipeline that endangered Florida's water supply was timed for simultaneous release with commercials on the same subject. In response, Graham held a press conference that featured leading environmentalists refuting the Hawkins charge, and he used footage from the press conference in his next wave of ads. Hawkins's ads on illegal drugs were complemented by a Washington press conference to introduce and explain new drug legislation, featuring her and members of the Republican leadership. A film crew from Republican party headquarters taped the conference and distributed it to Florida television stations. When President Reagan visited Tampa on Hawkins's behalf, his remarks closely mirrored her commercials.[21]

Such strategies usually work because of the relative lack of interest the press has in developing its own coverage, especially of Senate races. Even when reporters seek to present their own perspectives rather than the campaign perspective, candidates can thwart them by their lack of availability except in controlled situations. In the Florida case Hawkins remained in Washington almost continuously until ten days before the election, virtually forcing reporters to cover the campaign on her terms. When her opponent visited a media market, to achieve balanced coverage, television stations were reduced to running Hawkins's ad clips as her part of the story. An NBC reporter in Tampa observed in frustration: "We couldn't cover the campaign. TV needs video and we couldn't get any Hawkins video except her ads. She simply wasn't here." [22]

Candidates accused of manipulating the media with planned events counter by describing their inability to get the press to focus on policy-oriented matters. Hawkins's successful challenger, Bob Graham, recalled "learning a lesson" from his own early experiences with the press. In his 1977 gubernatorial campaign Graham got wide media attention with the first use of an often-imitated gimmick—"job days"—which he spent doing a variety of mundane tasks at which many constituents made their living. Arguing that, "If you want to make free news, you have to do something interesting and out of the ordinary," he recalled spending weeks preparing a major speech on higher education reform, delivered in Boca Raton. Graham noted that the speech "got zero coverage." He added: "Two days later I had a job driving a cement truck, also in Boca Raton. It got coverage by three TV stations and about a half-dozen newspapers." [23]

## Losing Control of Free Media

Press coverage creates problems for a Senate campaign only if the contest generates a great deal of conflict or has other elements the press can seize on as newsworthy. Such was the case confronting the liberal Democratic senators who were the victims of the first massive targeting effort by right-wing groups in 1980. Eve Lubalin, a strategist for one of the chief targets, Indiana senator Birch Bayh, described the effect of the conservative assault on Bayh:

> From the time NCPAC [the National Conservative Political Action Committee] put us on their list, I don't think there was one story I read in an Indiana paper that didn't start off, or have parenthetically in one of the first three paragraphs, "Birch Bayh, one of the five most liberal senators targeted by conservative groups. . . ." It began to dominate the news. Wherever Bayh went, instead of the thing being covered the way we wanted it, the story was these groups picketing him.
>
> When the oil companies demanded service station owners take down our posters, we were going to film Exxon coming in and forcing this little service station dealer to take down his Bayh poster, and Bayh talking about freedom of speech, freedom of the press. The pickets were there and the TV coverage was them heckling Bayh—we totally lost control of the event.

## Other Free Media Opportunities

Appearances before newspaper editorial boards, on news interview programs, and in debates with their opponents are the other forms of free media exposure available to Senate candidates. Candidates value these opportunities because, despite usually minuscule audiences, short excerpts from debates and interview programs become "sound bites"— brief items on the regular news programs—and a strong or weak performance influences the tone of other coverage. As strategist Bill Hamilton observed, "The impact of the debate is in what is written about it and what segment gets shown on the eleven o'clock news." [24] In Maine in 1984 the staff of challenger Libby Mitchell somehow confused her schedule; at the time of her last debate with Sen. William Cohen, she was at a hairdresser's appointment. Press coverage was savage. Meeting in Washington with the editorial board of New Jersey's largest newspaper, 1988 Senate challenger Pete Dawkins incautiously expressed enthusiasm about the possibility of joining the capital's movers and shakers, telling reporters that he would kill himself if he had to live in a small town. These remarks played into reporters' suspicions that Dawkins's recent move to New Jersey was solely for the purpose of a Senate run. They gave the unhappy challenger several days of negative coverage.[25]

## The Special Case
## of Gubernatorial Candidates

Because reporters attach more significance to gubernatorial races and give them heavier and earlier coverage than Senate contests, the free media play a greater role in governors' races. Issue content as opposed to "horse race" concerns also gets more attention.[26] Typically, when covering the concurrent 1986 senatorial and gubernatorial contests, California's leading newspaper, the *Los Angeles Times*, ran multipart series carefully analyzing the records of Gov. George Deukmejian and his challenger, Los Angeles mayor Tom Bradley. No such examination of the records of the Senate candidates was undertaken.

Like presidential campaign strategists, gubernatorial strategists attempt to use the press as a partial substitute for expensive advertising. It can be to the advantage of lesser known or underfinanced gubernatorial challengers that journalists arrive earlier in the campaign season than they do in Senate races, and they pay more attention to and are more knowledgeable about the issues. In most Senate races a challenger with little money for paid advertising and in an uphill battle for press coverage would be unable to get a theme out and would be well on the way to losing. A gubernatorial challenger, with some luck, can conserve funds for a last-minute advertising push and use the press to keep the campaign alive.

A single media event, for example, is credited with setting the 1987 Kentucky gubernatorial campaign of challenger Wallace Wilkinson on its winning track. Wilkinson had a great deal of money to spend on his Democratic primary race (the key election in Kentucky). His problem was that the other three candidates did also, and all were better known and politically more experienced than he. Wilkinson thus found it very difficult to get press attention.

Languishing at about 8 percent in the polls two months before the election, Wilkinson's strategists hit on a press announcement that would draw attention to his cause. They took the seemingly odd step of having the candidate call a press conference to denounce the arrival in

Kentucky of a Toyota plant with two thousand new jobs. Wilkinson's argument was that the state had to give Toyota $136,000 in tax concessions for each job and that more jobs could have been created by investing that money in local small businesses. Although this logic was greeted with a mixed reception, that was not the major point. As Wilkinson media consultant David Sawyer observed, the attack by itself was not a winning issue. "But it made people begin to take notice of Wallace by presenting something different." [27] After the press conference, which was accompanied by a wave of advertising on the same subject, Wilkinson got more press coverage. His numbers in the polls went up steadily, and the standings of his rivals fell; he wound up with a comfortable and convincing primary victory and won by a landslide in the general election. Had Wilkinson been a Senate candidate in a similar position, it is doubtful that even such a "man bites dog" announcement would have attracted the attention of the state press.

## Differences in Media Outlets

In deciding how to approach the press, candidates must finally consider the differences between radio, television, and print journalism and journalists. Radio presents the fewest difficulties but offers the fewest rewards. Aside from airing actualities or giving candidates an opportunity to participate in call-in shows, radio has little place in a campaign's free media plan. Candidates are looking with interest toward local cable television, which is similar in many respects to radio, but its audiences are still small. We address the possibilities of cable further in chapter 10.

The major concern for campaigns in planning media events is to strike a balance between the need for planned visuals, which television demands, and the cynicism with which print reporters for elite newspapers regard media events. A Senate press secretary with experience as both a print and television reporter said: "I tried to set up events that weren't insulting to the print guys for the sake of TV—because you can create a terrible backlash of being criticized as a media-conscious campaign, which of course every campaign is. It's an awful balance." A reporter for a state news program on New Jersey public television, which is closer in orientation to print than commercial TV, gave an example of the difference between print and television coverage of a media event in the campaign of Gov. Thomas Kean:

> Kean was campaigning with Jack Kemp in Camden. They were walking on this horrible, horrible street, talking about urban enterprise zones. We did a pretty harsh report. After all the other television crews left, we went and asked the neighbors what they thought about the visit.

That was a better story than their being there. You couldn't get away
with that on commercial TV. There's no action there at all. The parade's
gone. All the visuals have left.

In summary, press coverage can have some effect in nonpresidential
campaigns for statewide office, particularly for governors. But unlike its
role in presidential campaigns, it is clearly secondary to paid media in
advancing a campaign's central arguments. As one consultant mused: "If
you don't have money for media, the only way you build credibility is
with the press. . . . If you don't have money, you're probably going to
lose."

# The Increase in Negative Campaigning _____

We noted early in this chapter that more and more commercials have a
negative tone. The reasons for this increase cannot be discussed without
reference to the free media, because candidates and campaign personnel
regard the kind of free media coverage they get as one of the important
reasons negative advertising is necessary. In this section we analyze the
causes of the increase in negative advertising, examine the criticisms of
its effects, and assess their validity.

## The Causes of Negative Advertising

Consultants identify one overriding cause for the sharp rise in
negative advertising: It works. Democratic consultant Michael Kaye,
while regretting the trend, still believes that, "If you try to run a
positive, decent campaign, you're dead. If negative advertising didn't
work, it would stop tomorrow." [28]

Kaye's comments are supported by the research of political consultants who, unlike academic and media polling organizations, have
developed a substantial database on voters' reactions to various forms of
political advertising and to particular advertisements. Media consultant
Jill Buckley has described the findings: "People say they hate negative
advertising. They hate it and remember it at the same time. The problem
with positive is you have to run it again and again and again to make it
stick. With negative, the poll numbers will move in three or four days."
The same research shows that although candidates making the charges
lose ground temporarily they bounce back quickly; victims who do not
answer effective charges lose even more ground and take longer to
recover lost support. Pollster Ed Mellman has concluded: "When we ask
people about negative ads, they'll say they don't like them. But that's not
the point. The point is they absorb the information." [29]

Although this explains why campaigns are tempted to use negative advertising, it does not explain why negative ads have grown so rapidly in recent election cycles. Many political scientists contend that the decreased role of the political parties in structuring campaigns and the increased role of personalities in politics is responsible. Larry Sabato voices this position: "If you had a party organization that was prepared to mobilize people on behalf of its candidates and a party program, perhaps you wouldn't have to exploit as much of the negative emotions in people in an effort to get a turnout." [30]

This theory, however, ignores many prominent examples of vicious negative messages during the strong party era that even the most combative contemporary campaigners would eschew. Andrew Jackson, the founder of the modern Democratic party, was accused by his opponents of adultery and murder in handbills headed, "Some Account of the Bloody Deeds of General Jackson." His successor, Martin Van Buren, was denounced for misusing public funds to purchase expensive European furniture and gold tableware. Supporters of the Republicans' 1884 presidential candidate, James G. Blaine, taunted opponent Grover Cleveland, who allegedly fathered an illegitimate child, with cries of "Ma, Ma, where's my pa?" Cleveland's supporters retorted, "Gone to the White House, ha ha ha!" [31] More recently, as Jeff Greenfield has noted: "The *New York Times* described the negative political atmosphere as a nightmare in billingsgate. But they said that in 1950, before the TV age of politics was ever born." [32] American politics has always been so personal, and American parties so fragmented and nonideological, that strong party periods such as the late nineteenth century seem to produce more, not less, negative electioneering, as party organizations sought means to mobilize the faithful.

The weaker parties of today contribute to the rise in negative campaigning for a different reason. In periods of strong party identification, many challengers are swept into office as a result of national tides favoring a given party. Today such tides are weaker, and attachments to particular incumbents for reasons other than party are stronger. The result is, as we have noted previously, that challengers who hope to win must give voters compelling reasons to vote for them and must also explain why they should replace apparently satisfactory incumbents. Conversely, incumbents no longer protected by a majority party label can become vulnerable if challengers have enough resources to disseminate telling attacks widely. They must then answer such attacks and offer equally compelling reasons that voters should not choose the challenger. The process we have just described by definition requires negative and comparative messages.

Another cause of heavier negative advertising is the escalating cost of paid media, particularly in the densely populated states. In competitive 1988 Senate campaigns, for example, negative spots were a much greater part of the mix in California, Florida, and New Jersey than in Mississippi, Nebraska, and Wisconsin because advertising rates are so much higher in these states than in the less densely populated ones. In New Jersey rates increased during the short period between the time the Lautenberg campaign drew up its advertising budget and the time it began purchasing spots; this added about a million dollars to the campaign's planned advertising buy. Most of the candidates in the larger states could not afford to go on the air until the fall, and they aired only eight or ten different spots. In the smaller states, for the same or less money, candidates could air twenty or thirty different spots, for periods as long as a year before the election.[33]

It is, however, possible for campaigns to present such messages through vehicles other than thirty-second TV spots. Candidates could participate in a series of televised debates, or they could make their views known through explications of policy positions in newspaper articles. Many European democracies require television stations to offer candidates or parties free air time. But the lightly regulated, free enterprise American media cannot be forced to give up substantial amounts of air time, which they can sell at a profit, nor do they seem inclined to do so. The problem is compounded by the large number of American elections, compared with most other political systems, and by a Federal Election Commission ruling that the offer of free time for commercials constitutes an impermissible corporate campaign contribution. Finally, candidates cannot be forced to participate in debates, and well-known incumbents often refuse to give such exposure to lesser known challengers. Negative advertising, then, often represents a candidate's attempt to draw his or her opponent into a debate.

As we noted earlier, candidates complain with some justification that the press coverage they receive is not conducive to debate on the issues.[34] Consultant William Zimmerman argued: "TV demeans the news ... by presenting only cursory glances at substantive world events while reserving hours for in-depth coverage of the weather. Is it any wonder that negative ads work in such an environment?" His colleague, Daniel B. Payne, adds, "Politics will get better only if the press covers the content, not the techniques of campaigns."[35]

## The Effects of Negative Advertising

The debate about negative advertising would not be important if many people did not believe negative ads have deleterious effects on the tone and conduct of American politics. For once, prominent liberal columnist Tom Wicker and leading conservative columnist George Will agree. Wicker characterized the 1986 midterm campaigns, with their endless ads about missed votes, attendance records, and the like, as the "nastiest, least relevant [and] most fraudulent," while Will described them as "niggling tendentiousness." [36] Not only were the candidates accused of running on trivial issues and making baseless charges, but many people shared the belief of Curtis Gans, director of the Committee for the Study of the American Electorate, that the upsurge of negative advertising was responsible for so alienating the public from politics that turnout declined to the lowest figure for a midterm election since World War II.[37] The low turnout for the 1988 presidential election, compared with 1980 and 1984, was also ascribed to the negative tone of many races that year.

Closer analysis makes these interpretations suspect, however. First, in 1986, ten Senate elections were decided by a margin of four points or less. In all of them, as might be expected, negative advertising figured heavily. In four of these states, turnout was down from the 1982 midterm, but in six cases, it was up.[38] In two of the higher turnout states, there were also close gubernatorial elections, and the winning Senate and gubernatorial candidates were from different parties. Otherwise, no obvious explanation—such as open seat versus incumbent races, concurrent gubernatorial elections, ease of registration, region of the country, or demographic patterns—correlated with the increased or depressed turnout.

Furthermore, in the two 1986 statewide races in which a candidate locked in a close race made negative advertising a central issue, both lost. In the Pennsylvania gubernatorial election Republican William Scranton, with polls showing him ahead, stopped his negative advertising in the third week of October with great fanfare. Postelection analysis indicated that Democrat Robert Casey's final targeted negative ads were probably responsible for his narrow victory. Torn between the moral high ground and his experience with the effect of negative ads, Scranton's media adviser, John Deardourff, correctly prophesied at the time that pulling Scranton's ads "may be a kamikaze mission." [39]

Similarly, in the face of mixed press reaction, Missouri Democrat Harriet Woods pulled a controversial negative ad. The ad showed a crying farmer whose property had been foreclosed by a bank on whose board sat Woods's Senate opponent, Republican Christopher Bond. Woods fired her pollster and media consultant, who opposed her decision to pull the ad. They wanted to continue running the ad because farmers, to whom it was targeted, were responding positively. Woods never regained the momentum she lost after these decisions. Commenting sourly on her actions, the fired media consultant, Robert Squier, said of the candidate and her advisers, "All they have to do is pin wings on her and she'll fly to the Senate." [40] The pattern continued in 1988, when New Jersey Senate challenger Pete Dawkins called for an end to negative ads at the close of the race. Dawkins lost by nine points. Connecticut incumbent senator Lowell Weicker also ended his campaign by describing challenger Joe Lieberman's negative spots as "garbage." Weicker, too, was defeated.

These events give credence to the viewpoint of political analyst Alan Ehrenhalt:

> I don't see evidence that negative advertising contributed directly to the low turnout. In fact, I think there were places where it created excitement. . . . Not everybody who doesn't vote is somehow angry about the campaign or upset with the quality of the coverage. . . . They may be satisfied with the quality of representation they're getting. . . . There is evidence that when people are mad enough they will come out and vote.[41]

Another incorrect assumption in the debate about negative advertising is that all negative messages are created equal and have the same impact. But this is clearly not true. Negative ads differ in their content and in their effectiveness. Ads that are nasty and personal, unspecific, untrue, or irrelevant are ignored by viewers or redound to the discredit of those making the charges.[42] Among the issue-based attack ads, for every one that focuses on how many unimportant committee meetings a senator or representative has missed, there is another that raises substantive questions about budget, tax, or defense policy. Even the seemingly trivial ads on missed votes and the like influence voters only when they strike a real chord.

Such attacks defeated Kentucky's Dee Huddleston in 1984 and Connecticut's Lowell Weicker in 1988 because they did not make the affirmative case for themselves to their constituents. Negative ads did not defeat California's Alan Cranston in 1986 or New Jersey's Frank Lautenberg in 1988 because voters knew, or learned during their campaigns, of the incumbents' records of achievement in office. To think otherwise, Roger Ailes, creator of the anti-Huddleston ads (and architect of George Bush's 1988 presidential campaign), pointed out, "underestimates the intelligence of the voters. They are capable of weeding out garbage commercials—gratuitous commercials that are unfair or inaccurate." [43]

## Setting the Campaign's Agenda

Campaigns devote much of the early fall of election years to the demands of establishing the campaign's theme. The messages that campaigns transmit through the paid and free media are what enable them to set the campaign's agenda. Elections become close contests when two opposing campaigns are successful in setting out themes that penetrate the consciousness of voters and strike enough of a chord to produce a possible winning coalition. When strategists in close contests move into the final weeks, they seek to hold their coalitions together, look for appeals that will persuade undecided voters, respond to charges by their opponents, and get their supporters to the polls. In the next chapter we look at these final weeks of a campaign.

## Notes

1. *Congressional Quarterly Weekly Report,* July 18, 1987, 1552-1553.
2. These points are described in detail in Jerry Hagstrom and Robert Guskind, "Shopping for Airtime," *National Journal,* February 20, 1988, 462-467.
3. A similar problem plagued Republican Senate challenger Beau Boulter in Texas in his 1988 race. Although Boulter advertised heavily during the early fall primary and bested his competitors decisively, he was still unrecognized by 82 percent of Texas voters two months before the general election *(Dallas Morning News,* September 9, 1988). The costs of placing spots in Texas's eighteen media markets—many of which cover large metropolitan areas and are very costly—made Boulter's losing struggle against incumbent Lloyd Bentsen even more difficult that it would have been in other states.
4. See the *Washington Post,* October 8, 1986, for an extended discussion of the Florida campaign and general considerations relating to time buying.
5. Louis Sandy Maisel, *From Obscurity to Oblivion: Running in the Congressional Primary* (Knoxville: University of Tennessee Press, 1982), 111; Edie N. Goldenberg and Michael W. Traugott, *Campaigning for Congress* (Washington, D.C.: CQ Press, 1984), 116-119; John R. Alford and Keith Henry "TV Markets and Congressional Elections," *Legislative Studies Quarterly* 9 (November 1984): 665-675; Andrew D. McNitt, "Congressional Campaign Style in Illinois and Michigan," *Legislative Studies Quarterly* 10 (May 1985): 267-275; Margaret K. Latimer, "Information in State-Level Campaigns: How Do Electoral Factors Interact with the Media Message?" paper presented at the annual meeting of the American Political Science Association, Washington, D.C., September 1-4, 1988.
6. Goldenberg and Traugott, *Campaigning for Congress,* 116.
7. David J. Heller, "Mail, Money and Machiavelli," *Campaigns and Elections* 8 (November-December 1987): 45.
8. *Birmingham News,* September 30, 1986.
9. Some landmarks in a vast literature are Jeff Greenfield, *The Real Campaign* (New York: Summit Books, 1982); John Carey, "How Media Shapes Campaigns," *Journal of Communication* 26 (Spring 1976): 50-57; Thomas E. Patterson and Robert D. McClure, *The Unseeing Eye: The Myth of Television Power in National Politics* (New York: Putnam, 1976); Thomas E. Patterson, *The Mass Media Election: How Americans Choose Their President* (New York: Praeger, 1980); Michael J. Robinson and Margaret Sheehan, *Over the Wire and on TV* (New York: Russell Sage, 1983); Peter Clarke and Susan H. Evans, *Covering Campaigns: Journalism in Congressional Campaigns* (Stanford, Calif.: Stanford

University Press, 1983); Martin Schramm, *The Great American Video Game* (New York: Morrow, 1987); David Broder, *Behind the Front Page* (New York: Simon and Schuster, 1987); Timothy Crouse, *The Boys on the Bus* (New York: Random House, 1973).

10. Robinson and Sheehan, *Over the Wire and on TV*, 148.
11. Donald Matthews, "Winnowing: The News Media and the 1976 Presidential Nominations," in *Race for the Presidency: The Media and the Nominating Process*, ed. James David Barber (Englewood Cliffs, N.J.: Prentice-Hall, 1978), 66-67.
12. Clarke and Evans, *Covering Campaigns*, 43-46; Jan P. Vermeer, "Congressional Campaign Coverage in Rural Districts," in *Campaigns in the News: Mass Media and Congressional Elections*, ed. Jan Pons Vermeer (Westport, Conn.: Greenwood Press, 1987).
13. Clarke and Evans, *Covering Campaigns*, 5.
14. Robinson and Sheehan, *Over the Wire and on TV*, 76.
15. Quoted in *USA Today*, April 22, 1988, 1.
16. ABC and CBS did slightly better, offering coverage of forty-eight and forty-five minutes, respectively. All told, all 1984 nonpresidential contests got about 3 percent of network news time and about a tenth as much time as the presidential contest. See Doris A. Graber, "Kind Pictures and Harsh Words: How Television Presents the Candidates," in *Elections in America*, ed. Kay Lehman Schlozman (Boston: Allan and Unwin, 1987), 115-141.
17. Jonathan F. Hale, "The Scribes of Texas: Newspaper Coverage of the 1984 U.S. Senate Campaign," in *Campaigns in the News*, ed. Vermeer, 91-108.
18. *Charlotte Observer*, October 14, 1986.
19. Martin Schramm, "The Media Isn't the Message," *Washington Post National Weekly Edition*, April 16, 1984, 12.
20. Quoted in *St. Petersburg Times*, November 2, 1986, A1.
21. *Orlando Sun-Sentinel*, September 19, 1986; *St. Petersburg Times*, November 2, 1986, A1.
22. Bill Ratliff, quoted in the *Tampa Tribune*, October 29, 1986, 15B.
23. Ibid, Bob Graham quoted.
24. Quoted in the *Miami Herald*, October 20, 1986, 8A.
25. *Portland Press-Herald*, October 20, 1984; *Trenton Times*, November 7, 1988, A1.
26. Charles M. Tidmarch, "Press Issue Agendas in the 1982 Congressional and Gubernatorial Election Campaigns," *Journal of Politics* 46 (November 1984): 1230.
27. David Beiler, "White Knights, Dark Horses," *Campaigns and Elections* 8 (September-October 1987): 47.
28. *Las Vegas Review-Journal*, October 5, 1986.
29. Jill Buckley, quoted in *Congressional Quarterly Weekly Report*, December 7, 1985, 2561; Ed Mellman, quoted in the *Charlotte Observer*, October 15, 1986.
30. Quoted in *Political Report*, April 24, 1987, 8.
31. See Keith Melder's fascinating series of articles on nineteenth-century campaign messages in *Campaigns and Elections*: "The Birth of Modern Campaigning" 6 (Summer 1985): 48-53; "The First Media Campaign" 6 (Fall 1985): 62-68; "Creating Campaign Imagery, Part I: The Man on Horseback" 6 (Winter 1986): 4-11. See also M. J. Heale, *The Presidential Quest* (New York: Longman, 1982).
32. "Nightline," October 6, 1986.
33. Robert Guskind and Jerry Hagstrom, "In the Gutter," *National Journal*, November 5, 1988, 2787-2788.

34. We address this issue further in chapter 8.
35. Zimmerman and Payne are quoted in "Memos," *Campaigns and Elections* 7 (March-April 1987): 12.
36. Quoted in John Nugent, "Positively Negative," *Campaigns and Elections* 7 (March-April 1987): 47.
37. *Washington Post*, October 15, 1986; *Political Report*, May 29, 1987, 8.
38. The ten elections took place in Alabama, Colorado, Idaho, North Carolina, North Dakota, and South Dakota, where turnout was up, and in Georgia, Nevada, Washington State, and Wisconsin, where turnout was down. Turnout figures from *Congressional Quarterly Weekly Report*, November 8, 1986, 2805; March 14, 1987, 485.
39. *Philadelphia Inquirer*, October 21, 1986; November 6, 1986.
40. Quoted in Steven P. Roberts, "Politicking Goes High Tech," *New York Times Magazine*, November 2, 1986, 44.
41. Interviewed in *Political Report*, May 29, 1987, 6. Ehrenhalt's views on the reasons for nonvoting accord with the more systematic studies by Arthur T. Hadley, *The Empty Polling Booth* (New York: Prentice-Hall, 1978); Raymond E. Wolfinger and Stephen J. Rosenstone, *Who Votes?* (New Haven, Conn.: Yale University Press, 1980); and Ruy A. Teixeira, *Why Americans Don't Vote: Turnout Decline in the United States* (Westport, Conn.: Greenwood Press, 1987). These studies note that satisfaction, albeit apathetic, is a major reason many people do not vote; it should be noted also that nonvoting during the 1920s was higher than during the 1980s. Further, the severe 1982 recession resulted in that election exhibiting unusually heavy turnout.
42. See the examples in Nugent, "Positively Negative," 47-49.
43. *Washington Post*, October 6, 1986.

# Winning the Election = 8

*Even though we were down six points ten days before the election, I figured we were going to win because I felt we really controlled the dynamic of the race; we controlled the dialogue and the definition of what was at stake.*

Manager for a successful Senate challenger

As campaigns move into the final weeks, their course is determined by what has gone before. If one of the candidates—usually a weak challenger—has not acquired reasonably high levels of positive recognition or has not advanced an appealing theme, the race is effectively over, even though the balloting has not taken place. In some elections, however, the contest is spirited until the final moments.

When the race is a tossup, campaign organizations have two major tasks. The first is to continue advancing the candidate's arguments, reinforcing the candidate's base, and responding to the opponent's charges. The second is to ensure the highest possible turnout of the candidate's supporters on election day. In this chapter we look at the activities in this final stage of closely fought campaigns.

## The Electronic Debate

By the time a campaign has reached its final weeks, both candidates have had the opportunity to set the agenda and assume control of the dialogue. The degree of success achieved by the rival campaigns produces one of three patterns: (1) A candidate who is far ahead refuses to be drawn into debate and ignores opposition charges as long as there is no evidence that they are effective; (2) a candidate who was once far ahead is put on the defensive, ending up on the wrong side of the momentum in the race and in danger of losing control of the dialogue; or (3) both candidates have advanced persuasive themes capable of mobilizing a winning coalition. In the second and third cases campaigns take on the quality of an electronic debate—a volley of charges and countercharges on TV and radio and by direct mail. In their paid and free media appeals, candidates must respond to compelling accusations, rally the undecided, or convert weak supporters of the opposition to their cause.

The problem for each campaign is to determine which situation it faces. Electoral volatility has increased enormously in the past few decades. In the 1940s, when party identification was stronger, more than three-quarters of the voters made up their minds about which candidate to support before Labor Day. By the 1980s this figure frequently dwindled to a third. Another third did not decide until the last two weeks of the campaign or on election day itself.[1] Thus even candidates who seem safely ahead worry that a last-minute ploy of the rival camp or events on the national or world scene will erase an apparently secure lead. For their part, candidates who believe they are on the defensive or who are locked in a close race must deduce what appeals will swing the momentum in their direction.

All campaigns have difficulty in determining exactly which voters need shoring up, what the most effective last-minute appeals will be, and where and how to communicate their messages. The uncertainty of the final days can lead to strenuous efforts in many directions, with little sure knowledge about the effectiveness of any strategy. Veteran Republican campaign manager Merrick Carey likens this period to "being told you have six weeks to live." In Stimson Bullitt's classic formulation, "every cartridge must be fired because among the multitude of blanks one may be a bullet."[2]

## The Advent of Tracking Polls

Robert Caro has observed: In the "era before the widespread use of political polling, information was a commodity very difficult for a politician to obtain.... A candidate might wonder—might be desperate to know—how his strategy was working, but it was hard for him to find out."[3] Technological advances in polling, made possible by faster and cheaper personal computers and data entry, have now made available a source of useful last-minute information. Campaigns that use these *tracking polls*—scientific samplings of public opinion taken every day during the last few weeks of a campaign—can chart the considerable ups and downs in candidates' support. They can identify which groups in the electorate are particularly volatile and what issues concern the voters most. Pollster Bill Hamilton has remarked: "Nobody goes in with that much of a solid vote anymore. That's why tracking is so important."

All genuinely competitive statewide campaigns now use tracking polls. The usual recommendation is that they begin about a month before the election and continue until election day. In theory the same schedule applies to House races, but tracking is much less frequently done in these contests. For the reasons we discussed earlier—one-party dominance of many congressional districts, the lopsided margins in many races, and the low media profile—most House races are never in doubt. In the few that are real contests, tracking is often too expensive. Furthermore, competitive House races tend to be in the suburban areas of large population centers, where high media costs make it difficult for candidates to get new information to voters quickly.

No sophisticated campaign organization doubts the need for tracking polls; the problem is paying for them. Here Republican candidates have a distinct advantage. Polling is another function increasingly performed by their national party committees. The National Republican Senatorial Committee tracks close races for four to six weeks before election day. Although Federal Election Commission rules specify that the committee cannot transmit detailed findings to campaign organizations without charging them against permissible in-kind contributions, they *"are* allowed to describe general trends and suggest remedial action—which is, of course, all any campaign really needs to know." [4]

In 1984 the National Republican Congressional Committee took on this same function for House candidates in close races. As Republican consultant Vince Breglio said of the defeat of fourteen Republican House incumbents in 1982:

> There were incumbents who shouldn't have lost. They lost because they didn't know where they were going in the last two weeks of the campaign. They thought they were ahead, but the data they were looking at was from mid-September, and things had changed dramatically enough that they needed much more in the way of media and much more aggressive posturing. With that in mind, the congressional committee is going to do some tracking in selected races.

In competitive races, in the last four weeks or so of a campaign, daily polling of a volatile electorate has become a necessity.

## Tracking Polls and Campaign Money

Tracking is important to campaigns for reasons other than providing information that enables them to adjust their strategies. Reliable data that a once-hopeless candidate has come within striking distance of winning is critical for campaigns to raise the money necessary for their final paid advertising and get-out-the-vote efforts. In recent election cycles a quarter or more of all the PAC money contributed, particularly to challengers, has been given after October 1. Wyoming representative Richard Cheney described well the problems candidates have with late contributions: "Much of the money that is said to be available for campaigns really does not appear until after the race has already been decided." [5]

A candidate's failure to move up in tracking polls thus slows the flow of funds coming into the campaign. Even the well-funded Republican national committees stop short of maximum efforts when tracking shows their candidate trailing substantially. A former executive director of the National Republican Senatorial Committee observed: "This committee has a very strong interest in knowing exactly what's going on in each state so it can decide where to spend its dollars, where to direct supportive PACs or individuals. . . . We will be very bold and aggressive to try to make things happen, but we won't throw our money away."

## Last-Minute Strategies

If candidates have good information in the last few weeks of the campaign and enough money to effect a change in their strategy, the question is what should that strategy be. Usually, the negative tone of the contest will intensify. As we saw in chapter 6, the early themes of almost all successful challengers, who typically start the race behind, involve attacks against the incumbent. If the charges draw blood, they will probably continue until the end of the campaign; however, incumbents—or any frontrunners—who find their leads diminishing must counterattack. Only the most secure candidates can avoid an attack strategy in the closing weeks and continue to run positive campaigns that ignore the opponent.

In their 1986 gubernatorial campaigns New York's Mario Cuomo and Maryland's Donald Schaefer, who both won in record landslides, were almost able to disregard their opponents. A reporter noted that Cuomo's full day of political events the Saturday before the election was "unusual in a race in which Mr. Cuomo has declined to campaign, choosing to appear as gubernatorial as possible." Cuomo's manager explained: "The governor is governing. He has a government to run." He added that Cuomo's challenger "has more time to campaign because he has less responsibility." A week before the Maryland election, the state's leading newspaper was already examining how Schaefer would organize his transition team. It observed of his hapless and eccentric opponent, Thomas Mooney: "News organizations are covering the GOP campaign by poking fun at 'the Moonman,' or—more often—not covering him at all." [6]

Besides making negative charges against their opponents, candidates in tight races must also respond to accusations against them that seem to be influencing the electorate. This interchange is the electronic debate, to which we referred earlier. The responses must not sound as if a candidate is on the defensive and concerned about losing. One way to avoid a loser's image is to integrate the campaign's own theme into the response in such a way that the answer refutes the charge and at the same time reinforces the candidate's own message.

A classic example occurred in the 1986 Louisiana Senate race. The debate began with an ad by Republican hopeful Henson Moore, who like many other Republicans that year attacked his opponent's attendance record. The ad opened with a stark graphic showing the numbers *1083* in white on a black background; it continued with an announcer querying people on the street:

ANNOUNCER: The number 1083. Know what it stands for?
—1083? Haven't the remotest.
—Is it a tax form or something like that?
—How much money I made the last two months?
—Down payment on a car?
—I don't know.
ANNOUNCER: 1083 is the number of votes Congressman John Breaux missed in Congress; 1083 times he didn't show up for work.
—I wish I had a job like that!

The day after this ad appeared, another ad went on the air with the same opening graphic, a similar announcer's voice, and a similar set of bemused citizens:

ANNOUNCER: The number 1083. Know what it stands for?
—1083?
—The last time the Saints won a game?
—The temperature out here now?
ANNOUNCER: 1083 is the number of jobs lost in Louisiana every ten working days because of Reagan policies that Henson Moore promises to continue. The numbers that count are the eighteen effective pieces of legislation that John Breaux has passed and the zero for Henson Moore.
—That's incredible!

Breaux staffer Randy Thompson subsequently explained the campaign's quick reaction: "We knew when it was going to start. The day it started, we shot our response. And we were on the air with it the next day." Not only did the response incorporate a major theme of the Breaux campaign, but as Thompson continued: "You had both of them on the air at the same time and it confused the whole issue. And that was our goal with '1083'—to make the [attendance] issue a non-issue." [7]

Similar ripostes now occur in many other hotly contested races. In the Kentucky Senate race in 1984, Mitch McConnell's "bloodhound" ads, which questioned incumbent Dee Huddleston's attendance record, erased Huddleston's forty-plus point lead when he did not answer the charges. A lesson can be drawn from this contest: a seemingly credible charge unanswered is a charge admitted. Whether an attack is making headway with the voters and must be answered can be determined from tracking polls. Pollster Harrison Hickman has observed: "You have to know if your media is working and if your opponent's media is working. Information is now a much more important commodity." Comparing recent campaigns to those of the past, media consultant Robert Squier adds:

> Before, it was like trench warfare in World War I. You'd get the guns ready, and three weeks before the election you would fire off your stuff and then on Election Night you would count the bodies. Today you listen and talk back and listen again and talk back.[8]

Perhaps the ultimate example of anticipation and preparation occurred in the 1986 four-way Maine gubernatorial race, which was narrowly won by Republican John McKernan. In October, McKernan's camp ran a response ad showing the other candidates flipping and turning "Maine's record for clean politics upside down," while an indignant woman declared, "Anyone who would do this wouldn't be fit to be governor." Astute viewers noted that the green grass and leafy trees in the ad indicated it had been filmed during the summer, long before any of the attacks on McKernan were aired.[9]

Some candidates are fortunate enough to destroy their opponents' charges by proving them false. A candidate trapped in a highly publicized lie is unlikely to win. The Mississippi gubernatorial race of 1983 provides a bizarre example. Going into October, Democrat Bill Allain, who was then the state's attorney general, led Republican businessman Leon Bramlett by thirty points in the polls. Republicans had never won a gubernatorial race in Mississippi, although one candidate had come within four points. The state had two Republican representatives and a Republican senator and had voted for the Republican presidential candidate three times since 1964. A black candidate, who had previously run for the Senate, splitting the Democratic vote and permitting the Republican to win, was once again running as an independent in the gubernatorial race. A Republican victory by a strong candidate was therefore by no means out of the question. Bramlett's organization, which had fired its campaign manager and national consultants in September, was dominated by political amateurs, including the candidate himself. The campaign was frantically searching for a major issue to use against Allain.

The issue they came up with led to one of the strangest and dirtiest campaigns in recent American history. In mid-October a Jackson attorney appeared on Mississippi television in a paid political program to announce, "Our investigation has established by clear and convincing evidence, beyond a reasonable doubt, that Mr. Bill Allain has, over the years, frequently participated in homosexual activities with male prostitutes." Interviews, which followed, were intended to show that these alleged sexual contacts were black transvestites. With graphics identifying them as "Nicole Toy, AKA Grady Arrington" and "Davia Ross, AKA David Holiday," the transvestites were asked such questions as, "When you say *oral sex*, did he [Allain] want you to perform oral sex on him?" and, "Is it general knowledge in the gay community that he is dating men?" To all such questions, those interviewed replied affirmatively.

It was soon revealed that Bramlett supporters had paid the homosexuals to make their charges. Allain's advertisements denying the charge, while obviously necessary, were no less astounding. His ex-wife told voters she had had a normal married life. The candidate himself appeared, announcing: "I'm Bill Allain. Yesterday I passed an independent lie detector test, proving that the charges against me are false." Another Allain advertisement summarized the campaign's response: "There's a new word in our campaign for governor, and the word is smear. Here is what the smear merchants would like us to believe. Three male prostitutes. Each with criminal records. Each admittedly bribed [for] $300 and $50 a day."

Despite the spectacular charges and the introduction of sexual and racial elements into one of the most conservative and racially charged electorates in the nation, Bill Allain won 55 percent of the vote in a three-way race. After the election the homosexuals appearing in Bramlett's paid broadcasts confirmed the voters' opinion that the allegations were false and that none of them had ever met Allain.

In the final days of an election period, campaigns may also choose to level charges or respond to them in a quieter and more targeted fashion through direct mail. Direct mail reaches specific audiences. For example, Pennsylvania Democrat Robert Casey's own tracking polls showed that he suffered severe voter defections after an October 20 debate with his gubernatorial opponent, William Scranton, in which Casey opposed legalized abortion. His pollster, Pat Caddell, remembered: "Overnight it drove huge numbers of young women and liberal Democrats to the Republicans. It almost sank him." By the Thursday before the election, Casey was almost back to even. His campaign decided to try to go over the top by appealing to conservative Democrats and dissuading conservative Republicans from voting at all.

During the final weekend the Casey campaign sent mailgrams to fifty thousand Republican households in central Pennsylvania; they were accompanied by fifteen-year-old pictures of a long-haired Scranton in the company of guru Maharishi Mahesh Yogi. Similar television ads ran in every state market save liberal-leaning Philadelphia. The mailgram, signed by a respected local Republican, asked, "What message would it send our young people if someone with Bill Scranton's character and values became our governor?" It suggested that recipients refrain from voting at all in the gubernatorial election. Both turnout and the Republican margin were unexpectedly low in central Pennsylvania's Republican heartland, and Casey won by 75,000 votes out of more than 3.3 million cast. Caddell asserted, "I look at the vote margin and I am damn glad I made that decision." [10] Such mailings illustrate the observation of Republican direct mail strategist John Simms: "A TV message can't be very specialized. That's not true with mail. You can mail a very specialized message that has no bleed into other groups."

In the last weeks of a closely contested campaign, candidates use advertising to level accusations against their opponents and to reply to charges made against them. At the same time the press is stepping up its coverage. The interaction of campaigns with the press in this period is our next subject.

## The Role of Free Media

When campaigns move into their final phase, coverage by print and television journalists increases, but it does not change in any important thematic or substantive respect. Indeed, if anything, reporters' interest in the horse race aspects intensifies. Sophisticated campaigns quickly learn that the press will report the charges and countercharges typical of the final stage of a campaign, but it will draw back from assessing their validity or accuracy. A journalist for a major state newspaper in Texas complains: "It's hard to figure out exactly what's going on. The other guy always has an explanation." [11] Because campaign strategists are aware that independent judgments are more credible than statements by candidates or their supporters, however, they seek external confirmation of their positions from outside institutions such as the media.

As we indicated in chapter 7, campaigns are not likely to get media confirmation. In the 1980 presidential election CBS and UPI were almost eight times more willing to draw explicit conclusions about the chances of presidential candidates than about their leadership qualities. Studies of the coverage of the 1984 presidential election and of the 1988 presidential primary races yielded similar findings. Two of the researchers concluded, "Saying nothing about the issues, beyond what others have said, strikes us as being the first commandment in campaign news coverage."[12] Similarly, an analysis of congressional campaign coverage discovered that although reporters agreed that the candidates emphasized the issues above anything else, in their stories the journalists stressed the candidates' personal characteristics and political attributes such as experience and name recognition.[13] A reporter elaborated:

> The reporter thinks—the charge, the countercharge, and it's covered like that. The middle ground—who's correct and who's wrong—there's no time to find that out. Or someone will get dispatched to find out and will write a Sunday story. That's the catch basin in journalism. Correct it on Sunday, but let it go wrong for six days.

All the characteristics of the press described in chapter 7—the journalists' lack of substantive background, the pressure on them to move on to the next assignment, and the premium on hard facts and events as opposed to judgments—operate as reporters cover the end stages of a campaign. How, then, do campaigns get their stories out?

## The Techniques of Charge and Countercharge

Since campaigns cannot rely on reporters to press their charges and responses effectively, they must place primary emphasis on their own paid media. Thomas Patterson and Robert McClure have found that, given the press's attention to campaign hoopla and the horse race, voters learn more about candidates' issue positions and criticisms of them from political advertising than from political journalism. In an experiment that used actual ads, other political scientists discovered that their subjects retained information about issues from thirty-second spots as well as they did from the same subjects discussed in debates.[14]

Dramatic new charges made in advertisements often rate a news story. Candidates now routinely call press conferences to screen new advertising spots for reporters. The purveyors of the sexual charges against Mississippi gubernatorial candidate Bill Allain, for instance, decided to buy advertising time only after they were unable to persuade the leading Mississippi media to investigate. Once the ads were aired, investigation was minimal, but coverage was not.

Still, as Republican media consultant Roger Ailes has said:

> In the beginning, when a candidate is totally unknown, paid media tend to define a candidate's background. But then as the public gets to know the candidate, and Election Day approaches, I think the importance of the so-called free media increases and the paid media decreases.[15]

Thus to get effective press coverage of the messages they want to disseminate, campaigns seek other ways than the usually ineffective strategy of giving reporters a lead to follow. Playing to reporters' own preferences, they try to create a news story, through either a new series of advertisements or a staged event.

To be effective, strategists must keep in mind several factors that make it more likely that the press will pick up the story and that it will be credible and persuasive to the journalistic community and to the public. We examine those factors in the following sections.

**Staying Off the Defensive.** It is generally unwise for candidates to defend themselves personally against hostile accusations made by an opponent. When candidates try to explain away charges that are matters of judgment rather than fact, they are usually perceived as having been forced on the defensive, and that is the explanation which will be reported. A classic example is Richard Nixon's "I am not a crook" defense at the height of the Watergate investigation.

In 1986 many Republican senators felt compelled to respond to charges that they would cut Social Security benefits (collected by 16 percent of the entire population and 21 percent of voters). Nearly all these senators enlisted beneficiaries of the program to make the case for them, sometimes bringing in their own relatives. In Alabama incumbent Jeremiah Denton's mother told viewers:

—I just want to thank the people of Alabama for all the nice letters you've written my son, Jeremiah, about how you appreciate what Jeremiah's done to save Social Security for millions of Americans. But when some politician attacks my son wrongly, it's a mother's right to speak up, and I did.
DENTON: You tell 'em, Mom!
—I did, Jeremiah.

In New Hampshire, where Sen. Gordon Humphrey's parents were perhaps reluctant to go on camera, an elderly female constituent stood in for them:

What do you do about a politician who tries to frighten the elderly? Well, Norm D'Amours is trying to do just that. He claims Senator Humphrey does not believe in the Social Security system when his own parents are on it, I'm on it, and many of his constituents in New Hampshire are on it. Mr. D'Amours knows this is a lie. Shame on you, Mr. D'Amours. Senator Humphrey is a very strong supporter of Social Security.

**Basing the Charges on Facts.** Effective charges, from the point of view of the media and the public, must be based on hard facts and not on judgments. Claims or accusations based on questionable data tend to backfire on those who make them. When the Colorado Republican state chair accused Democratic Senate candidate Tim Wirth of accepting a certain PAC's money to influence his vote, it turned out that Wirth had taken the contribution but voted against the PAC's position. The *Denver Post* headline read, "For the second day in a row, Republican blasts against Democratic Senate candidate Tim Wirth may have misfired"— not the coverage Republicans hoped for when they made the charge.[16]

**Using Respected Outside Figures to Accuse or Respond.**   A third precept campaigns follow in making or responding to attacks is having outside parties, rather than the candidate or the campaign organization, deal with a charge. Allegations or responses are usually more credible when respected external figures make them. When 1988 Senate challenger George Voinovich accused incumbent Howard Metzenbaum of voting against measures restricting child pornography, Ohio's other highly popular Democratic senator, John Glenn, took to the airwaves to denounce Voinovich:

> In the past I've known George Voinovich as an honorable man. But his new TV ad is the lowest gutter politics I've seen in a long time. To imply that Howard Metzenbaum, with four daughters and six grandchildren, is somehow soft on pornography is disgusting. Howard Metzenbaum has voted for every law we have to stop child pornography. These ads tell more about George Voinovich than they do about Howard Metzenbaum. Think about it.

Similarly, to deflate California Republican challenger Ed Zschau's claim that he had successfully led a high-tech company, Sen. Alan Cranston held a press conference featuring Zschau's replacement on the company's board and Thomas Peters, author of the best-selling book on entrepreneurial companies, *In Search of Excellence*. The business executive told reporters: "The company was in shambles when he left. . . . It was not a leading edge company and it did not fight international trade competition. I think if it were not for the people who replaced Ed, it would not be around today." Peters detailed Zschau's alleged flip-flops on international trade issues.[17]

**Exceptions to the Guidelines.**   In making accusations or responding to them, candidates ideally should employ third parties, who present the case on the facts. The only time candidates should be personally involved is when their appearance alone will make an allegation or a response credible. Bill Allain in Mississippi, for instance, could not duck comment on the homosexuality charges leveled against him. At least part of a believable response had to involve the candidate himself. Allain's success in refuting the charges points up again the general rule that facts are more convincing than opinions or emotional appeals. Allain did not emotionally and defensively say, "I am not a homosexual," as Nixon had unpersuasively argued, "I am not a crook." Instead, he produced hard evidence—the payments made to his accusers and an "independent lie detector test"—to prove that the charges against him were false. Allain was believed; Nixon was not.

If personal intervention by the candidates is so rarely effective, why do so many of them come to their own defense? The most frequent answer is that such candidates are often underfinanced challengers who may not be experienced enough to know that this is a poor strategy or, more often, do not have the money to advance their messages through the paid media.

Eventually, time runs out for all campaigns, and election day is upon them. The opportunity to attack the opponent or defend the candidate is over. Campaigns hope their arguments have carried the day and that the large volatile element of the electorate will swing in their direction. But in those races where few votes appear to separate the candidates, the get-out-the-vote (dubbed GOTV by campaign participants) activities on election day become crucial, as do the voter targeting activities that must precede them.

## The Role of GOTV and Targeting _____

Get-out-the-vote efforts are designed to do what the name suggests—to bring as many of a candidate's supporters as possible to the polls on election day. Most simply, this means finding out which voters support a candidate and making sure they actually vote.

The second task is relatively straightforward, but determining which voters support a candidate is more complicated. Voters may support candidates strongly, oppose them strongly, be undecided, or have weak preferences, which could change as a result of information received during the campaign. In a competitive race voters in the last two categories decide its outcome. Devising and carrying out a strategy to assess correctly who those swing voters are is a process known as *targeting*. A candidate's strong supporters must not be forgotten, either. Voter contact specialist Pete Curtin has observed of GOTV efforts directed at strong supporters: "There's a tremendous need to do that. I've seen campaigns that lost because they took their core vote for granted."

It bears repeating that GOTV makes a difference only in campaigns that have already created the conditions that give them a potential majority:

> Identification and turnout programs presume that campaigns have created a winning strategy and implemented it by effective tactics. . . .

Identifying and turning out every supporter in the district will not produce a victory unless the candidate has more backers than does his opponent.[18]

## GOTV, Old Style

Historically, GOTV was the province of the political party organizations. Harold Gosnell describes the role of the dominant Democratic Chicago machine in the 1930s: "Efficient precinct captains saw that a thorough canvass was made before each general or intermediate registration, so that they could be sure that the names of all their potential supporters were on the books." [19] On election day, fueled with organization street money, party workers fanned out over the district to get supporters to the polls. Their success in this vote-pulling operation strongly influenced the award of the party's patronage resources.

Today, party organizations still play a role, particularly in less visible, low-turnout elections at the county and municipal levels, but most have become enfeebled. Consultant Curtin, a close observer of the fabled Hudson County, New Jersey, machine, which controlled state elections in the days of the legendary Boss Hague, said:

My sense is that the organizations don't understand that times have changed, that people with twenty or thirty years of service as county committeemen are slowing down—actually slowing down. They do have these tiny notebooks with their lists, but the list used to be fifty, and now it's thirty. They can get a vote out, but it's not sufficient to win.

Another consultant who has worked closely with organization politicians in the same state agreed:

It's a function of not moving into the modern era of politics. They're still twenty years back. It's not that they don't have the resources. They still have some jobs, a lot of things you need. But in terms of mobilization, they're not very good.

A special problem for candidates is how to relate to local party organizations that want to be involved. The issue rarely arises west of the Mississippi, where party machines never fully developed. "You've got to understand," noted one strategist, "that traditionally in the West, the party is not as influential as in the East. There's really nothing west of Natchez, there never has been. It's a throwback to the Progressives."

In the East, where vestiges of the party machines remain, campaign organizations are unenthusiastic about heavy dependence on party activists, who are considered unreliable and not conversant with modern techniques. In a strong but fairly typical comment, a campaign manager for a House incumbent said of the local party organization:

They weren't useful, they weren't dependable, they weren't helpful. We didn't want to rely on county organization people; they're more trouble than they're worth. They're more concerned if their name is in the right place on the invitation. They just don't produce. We don't need them.

Campaigners do not feel safe if they entirely ignore the party activists, however. When election day comes, party organizations can often supplement the campaign's own efforts in mobilizing the voters. Another campaign manager observed: " The Democratic regulars and the traditional elements of the Democratic base like labor are real utilities in the last ten days of the campaign. If they're going to make any contribution, it's getting out the vote. There's really one day when all that matters."

Moreover, strategists believe that although party activists may be of limited assistance, they can seriously damage a campaign if they turn hostile. One adviser noted:

Party organizations are capable of generating intense negative energy. They will just distract you for the whole race if you don't pay attention to them, if you don't court them. If you're suddenly having to deal with a county chairman who's bad-mouthing you to the press or a state chair who says you're not running a good campaign, it just screws up the inside of your campaign. It gives inside people with dissent an occasion to question the whole strategy.

Another campaign staffer agreed:

How much they can help you is questionable, but how much they can hurt is documentable. People can bad-mouth and destroy you. If they're out in the cold, they're going to be bad-mouthing you. Somehow you've got to keep them separate because you don't want them mucking around.

Campaigns deal with this situation in two ways. First, they send their own paid field staff to serve as liaisons with the party organizations. One House campaign assigned paid field staff to party offices during the final three weeks of the campaign. A Senate campaign had a paid operative in every county of the state by Labor Day. This tactic gives the campaign organization information about what the party people are doing and an opportunity to offer them advice and manage crises before they get out of control. It is also part of the second and more important strategy in dealing with the party regulars: It keeps party activists happy so that they will not denigrate the campaign and will do whatever they can on election day. A campaign manager described his "party pacification" operation:

We would call party leaders every time we went into a county; we would call every party leader and say the candidate was coming. Not that they wanted to come, but they were offended if they didn't know. We'd call them at least once a week to give them inside gossip. The candidate would call them—he'd make a couple of hundred calls every week. At the end of the campaign, we sent them all a paperweight or something.

Because of shrinking bases in their communities, the aging and old-style politicians who dominate what remains of local and county organizations have become ineffective at mobilizing voters. As we discussed in chapter 3, patronage jobs are fewer. Once-prized positions as precinct captains are less attractive and more difficult to fill. More voters are self-declared independents, and many partisans split their tickets. Campaign organizations thus have to look beyond their local parties for an effective get-out-the-vote operation.

At first, volunteer canvassers, moving from house to house or calling residents listed in telephone directories, replaced or supplemented party workers. But through the early 1970s such GOTV drives were not notably successful from the perspective of the campaigns that conducted them. It was not that the activities did not boost turnout—they did. The difficulty was that they increased turnout indiscriminately. More voters showed up at the polls if contacted by campaign organizations, but their preferences were not significantly different from those of voters on the whole. One analyst noted:

> To be effective, a canvass should concentrate on turning out the vote among voters and in neighborhoods which are likely to support the party; and it must avoid contacting opposition voters. (It is worth noting that despite the rather obvious nature of this advice, neither party is particularly successful in concentrating its efforts in this manner.) [20]

"Blanket" canvasses, another observer added, always benefited the normal majority, which probably did not even need such efforts to win.[21] Sophisticated campaign organizations understood this. But the absence of party registration in many states, the growing numbers of voters registering as independents, and the proclivity of partisan voters to split their tickets all made it difficult for campaigns to figure out how to avoid contacting and mobilizing those who would not support them at the polls. In the next section we examine technology's answer to the problem.

# The New Technology and GOTV

The advent of sophisticated data-processing techniques revolutionized the means by which campaigns could identify, contact, and mobilize the critical swing voters. Once computers permitted the analysis of large amounts of data, those data could be organized in ways that greatly increased the ability of campaigns to target the "right" voters to contact. Election districts could be classified according to party strength, propensity of voters to swing from one party to another in succeeding elections, and levels of turnout. The swings and turnout variations could be refined further: Were they related in specific ways to certain offices or kinds of candidates? Would higher turnout in a given district be likely to help or hurt the candidate? Analyses could be conducted not only of election districts but of particular voters within them to determine their voting histories: How often and for which elections did they turn out? Were they regular primary voters, an indicator of strong attachment to a party?

By the late 1970s further refinements emerged as political consultants took up what became known as *geodemographic targeting*. Using detailed data from small, homogeneous tracts identified in the U.S. census, companies such as the pioneering Claritas Corporation divided these areas into different groups, or clusters, with distinct patterns of ethnicity, race, housing style, family life cycle, and other variables. Each cluster was given an evocative name—"Old Melting Pot" or "Blueblood Estates," for example. It was possible to identify by cluster type all areas of a given constituency. Polling data on opinions and attitudes could be integrated with the other information about the clusters. Using these data, campaigns could determine the kinds of messages that would be most effective in each cluster. The availability of inexpensive personal computers in the 1980s gave rise to many firms that purveyed targeting software within the price range of even state legislative campaigns.

These developments greatly enhanced the ability of a campaign to zero in on its own present and potential supporters without mobilizing its opponent's as well. Studies of the new, more targeted GOTV approaches indicated that they have the desired effect. In a special election for the Washington, D.C., City Council, for instance, turnout rose 9 percent among sympathetic voters contacted by a phone bank, compared to the turnout of a matched control group that was not contacted.[22] Some analysts argue that only in races such as this, which have little media visibility and low turnouts, does GOTV make a difference.[23] Barry Brendel, the voter contact specialist for Frank Lautenberg in the 1982 New Jersey Senate race, however, found almost exactly the same effect on turnout as in the D.C. contest. The turnout rate in solid Democratic precincts in New Jersey that were left as an uncontacted control group was 7 percent lower than in similar precincts where Lautenberg's campaign had carried out targeting and GOTV activities.

The richness of this new targeting information and the variety of ways in which it can be organized and analyzed meant that campaigns could adapt their targeting plans to their particular situations. Some of the variations can be seen by examining the voter contact programs in several Republican House campaigns. One candidate was running in a race in which the state party assumed responsibility for calling registered Republicans; he therefore contacted only independents. Two other candidates contacted all voters in swing districts; in one case the state had no party registration, and in the other the Republicans were in such a minority that the candidate needed many Democratic voters as well as independents to win. Still another contacted only registered Republicans who had specific demographic characteristics associated with consistent party-line voting, because the district contained areas with a large number of registered Republicans who often voted Democratic.[24]

We should not conclude that the apparent precision of these techniques is foolproof or that all campaigns use targeting as skillfully as they might. First, the quality of the available data and the time required to put it in usable form vary significantly. In some states voters must register by party, and their telephone numbers and addresses are recorded; all this information, centrally located on computer tapes, can be purchased at a reasonable price. At the other extreme, in some states there is no party registration; registration records are maintained by the counties; phone numbers are not recorded; and the data are not available in computer-readable form. The situation faced by each campaign can substantially affect when voter contact is begun and whether it can be completed in time.

Second, the more sophisticated the targeting plan required and the more work needed to carry it out, the more expensive it will be. Campaigns may know what needs to be done organizationally but simply may not have the financial resources to follow the plan through.

Bearing in mind these important caveats, we can now examine the typical organization of targeting efforts, the factors that affect them, the way they feed into the final GOTV efforts, and the activities that take place on election day.

## The Targeting Plan

An effective voter identification and contact effort begins in the late summer before the election. At that time campaign organizations acquire the names, addresses, and telephone numbers of the groups of voters they have decided to contact. Most of the voter identification and contact is done at central telephone banks set up by the campaign or, particularly in statewide races, by businesses that specialize in telephone soliciting and interviewing. The callers can be volunteers, paid workers, or a mixture. Increasingly, volunteers are used only when financial constraints make it necessary. No matter how dedicated the volunteer corps, they cannot be depended on to staff a phone bank reliably at the right hours. Voter contact specialist Curtin explained: "We use the volunteers for other activities. No matter how large a turnout you get, it's still unpredictable. You can't do systematic voter contact work with volunteers. When you have paid workers, it's a job."

The first calls go to those groups the campaign has identified as critical to its efforts. In North Carolina, for example, where statewide Republican victories depend on a large crossover vote from conservative Democrats, Republican Senate candidate Jim Broyhill's campaign benefited from a $700,000 paid phone bank effort financed by the Republican National Committee. Callers contacted eighteen thousand registered Democrats each night, attempting to identify those who were undecided or favorable toward Broyhill.[25]

The two major factors that affect campaign targeting plans are the resources available and the office sought. The less visible the campaign is in the mass media and the lower normal turnout tends to be, the more important targeting, telephoning, and direct mail are in the overall plan. Statewide campaigns must expend enormous resources on broadcast advertising. The sophisticated geodemographic efforts recommended by voter contact specialists for a closely contested race in a large and heterogeneous electorate are extremely costly and therefore are not used as frequently as they might be. Although targeting efforts are not ignored, they do not loom as large in statewide campaigns as in smaller constituency races, where they are often considered crucial.

Republican representative Frank Wolf of Virginia provides an instructive example of a major congressional GOTV campaign, showing how new technology aids such efforts. Wolf, whose marginal suburban Washington district was represented by a Democrat for three terms before he carried it for the Republicans in the 1980 Reagan landslide, was opposed by a popular, well-financed Democratic challenger in 1986.

The Wolf campaign set a target of identifying 42,500 favorable households. In early 1986 the district's voter list was entered into the campaign's computer. A list vendor was able to check, correct, and supply phone numbers for 70 percent of the list. Campaign workers, using PTA and club membership lists and door-to-door canvassing, worked on completing it. A paid phone bank with three supervisors and twenty-five callers contacted voters, first implying they were from a survey research firm. Voters who indicated they supported Wolf were asked whether they wanted absentee ballots or yard signs or were willing to volunteer in the campaign. Each voter received three subsequent mailings, keyed to the issues Wolf was stressing in his other paid and free media. Undecided voters received a follow-up letter within seventy-two hours of the initial contact.

A postcard reminding favorable voters to go to the polls was mailed during the week before election day. Six temporary phone banks, now staffed by volunteers, called favorable voters during the three days before the election. Poll watchers in 75 percent of the precincts reported the names of those who had still not voted by 2:00 p.m. so that the phone banks could call them again. In districts where there were no poll watchers on duty, everyone on the favorable list was called. When the election was over, and Wolf had won 60 percent of the vote, the campaign had exceeded its voter identification goal by a third, and turnout was seven points higher than expected.[26]

## Voter Registration Drives

Closely related to targeting are voter registration drives. To vote, a person must be registered, and in most areas more than a quarter of the potential electorate is not. Traditionally, voter registration drives have been conducted by the Democratic party and organizations sympathetic to it since nonregistration is concentrated among low-income groups and minorities, who tend to be Democratic voters. The usual Democratic technique is to conduct blanket registration drives in favorable areas. Republicans, whose core supporters are much more likely to be registered, have in the past generally eschewed this activity.

Spurred by the increased turnout in 1982, which benefited the Democrats, however, the Republican National Committee and the Reagan-Bush campaign committee embarked in 1984 on a $10 million high-tech effort to find and register likely Republican voters. Because they lack the solid group support that Democrats have in many areas, Republicans would not benefit from the blanket drives conducted by their opponents. Instead, the Republicans used what data-processing professionals call "merge and purge" to create lists of individuals to contact. In Colorado, for example, direct mail consultants matched the names of 2.2 million driver's license holders against those of 1.2 million registered voters, which yielded 800,000 names of persons eighteen and over who had licenses but were unregistered. They eliminated all those living in ZIP code areas with heavy Democratic voting patterns, reducing the list to 120,000 names. These names were matched with phone numbers, which were available for 60,000 names.

A phone bank in Denver called these 60,000 households to ascertain whether the individuals had recently registered, whether they intended to vote in the 1984 election, and whether they were favorable to either

President Reagan or incumbent Republican senator William Armstrong. Those not registered but intending to vote and inclined toward the Republican candidates totaled 20,000 individuals. They received a personalized letter from the state party chairman telling them where to register. The names were then transmitted to county Republican organizations, which were to make sure the people got registered.

In states such as New Mexico and Florida human intervention was eliminated. Computer-dialed phone calls, when answered, activated a tape recorded message asking the respondents whether they were registered and whether they favored President Reagan.[27] Such reliance on modern-day technology is expensive, and the Republicans invested as much as $7 for each new voter registered.

After a registration and GOTV program that produced more new voters than the Democrats' efforts in 1984, the Republicans in 1986 increased their GOTV activities, making eleven million calls in twenty-five states that had important midterm contests and sending out twelve million pieces of mail. About half of all those contacted, who were identified as favorable or persuadable, received an election week taped phone message from President Reagan, urging them to vote.[28]

A final GOTV technique perfected by the Republicans through the 1980s was efficient use of absentee ballot programs, particularly in states with large numbers of retired people and military personnel. In 1988 the Republican National Committee spent $5 million informing voters about how to cast absentee ballots in states such as California, Florida, and Texas. On election night two Florida Republicans, Senate challenger Connie Mack and House challenger Craig James, appeared to have lost. When the absentee ballots were counted, however, both emerged as narrow victors.[29]

## The Remnants of Old-Style GOTV

Blanket pulls by telephone and door-to-door canvassing, which might bring out the opposition's supporters, can be done only in the most solidly partisan localities, particularly those with a history of low turnout. In the current era of split-ticket voting and mostly heterogeneous neighborhoods, heavily black districts most often fit this description. As the one easily identifiable group that still tends to be geographically concentrated and overwhelmingly Democratic, it merits special attention from Democratic candidates on election day. The orchestrator of the field operation in one urban congressional district said, "We worked the black districts down to the bone." Another Democratic strategist noted that "you don't have to persuade black voters to vote for you; you just have to persuade them to vote at all."

The "graveyard vote" and other forms of election day corruption from the party machine era are generally a thing of the past, disappearing in the wake of a more educated and affluent electorate and stricter reporting of campaign expenditures. Election day workers are still often paid sums ranging from $5 to $100, but in the words of one field organizer, "Every bit of it has receipts and Social Security numbers." Although widespread corruption has stopped, pockets continue, particularly in the old machine-dominated cities such as New York, Philadelphia, and Chicago and in the rural South and Midwest.

Urban corruption most often takes the form of "graveyard registration" and encouragement of voting by illegal aliens, while rural areas see the theft or illegal purchase of absentee ballots and "vote buying." [30] A campaign worker for a local politician in Hudson County, New Jersey, recounted his trips to the county administration building: "I used to read the names of the people who turned in absentee ballots. A typical case was Mayor X's mother who turned in four ballots. This is quite an accomplishment for someone who died in 1979." Another participant in a southern campaign that attracted a large poor and rural vote described the election day GOTV effort there:

> It depends on paying off the right people at the right time with the right credibility in the right neighborhoods. A lot of bad things happen on election day, which we didn't get into too much. We paid off what we thought were the right people and let it lie. We didn't really have a strong election day operation, just a set of people we thought we could depend on.

Because of the dissimilar constituencies of the two major parties, blanket pulls and the use of groups outside the campaign to do GOTV activities are phenomena almost entirely associated with Democratic campaigns. The Republican party has not had identifiable groups who could play the role that labor unions and others have played for the Democrats, except for the white religious fundamentalists and organizations such as the right-to-life movement of recent years. As a general rule, the core Republican vote is better educated, more politically aware, and more likely to turn out on election day anyway. One Democratic strategist said: "Phones are a much more important tool for Democratic candidates than Republicans. What is the real return for Republicans? Their vote is going to come out anyway. Democrats are the ones who need to mobilize."

Republican strategists accept this assessment of their core vote, but as the minority party in most areas, the core party vote is not enough to produce victory. Republican victories often depend upon carefully identifying and bringing out independents and "persuadable" Democrats. Republican consultant David Murray explained:

If you're a Republican, the independent voter is the prize. The problem with them is they're the most difficult voters to bring out. The Democrats physically deliver their votes, working with unions and their party organizations and municipal and county employees. Republicans don't have it.

Precise and extensive targeting is crucial. Former National Republican Senatorial Committee executive director Mitch Daniels gave this colorful analogy: "It's like the U.S.-Soviet strategic balance. The Democrats have throw weight, so we have to have accuracy. They have quantity; we have to have technical advantage." A staffer at the National Republican Congressional Committee elaborated:

> The Republican party—Republican institutions—have perfected certain things over the years—small-giver fund-raising; candidate improvement and training; the whole range of direct candidate services. The Democratic side has perfected turnout.
> I don't know if that's directly the Democratic party institutions; it's more prevalent in institutions such as labor. But clearly their forte is mobilizing bodies in the last three weeks.... That is the mandate for our party.[31]

This line of thinking among Republicans has brought about the voter registration activities described earlier in this chapter. And as a Texas GOP strategist observed:

> We are not going to pay $5 for every new Republican and then let that person stay at home on election day. We are going to check those names against our computers all day ... and if some guy hasn't shown up by 6:00 p.m., we'll carry him to the polls.[32]

Election day, the day of decision, finally arrives. In the year or more preceding it, candidates have decided to run and have sought the informational and financial resources they need for the race. Within the constraints imposed by their individual beliefs and their constituencies, they have framed the arguments that constitute a case for their election and have tried to present them to the public as effectively as possible. They have made every effort to get their supporters to the polls. If they neglect these tasks or do not do them as well as their opponents, they will probably fail in the voting booth as well. If they carry out these functions, they will probably win. In the next chapter we look at how these lessons have played out in a variety of campaigns.

# Notes

1. See the data in Stuart Rothenberg, *Winners and Losers* (Washington, D.C.: Free Congress Research and Education Foundation, 1983), 54-58.
2. Stimson Bullitt, *To Be a Politician* (Garden City, N.Y.: Doubleday, 1961), 90.
3. Robert Caro, *The Years of Lyndon Johnson: The Path to Power* (New York: Knopf, 1982), 644.
4. Larry Sabato, "Parties, PACs and Independent Groups," in *The American Elections of 1982*, ed. Thomas E. Mann and Norman J. Ornstein (Washington, D.C.: American Enterprise Institute, 1983), 106 n.
5. PAC data from presentation by Larry Sabato at the Roundtable on Congressional Recruitment, annual meeting of the *American Political Science Association*, Washington, D.C., August 29, 1986; Richard Cheney, "The Law's Impact on Presidential and Congressional Election Campaigns," in *Parties, Interest Groups and Campaign Finance Laws*, ed. Michael J. Malbin (Washington, D.C.: American Enterprise Institute, 1980), 252.
6. *New York Times*, November 4, 1986; *New York Post*, September 11, 1986; *Baltimore Sun*, October 31, 1986.
7. "*C & E* Interview with Lance Tarrance, Bill Hamilton, Adam Goodman and Randy Thompson," *Campaigns and Elections* 7 (January-February 1987): 29.
8. Jerry Hagstrom and Robert Guskind, "Calling the Races," *National Journal*, July 30, 1988, 1972-1976.
9. *Congressional Quarterly Weekly Report*, December 7, 1985, 2560; December 19, 1987, 3145; *Portland Press-Herald*, October 17, 1986.
10. *Philadelphia Inquirer*, November 6, 1986.
11. Jon F. Hale, "The Scribes of Texas: Newspaper Coverage of the 1984 U.S. Senate Campaign," paper presented at the Dwight Griswold-E. C. Ames Conference on Mass Media and Congressional Elections, Nebraska Wesleyan University, Lincoln, Nebraska, March 7-8, 1986, 19.
12. Michael J. Robinson and Margaret Sheehan, *Over the Wire and on TV* (New York: Russell Sage, 1983), 49; Maura Clancey and Michael J. Robinson, "General Election Coverage: Part I," *Public Opinion* 7 (December-January 1985): 49-54; 1988 data gathered by John Merriam of the Conference on Issues and Media and reported in *USA Today*, April 22, 1988, 1.
13. Peter Clarke and Susan H. Evans, *Covering Campaigns: Journalism in Congressional Elections* (Stanford, Calif.: Stanford University Press, 1983), 39-41.
14. Thomas E. Patterson and Robert D. McClure, *The Unseeing Eye: The Myth of Television Power in National Politics* (New York: Putnam, 1976), chapter 6; Marian Just et al., "Thirty Seconds or Thirty Minutes: Political Learning in an Election," paper presented at the annual meeting of the Midwest Political Science Association, Chicago, Illinois, April 9-11, 1987.
15. *New York Times*, November 1, 1982, B1.
16. *Denver Post*, October 10, 1986.
17. *Los Angeles Times*, October 25, 1986, 33.
18. Rothenberg, *Winners and Losers*, 89.
19. Harold Gosnell, *Machine Politics: Chicago Model*, 2d ed. (Chicago: University of Chicago Press, 1968), 81.
20. Gerald H. Kramer, "The Effects of Precinct-Level Canvassing on Voter Behavior," *Public Opinion Quarterly* 35 (Winter 1970-1971): 572.
21. John C. Blydenburgh, "A Controlled Experiment to Measure the Effect of

Personal Contact Campaigning," *Midwest Journal of Political Science* 15 (May 1971): 381.

22. William C. Adams and Dennis J. Smith, "Effects of Telephone Canvassing on Turnout and Preference: A Field Experiment," *Public Opinion Quarterly* 44 (Fall 1980): 389-395.

23. Blydenburgh, "A Controlled Experiment," passim.

24. Rothenberg, *Winners and Losers,* 85-86.

25. *Charlotte Observer,* October 14, 1986.

26. Thomas Herrity and John D. Brady, "Saving Money with a PC," *Campaigns and Elections* 8 (March-April 1988): 53-56.

27. For a full description of the program, see T. B. Edsall and Haynes Johnson, "The GOP's Search for Voters," *Washington Post National Weekly Edition,* May 7, 1984, 9-10.

28. See the *Washington Post,* October 6, 1986; Larry J. Sabato, *The Party's Just Begun* (Glenview, Ill.: Scott, Foresman, 1988), 83.

29. Charles R. Babcock, "Getting Out the Vote Using Those Who Stay at Home," *Washington Post National Weekly Edition,* December 5-11, 1988, 13.

30. Robert Goldberg, "Electoral Fraud—An American Vice," in *Elections American Style,* ed. A. James Reichley (Washington, D.C.: Brookings Institution, 1987), 185.

31. *New York Times,* November 7, 1982, B3.

32. Ibid.

# Campaigns in Context    9

*Political campaigns are a lot like bridge; they depend on the cards you were dealt and the way you play the hand.*

Jeff Greenfield[1]

In the preceding five chapters we looked at how incumbents and challengers organize their races and find the money to finance them, acquire the necessary information about their constituents, decide on campaign themes, get the themes out through paid and free media, respond to charges against them, and mobilize their supporters to vote. We described the hurdles they face at each step of their campaigns and considered some of the factors that determine whether the difficulties will be surmounted.

In this chapter we look at how a variety of candidates put it all together—or failed to do so. Each example illustrates some of the points we discussed and shows how the various elements of a campaign interact to produce success or failure. Because the office sought is, next to incumbency, the most significant element in determining campaign strategy, we will look in turn at campaigns that illuminate House, senatorial, and gubernatorial races.

## A House Race

With the number of voluntary House retirements dwindling and with more than nine in ten incumbents successfully reelected in recent election cycles, House challengers have the smallest statistical chance of victory of all challengers for political office. In 1986, when political hopefuls looked at the few targets of opportunity among House seats, one object of interest to Democrats was New Jersey's Twelfth District, represented by Republican Jim Courter.

Although the four-term incumbent had won by large margins in his previous three outings, the Democrats had some reason for hope. After the 1980 census, because of partisan disputes over redistricting that eventually required court intervention, Courter's district had been redrawn twice, in 1982 and again in 1984. Both times he found himself with a majority of new constituents whom he had not previously represented.

The Republicans seemed to have a clear edge in all the redistricting plans, but each one introduced more Democratic areas into the Twelfth District. In the presidential contest Democrat Walter Mondale was able to win 44 percent of the district's vote in 1984, five points better than his statewide showing. Despite facing underfinanced and unknown opponents, Courter dropped seven points in the vote between 1980 and 1984, although his margins remained very healthy. A top Courter staffer, Merrick Carey, recalled, "We used to joke that a millionaire Democrat could do a lot of damage."

It was widely believed that Courter had aspirations for higher office. From the Democrats' point of view, the Twelfth was worth investing in even if Courter could not be defeated. His future political position could be weakened by a brush with defeat, and he could be forced to spend large amounts that might otherwise be put away for a future statewide race. What the Democrats needed was a classic strong challenger: someone with political experience, recognition, and a fundraising and organizational base. They came up with Middlesex County freeholder David B. Crabiel.

## The Democratic Challenger

On paper, Crabiel filled the bill. The owner of five funeral homes in the district, all bearing his name, he had held local office continuously since 1961 and was serving his third term on the county governing body. His brother had been a powerful figure in the state senate. The Middlesex County Democratic party was one of the few remaining robust county political machines that had access to important contribution sources. With help from the staff of Sen. Frank Lautenberg, who saw Courter as a potential opponent, the Crabiel campaign engaged Hickman-Maslin, a first-tier national Democratic polling firm, and several local media and direct mail consultants who had impressive records in past state contests.

The first Hickman-Maslin poll showed that 40 percent of Courter's constituents did not know enough about their representative to rate him favorably or unfavorably. Only 39 percent said that he definitely deserved to be reelected, rather than giving a new person a chance, or that they were undecided. Courter had spent most of his time in the House concentrating on foreign policy issues and was a leading supporter of President Reagan's policies on the Nicaraguan contras and on "Star Wars" (the Strategic Defense Initiative, or SDI). Both positions were unpopular with his constituents. All these factors led the Democratic Congressional Campaign Committee to designate the Twelfth a targeted district, and Crabiel was eventually able to raise well over $300,000—about three-quarters of what incumbent Courter had spent in 1984 and more than triple the war chest of his previous opponent. Staffer Carey remembered the Courter campaign's concern when Crabiel's first fund-raising report was released: "He was raising serious money."

On election day David Crabiel got 37 percent of the vote, about two points more than any other Courter opponent since 1980 but a small payoff for such a large investment of money and talent. The district's Republican leanings and the incumbent's textbook high-tech campaign surely played a role in this disappointing showing, but the Crabiel campaign made almost every mistake a congressional challenger could.

The first error, which led to many others, was the candidate's insistence on strong personal involvement in every phase of the campaign. A despairing staff member observed, "The candidate was obsessed with his own concepts of what was important and wanted to keep every aspect of the campaign (even those he couldn't understand) under his thumb."

Not only was this micromanagement a drain on the candidate's time, but it quickly became clear that Crabiel did not understand the difference between the disappearing traditional political style of his Middlesex County base (which was only a fraction of the district) and that of the Republican or independent-leaning well-to-do suburbs that made up the majority of the Twelfth District. A staff member described the situation:

> Crabiel, a veteran of nearly thirty years of local and county campaigns, didn't have the first clue about how to go about organizing his effort. His orientation was extremely provincial—limited to the Middlesex County machine way of doing things. ... He could not understand the basic difference between how things operate in Middlesex County and how they operate in areas where Democrats are not dominant and no machine exists.

As a result there were constant clashes between the candidate and the professionals he had engaged. His manager did not get access to the poll results until a week after Crabiel received them. When his fund raiser signed up Sen. Joseph Biden, then a Democratic presidential contender, for a fund-raising luncheon, Crabiel decreed that the planned $100 to $150 ticket price be cut to $35—in line with the price of county events. The candidate also canceled two summer fund-raising events, saying everyone he knew went on vacation then. He invested $1,000 a month in a station wagon bearing a large roof sign with his name. He said it would improve his recognition in the district. A staffer reported, "He thought I was out of my mind when I suggested the money would be better used on radio."

There were also disputes about how to use the funds that were available in the early fall. Crabiel decided polls were too expensive, commenting: "The best poll in the world is the one the candidate takes himself. I don't believe in 'em anyway, and neither does [the Middlesex County party chair]." Instead, he added a San Francisco trolley-type bus to his motorized fleet. The campaign's staff and "free" resources were not used effectively. Crabiel refused to speak to the Democratic Congressional Campaign Committee operatives who arrived from Washington, telling everyone they were spies. The press secretary was ordered to produce no more than one press release each week, for fear of boring the media, and the releases were not to include any controversial issues, such as Courter's foreign policy positions, because Crabiel believed "people don't want to hear that stuff."

Crabiel could not imagine what his campaign manager might be doing in the office in his absence and insisted that the manager accompany him everywhere. Since the candidate had as little comprehension of targeting techniques as he did of polls, his extensive door-to-door canvassing in the campaign bus and station wagon took him to every railroad station or shopping center, even to those in the heart of "enemy territory," rather than to chosen swing locations. Another staffer remembered that the candidate, "obsessed with his 'insights,' was a nightmare to try to control."

## The Incumbent's Response

By mid-October, despite the chaos of the Crabiel campaign and the absence of any polling information, there was reason to believe that the incumbent was concerned. Courter had begun to respond to some of Crabiel's attacks. The Courter campaign had done an October poll, which showed the challenger still far behind, but the incumbent's vote had dropped below 50 percent and the number of undecided voters had increased. There was real concern that "Crabiel could break 40 percent or even better."

Courter began a number of coordinated responses to the challenger's criticisms. On letterhead almost identical to official House stationery, he wrote his constituents, saying, "Let me take just a minute of your time to review my record in Congress." After noting that "over my eight years in Congress I have voted to restrain federal spending and to eliminate waste," the candidate underlined his votes to "increase funding to accelerate the clean up of New Jersey's toxic waste sites" and his position of "consistently opposing cuts in social security benefits." The only reference to his concentration on defense issues was a note at the end that he had "fought for New Jersey's fair share of the defense budget."

Courter's letter was quickly followed by a direct mail piece from the popular incumbent Republican governor. Designed to look like a telegram, it denied the Crabiel campaign's charges that Courter would cut Social Security and pointed up his opposition to wasteful defense spending and support for environmental programs. Courter also revised his radio ads. After airing endorsements from representatives of classic Democratic constituency groups such as labor unions, he saturated the airwaves with constituent testimonials to his effectiveness at cleaning up a local toxic waste dump, a major district concern.

By this time the Crabiel forces had inadequate money to respond to Courter. During the last five weeks of the campaign, Crabiel was able to send out only three mailings, compared to five Courter mailings in the last two weeks. On election day Courter emerged $700,000 poorer but virtually unscathed. By 1988 he was an all-but-announced 1989 gubernatorial candidate.

## Lessons of the Campaign

The Crabiel campaign illustrates, first, that naive congressional candidates need the help of experienced consultants and, second, that they often ignore the consultants they hire. Moving beyond his base into a different kind of constituency, the candidate needed to change his technique. Crabiel was the product of one of the few old-style county machine organizations that, within narrow geographic confines, can conduct a campaign based on indiscriminate mobilization of an assured partisan vote. In the House race he was running in a district populated by large numbers of independent voters more swayed by issues and candidate images than by party loyalty. With limits to money and time, he needed to identify swing areas to add to his base, reserve his own energy and time for those areas and for fund raising, flood the targeted areas with radio advertising and direct mail, stick to the issues identified as powerful in his early polling, mobilize groups attracted by those issues, and let his expensive consultants run his campaign as long as it was consistent with his beliefs about basic thematic strategy rather than tactics. In other words he needed to organize a campaign similar in design to that of his opponent.

Instead, Crabiel exemplified the difference between media-savvy House candidates such as Courter and those described by consultant Michael Murphy: "People win for sewer commissioner because they mailed out 25,000 potholders. They think the way to win for Congress is to mail out 50,000 potholders." [2]

# A Senate Contest

Candidates for a statewide legislative office must perform the same things that House contestants accomplish, but with a larger and more complex constituency their efforts are correspondingly greater and more intricate. The successful 1986 Georgia Senate race of Democratic representative Wyche Fowler, who defeated freshman Republican senator Mack Mattingly, illustrates several themes: (1) preparation for a race early enough, (2) emphasis on those aspects of one's image that fit best with a new and broader constituency, and (3) use of the greater availability and credibility of the press coverage available in statewide races. It also shows the different partisan styles and strategies that characterize many Republican and Democratic races for Senate seats.

## Early Days of the Campaign and the Primary

Fowler began planning for his contest with Mattingly at least two years before election day. He had entered the House in a 1977 special election to replace newly named UN ambassador Andrew Young—the first time a white had replaced a black in a congressional election since 1900.[3] By 1982 his district had a majority of black registered voters. With pressure on him to step aside and permit a black to represent the district, Fowler saw the opportunity to move up to the Senate in 1986.

Fowler had several unusual assets for a challenger when he began his preparations. As a member of the tax-writing House Ways and Means Committee, he had good access to PAC money (which made up 42 percent of his 1984 campaign expenditures) for financing his early campaign requirements. In February 1986 he bought a two-week flight of advertising to build statewide recognition. Serving an Atlanta district, he had established good relations with the Atlanta *Journal* and *Constitution*, the largest newspapers in the state, and he had access to the television market that reaches about 60 percent of Georgia's general-election voters. All these considerations helped him establish good recognition levels for a challenger. Furthermore, as Atlanta's hometown candidate, he could expect somewhat earlier and heavier major media coverage than many Senate challengers receive.

Mattingly was a less imposing incumbent than many others running that year. Formerly a sales representative for IBM in his native Indiana, he had been Georgia state Republican chairman but had never previously run for office. He was widely viewed as a surprise winner, who squeaked by in the 1980 Reagan landslide, helped by several scandals surrounding Democratic incumbent Herman Talmadge. Mattingly could have done more during his first term to solidify his position in Georgia. He had built a good reputation among other Senate Republicans as manager of Alaska senator Ted Stevens's almost successful candidacy for majority leader and as President Reagan's point man in the fight against the legislative veto. But he had never visited several Georgia counties, and his 1980 victory resulted from a particularly strong showing in metropolitan Atlanta, his 1986 opponent's home turf. When the campaign season opened, polls indicated that although Mattingly had a high positive job rating, a full one-third of the electorate knew little or nothing specific about him.[4]

Poised against these factors were a number of less positive ones for Fowler. The first was the historic disinclination of Georgians to vote for a "national" (that is, liberal-leaning) Democratic Senate candidate. The state's revered senior senator, Sam Nunn, was firmly in the conservative mold of Georgia senators. (In 1986 Nunn had the eighth highest support score for President Reagan among all Democratic senators.)

Fowler's image as an urban liberal was reinforced early in the campaign season by his Democratic primary opponent, Hamilton Jordan. Jordan, former chief of staff to President Jimmy Carter, positioned himself as the moderate-to-conservative "courthouse crowd" alternative to the congressman from the big city. The "Sam and Ham" buttons that sprouted among his supporters symbolized Jordan's identification with Nunn and the conservative Democratic establishment. The credible primary challenge from Jordan (and from two other candidates) meant that Fowler had to spend heavily and stay somewhat to the left of the field to keep his voting base during the primary. There was a danger, too, that failing a majority in the August 12 primary, a runoff election would be held barely a month before the general election. A runoff would further deplete Fowler's resources and leave him more to the left than he wanted to be.

Mattingly had the Republican field to himself and could concentrate on building up his local reputation. To do so, he began running his television commercials almost continuously in January 1986. Mattingly could afford this much early exposure because by the end of 1985 he had raised $1.74 million, about three times as much as Fowler had raised.

Fowler had a stroke of luck when the primary candidate politically closest to him withdrew, setting up essentially a two-person race between himself and Jordan. The spirited contest for Fowler's seat in the House brought a high turnout in his old congressional district and was a boon for him. Working against Jordan was his late start and lack of money to buy television in the Atlanta market. Fowler won 50.2 percent of the primary vote, thus barely avoiding a runoff. This victory brought him much publicity and positive recognition fewer than three months before the general election.

The challenger was still decidedly an underdog, however. Mattingly was able to sap Fowler's momentum with a heavy negative advertising campaign immediately after the primary. It characterized Fowler as a "big spender" and, like many Republican Senate campaigns that year, focused on Fowler's poor attendance record while he was campaigning for the primary, encapsulated in the slogan, "Fowler— Absent for Georgia." Fowler did not have the money to respond to these charges, leaving the impression they might be true.

## The Challenger Pulls Ahead

Through mid-October the challenger languished in the polls, consistently about sixteen to eighteen points behind Mattingly. The local media agreed with the assessment in the *New York Times* on September 30 that Fowler had "little chance to win unless he can somehow get off the defensive." On October 13 the *Atlanta Constitution* observed, "The Republicans have controlled the dialogue ... giving a classic example of their highly developed skills in re-electing shaky incumbents." The "smart money" in Washington also appeared to agree with the gleeful assessment of Reagan-Bush consultant Lee Atwater, "I don't think Senator Mattingly could have had a better opponent from political central casting."[5] By early October the Democratic Senate Campaign Committee, which had "maxed out" for challenger John Breaux in Louisiana and had contributed 62 percent of the maximum to Alabama challenger Richard Shelby, had given only $175,000 (44 percent of the maximum) to Fowler. Mattingly, by this time, had received virtually his full allotment from the Republican Senate Campaign Committee.

Fowler, however, had a plan and stuck to it. Recognizing that he could never match Mattingly's expenditures, he reserved most of his media buys for the last few weeks of the campaign. He spent September and October solidifying his position with the Georgia Democratic establishment. Like other southern Democratic politicians, the Georgia courthouse crowd—led by the governor, the lieutenant governor, state House Speaker Tom Murphy, and Senator Nunn—had recently become cooperative, a receptivity that stemmed from their fear of further Republican gains at the local level. The possibility that a Fowler victory would help the Democrats regain control of the Senate in 1986 was also of some local interest, since Democratic control would make Senator Nunn chairman of the Armed Services Committee.

Fowler began his public courtship of the courthouse Democrats with a "podium-pounding, Bible-quoting" speech to the state party convention in late September.[6] It was not long before many of these formerly suspicious Democrats were talking like the county commissioner who, referring to his local state legislator, observed, "If Charlie says Fowler ain't got horns, then he must be okay."[7] The strong endorsement of Senator Nunn, who had previously kept his distance from nominal fellow partisans, was particularly important in gaining Fowler credibility among these voters.

The Atlanta representative spent much of the fall crisscrossing the state's rural hamlets. His television advertising, which began in earnest in mid-October, further conveyed to the public that Fowler was "just folks" and shared their values, while Mattingly did not. In one spot Fowler was pictured with a Georgia mule; in another he appeared relaxing in his mother's backyard, playing with some puppies. While his mother sat nearby, he told viewers:

> I'm Wyche Fowler—the guy Mack Mattingly's been attacking with his millions in slick ads. If half the stuff he claims was true, my momma wouldn't let me come home for Sunday dinner. The choice is yours—a proven, effective partner you can get to and talk to and trust or a senator you'll never see except on TV. Hey, I may not be perfect, but in this race I'm definitely the pick of the litter.

Fowler's advertising messages were consistently predicated on the benchmark poll finding in the fall of 1985 that showed Georgians' strong preference for a senator "representing the average person."[8] Even the early winter spot designed to familiarize voters with his unusual first name implicitly spoke to traditional values, as a teacher and school children repeated, "Wy*che*—like in chur*ch*."

## Pressure on the Incumbent

Meanwhile, Mattingly continued to spend most of his time in Washington, while his consultants held press conferences in Georgia to preview his new television ads. With Mattingly refusing to debate his opponent, television stations were reduced to showing a debate between the candidates' media consultants. Mattingly's presence only in his paid advertising led to criticism from the press, which characterized him as the "electronic senator" and the "Max Headroom of Georgia politics." Such coverage played into Fowler's advertising and his oft-repeated theme in personal appearances, "We're having an election; we're not having an auction." On October 15 the *Constitution's* premier political columnist scathingly wrote, "When Joe Louis said you can run but you can't hide, he obviously had never met Mack Mattingly."

Pressure grew on Mattingly to reverse his decision not to debate the challenger, and he finally agreed to do so on October 20. The delay, coupled with the crescendo of negative press coverage, made the debate of extraordinary public interest, doubtless much greater than earlier or more frequent encounters between the opponents might have been. In a tone reminiscent of the "Rocky" films, the media dramatically described the debate as Fowler's last chance to get "momentum for a campaign that is far behind in the polls." [9] Aired mostly on public television stations, the debate drew a larger audience in Georgia than any of the national network offerings that evening. An independent estimate put the audience size at 60 percent of the state's viewers.[10]

As both sides had respectively hoped and feared, the debate worked strongly to the advantage of the challenger. Follow-up polls immediately after the debate showed Mattingly's lead cut in half. Fowler then poured his remaining resources into a variety of messages further portraying him as the candidate of ordinary Georgians and Mattingly as the creation of out-of-state consultants and national party bureaucrats.

On October 28 the challenger ran a one-hour call-in show, broadcast over ninety radio stations. On "Wyche Fowler Listens to Georgians" he chatted amiably with callers and even sang the gospel tune, "Farther Along." The call-in format was repeated every weekday until the election. Positive advertising continued to stress Fowler's down-home roots. Contrapuntal negative advertising attacked various Senate votes cast by Mattingly and continued to distance Mattingly from the image of a senator "representing the average person" that polls showed Georgians desired. A Fowler ad listing big out-of-state corporations that paid no taxes and contributed to the Mattingly campaign ended with the tag line: "Senator Mattingly votes against Georgia. He votes against us."

On October 30 the Sunday *Atlanta Journal-Constitution* banner-headlined the results of a final poll, "Fowler, Mattingly in Dead Heat." On election day Wyche Fowler eked out a 51 percent victory, carrying both metropolitan Atlanta and rural congressional districts in south Georgia. He won the votes of a majority of blue-collar workers, about 25 percent of 1984 Reagan supporters, and about 80 percent of the black vote and 40 percent of the white vote. This was a strong showing for a political figure whose record indeed revealed him to be the relatively liberal "national Democrat" portrayed by the opposition.[11]

## Lessons of the Georgia Race

What can we learn from this Georgia challenger victory? First, Fowler benefited greatly from his experience in the House. He could use the two years before the election that normally would have been devoted to his House campaign to organize and raise the seed money for his Senate effort. His position on the Ways and Means Committee gave him unusually early access for a challenger to PAC money. At the same time, Fowler's opponent did not use his Senate term to solidify his image or to build a personal organization.

Second, Fowler was able to gain greater coverage by important state media organs than any House challenger could hope for—and more than most Senate challengers, particularly those being outspent more than two to one as he was. His contest had an unusually large number of the characteristics that draw reporters' interest. He was already well known to journalists in Georgia's largest media market. His opponent made the kinds of tactical errors that excite political reporters. And the Georgia Senate race was important in that year's major political story—whether the Democrats could recapture control of the Senate by blunting Republican gains in the South.

Third, this race demonstrates that national issues play a greater role in Senate campaigns than they do in House campaigns. It also exemplifies the adage of former House Speaker Tip O'Neill: "All politics is local." In 1980 Mattingly was swept in by a combination of the shortcomings of the incumbent and the powerful national trends that were working in the Republicans' favor. In 1986 he lost because the Republican national message was less convincing, and, in midterm races, when there are no presidential candidates to articulate national concerns, local issues loom larger. Mattingly's more charismatic opponent was also able to redraw his image, skillfully emphasizing his Georgia roots and making the Indiana-born Mattingly rather than himself the candidate of alien national or external forces. Finally, to the extent that coattails still matter, Fowler did not have to contend with Ronald Reagan at the top of the ticket. Instead, heading it was a popular Democratic governor who captured 71 percent of the vote in his contest.

The 1986 Georgia race is a microcosm of the various recruitment, thematic, and campaigning strategies of Republicans and Democrats in recent years. Many Republican hopefuls are, like Mattingly, relatively inexperienced and are helped to their first victories by their party's national message and financial and organizational resources. Many

Democrats are, like Fowler, veterans of state and local office, who must depend more heavily on the residual psychological identification of voters with their party, the remnants of its local organizational base, and the support of traditional constituency groups.

# Gubernatorial Races in Two States

Recent gubernatorial races in Texas and New Jersey illustrate some of the similarities and differences between these contests and Senate matches. Gubernatorial candidates must also build recognition, raise money, and deal with time constraints; however, they must offer different themes, emphasize different issues, and raise money from other sources. These elections also illustrate some differences between hard-fought and low-key contests.

## Texas

In the 1986 Texas gubernatorial race Democratic incumbent Mark White lost to his challenger, former Republican governor Bill Clements, 48 percent to 52 percent. This election was a rematch of the 1982 contest in which White turned Clements out of office by a similar margin. Both races revolved around the same themes: the incumbent's leadership and competence in dealing with major state issues while in office. Both illustrate the fund-raising problems that even strong challengers have.

Although Texas's oil-based economy would not collapse for another few years, the 1982 White campaign was still able to play on the theme, in the midst of the worst national recession in fifty years, that incumbent Clements shared the Republican disdain for the "little guy." White's strategist, David Doak, described the campaign's strategy:

> We wanted to run Clements as the candidate of the rich, a guy who constantly sided with the rich against the average guy—not the poor, the hungry, the disadvantaged, but *everyone*. We wanted to drive a wedge in the electorate between the rich and everybody else. Clements was rich personally; his negatives fit that mold. He was a big oil man. His biggest single negative in the polls was a big oil spill where he had sided with the big oil companies against the environment, against Texans.

The issue that best conveyed White's theme was an attack on utility rates, which had risen dramatically during Clements's term in office. Polls showed that this charge was very effective; however, getting the message out to the public, which was spread among almost thirty media markets, was not easy. Despite raising more than $7 million, White was being outspent by the wealthy Clements almost two to one. White chose to conserve his money for the end of the race, hoping that press coverage would keep him in contention. David Doak explained:

> The strategy of the campaign was to fight a holding action until the last three weeks. We couldn't match Clements's money.... We made the strategic decision to try to keep the race on hold until the last three weeks when we could match him dollar for dollar.... One of the keys to that was trapping Clements into a series of debates.... The most important part was the debates would give the press something to focus on in that intervening period while we saved our money up; something to focus on other than Clements's paid media.

The underfunded Democratic challenger narrowly defeated the wealthy Republican incumbent on election day. White's slender victory was attributed to voter distaste for Clements's arrogance, the challenger's populist appeal, and the unity of Democratic officeholders brought by a rising local Republican threat.[12]

**A Rematch.** The tables were turned on White in 1986, when he was the incumbent with a record to defend. On the surface it appeared that the now-crippled Texas economy, victimized by the "oil bust," would be his major problem. Because of the loss of oil revenues, the state had been forced to raise taxes midway through White's term. In 1984, aware of the effect this could have on his reelection contest two years away, White moved to frame the issue in an extensive four-week statewide advertising campaign. The ads featured the governor telling Texans:

> When I ran for governor, I made a promise to you and to myself: To give Texas first-class schools. To raise teacher pay and to toughen academic standards. But that costs money. We had to raise taxes on things like liquor, cigarettes, and beer. I had hoped we could avoid raising taxes. But times changed, and the economic slowdown and the drop in oil prices forced me to choose between keeping down taxes or helping our kids. The legislators and I made a decision. Our kids come first.

To a substantial extent, this strategy worked. Polls shortly before the 1986 election showed that favorable attitudes toward White's educational policies were the dominant factor in shaping voter choices and that the tax increase was a relatively minor concern.[13]

In his second race for the governorship, White, as the incumbent, had no problems raising the money to get his message across. By the end of September, he had already raised more than he did in his entire 1982 campaign. White's fund raising was outpacing his challenger's four to three, and he was gaining his biggest comparative advantage from donors doing business with the state—among them, developers, bankers, highway contractors, and beer distributors. Moreover, White's campaign was essentially debt-free, while the wealthy Clements had already lent his campaign more than a million and a half dollars.[14]

Another difference between the 1982 and 1986 campaigns was that in 1982 voters had traded a well-known quantity—Clements—for a largely unknown one—White. Although White had served four years as the state's elected attorney general and had spent more than a million dollars to win the contested 1982 gubernatorial primary, his statewide recognition level after the primary was only 50 percent. Discussing the 1982 campaign, strategist Doak observed: "Mark never had a big negative. He was not well known; not many people knew much about him."

But in 1986 voters were judging the state's two most recent governors against each other, as both campaigns were aware when they framed their strategies. Consultant Harris Diamond of the White campaign noted that a major component of White's message was "let the voters of Texas remember why they didn't vote for Bill Clements the last time." A spokesman for Clements made a similar argument: "We're saying both men have been governors, they both have records, and let's compare their records."[15]

Polls confirmed the high level of information voters had received about both candidates and their past performances in office. In a Gallup poll the weekend before the election, more than three-quarters of each candidate's supporters said they had decided which candidate they would support more than a year before. Only one-sixth said they had seriously considered the other candidate. The close 1986 race would turn on the relatively few voters who were still undecided about which candidate had a superior record in office. The 1982 election was a referendum on one candidate's performance; the 1986 election was a comparison between them. The candidates' personal attributes and their records in office were, after education, the reasons most frequently given by voters for supporting or opposing either of them.[16]

If voters were generally supportive of White's education initiatives and were not unduly disturbed about the tax increases during his term, why did he lose narrowly in 1986 rather than winning narrowly as he had in 1982? The answer lies with the relatively small number of populist-leaning swing voters who had responded to White's appeal in 1982. In 1982 these swing voters had considered the utility rate increases the epitome of "establishment" arrogance. In 1986 that arrogance was symbolized by one of the education reforms: "No pass, no play." White had banned high school athletes with poor academic records from engaging in team sports for a six-week grading period. He resisted suggestions that the suspension period be cut to three weeks. In rural

Texas, where high school football is practically a religion, this policy was unpopular. A second White initiative—a mandatory seat-belt law—generated a similar reaction from the same voters.

The major difference between the patterns of the two elections was that Clements carried the rural vote two to one in 1986, a reversal of the 1982 pattern.[17] Although in 1986 Democrats won seven other statewide offices with victories ranging from 52 to 92 percent, Republican Clements avenged his 1982 defeat.

**Comparison of Gubernatorial and Senate Races.**   A number of the similarities and differences between Senate and gubernatorial races emerge if we compare these Texas races to the 1986 Georgia Senate race. They are similar in that competitive statewide races against an incumbent almost always involve experienced challengers who have built some recognition. In such contests the candidates must convince voters at the margins. The battle is fought for the relatively few swing voters, conducted primarily over the airwaves. Even experienced challengers, however, have trouble achieving the financial wherewithal to build enough recognition to compete. Furthermore, for challengers to defeat an incumbent, it is as important for them to give voters a reason to turn out the officeholder as it is to convey their own credentials for the job.

In races for the governorship different themes emerge. Senate victories often turn on the candidates' identification and empathy with the state; executive races are more concerned with competence and leadership. Senate incumbents are judged on how well they have maintained connections with the state while participating in national politics; gubernatorial incumbents are judged more on policy performance. The dialogue in races for governorships is also about different issues. National concerns are peripheral, and idiosyncratic state issues—taxes, the state's economy, educational programs, the criminal justice system, and the like—come to the fore. Gubernatorial candidates can expect more and earlier media coverage (and scrutiny), but their contests still depend on raising enough funds to buy paid advertising. With national parties and federal PACs giving little support to gubernatorial races, candidates must turn to individuals and businesses who are objects of state regulation or beneficiaries of state contracts—or to their own resources.

# New Jersey

Like the Texas campaigns, the 1981 and 1985 gubernatorial races in New Jersey featured a candidate, Republican Thomas Kean, who figured in both of them. Aside from this similarity, the New Jersey and Texas contests were different in many ways that permit us to explore other characteristics of statewide executive contests. First, unlike either Texas race, the 1981 New Jersey competition was for an open seat; no incumbent was running. Second, in the 1985 New Jersey election an incumbent not only successfully held his seat but won a landslide victory. This election permits us to examine the dynamics of a low-key race rather than a hard-fought one. Third, like presidential elections and a few other gubernatorial contests, the New Jersey races were substantially underwritten by taxpayer dollars. The state's campaign finance law leveled the financial playing field for the candidates and kept a lid on candidate expenditures.

**An Open Seat Election.**   In 1981 New Jersey experienced its first gubernatorial election with no incumbent since 1969. This opportunity, combined with generous public financing for the primary contests, produced a field of almost twenty "serious" candidates in both parties. The primary winners on both sides were typical strong challengers. Democrat James Florio was a popular four-term U.S. representative who had run for his party's gubernatorial nomination in 1977. He had served in the state legislature before entering Congress. Republican Tom Kean had served ten years in the state assembly, rising to the leadership of the lower house before leaving to run unsuccessfully for the governorship in his party's 1977 primary.

State economic conditions, particularly unemployment, inflation, and taxes, dominated the thoughts of the electorate in 1981. In polls, voters named the economy the most important problem facing the state three times as often as any other issue.[18] Public opinion was almost evenly divided over President Reagan's recently passed tax and domestic spending cuts, and both gubernatorial candidates made the general stands of their national parties their principal platforms for this state election.[19]

Kean's campaign, directed by Roger Stone, Reagan's 1980 northeastern campaign coordinator, was a virtual replay of the president's message. Kean promised to cut business taxes and reduce the state sales tax "eventually." He argued that the resulting economic growth would produce the same state revenue or greater amounts. Florio, skeptical about this plan, argued for small, carefully targeted tax cuts.

Both candidates had some difficulty in conveying their themes to the public. In mid-September 65 percent of New Jersey voters said they knew little or nothing about Florio, 70 percent said the same about Kean, and only 26 percent believed they could cast an informed vote. More than half could not characterize either candidate as liberal, moderate, or conservative, even though about nine voters in ten could remember hearing radio or television advertisements from both candidates. About the same number could identify the names of the two party standard-bearers.

In other words, six weeks before the election, most voters had been exposed to the campaign and knew who the candidates were but not much else. A major reason for this lack of information was the spending limits that public funding placed on candidates' advertising in New Jersey's expensive media markets. The limits made it difficult for candidates to penetrate voters' consciousness in any significant way.

Throughout September and October polls showed little voter movement. Florio led Kean by six or seven points, and one-fifth of the voters were undecided. In late October, however, when voters who were still undecided were pushed to make a choice, Florio's lead dropped to four points. Among those who made their choices in the final week of October, the candidates were separated by a single point.

On the Sunday before the election the Eagleton Poll, the only organization that regularly tracked the race, contacted its undecided late-October respondents again. Interviews revealed that most of these voters were still undecided, but of those who had made a choice, twice as many chose Kean as chose Florio. The poll director commented, "There is a clear trend in Kean's direction, and perhaps a great deal of movement." [20]

The next day with more than two million votes cast, Kean defeated Florio by fewer than two thousand votes. It was the closest election in the state's history. How did Kean accomplish this come-from-behind victory in a state where registered Democrats dominated and Democrats had won six of the seven previous gubernatorial elections? His campaign, following the advice of his consultants, made better use of the limited public funds available.

After the election Florio admitted that he had modeled this race on his congressional contests: "I was conducting the gubernatorial campaign as the type of campaign a congressman can still do—a very personal thing. The coffee klatsches, the plant gates—you can't do that on a statewide basis. It's all a media campaign."

Rather than spending his limited funds primarily on television, Florio invested heavily in direct mail and in a campaign field organization. He spent his time making public appearances. Rather than hiring media consultants familiar with statewide contests, Florio employed the same company that had produced radio advertising for his congressional races. This company had never before worked in a statewide race.

Intense and intellectual, Florio appeared cold and distant in the issue-oriented commercials he directed his media consultant to produce. As the candidate himself observed later:

> The image I had—in my area, I'm regarded as independent, but in the
> state, I'm seen as a loner. If you're conscientious and hard-working,
> that's one thing. But to go beyond the pale and look driven—that's a
> negative.... I came across too intensely on TV. If you're trying to
> moderate an image of a hard-driving person, you don't put that hard-
> driving person on TV, who seems to say, "Vote for me, or else!"

Finally, despite the known volatility of an electorate that had
recently given landslide victories to statewide candidates of both parties,
Florio spent his legally limited funds evenly throughout the campaign,
and there was little money left when the race tightened at the end.

Tom Kean, on the other hand, was a Republican politician in a
predominantly Democratic state and resident of a predominantly Democratic county. He learned early the value of good polling and targeting
programs to a Republican candidate. Kean's warm, low-key, friendly
personality came over well on television, and he was comfortable with
the medium. After losing the 1977 primary, he had taken a job as a
commentator on the state's public television nightly news program.

In 1981 Kean quickly hired several of the country's premier
Republican statewide consultants. The important media consulting job
was filled by Bailey-Deardourff, then "considered [the] most prominent
Republican media firm." [21]

Studying their polling data, the Republican team saw that a theme
similar to President Reagan's emphasis on economic growth, optimism,
and state pride was the best message for a genial, moderate Republican
candidate such as Kean. Historically, New Jersey politics had been beset
with corruption and scandal. Its senior Democratic senator, Harrison
Williams, was then enmeshed in an FBI sting operation designed to
ferret out lawmakers suspected of taking bribes. Williams would soon be
forced to resign. The state also had an inferiority complex about its role
as a bedroom (and garbage dump) for neighboring Philadelphia and
New York.

But in the late 1970s New Jerseyans were cheered by the move of
several New York-based corporate headquarters and sports teams to
their state and by the resurrection of Atlantic City as a resort mecca with
legalized gambling. A sense of state pride slowly began to grow. [22]
Kean's advertising stressed the themes of economic growth and optimism. In late October, when the one-fifth of the electorate that was
undecided began to pay attention to the race, Kean, unlike Florio, had
the resources to reinforce his message repeatedly. In the final week of
the contest, he had four times as much money left to spend as did his opponent. [23] The poll data showed that late deciders who received much of
their information about the election from television swung his way and
gave him his breathtakingly narrow victory.

The Republican hopeful, unlike his opponent, had a grasp of the requirements of a statewide race. In his review of the contest Kean noted the difficulties he had with those supporters who did not understand where a gubernatorial campaign effort must place its resources:

> Party leaders complained that I wasn't going to all the party dinners and meetings.... Few felt that our plan to save our money for a final television, radio, and direct mail blitz made any sense.... My opponent was attending fourteen events a day, flying all over the state, and shaking as many hands as humanly possible.[24]

**Four Years Later.** When Kean stood for reelection in 1985, the comparisons between the New Jersey governor and President Reagan seemed to have become more pronounced. Like the president, Kean quickly found that some of the promises of supply-side economics did not pan out. Unemployment had risen to 10 percent in 1982, and the state, collecting less revenue but having greater needs after the Reagan budget cuts, faced a fiscal crisis. Furthermore, New Jersey, like most states (but unlike the federal government), was constitutionally required to balance its budget. Kean was forced to raise the state sales tax rather than lower it and to increase the state income tax as well.

Like President Reagan, Kean dealt with these unpleasant tasks early in his first term. By the time 1985 rolled around, the New Jersey economy had rebounded even more sharply than the national economy, and its unemployment rate was one of the lowest in the country. These events were reflected in periodic measurings of Kean's job approval rating. In September 1982 negative assessments of his performance outnumbered positive ones 46 percent to 39 percent. By August 1984 the figures had changed to 52 percent positive and 38 percent negative. In August 1985 the governor's positive rating had shot up to a remarkable 76 percent.[25]

Kean's impressive poll standings led his 1981 opponent, Jim Florio, to decide to wait for the 1989 governor's contest, when Kean would constitutionally be barred from a third term. The availability of public funds, however, and the example set by both Kean and Florio in converting early primary losses into subsequent nominations persuaded several credible candidates to enter the Democratic fray. The two leading contenders were the majority leader of the state senate and the eventual primary winner, Essex County Executive Peter Shapiro.

Shapiro, who was only thirty-two at the time of the primary, was a *wunderkind* of state politics. Immediately after graduating from Harvard University, he began a successful campaign for the state legislature and was elected when he was twenty-three. At twenty-six, Shapiro was elected to head the state's second largest county, thus becoming the youngest county executive in the United States. In a 1983 cover story that discussed New Jersey's possible future leaders, the state's leading political journal placed Shapiro first. He was described as "unquestionably the brightest of the rising political stars in the Garden State." The article continued:

> It is said that Essex County Executive Peter Shapiro can write his own ticket—to the governor's mansion, to Capitol Hill, even to the White House.... That's possible of course; but it is far more probable that Shapiro will one day be governor of New Jersey.[26]

Even the stellar Shapiro, however, seemed to have little chance of defeating the popular incumbent. When the state's voters were asked in May 1985 whether they would be inclined to vote for Kean or *any* Democrat, Kean led, 50 percent to 18 percent. Almost as many professed Democrats chose Kean as those who chose their still unknown standard-bearer.[27] Once Shapiro was selected, in a low turnout primary with a minority of the vote, his position deteriorated rather than improved. In late August, Kean led Shapiro in the polls, 68 percent to 19 percent. Only 15 percent of the Democrats preferred the challenger, 41 percent opted for Kean, and 44 percent were uncertain.[28] The disaster that appeared to be in the making was confirmed on election day. Kean defeated Shapiro, 70 percent to 30 percent, the largest margin in state history.

**The Advantages of Incumbency.**   How did the Democratic rising star come to suffer such an ignominious loss, while his opponent, within a space of four years, performed the remarkable feat of winning office by both the smallest and largest margins in his state's history? A close look at their campaigns explains much.

Like many incumbents, Tom Kean effectively began his reelection campaign two years before election day. During the 1983 midterm legislative elections, as we described in chapter 4, Kean ran extensive advertising to promote himself at least as much as the Republican legislative candidates. Responding to a Democratic complaint, the state Election Law Enforcement Commission ruled that this expenditure did not count against Kean's 1985 spending limits but was permissible because of his role as a leader of the state Republican party. Kean also conducted an extensive advertising campaign during the primary season, partly financed with public money, although he was unopposed for his party's nomination.

Kean used his incumbency effectively in other ways. Early in the fall of 1985, the state tourism agency began an expensive advertising campaign, prominently featuring the governor, who smilingly told viewers, "New Jersey and you—perfect together." This ad campaign ran through election day. Finally, many state employees volunteered to take part in the campaign after work. Kean was able to spend less than 9 percent of his budget on campaign administration, compared with his challenger's 15 percent.[29]

Of the $2.2 million in public money available to him, the incumbent could therefore allot 90 percent to paid media, principally television. Kean's advertising ignored Shapiro, concentrated on the state's economic renewal and other achievements of his tenure, and reiterated the themes of optimism and pride he had used in 1981. Each ad ended with the slogan "Governor Tom Kean—building pride in New Jersey."

**The Challenger's Problems.** Shapiro, on the other hand, suffered from both external events and self-inflicted wounds. Shortly after the June primary his first child was born prematurely and in grave physical condition. He left the campaign trail for the entire summer, slowing a fund-raising effort that was already hampered by his standing in the polls and preventing him from gaining any momentum from his June victory. September found him in worse shape than he had been in June.

The challenger's campaign themes did nothing to help his cause. The June primary advertising, which featured colorful graphics, pictures of the candidate with smiling citizens, upbeat jingles, and the slogan "A Better Way," was almost totally without substantive content.[30] Although it made viewers feel good, it told them virtually nothing about Shapiro. Not a single advertisement ever mentioned any of the government positions that he had held or any of his other accomplishments. In August 83 percent of the state's voters reported that they did not know how Shapiro was currently employed, and only 19 percent felt they knew "a lot or some" about the Democratic candidate.[31]

When the fall campaign began, Shapiro still had not raised enough money to collect the full state matching grant. His financial situation and poll standings led the state's press to write him off. The big story in the print media became whether Kean's expected massive victory would cause the Democrats to lose control of the state assembly, up for election at the same time. Television news coverage by New York and Philadelphia stations, always problematic, was almost nonexistent.

When Shapiro finally began his fall advertising, he had to attempt within a few weeks to identify himself and also to explain why he should be preferred to the incumbent. With the state's economy—a staple of gubernatorial campaign dialogue—booming, Shapiro focused his criticisms of Kean on the other issue that polls showed was very important to New Jersey voters—the Garden State's environmental problems.

The Kean campaign successfully deflected this attack as well. The state's environmental problems were indeed serious and on voters' minds. But during his first term, the governor had put in place several effective programs, which he detailed in his primary and general election advertising as reasons for New Jersey's new pride in itself. Voters accepted Kean's argument that the mistakes of a half-century would take a long time to remedy but that the governor had begun to do the job. Kean correctly assessed the problem with Shapiro's approach: "He erred in his choice of issues. . . . He had mistakenly taken us on where our armor was strongest. Never breaking through on toxic waste, Peter had no way to convince people, even Democrats, that they should vote out the Kean administration." [32]

Because of Shapiro's limited budget and desperate need for recognition, all his ads were black-and-white "talking head" shots of the candidate. Apparently afraid of attacking the popular incumbent by name, Shapiro made obscure references. "*They* say we have to wait" to deal with various state problems such as environmental pollution and high auto insurance rates, he repeatedly told mystified viewers, who had no context to help them identify to whom he was referring. When it became clear that many viewers could not even recognize the speaker, the ads began running with a caption that gave Shapiro's name and finally his party identification, as if imploring Democratic defectors to come home to their partisan roots. Unable to deal with the classic challenger problems of insufficient time, money, and recognition, Peter Shapiro went down to crushing defeat.

**Other Considerations in Gubernatorial Races.** These two New Jersey contests illustrate some further points about hard-fought and low-key gubernatorial contests and about the role of money. Open seat contests such as the 1981 Kean-Florio race are almost always close and attract strong candidates—often many of them—in the primaries. Races featuring popular incumbents such as the 1985 Kean-Shapiro contest draw fewer, less experienced challengers. The strongest potential candidates bide their time for a better opportunity.

Generally, campaigns that feature seemingly unbeatable incumbents make it much more difficult for a challenger to raise sufficient funds and become known. Without recognition, upward movement in the polls, and "smart-money" backing, a challenger has less chance to get free media coverage. The free media can often inflict further damage on a challenger. Since the press usually gives any governor's race more coverage than legislators' races, the free media can underscore an incumbent's invincibility and reinforce a challenger's "sure loser" image.

A campaign such as Shapiro's early effort, in which the challenger failed to make an effective case for himself or against the incumbent, probably could not have attracted a large amount of money from the typical contributors to gubernatorial races anyway. But limited by public funding to the same expenditures as a popular, much better known, and reasonably effective incumbent (and without the degree of media exposure enjoyed by presidential candidates), a challenger has almost no chance to triumph.

In the previous six chapters we detailed how modern-day American campaigns negotiate predictable hurdles. In the final two chapters we consider what the future may hold for campaigns and candidates. We also offer some thoughts about the effects of candidate-centered and media-centered campaigns on political culture, political institutions, and policy processes. Ultimately, beyond the color, drama, and excitement of political campaigns, it is because of such consequences that campaigns demand our careful and thoughtful attention.

## Notes

1. Jeff Greenfield, *Running to Win* (New York: Simon and Schuster, 1980), 28.
2. *Congressional Quarterly Weekly Report*, December 7, 1985, 2564.
3. Alan Ehrenhalt, ed., *Politics in America 1986* (Washington, D.C.: CQ Press, 1985), 374.
4. Alan Secrest, "Learning the Lessons of 1986," *Election Politics* 4 (Winter 1986-1987): 8.
5. Transcribed remarks from a presentation at the annual meeting of the American Political Science Association, Washington, D.C., August 29, 1986.
6. *Atlanta Constitution*, September 28, 1986, 2.
7. *Atlanta Constitution*, October 9, 1988.
8. Secrest, "Learning the Lessons of 1986," 8.
9. *Atlanta Constitution*, October 20, 1986.
10. *Political Report*, February 20, 1987, 3; *Atlanta Constitution*, October 21, 1986. The debate was carried by commercial stations in Atlanta, Albany, Columbus, and Macon.
11. Although Fowler swung somewhat to the right in 1986, his 1985 rating of 50 from the liberal Americans for Democratic Action was twenty points higher than Senator Nunn's; his rating on labor issues from the AFL-CIO's Committee on Political Education was twenty-nine points higher, and his American Conservative Union rating, thirty-one points lower (Michael Barone and Grant Ujifusa, ed., *Almanac of American Politics* [Washington, D.C.: National Journal, 1988], 288-289). Fowler's ideological shift and large number of missed votes are typical examples of the general findings of John R. Hibbing, "Ambition in the House: Behavioral Consequences of Higher Office Goals," *American Journal of Political Science* 30 (August 1986): 651-663.
12. Anthony Champagne and Rick Collis, "Texas," in *The Political Life of the American States*, ed. Alan Rosenthal and Maureen Moakley (New York: Praeger, 1984), 136-137.
13. *Dallas Morning News*, October 22, 1986, 12.
14. *Dallas Morning News*, October 26, 1986.

15. *Dallas Morning News,* October 22, 1986, 9A, and October 26, 1986.
16. *Dallas Morning News,* November 2, 1986.
17. Jeannie R. Stanley, "Party Realignment in the States: Texas," *Comparative State Politics Newsletter* 8 (December 1987): 21.
18. Eagleton Poll, May 6-18, 1981.
19. Unless otherwise noted, these and subsequent poll data reports are from the Eagleton Poll, September 15-27, 1981.
20. Eagleton Poll, November 2, 1981.
21. Larry J. Sabato, *The Rise of Political Consultants* (New York: Basic Books, 1981), Appendix C.
22. Maureen Moakley, "New Jersey," in Rosenthal and Moakely, ed., *Political Life of the American States,* 219-235; Cliff Zukin, "Political Culture and Public Opinion," in Gerald M. Pomper, ed., *The Political State of New Jersey* (New Brunswick, N.J.: Rutgers University Press, 1986).
23. Data provided by the New Jersey Election Law Enforcement Commission (NJELEC).
24. Thomas H. Kean, *The Politics of Inclusion* (New York: Free Press, 1988), 45, 47.
25. *Star-Ledger*-Eagleton Poll, September 1, 1985.
26. "Nine for the Nineties: The Powers to Be," *New Jersey Reporter* 12 (May 1983): 7-8.
27. *Star-Ledger*-Eagleton Poll, April 29-May 8, 1985.
28. *Star-Ledger*-Eagleton Poll, August 15-25, 1985.
29. These and other data on spending in the 1985 election are from the New Jersey Election Law Enforcement Commission, *New Jersey Public Financing: 1985 Gubernatorial Elections* (Trenton: NJELEC, September 1986).
30. Shapiro confirms that the slogan was "lifted" from the fictional campaign in a 1972 Robert Redford film he admired, *The Candidate.* The message of this film is about the dangers of emphasizing style over substance.
31. *Star-Ledger*-Eagleton Poll, September 1, 1985.
32. Kean, *Politics of Inclusion,* 127-128.

# The Play and the Players: Future Directions in Campaigns

# 10

*The party campaign committees can be very helpful. They can also be a pain in the neck. If you're doing a race they've targeted, there's the financial advantage that's very great. But other than giving us the money, access to contributor lists, getting national speakers to do fund-raising events—other than that, I don't look for them to do a damn thing.*

Jay Smith, political consultant

*With consultants, you have to assemble a campaign à la carte from a very expensive and unaccountable menu. There will always be a role for those people in a complex, technology-based election system. But in my judgment they are not sufficient all by themselves. The most successful campaigns will be those that are in a position to draw on a standing organization, the party, for resources, technical help, and money.*

Mitch Daniels, NRSC

The replacement of the traditional political party organization by technology and those who know how to use it is the crucial change that engendered this observation by political scientist Larry Sabato: "There has been no greater change in American politics in recent years than the manner in which candidates run for public office. The very character of electioneering has been altered irrevocably by the revolution in campaign techniques." [1] The role of the party boss has been taken over by the political consultant, that of the volunteer party worker by the paid telephone bank caller. Most voters learn about candidates not at political rallies but from television advertising and computer-generated direct mail; candidates generally gather information about voters not from the ward leader but from the pollster. The money to fuel campaigns comes less from the party organizations and "fat cats" and more from direct mail solicitation of individuals and special-interest political action committees. In short, candidates have become individual entrepreneurs, largely set free from party control or discipline.

Although the changes in campaigns have been real and vast, there are also some less obvious continuities. Campaigners have always used the major means of mass communication and public relations in each historical era. Alexander Hamilton served as ghost writer for George Washington's farewell address. Thomas Jefferson's political success stemmed in part from his command of the written word, when tracts and pamphlets were the major forms of political communication, and Franklin Roosevelt was a master of the radio. Television and the computer are in an important sense only the most current incarnations of these communication tools. Nor are the special-interest groups prominent in contemporary American politics an entirely new phenomenon. They are direct descendants of the nineteenth-century abolitionists, prohibitionists, and suffragists. As for business, its role in politics has been active and controversial since the founding of the country.

And there is also a continuing but changed role for political parties. The Republican national committees, which were moribund and almost bankrupt not many years ago, have assumed a place of some importance in Republican campaigns. The Democratic national committees, stung by their defeats in 1980, followed suit. Parties now seek to shape a place for themselves consonant with their new environment. Under the old system parties provided two vital resources: money and strategy. The emergence of political action committees and professional political consultants gave candidates alternatives to the party. The future roles of the political parties in campaigns will therefore depend not only on what they do but also on the future roles of these other actors.

We begin this chapter by looking at new developments and likely directions for political consultants and campaign technology. We then examine the emerging roles of the more traditional campaign actors—special-interest groups and the parties—as they adapt to technologically driven and candidate-centered races.

# Institutionalizing the Campaign Industry

The past few decades have seen the emergence of a new industry made up of people and institutions whose livelihood comes from working on political campaigns. The early professional consultants viewed campaigns as seasonal work. To advertising agencies, public relations firms, survey research companies, and documentary filmmakers, campaigns were one class of clients among many. Although generalists have not disappeared, political consultants are increasingly specialists whose livelihood depends entirely on politics. It is not surprising, then, that they would seek, as do any executives, to expand, systematize, and rationalize their businesses. At least three distinct but overlapping developments in the campaign industry have resulted from its growing specialization and institutionalization: moves toward the reduction of seasonal business fluctuation, market expansion, and the generation of new products and services. We discuss these in turn.

## Reducing Seasonal Fluctuations: The Permanent Campaign

Political consultants are moving in a variety of ways to ensure that they have business outside the traditional campaign period. Not only is the period itself lengthening, but consultants are also successfully looking for ways to sell their products day in and day out, throughout the year. One development is the practice of the national party organizations and certain interest groups to put consultants on annual retainers. For example, pollsters Richard Wirthlin, Robert Teeter, and Linda DiVall all have lucrative continuing contracts with the Republican national committees, and the American Association of Retired Persons (AARP) has a continuing relationship with pollster William Hamilton and media consultant Jill Buckley.

Another development is year-round business from successful candidates, especially for executive office. Some consultants have convinced their clients, particularly governors, that there is value in paid media outside election periods. Gov. Bill Clinton of Arkansas was the first to buy advertising shortly after election day. His ads were intended to explain the need for tax increases. Clinton had been elected to a two-year term in 1978 with 63 percent of the vote, but he was narrowly defeated in 1980. Public opposition to tax increases played an important role in his defeat. Clinton's 1980 opponent, who ran against the tax increases, wound up raising taxes himself and lost to Clinton by ten points in 1982. By then more taxes were required for sorely needed educational programs, and Clinton faced another race in 1984. A consultant to Clinton said of the events beginning with the 1980 defeat:

> I always felt something could have been done to have prevented that. In Clinton's second term almost the same thing was materializing. In order to get an education package through, he had to pass new taxes,

and he didn't want to go down the tube again. I suggested these ads to shape the public perception of what was going on. Essentially, we were trying to explain the tradeoff between improving education and taxes. Instead of having it fixed in the public's mind that he raised taxes, we wanted it fixed in the public's mind that he improved education.

The response in Arkansas encouraged the same consultant to suggest a similar strategy to Texas governor Mark White, when White guided a tax package through the state legislature in 1984, midway through his four-year term. Clinton was easily reelected in 1984, and although White narrowly failed in his reelection bid, his loss had little to do with the education tax increase. Since then governors Thomas Kean of New Jersey and Robert Casey of Pennsylvania have also used print and television advertising midway in their terms to explain their programs.

This trend may be largely confined to executive officeholders, for whom it serves the same purpose as the televised presidential speech. Other executive officeholders cannot command the free television time the president gets, nor would their talks usually generate large audiences. A thirty-second spot inserted into a television program does not overtax viewers, yet it gets a message across when repeated over a period of time.

Legislative officeholders traditionally do not have opportunities for extended televised appearances such as executives' press conferences, speeches, or televised town meetings. Television media markets, as we have seen, do not often cover congressional districts efficiently. House members, however, can communicate regularly, easily, and cheaply by sending franked newsletters. Senators might seem likely advertisers outside election periods, particularly since their constituents may forget who they are during their six-year terms, but many are wary of this technique. A consultant reported:

> I suggested [advertising] to a senator. But he says he's not going to do it; it would be a sign of weakness. There is the problem that when a governor does it, he's clearly explaining his program. A senator doesn't have as clear a program.

In his 1988 senatorial race, however, North Dakota's Quentin Burdick made good use of a paid video press release. When polls showed the eighty-year-old veteran far behind a much younger primary challenger early in 1987, Burdick commissioned television ads to let voters know he had just been awarded the chairmanships of the Senate Appropriations Agriculture Subcommittee and the Environment and Public Works Committee, the first such seats for a North Dakota senator since World War II. In the cheap North Dakota media markets, his annoucement could be shown statewide a dozen times for less than

$7,000. This information helped solidify Democratic support for Burdick, and shortly thereafter his primary challenger withdrew from the race.

Executive client-candidates, in contrast to those from the legislature, generate other business for consultants outside the election season. Pollster Bill Hamilton elaborated:

> If a governor is elected, there's a lot of polling you can do in that state—whether it's special-interest groups the governor is close to, constitutional referenda, even occasionally state agencies—very legitimate stuff. A Senate campaign helps your reputation, but there's never any continuing business. You sell them once every six years. They're not executives. There's not as much of a continuing relationship with a senator as there can be with a governor.

In the consultant community, campaign managers are often out in the cold after the campaign season is over. Winning managers return to or land jobs on incumbents' office staffs, but this is often not possible for the talented professional manager who happens to lose. Moreover, having gone through one campaign, even successful managers are loath to take on the job again. As an ex-manager described the problem, "A person who sits around a House office makes a lot more, and they don't have to kill themselves for the money." Both national party organizations recognize the manager problem and are beginning to think about solutions. So far, this has mainly taken the shape of trying to supply a flow of new talent. In 1987 the Republican National Committee institutionalized its training sessions by establishing a formal Campaign Academy for managers. The Democrats offer similar sessions on a less regular basis.

Retaining experienced people, however, remains a problem. A staffer at the Democratic Congressional Campaign Committee has said:

> I'd like to see the day when this party trains campaign managers, puts them in the field on an apprentice run. After the campaign we put them in a job—with a law firm, a PAC, a trade association—where they can work in the off-year, and in the campaign year we can call them back. They're tried and true and proven, and they don't have to worry about being out on the street in the off-year.

Naturally, all consultants applaud any developments that will smooth out seasonal fluctuations in their business activities and prevent them from being out of work during the noncampaign season. Their clients are becoming more and more convinced that consultants can help them build a record in office that will serve them well when the campaign season returns. Thus both sides see value in what is becoming a permanent campaign.

The campaign industry has also become large enough that some firms can offer services to each other. A prime example is John Aristotle

Phillips's Aristotle Industries. Since 1983 it has marketed campaign software that generates direct mail, organizes scheduling, and produces financial reports. In 1986 the company acquired part of ITT-Dialcom, which maintains a large computer that helps about 170 House members answer constituent mail. As Dialcom's manager explains, "Aristotle Industries is in the business of helping congressmen get elected; ITT-Dialcom is in the business of helping congressmen stay elected." [2]

Another new, primarily intraindustry, service is the *Campaign Hotline*, introduced in 1988 by Republican consultant Doug Bailey and Democratic consultant Roger Craver. During the 1988 campaign season the *Hotline* provided a daily summary of media coverage of campaign events in major national and statewide races, poll results, candidate appearances and statements, interviews with leading political players, and the like. Candidate campaign organizations and the national party committees were guaranteed daily inclusion of short reports of their choosing, and other subscribers could also submit items. After the election the *Hotline* continued as a more general compilation of current political happenings. Subscribers can download it and submit items through a computer service bureau every morning.

## Market Expansion: High-Tech
## Campaigns at the Local Level

Since the early 1980s high-tech practices have reached the local level. Several factors contribute to this trend. One is the advent of the inexpensive personal computer. Home computers make it financially feasible for local candidates to manage voter and contributor lists and to generate specialized mail messages. Another is the growing professionalization of state and local government and thus greater interest in serving in state and local office. State legislatures and county governments have been taking on new responsibilities since the early 1970s, and this trend intensified in the Reagan era. With new responsibilities came higher salaries and more perquisites for local officeholders, an increasing desire to stay in office, more competition, and greater use of consultants.

Finally, the Republican national committees, unable to spend all their available resources on federal candidates, began funneling them to state and local organizations. A Republican national staffer explained: "While we have these limits on federal expenditures, the next logical place to go with our dollars is to build stronger state parties beneath these [state and local] campaigns. Those transfers are not limited." These Republican initiatives beginning in the late 1970s were quickly emulated by the Democrats. This section elaborates on these developments.

**Computerizing Smaller Campaigns.** The campaign functions at which computerized database management excels—targeting programs, direct mail generation, list development, and so on—are of increasing interest to local campaigns. Each week seems to bring a new company offering software that can be used on local candidates' personal computers. A typical basic package includes modules for list management, targeting, and budgeting. Options include programs that generate press releases, organize scheduling, run simple poll analyses, and upload or download data to other computers. A leading industry journal founded in 1979, *Campaigns and Elections,* devotes much space to advertising from such companies, reviews of software packages, and articles explaining how to use them effectively in local campaigns.

State legislative candidates and congressional candidates with modest budgets need similar database management programs but of greater size and complexity and requiring more technical knowledge and equipment. These campaigns can purchase prepared voter lists containing names matched with telephone numbers and coded for probable ethnic origin, gender, and post office carrier routes.

The same information is also available on three-by-five cards upon which telephone bank operators in voter-identification operations can record voting preferences, or it can be printed on labels for mailings. Companies will also prepare targeting and demographic reports based on these data. A targeting report for a congressional district might include demographic estimates for as many as three hundred groups, broken down as finely, for example, as the number of black males, ages thirty to forty, who are renters and registered Democratic voters. These reports can set vote goals for each group in each voting precinct.

Additionally, computer graphics packages can portray maps of congressional districts showing demographic and voting patterns and trace suitable routes for canvassers. High-speed laser printers produce hundreds, even thousands, of personalized direct mail pieces per hour.[3] One estimate is that candidates for all offices in 1986 spent $2 million on computer software and $20 million including hardware and services. The Republican National Committee estimated that computers and direct mail would account for 15 to 25 percent of all 1988 spending.[4]

Campaigns can choose from the large number of local and regional political consultants who have sprung up in recent years to implement these programs. Some software companies now offer site licenses to regional consultants. A consultant can purchase a master copy of a computer package and make unlimited copies for clients. The parent firm provides the consultant with help and customer support.

**New Roles for State and Local Parties.** Because of the high costs of elaborate computer programs, local candidates, particularly for the state legislature, are banding together to purchase services in volume. The state party organizations are one group of frequent customers representing multiple legislative candidates.

The Republican state organizations benefit heavily from the assistance provided by their strong and wealthy national committee. According to a 1984 survey, the national Republican party provided at least two-thirds of its state affiliates with direct financial aid for both the parties and their individual candidates; assistance in fund raising, polling, and data processing; and help with candidate recruitment and training. Of the state Democratic organizations, a quarter or fewer got such assistance from their less wealthy national committees. On average, across the country approximately two-thirds of the Republican state party funds came from their national committees. The state Democratic parties, with much lower average budgets, received only a third of their money from the Washington committees.

Despite less money from Washington, the Democrats did fairly well at providing their state legislative candidates with services. Although 90 percent or more of the state Republican parties contributed money to candidates, assisted them with fund raising, and ran campaign seminars, two-thirds or more of the Democratic organizations also offered these services. About three-quarters of the Republican state organizations offered some polling and media consulting, but so did half of the Democratic organizations.[5]

In the last few years, however, particularly on the Democratic side, state legislative candidates have come to rely for such services on a different party organ—the partisan legislative caucus. In most states outside the South, all members of each house of the legislature that share the same partisan affiliation belong to a formal organization—the caucus—which elects a leader and hires professional staff.

Caucus campaign committees, headed by the majority and minority leaders in each house, now raise funds to support legislative campaigns and contract for campaign services such as polling and direct mail. Although both the minority and majority legislative caucuses solicit money and offer services, it is obviously easier for the majority to attract contributions, particularly from the political action committees that provide a large portion of such funds.

Generally, state-level PACs contribute heavily to individual incumbents and expect that challengers will be supported by the large sums these PACs also contribute to the legislative caucus campaign committees. With the Democrats in control of about two-thirds of all state legislative houses throughout the 1980s, and with many of their state party organizations bankrupt, it is evident why the caucuses are a more important tool for them than for the Republicans.[6]

Some examples give an idea of the scope of these activities. In California the Democratic senate and assembly leaders raised well over $5 million for 1986 state legislative campaigns. The assembly leader was able to dole out as much $350,000 to a hopeful for an open seat in the assembly, considerably more than many California incumbent congressional representatives spent on their reelections.[7] In Illinois, where the most expensive campaigns for contested seats cost in the range of $100,000 that same year, the four party caucuses raised and spent almost $3 million. This amount exceeded the 23 percent of all campaign funds for which the caucuses were the source in Illinois's previous legislative cycle.[8]

A major reason for greater party caucus activity is the increased competition for legislative seats in the growing number of areas where party voting is weak even at the state and local level. In Wisconsin the legislative campaign committees of both parties were galvanized by the 1984 elections, when the Reagan landslide produced a seven-seat gain in the assembly for the Republicans, dangerously narrowing the Democrats' long-term margin. The Democrats faced the further disadvantage of an unpopular governor at the top of the ticket in 1986. Competition brought the advent of several new caucus functions, in addition to refining voter lists, which had been their staple activity. Targeting of resources became the ruling principle. For the first time both safe and hopeless candidates were completely shut out. Cash donations to individual campaigns was replaced by in-kind contributions. Money was spent on generic television advertising, individualized radio advertising, polls, and phone banks. The caucuses also provided issue papers, press releases, and speakers. Similarly, in New Jersey's 1987 legislative elections, the leaders of the Democratic senate majority and the Republican assembly majority each raised more than a million dollars to support their party's legislative candidates.[9] With more state legislative chambers having smaller partisan majorities and redistricting looming in 1990, such activities in 1988 could only increase.

## New Products and Services: Increased "Narrowcasting"

A final likely trend in future campaigns is the use of less "broadcasting" and more "narrowcasting." Rather than sending general messages to entire constituencies, candidates will be able to send specialized messages to identifiable constituency groups.

Some increasingly precise and ubiquitous forms of narrowcasting that we have already described are direct mail and computerized telephone dialing and taped phone message delivery. Less technologically developed but growing rapidly is narrowcast television, delivered by cable systems and videocassette recorders.

By 1988, 51 percent of all American households were connected to local cable television systems, up from only 19 percent in 1980. In the same period the average proportion of the television audience watching a network TV station rather than alternatives such as independent stations, VCR tapes, or cable slipped from about 60 percent to just under half. Even in prime time the network share dropped from 90 percent of viewers in 1978 to 70 percent ten years later.

Furthermore, the average time spent by the public viewing the large cable-based networks such as CNN, ESPN, and Lifetime rose from about two hours each week in 1980-1981 to more than eight hours in 1985-1986. With town-specific franchises and inexpensive local rates, many local candidates—such as the county executive candidates in Suffolk and Erie counties in New York and state legislative and county candidates in New Jersey and Louisiana—have recently bought local cable advertising.

Newly available interconnects between cable networks also now permit simultaneous advertising across stations and cable franchises. An on-line computer service sponsored by the National Cable Television Association and the Nielsen rating service has made purchasing the appropriate advertising easier. The service describes cable audiences by congressional district and standard demographic categories and lists available programs and rates. Several networks have established sales representatives in common.

Some cable networks such as MTV, ESPN, and Spanish-language stations also offer highly targeted audiences; surveys show that others such as CNN have viewers who are unusually politically attentive and participatory. As early as 1982, cable was credited with substantially assisting Massachusetts representative Barney Frank in his defeat of Margaret Heckler (later a Reagan Cabinet secretary) when redistricting put them in opposition. Frank ran particularly effective advertising on a Portuguese-language station in his district.

With VCR sales rates in the 1980s resembling the sales of televisions in the 1950s, political players are also showing interest in this medium. In volume, programs on VCR tapes can cost as little as $5 per unit to produce. In 1988 the AFL-CIO taped four-minute presentations by thirteen of the early presidential candidates and distributed fifteen thousand copies to union halls. Their intent was to encourage members to get involved with the race and consider running as national convention delegates.

The national party congressional committees also distribute tapes to candidates. A recent Democratic effort, hoping to take advantage of the "gender gap," analyzed women's voting behavior and advised candidates to campaign at female-dominated workplaces such as hospitals as well as at the traditional factory gates. Republican tapes have ranged from debate strategy to analysis of the budget deficit. Candidates at the state level have used tapes to "speak" simultaneously at multiple gatherings of campaign workers or have distributed them as campaign souvenirs—what one writer calls an "electronic potholder." [10]

Thus technology will play a greater role in the smaller political units and make larger political units approachable in a more targeted way.

## The Changing Role of Special-Interest Groups

Along with consultants, special-interest groups and their associated political action committees now are vital forces in campaigns. In this section we look more closely at their activities.

Although the distinction is not perfect, special-interest groups, as we discussed in chapter 3, are divided between those whose interests are primarily economic, personal, and tangible and those with a more ideological bent.

For several years after PACs entered the political fray in 1978, those with mainly economic interests—corporations, trade associations, and labor unions—confined their candidate support activities almost entirely to financial contributions to candidates. The more ideological "nonconnected" PACs, while making some direct contributions, were more inclined than other PACs to offer in-kind expenditures. On the right, groups such as the Committee for the Survival of a Free Congress (CSFC) provided conservative candidates with staff and organizational support. On the left, organizations such as the National Committee for an Effective Congress (NCEC) provided liberal contenders with elaborate targeting plans.

The two kinds of PACs also differed in the ways they treated challengers and incumbents and in the ways they made independent expenditures. The numerically dominant economically oriented groups, which provide most PAC dollars, directed their contributions heavily to incumbents, a pattern that grew stronger over time. In 1978 challengers to House incumbents received 19 percent of all PAC money contributed to House races, while their Senate counterparts collected 30 percent of the PAC money going to those races. By 1986 the comparable figures had dropped steadily to 14 percent and 21 percent, respectively, and they went even lower in 1988.[11]

The fear of antagonizing incumbents who served on committees that regulate their industries and the anemic success rate of challengers contributed to these developments. Because so many more Democrats, particularly in the House, were incumbents, Republican House challengers suffered the most from a dearth of PAC money. As late as June 1988, the hundreds of Republican challengers in House races had received a cumulative total of $317,000 from PACs—less than the amount collected by one Indiana freshman Democratic incumbent.[12]

Another consideration was the influence of local PAC affiliates, which often successfully urged their parent bodies to support incumbents who might have less-than-perfect "big picture" records but who had been helpful on district matters. Thus California senator Alan Cranston, who achieved a 1986 rating of 95 from the liberal Americans for Democratic Action and only a 32 from the Chamber of Commerce, was able to collect more than $600,000 in corporate and trade association PAC money in his race that year. Local sentiment also determined which of two equally appealing candidates would be supported. The national Chamber of Commerce, for example, recommended support of Alabama Senate incumbent Jeremiah Denton rather than an opponent also friendly to business because a survey of the Alabama Chamber members had shown "17 to 1 support for Denton." [13]

The more ideological PACs were more receptive to challengers, particularly early in the campaign season when challengers need seed money to get their efforts off the ground. To win support even from those PACs, however, challengers needed to make a powerful case. In a report to contributors on the 1986 Senate races, NCEC indicated that it was not assisting the Democratic candidates in Lousiana and Alabama because they were ideologically unacceptable. And otherwise acceptable Democratic challengers in states such as Alaska, Arizona, Indiana, and New Hampshire were denied support because their races were considered hopeless.[14]

In addition to giving candidates' campaign committees direct contributions and in-kind support, PACs are also conducting a slowly increasing number of independent expenditure campaigns. As we said in chapter 3, independent expenditures are individual or group efforts supporting or opposing a candidacy that are not organized or coordinated by the campaign that benefits from them. They include such activities as informational mailings to group members or the purchase of broadcast advertising.

Although direct and in-kind contributions to candidate campaign committees outpaced independent expenditures sixteen to one in 1986, the amounts of independent spending rose steadily from $2.2 million in 1980 to almost $9.4 million six years later, and groups rather than individuals were responsible for 90 percent of them.[15] The character and sponsorship of independent expenditures have changed in the most recent election cycles. The most important of these changes are the increasing number of independent campaigns by nonideological rather than ideological groups and a concomitant shift from predominantly negative to predominantly positive independent messages.

In the late 1970s and early 1980s a conservative trend among voters and Ronald Reagan's success generated the creation of conservative "New Right" ideological groups that were able to raise large sums. There were a number of such groups, including the Conservative Victory Fund, the Conservative Caucus, Christian Voice, and the Congressional Club, but the largest, most visible, and best-funded group was the National Conservative Political Action Committee (NCPAC). NCPAC and many of the other groups specialized in independent expenditures for negative broadcast media. They claimed predominant credit for the defeat of several liberal Democratic senators in 1980.

By 1984, however, with endangered liberals in shorter supply and better able to use past experience to defend themselves, the New Right groups switched their focus to support imperiled conservative idols such as North Carolina senator Jesse Helms.[16] Enormous amounts were also spent on direct mail to promote President Reagan, not because he was in jeopardy but because there with fewer liberal demons available to alarm their supporters, and the Reagan appeals were the best way to raise funds for the groups' activities.

By the 1988 election cycle almost all the New Right groups were in dire financial straits. Among the reasons were the accomplishment of some conservative goals, some disenchantment among contributors with the Reagan administration, oversolicitation by too many groups, and the death of NCPAC's founder and leading New Right strategist, John T. "Terry" Dolan. Their opponents had also won several legal challenges maintaining that the groups' activities were not really independent but coordinated with candidate campaigns and hence illegal. NCPAC, which had raised $9.3 million in the 1986 election cycle, was able to garner only $1.7 million in 1987, and it was more than $4 million in debt. The Congressional Club, which raised $15 million in 1985-1986— the most of any PAC in the country—was down to $2.2 million in receipts and also owed a million dollars. New Right groups were minor players on the independent expenditure front by 1986 and were almost invisible in 1988.[17]

The sharp upsurge in independent expenditures came from increased activities by more traditional nonideological PACs. The three leading independent spending groups in 1986 were the National Committee to Preserve Social Security, the Realtors' RPAC, and the

American Medical Association's AMPAC. Together they accounted for almost two-thirds of all independent outlays. Instead of negative and ideological messages, these groups concentrated on general positive appeals for preferred candidates, often indistinguishable in tone and style from the candidates' own messages. AMPAC's Peter Lauer explained: "We don't believe that issues are the way independent expenditures should be promoted. Name ID and GOTV are the most important goals." [18]

AMPAC began limited independent expenditures in 1978, with a modest $48,000 investment for campaign buttons and print ads supporting ten House candidates in local editions of *Time, Newsweek,* and *Sports Illustrated.* Two years later a more sophisticated effort on behalf of twenty House candidates saw expenditures of $200,000 for television ads and $90,000 for direct mail. Similar programs, also including some polling, were conducted from 1984 to 1988, with independent expenditures rising to a peak of $1.5 million in 1986.

Although groups such as AMPAC and RPAC continued making direct contributions to candidates, independent expenditures, which are not limited by the campaign finance laws, were increasingly embraced as a way to support the groups' most favored candidates. For example, Mississippi senator Trent Lott could receive a maximum of $10,000 from any PAC for his tough 1988 open seat race. RPAC, however, spent $344,000 on polling and producing and airing ads for Lott in an August and September independent expenditure. In the closing days of his contest, beginning in mid-October, the Auto Dealers and Drivers for Free Trade PAC (representing imported-car dealers) weighed in with a similar purchase, spending at least $319,000.

An AMPAC operative explained the strategy behind such spending decisions: "As long as the government places limits on our [direct contribution] activities—and holds out the promise of future limitations—independent expenditures remain one of the best ways to exercise our ... constitutionally protected right to freedom of speech." [19]

An important result of the more pragmatic attitudes of the trade association PACs, in contrast to the New Right groups, is that, with the fading of NCPAC, which spent mostly on Senate campaigns and almost exclusively to advance Republicans, both House members and Democrats have improved their share of the independent expenditure pool. The five-to-one Republican financial advantage in 1982 dropped to barely better than even in 1986, when relatively liberal Democrats such as Montana senator Max Baucus and New York representative Robert Mrazek benefited substantially from AMPAC or RPAC independent spending. Other Democrats, including Ohio senator Howard Metzenbaum and representatives Liz Patterson of South Carolina, Mike Parker of Mississippi, and Ben Nighthorse Campbell of Colorado, did the same in 1988.

Finally, although independent expenditures by individuals are still a very small part of the total, they represent another possible major new source of political spending. One strong supporter of Israel spent more than $400,000 on negative television advertising against Illinois senator Charles Percy in 1984. Percy eventually lost to challenger Paul Simon by only two points. Although it could not be proven, there were strong suspicions that the same person financed a conservative third-party candidate in the 1986 California Senate race. That candidate's vote total was more than the margin separating winning Democrat Alan Cranston and losing Republican Ed Zschau.[20]

PACs outspent parties by a ratio of five to two in 1986 (up from three to two in 1978), in considerable part because of the limits placed on parties by the campaign finance laws. But the political parties have grown much stronger in the past few years and perform many functions for campaigns besides contributing money.

# Revival of the
# Party Role in Campaigns

When modern technology first became important in campaigns with the advent of television in the presidential contests of the 1950s, it was, as we saw in chapter 3, at party initiative. The Republican National Committee commissioned and paid for Eisenhower's advertising. Party control of the technological delivery of campaign messages, however, had a short history and one that ended just as campaign technology was fully flowering. In 1968 the Nixon campaign set up the first technology-based campaign organization independent of the party structure. By the early 1970s the limits on contributions built into the new campaign finance laws made it rational for other candidates for federal office to follow the Nixon campaign's lead. Only in the late 1970s did the American political parties leap on the technology bandwagon and reenter campaigns in a significant way.

An observer in the mid-1970s might reasonably have concluded that American political parties were one of the lesser noticed casualties of the preceding cataclysmic decade. In little more than ten years the United States witnessed three political assassinations, decisively lost a major military engagement for the first time, saw destruction of fundamental elements of the social order in the civil rights and women's movements, watched its economy brought to the brink by a handful of "unimportant" oil-producing countries, and suffered through a far-reaching political scandal in the Watergate affair. These events engendered strong feelings of cynicism and alienation that affected all political institutions, including the parties. Americans turned less to the parties for voting cues, and, helped by technology, the candidates depended less upon them as well.

The national committees of both major parties were moribund. Organizational weakness at the top worked its way downward. The Democratic party was struggling to pay off a multimillion dollar debt it had assumed from Hubert Humphrey's presidential campaign in 1968. The Republican National Committee could raise only $300,000 toward its $2.3 million budget in 1975. Ideological activists in both parties launched serious attacks on organization-favored presidential candidates. After unseating the Illinois delegation loyal to the consummate organizational pol, Chicago mayor Richard Daley, at the 1968 Democratic National Convention, left-wing activists succeeded in nominating George McGovern in 1972. Former governor Jimmy Carter of Georgia, running as an outsider, bested "regular" Democrats such as Washington senator Henry Jackson in the 1976 nomination race. Despite party attempts to make outsider campaigns more difficult in 1984, two more consummate outsiders, Gary Hart and Jesse Jackson, between them won more than half the votes in Democratic primaries that year, and Jackson ran second in a large field in 1988.

On the Republican side, right-wing activists, rising from the ashes of the 1964 Goldwater debacle, almost succeeded in nominating their hero, former California governor Ronald Reagan, in 1976 and toppling incumbent president Gerald Ford, another party organization stalwart. In 1980 their triumph at the presidential level was complete, and in 1984 they dictated the Republican platform and turned back attempts to dilute their strength by changing the representation rules in the 1988 national convention. In 1988 some of them backed the presidential campaign of televangelist Pat Robertson. Although Robertson made a weak showing and dropped out early, his followers took over significant factions of the state Republican parties in places such as Hawaii, Nevada, and Washington State.

Senate, House, and gubernatorial candidates increasingly engaged in candidate-centered campaigns, ignoring the parties and triumphing in primaries through their own efforts. State party organizations had reported recruiting candidates for an average of 3.5 offices in the early 1960s, but this number had declined to 2.6 in the late 1970s. Researchers further found no relationship between the state parties' organizational strength and their standard-bearers' electoral strength.[21]

Federal candidates saw little utility in either the state committees or the congressional and senatorial committees in Washington. A Democratic Congressional Campaign Committee staffer commented: "The congressional committee frankly didn't have a lot of visibility or credibility with members of Congress. They didn't think the committee had to be alive, alert, energetic, or involved." A National Republican Senatorial Committee aide described the committee as "a sleepy, inconspicuous one-horse operation" in the early and mid-1970s. Observing that thirty-two of the states had no provision for party endorsement of gubernatorial candidates and that such endorsement played little role in most of the others, Sarah McCally Morehouse noted that in two-thirds of the states, candidates "enter the governor's office as self-made tribunes who got where they are under their own power." [22]

## Changing Roles for the Parties

The events of the 1970s and early 1980s, however, pushed the parties in new and revitalizing directions. In some ways the developments were similar for the two parties; in others, they were different. One similarity was that candidates and campaigns both turned to their parties as a result of defeat. The Republicans suffered devastating losses in the House and in the states as a fallout from the Watergate affair of the early 1970s, although the picture was not as grim at the presidential level. Although the Republicans were heavily outnumbered in state governments and in Congress, they won three of the four presidential contests between 1968 and 1980, two of them in landslides. For the Democrats the situation was reversed: they maintained their majorities in both houses of the national legislature and in the majority of states, but there was discord and serious weakness at the presidential level. Not until their losses of 1980 did Democratic Senate and House candidates show much interest in a possible role for the party.

A second similarity, and one with important implications for American politics generally, was the growing nationalization and centralization of the parties. For a century or more the distinguishing feature of American politics had been decentralization. The lifeblood of the political parties was their state and local organizations. The national committees were little more than an organizing locus for the state and local chieftains, who met every four years to nominate a president. The strength of the local parties was rooted in control of political patronage and nominations. Gradually, as we have seen, both died out. Conversely, the increasingly important and expensive role of technology in campaigns argued for the centralization of expertise and the growth of a national clearinghouse function for the parties. The old flow of communications and influence had been from the local party organizations to the national. Centralization reversed its direction.

Television's homogenizing of national politics also contributed to party centralization. In the pretelevision era, northern blacks and southern segregationists could coexist in the Democratic party, as could eastern internationalists and midwestern isolationists in the Republican party. National television resulted in "Democrats" and "Republicans" all over the country sharing similar views and attitudes, and for the first time it allowed a vigorous national party role.

The electorate's increasingly well defined view of each party gave rise to a substantial amount of party switching by officeholders, particularly after the victory of the conservative Goldwaterites at the 1964 Republican National Convention and again after the Reagan triumph in 1980. In the earlier period well-known politicians such as South Carolina's Strom Thurmond and Texas's John Connally moved from the Democratic party to the Republican party, while New York City mayor John Lindsay and Michigan senator Don Riegle went in the other direction. In the later period Democratic House members in Arizona, Florida, Pennsylvania, and Texas became Republicans, and many southern Democrats decided to make runs for office as Republicans. Representatives who found themselves in the "wrong" party, based on their policy views and voting habits, even acquired well-known nicknames. The liberal or moderate Republicans, concentrated in the Northeast, became known as gypsy moths, and the conservative Democrats, centered in the South, were styled boll weevils.

A third similarity between the parties was a stress on electability over ideology in choosing which candidates to support. Unlike the other two developments, this was a carryover from earlier periods. Despite the increasing homogeneity of both parties, the gypsy moths and boll weevils were a fact of life, and even greater diversity continued to exist among the party delegations in the Senate and among the governors. Neither party denied resources to any incumbents or promising challengers, no matter how uncooperative they might be.

A Democratic Congressional Campaign Committee staffer said: "This committee is not ideological at all. We want to make sure those folks are representing the district, not us." In explaining why the national party committees intervened for the first time in 1984 Senate primary contests, the National Republican Senatorial Committee executive director dismissed ideology and stressed electability and its importance for the Republicans in maintaining their control of the Senate:

> In this particular election we are not going to tie our hands. It's the first time the majority hangs by a hair. For us to take a fastidious hands-off policy would be very short-sighted if we can influence the nomination of somebody who can win and might be our fifty-first seat. Our first mission is to win a majority.

By emphasizing local issues, the Democrats, who had been practically shut out of federal representation in many western states, were able to elect governors somewhat to the right of the popular perception of the national party. Conversely, heavily Democratic northern states such as Rhode Island sometimes chose moderate or liberal Republicans as statewide officeholders.

The renewed strength of both parties was caused by increased competition, and the result for both Republicans and Democrats was a centralized, Washington-based organization that stressed electability over ideology. These new party organizations, however, also exhibited significant differences in their development and operating procedures. The differences are broadly related to the extent to which each party's campaign organizations emphasize national messages and resource allocation. Strangely enough, the Republicans, who are stereotypically viewed as the party favoring local control and deregulation, exert significantly more centralized control over campaign activities than do the Democrats.

## The Republicans: Centralized Organization and National Messages

In earlier chapters we noted the many campaign functions the Republican party was able to assume with the huge infusion of funds from its successful direct mail program begun in the mid-1970s. The Republicans set up a media center to produce low-cost, high-quality advertising for candidates and for the national party and to test the effect of advertising messages. Paid mailings for candidates flooded from party headquarters.

The party conducted hundreds of polls and actively recruited candidates. Its computers maintained voting record histories and accessed indexes to the nation's leading newspapers and magazines. State parties could tie in to the national party's data-processing facilities, and regional field and finance directors detailed from Washington assisted them. Millions of election-eve taped phone messages urging supporters to get out and vote emanated from RNC-financed professional phone banks. If the Republicans did not pioneer any electoral technology, they soon acquired it. The only financial problem was deciding how to spend all the money that was available. To carry out these tasks, the National Republican Congressional Committee increased its staff over the next decade to 130 and its annual budget to $60 million. (In 1975 it had had a staff of 6 and a budget of under $2 million, directed almost entirely toward incumbents.) The Senate campaign committee grew at a similar pace during the same period.[23]

The Republican strategy was driven by the party's minority status among both voters and officeholders and by their greater homogeneity. Unlike the heterogeneous and often feuding Democrats, who until recently had little incentive to band together as a party, the Republicans did unite. A staffer who switched to a Republican Senate office after the defeat of his former Democratic employer described the difference between the parties:

> Republican campaigns tend to be more structured, more thoroughly planned. Democrats tend to go off and hire a pollster there and a media adviser here. There's more of a Republican network where the various campaigns work well together, meshing with the national organizations. The Senate campaign committee is very good at sharing. Consultants use it as a clearinghouse. The Democratic party is all over the place.... It's not just the cohesive structure Republicans have. It's not just money. It's an attitude. The Republicans, despite the ideological differences from a Weicker to a Chafee to a Helms—there still tends to be an attitude that "we're all in this together."

As we have indicated, the Republicans' development of a national and centralized structure to wage campaigns was substantially an example of the old saying that necessity is the mother of invention. The Republicans had to recruit candidates and aid them from a central organization because they were so weak on the local level, particularly in large cities and in the South. Unlike the Democrats, they did not have a plethora of local elected officials ambitious to move up to higher office nor many strong local organizations and nonparty entitities such as labor unions to mobilize their vote. A party field manager dolefully remarked, "It's very frustrating to spend three hours in a coffee shop in Nowhere, Pennsylvania, with some county clerk who might run for Congress some day."

The Republicans' focus on their national organization had many historic roots. The party arose in the Civil War era as a response to the national issues of slavery and preservation of the Union. During much of the late nineteenth century, it financed its campaigns by assessing federal patronage employees. Even when its state party organizations were strongest in the first half of the twentieth century and provided the national committee with most of its funds, the Washington organization set fund-raising quotas for states and counties, in contrast to the "informality and confusion" of the Democrats.[24]

On the surface the development of the national Republican party organization would seem to be entirely positive from the point of view of candidates and those who wish the party well. There is apparently compelling evidence that Republican tactics have worked just as they were intended. In the 1978 elections, the first in which the full weight of the new Republican activities was felt, the party picked up seats in both the House and the Senate. It followed with a very strong performance in 1980 and sustained fewer losses than many expected in 1982. The influx of money and expertise appeared to have saved many marginal candidates.[25]

The rise of the mighty Republican apparatus has not brought unalloyed pleasure to all of its candidates, however, and there is evidence that in some cases it has been counterproductive. Inexperienced first-time challengers are much more enthusiastic about the national committees and their services than are the party's incumbents. Challengers in competitive Republican House campaigns are the only candidates in either party who see the party organizations as highly useful for anything but election day GOTV operations.[26] One participant in a neophyte campaign sounded the typical appreciative note: "I was really impressed. They had good polls, they did mailings, they paid for so many things and had very exact kinds of measuring tools. They were most cooperative." But more experienced campaigners often wish the party would simply give them financial help and otherwise stay away. One, calling the RNC arrogant, observed, "They tried to tell us how to run the campaign, and the advice was worthless."

A manager for a House incumbent was more specific in his indictment:

> I think the campaign committee is a superfluous bureaucracy. It doesn't do a thing for incumbents. I think it's a great organization for the president, a great organization to sustain your fund-raising mailing lists, but beyond their giving money, the most valuable thing they have is their campaign seminars for challengers.
>
> The RNC has a beautiful actuality service, a nicer office than I do, and sixteen cute little girls whose daddies are from Texas and gave to the Eagles [an organization of large contributors]. But it doesn't run on Sundays or after six in the afternoon. How the hell can you get something on drive time Monday morning? That's the living proof of bureaucracy.

Another problem identified by some Republican candidates is the difficulty generated by the committees' national outlook and their lack of familiarity with local problems. For example, the 1982 national party advertising theme—staying the course with President Reagan—struck the right note in areas where the president remained popular, but it was unhelpful or even detrimental in the many communities in which the severe economic recession was associated with the president's economic policies.[27] As one Republican incumbent who lost in 1982 argued, "To put out one theme and expect it to play in 435 districts is like Ford making one color car." [28]

In 1986, when the Republicans lost control of the Senate, similar complaints arose. Campaign staffers on both sides of the Louisiana Senate race ascribed the narrow loss by Republican Henson Moore to a national party "ballot integrity program" that garnered much unfavorable publicity. In an effort to purge the voting rolls of illegal or "nonexistent" participants likely to favor Democrat John Breaux, the Republicans sent mail to 1984 registrants in precincts that had produced at least an 80 percent vote for Democratic presidential candidate Walter Mondale, to see whether it would be returned to the post office as undeliverable. Since these precincts were overwhelmingly black residential areas, the program was, fairly or not, seen as racist.

This effort redounded to the discredit of the Moore campaign, whose theme—"It's morning in Louisiana"—was intended to paint Moore as a fresh new face, unsullied by the malicious tactics often used in Louisiana elections. Adam Goodman, Moore's media consultant, protested, "We really had problems trying to compete with the unfortunate problems that were brought on us by the RNC." Bill Hamilton, Breaux's strategist, agreed that Moore would probably have won without the furor generated by the ballot integrity program.[29] In the 1988 campaign a similar uproar occurred when a National Republican Senatorial Committee briefing memo advised an attack strategy linking Ohio Democratic senator Howard Metzenbaum to Communists.[30]

Republican committee staffers saw it differently, assigning much of the blame for the 1986 showing to weak candidates and their staffs. NRSC director Tom Griscom commented:

> The fallacy of this committee is that we are looked at as the driving force for all Republican campaigns. But some candidates want to run their own races . . . so that we are neither fish nor fowl. We need to make the fundamental decision whether, if this committee is going to make expenditures on a campaign, there should be full access and knowledge of what is happening.[31]

These controversies would not be important if there was hard evidence that the party's role did make a substantial difference to campaigns. But the apparently stunning recent Republican successes can be looked at in a framework that makes the party's role in them more problematic. For example, formerly accurate statistical models predicted that the Republicans would lose roughly twice as many House seats in the 1982 midterm election as they did. Another measure—seats lost by the president's party in his first midterm election—shows that the average since 1950 is eighteen, eight *fewer* than the Republicans lost in 1982. On the Senate side the Republicans did better than average in 1982, by not losing any seats. In 1962 and 1970, however, the president's party *gained* Senate seats in comparable midterm elections, and the net loss of eight Senate seats in 1986 also exceeded historical averages for a presidential sixth-year midterm. Despite two Reagan presidential landslides, the Republicans also ended the Reagan era with fewer House seats than they held when it began.

Other scattered evidence casts some doubt on the efficacy of the Republican campaign machine. A study of eight closely contested 1982 congressional races found that the presence or absence of National Republican Congressional Committee field staff had no effect on their outcomes. Furthermore, national party support did not always translate into electoral success in the district. Rather, a candidate's ability to attract contributions from individuals was the most important predictor of victory.[32]

The important point, however, may be that the entire political establishment—both Democrats and Republicans and political analysts from both the media and academia—*believed* that what the Republicans did made a difference. It is also indisputable that the Republican party's new activities coincided with their longest period of Senate control in the past half-century.

## The Democrats: Centralized Organization and Decentralized Messages

In 1980 the Democrats lost control of the presidency and the Senate and, much of the time, effective control of the House. Their defeat persuaded Democratic legislators to take their national committees more seriously. As a national staffer described it:

> It finally dawned on some folks in the House that the Republicans and their congressional committee were doing a tremendous amount of in-kind services for one-third what our incumbents had to pay for the same services. The votes that Reagan was getting in the House kind of pushed it along.[33]

The House campaign committee moved aggressively to raise money through direct mail and to plow much of what was collected not into campaign-related expenditures but into further direct mail fund-raising appeals. The congressional committee donor base grew from three thousand contributors in 1978 to more than a hundred thousand. The committee's staff, which had consisted of four people working out of the basement of a House office building, grew to about a hundred and moved into a new party building.

Democratic congressional candidates at first looked askance at how the newly flush congressional committee was spending its money. Incumbents particularly were annoyed that the committee was not supporting them. The manager for a Democratic committee chairman recalled: "I was one of the campaigns bitching and moaning in '82 that when we needed an extra check or an in-kind service they were tight as could be. This congressman went out and raised $150,000 for the DCCC." The strategy paid off, however. By 1984 the Democrats had opened a state-of-the-art media center that produced low-cost advertising spots for candidates. The almost nonexistent formal communication with PACs was greatly improved. For the 1988 elections, the Democrats deployed five regional coordinators; there had been none in 1980.

The Democrats' Senate campaign committee moved in the same direction, albeit more slowly. Through the 1982 elections it continued to concentrate on large-donor fund raising that primarily benefited incumbents. Thereafter, it began a direct mail program, candidate recruiting activities, and some polling. The DSCC still could not raise close to what it could legally spend in competitive races (much less could it fully fund virtually all Senate candidates, no matter what their chances, as the Republicans did). But its 1986 fund-raising capabilities improved to the point where by the end of September it had already "maxed out" for eight competitive candidates in small states where the total party contribution limits were under about $350,000.[34] The DSCC remained the smallest of the four party legislative campaign committees, with only about half the staff of either its Republican Senate or Democratic congressional counterparts.[35]

Despite the Democrats' somewhat successful imitation of the Republican national operation, there remain important differences between the parties—principally having to do with the Democrats' more decentralized decision-making processes and less thematic party messages. Gary Wekkin described the Republican bureaucratic model as one of inclusive authority and the Democratic model as one of overlapping authority.[36] The Republican party organizations hold a monopoly on many "service bureau" functions, give allocation decisions to the party bureaucracies, and minimize officeholder complaints by spreading resources around liberally. Democratic officeholders, on the other hand, participate much more fully in allocation decisions. The senators serving on the DSCC are heavily involved in making financial allocations, as are DCCC members and the Democratic House leadership.[37]

Additionally, the Democrats suffer less than might be expected from their relative financial disadvantage because a number of extra-party organizations perform some of the service functions that are the province of the Republican party organizations. The National Committee for an Effective Congress provides most Democrats with targeting plans. A PAC called Democrats for the Eighties, founded by party fund raiser Pamela Harriman, prepares issue materials. Labor unions, environmental groups, and others run effective Democratic GOTV operations. And because for the past half-century there have usually been more Democrats than Republicans in both national legislative houses, more Democrats benefit from the perquisites of incumbency.

As is true of the Republicans, these patterns are as much the product of history as of design. The Democratic party arose in the Jackson era as a set of locally based organizations. Their powerful local machines were a counterweight to Republican national domination for most of the period between 1860 and 1932. The Civil War split their northern and southern constituencies and organizations in ways that to some extent still persist. The Democratic Leadership Council, primarily a southern-based organization of elected officeholders that is virtually an announced competitor to the Democratic National Committee, is almost unimaginable on the Republican side.

The Republicans emphasize national themes and nationally based organizational activities and do relatively better in presidential years. The Democrats emphasize local themes and more decentralized resource allocation and do relatively better in midterm years. These tendencies arise less from conscious choice than from real and longstanding historical circumstances. Arguments that the Democrats suffer from the lack of a national theme or that Republicans should emphasize money less and a local base more substantially miss the mark.[38] The Democrats cannot homogenize their disparate and sometimes antagonistic elements. The Republicans, in an era of weak party loyalties and disappearing patronage, cannot create genuine deeply based local party organizations or allied constituency-based groups where none have existed.

A sharp drop in Republican party fund raising for the 1988 cycle and the modest Democratic increase were probably related less to their organizational performances than to the weakening appeal of the Republicans' national themes and the growing relevance of regional issues such as protectionism and agricultural policy—both local issues that tend to benefit Democrats.[39]

Although the party organizations are clearly important players in some campaigns, particularly in those of challengers, we should reiterate that the party is "but one of several sources of electoral support, and by no means the greatest, despite its recent growth."[40]

# Parties, PACs, and Consultants in Campaigns

One interpretation of the developments discussed in this chapter is that in the last few years American campaign practices have come almost full circle. As the traditional parties declined, political consultants, armed with technological skills, moved forward to take their place. Additionally, emerging independent groups such as the National Committee for an Effective Congress on the left and NCPAC and Committee for the Survival of a Free Congress on the right were a source of low-cost or no-cost professional services to candidates. The Republican party and to some extent the Democratic party then retaliated by positioning themselves either to fund or to provide the same services, with neither ideological nor mercenary incentives. To what extent have parties reassumed the central role in campaigns? What is their relationship to the consultants and political action committees that have usurped many of their traditional functions?

Perhaps naturally the consultants, the PACs, and the party professionals have somewhat critical views of each other's work, particularly in the Republican community, where the overlap has become greater and the competition more obvious. From the point of view of party organization staff, the consultants put the candidates second to their own profits and the special-interest groups are an unwelcome development. As Mitch Daniels described the party's role in campaigns:

> I think it's a very healthy thing to create a source of support for candidates that is not tied to a special interest and is not purely on a mercenary basis. We care about candidates, back them to the hilt, and don't ask anything from them except their own best efforts. We're going to be there every day, not just when the bill is overdue.

The consultants and independent PACs, on the other hand, believe that the party committees are bureaucratic, inflexible, and riddled with patronage. A New Right operative observed: "The NRCC doesn't have 'campaign managers,' they have 'administrative aides.' They homogenize all campaigns. There are NRCC 'managers' that have lost two or three races. They go back to their friends at the committee and get another campaign to screw up." One consultant said of the national committee field staff deployed to campaigns: "We don't allow them to interfere. By 'them,' I mean typically a field person, a young guy; this is his first real campaign. He may desire to get involved. His activities might be counterproductive. We won't allow it." Another is more direct: "The political staffs of the committees are on salary, and if they were any good, they would be running their own firms. All the good talent is freelancing." The perspective of both sides is thoughtfully summed up by Vince Breglio, a former director of the NRSC, who now heads his own independent consulting company:

> I've been on both sides, and the fact of the matter is that campaigns do get ripped off by their consultants. But my own personal view is that by the very nature of the party structure, the party will never accomplish its goal because really talented people can't survive in the pressure

cooker of the committees. Whenever an incumbent senator or congressman calls up and says "Hire X," you have to hire X. You can't maintain
the highest professional standards of advancement until you move
away from that into the private sector, where you are controlling the
dynamics that make an organization efficient. The national committees
will never have the kind of efficiency or personnel that will allow them
to take over some of the functions they'd like to.

In the final analysis, both the consultants and the party committees
admit that the future will probably include them both, although the
admission is somewhat grudging. From a consultant's point of view, the
chief advantage of working with the committees is that they are clients
with a long-term existence and, unlike some individual candidates,
provide repeat business; they can be depended upon to pay their bills;
and they make the consultant's life easier. Still, most consultants think
of the committees primarily as organizations that can help them with
their individual candidates and not as ends in themselves. From the
party's point of view, the consultants are a necessary evil in a technol-
ogy-dominated campaign system. The party's role is to attempt to
displace and replace the consultants as much as possible and where this
is not possible to control their behavior through the party's financial
resources.

In summary, the party is not the only repository of campaign
resources, technical or financial. A growing number of candidates in
both parties and of all ideological persuasions are wealthy enough to use
their own money to purchase the necessary resources and technical
help. The independent political action committees can also provide
these campaign needs. An adept and promising candidate can shop for
money and other resources among other special-interest groups—labor,
business, feminist, environmental, senior citizens, moralistic, or whatever. For better or worse, the parties' renascence has not yet returned us
to a party-based campaign system nor to a system in which most
candidates who become officeholders owe much to their party organizations. In the final chapter we analyze the broader political effects of this
state of affairs and the forces that might hinder or favor its continuation.

## Notes

1. Larry J. Sabato, *The Rise of Political Consultants: New Ways of Winning Elections*
   (New York: Basic Books, 1981), 336.
2. *Washington Post National Weekly Edition*, February 3, 1986, 13.
3. See the discussion of these techniques in David J. Heller, "Mail, Money and
   Machiavelli," *Campaigns and Elections* 8 (November-December 1987): 32-45;

Larry Sabato and David Beiler, *Magic or Blue Smoke and Mirrors: Reflections on New Trends and Technologies in the Political Consultant Trade*, prepared for the Annenberg Washington Program in Communications Policy Studies, Evanston, Ill., Northwestern University, 1988; Robert G. Meadow, "The Electronic Machine: New Technologies in Political Campaigns," *Election Politics* 3 (Fall 1986): 26-31.

4. *Washington Post National Weekly Edition*, March 28-April 3, 1988.

5. The statistics in the discussion of state parties come from a mail survey of state party chairs conducted from October 1983 through February 1984 by the Advisory Commission on Intergovermental Relations, in cooperation with the Democratic and Republican national committees. The survey probably somewhat overstates state party activity, since 30 percent of all state party organizations (ten Republican and twenty Democratic) did not respond; it seems reasonable to assume the nonrespondents would be concentrated among the less active and less well staffed organizations. The results are published in Timothy Conlan, Ann Martino, and Robert Dilger, "State Parties in the 1980s," *Intergovernmental Perspective* 10 (Fall 1984): 6-13, and *The Transformation of American Politics* (Washington, D.C.: Advisory Commission on Intergovernmental Relations, 1986).

6. See the summary of these developments in Malcolm Jewell and David Olson, *Political Parties and Elections in American States*, 3d ed. (Chicago: Dorsey, 1988), chapter 7.

7. A successful California ballot initiative in June 1988 apparently places future limits on the ability of the caucus leadership to transmit large sums to individual candidates, although the full implications are not yet clear. See the *New York Times*, June 9, 1988, B11.

8. R. R. Johnson, "Partisan Legislative Campaign Committees: New Power, New Problems," *Comparative State Politics Newsletter*, August 1987, 14-18.

9. For a description of the New Jersey Democratic Senate Campaign Committee program, see Joel Bradshaw and Elizabeth Sullivan, "The Case for Cooperation," *Campaigns and Elections* 8 (March-April 1988): 57-61.

10. Meadow, "The Electronic Machine," 27. For further discussion of cable and VCRs in campaigns, see Sabato and Beiler, *Magic or Blue Smoke and Mirrors*; John Power, "Plug into Cable TV," *Campaigns and Elections* 8 (September-October 1987): 55-57; *Washington Post National Weekly Edition*, June 6-12, 1988, 21; *New York Times*, July 1, 1988.

11. As of September 30, 1988, PACs had donated $62.4 million to 408 House incumbents and only $5.7 million to their challengers. Senate incumbents had received $28.5 million from PACs, while Senate challengers collected only $5.7 million (*National Journal*, November 5, 1988, 2818).

12. *New York Times*, August 30, 1988.

13. National Chamber Alliance for Politics, *Endorsement Report 1986* (Washington, D.C.: National Chamber Alliance for Politics, October 1986).

14. National Committee for an Effective Congress, *A Guide to the 1986 Campaigns for the U.S. Senate* (Washington, D.C.: National Committee for an Effective Congress, no date).

15. Frank J. Sorauf, *Money in American Elections* (Glenview: Ill.: Scott, Foresman, 1988), 111; *Congressional Quarterly Weekly Report*, November 5, 1988, 3185-3187.

16. See the account of their activities in Lisa De Maio Brewster, "PACS on the Warpath: How Independent Efforts Re-Elected Jesse Helms," *Campaigns and Elections* 6 (Summer 1985): 5-11.

17. For discussion of the groups' difficulties, see *National Journal*, February 27, 1988, 537, and April 23, 1988, 1087; *Washington Post National Weekly Edition*, November 10, 1986, 12.
18. *National Journal*, June 21, 1986, 1537.
19. Thomas R. Berglund, M. D., and Peter Lauer, "Political Prescriptions: AMPAC and Independent Expenditures," *Election Politics* 3 (Fall 1986): 20; *New York Times*, October 26, 1988, A23. For further discussion of independent expenditures by these groups, see Diana Owen, "The Information Environment for PAC Decision-Making," paper presented at the 1986 annual meeting of the American Political Science Association, Washington, D.C., August 28-31, 1986; Sorauf, *Money in American Elections*, 110-113.
20. Sorauf, *Money in American Elections*, 65.
21. James L. Gibson et al., "Assessing Party Organizational Strength," *American Journal of Political Science* 27 (May 1983): 206; Cornelius Cotter et al., *Party Organizations in American Politics* (New York: Praeger, 1984), 88-89.
22. Sarah McCally Morehouse, "The Politics of Gubernatorial Nominations," *State Government* 53 (Summer 1980): 128. See also Malcolm E. Jewell, *Parties and Primaries: Nominating State Governors* (New York: Praeger, 1984), parts IV and V.
23. Paul S. Herrnson and David Menafe-Libey, "The Transformation of American Political Parties: A Theory of Party Organizational Development," paper presented at the annual meeting of the Midwestern Political Science Association, Chicago, Illinois, April 14-16, 1988, 16-28. Another historical account of the development of Republican party activities can be found in Dan Nimmo, "Teleparty Politics," *Campaigns and Elections* 8 (Winter 1986-1987): 75-78.
24. Alexander Heard, *The Costs of Democracy* (Garden City, N.Y.: Doubleday, 1962), 196. A superb study of the Civil War era that discusses the formation of the Republican party is James McPherson, *Battle Cry of Freedom* (New York: Oxford University Press, 1988). On patronage assessments, see David Mayhew, *Placing Parties in American Politics* (Princeton, N.J.: Princeton University Press, 1986), chapter 1, and Heard, *Costs of Democracy*, 186.
25. See Larry Sabato, "Parties, PACs and Independent Groups," in *The American Elections of 1982*, ed. Thomas E. Mann and Norman J. Ornstein (Washington, D.C.: American Enterprise Institute, 1983), 72-110.
26. See the data reported in Paul S. Herrnson, "Do Parties Make a Difference? The Role of Party Organizations in Congressional Elections," *Journal of Politics* 48 (August 1986): 589-615.
27. See the findings in Alan I. Abramowitz, "National Issues, Strategic Politicians, and Voting Behavior in the 1980 and 1982 Congressional Elections," *American Journal of Political Science* 28 (November 1984): 710-721.
28. *Congressional Quarterly Weekly Report*, July 2, 1983, 1351.
29. "C & E Interview with Lance Tarrance, Bill Hamilton, Adam Goodman, and Randy Thompson," *Campaigns and Elections* 7 (January-February 1987): 26-31. There was further outrage when it was revealed that NRSC staffers awarded themselves large bonuses the day after their dismal 1986 showing (*Congressional Quarterly Weekly Report*, October 3, 1987, 2371).
30. *National Journal*, December 20, 1986, 3086-3087.
31. Ibid.
32. Stuart Rothenberg, *Winners and Losers* (Washington, D.C.: Free Congress Research and Education Foundation, 1983), 94.

33. The Democratic Congressional Campaign Committee, under the chairman-ship of (later House Speaker) Tip O'Neill, moved aggressively to raise money and provide some campaign services in 1972, when members feared they would be swept away in the Nixon landslide; however, the money came in large fat cat chunks, which were impermissible under the new campaign finance laws. House Democrats apparently once again grew complacent after the Republicans' heavy Watergate-related defeats. See Tip O'Neill with William Novak, *Man of the House: The Life and Political Memoirs of Speaker Tip O'Neill* (New York: Random House, 1987), 205-208.

34. Of these eight (Idaho, Louisiana, Maryland, Missouri, Nevada, North Dakota, South Dakota, and Washington State), the Democrats eventually won six. On the other hand, some promising Senate hopefuls in large states did not fare as well. Pennsylvania's Bob Edgar, for instance, had received only 29 percent of his allotment by this date. Unable to purchase enough television time in expensive markets such as Philadelphia and Pittsburgh, Edgar, who was widely regarded as a strong candidate with an excellent campaign organization, never became well known in the state and lost by a large margin.

35. Herrnson and Menafe-Libey, "Transformation of American Political Parties," 28.

36. Gary D. Wekkin, "Political Parties and Intergovernmental Relations in 1984: The Consequences of Party Renewal for Territorial Constituencies," *Publius* 15 (Summer 1985): 19-37.

37. See the extended discussion in Paul Herrnson, " Party Strategies and Resource Distribution in the 1984 Congressional Elections," and Barbara G. Salmore and Stephen A. Salmore, "Back to Basics: Party as Legislative Caucus," papers presented at the annual meeting of the Midwest Political Science Association, Chicago, Ill., April 9-12, 1987.

38. See, for example, Steve Lilienthal and Stuart Rothenberg, "Did the Republicans Get What They Paid For?" *Election Politics* 4 (Spring 1987): 19-21.

39. In the first eighteen months of the 1988 election cycle, National Republican Senatorial Committee fund raising was down about a third as compared with 1986; National Republican Congressional Committee receipts dropped by half compared with 1984. Although, as usual, well ahead of the Democrats, the Republicans' relative lead was a third smaller than it had been in both 1984 and 1986. (*Federal Election Commission Report*, August 29, 1988.) The Democrats lagged far behind (30 percent to 61 percent) in poll findings on which party would better be able to maintain a strong national defense, and they led only narrowly on the question of which party better represented respondents' views on national policy (48 percent to 43 percent). But they had a wide lead (51 percent to 38 percent) on which party better represented views on local issues. (ABC-*Washington Post* poll, January 1988, of 1,505 adult respondents.)

40. Leon Epstein, *Political Parties in the American Mold* (Madison: University of Wisconsin Press, 1986), 70.

# Campaigns and American Politics  11

*You can look around the floor of the House and see a handful—
twenty years ago, you saw a lot of them—today you can see just a
handful of hacks that were put there by the party organization, and
there are very, very few of them left. It is just mostly people who
went out and took the election.*

U.S. representative, 1983[1]

In the preceding chapters we discussed the importance of individual
candidates' campaigns and the declining role of the political parties.
Party organizations have become only one of several actors in candidate-
centered campaigns, and usually they are not the most significant. It is
important for anyone thinking about the future course of American
politics and governance to examine the declining role of parties in
campaigns. In this chapter we explain why.

Political parties have been central to the functioning of our democratic system. From James Bryce in the nineteenth century, who wrote
that "parties are inevitable. . . . No one has ever shown how representative government could work without them"[2] to E. E. Schattschneider
in this one, who argued that "democracy is unthinkable save in terms of
the parties,"[3] serious political analysts have "shared an underlying
agreement that effective parties are desirable and probably essential in
American politics as in democratic politics elsewhere."[4] Parties play
many vital roles in democratic systems, but these roles can be broadly
classified in terms of their functions for the electorate, as political
organizations, and in government.[5]

The way the American parties fulfill these roles, or fail to, is crucial to understanding how American democracy now operates. Of the three major party roles, campaigns are most directly related to the party as a political organization because the main purpose of the party's organizational role is nominating and electing candidates. Candidate-centered campaigns have given the parties a major competitor and, at the present time, one that is acknowledged to be dominant. The effects of candidate-centered campaigns, however, have also spilled over in important ways to the parties' other major roles. In the next section we discuss the various roles of the parties more fully, exploring the extent to which candidate-centered campaigns have been both causes and effects of party decline.

## The Decline of Parties ─────────────────────────

In the 1960s and 1970s scholars became disturbed by the apparent decay of the American parties in all their aspects. Their concern stemmed from the implications of party decline for the democratic process. One observer warned, "When parties are absent or . . . have become Cheshire cats of which very little is left except the smile, pathologies multiply." [6] The presumed pathologies included a state of affairs in which political debate was "more negative and bitter, and policy compromises are much harder to come by." [7] Scholars observed signs of party decay everywhere, pervading all its roles.

Within the electorate parties seemed increasingly unable to structure the voters' choices of candidates.[8] As we discussed in chapter 3, the electorate's psychological identification with the parties steadily weakened. Not only were fewer voters partisan identifiers, but those who did identify with a party reported weaker attachments.

Perhaps most damning was the voters' lack of interest in the parties. From 1952 to 1980, the percentage of the electorate that had no opinions about America's parties—either good or ill—rose from slightly less than one-tenth to somewhat more than one-third. More than two-thirds opposed the idea of voters registering as partisans, and almost as many rejected a proposal for a party lever on voting machines.[9] The parties, more and more, were not supported or rejected but were considered irrelevant. By a margin of 45 percent to 37 percent, the American public in 1983 believed that "organized special interest groups" spoke to their concerns better than the parties did.[10]

The decline of the parties' organizational role as the vehicle for nomination and election is what this book bears witness to. Local party organizations and their vaunted machines have almost passed into history. Little more than one-tenth of all Democratic and Republican county organizations now have permanent headquarters; even fewer have paid staff.[11] State party strength rebounded a bit from its nadir, but, as we saw in chapter 10, "the evidence is not overwhelming." [12]

At the national level, traditionally the weakest link in the party chain, growth was impressive. The fact remained, however, that the direct primary robbed the parties of their monopoly on nominations, just as the advent of television and computerized direct mail robbed them of their monopoly on campaign communication. In the late 1980s two-thirds of the public declared themselves in favor of primaries as the vehicle for choosing candidates rather than "open meetings of party activists"; 59 percent favored doing away with the national party conventions entirely and having voters select presidential candidates directly.[13] Campaign finance laws made it impossible for candidates to obtain from the parties the large amounts of money required to wage campaigns. Candidates turned to alternative sources such as political action committees, the candidates' personal resources, and direct solicitation of the public.

The parties' role in government suffered as well. Traditionally, parties were able to structure government policy because one party usually controlled both major policy-making institutions—the presidency and the Congress. Until the turn of the century, the president's party controlled the Senate almost 90 percent of the time, and the House more than two-thirds of the time. Most of the rare victories of the out-party occurred in midterm elections. Only twice in more than a hundred years—in the disputed Hayes-Tilden election of 1876 and the second election of Grover Cleveland, in 1892—did the president fail to carry both houses in a presidential election year. Between 1900 and 1954, despite the Populist and Progressive crusades against party control, the trend grew even stronger. The president's party controlled the Senate better than 90 percent of the time and the House more than 80 percent of the time. Not once in all the presidential elections between William McKinley's second campaign and Dwight D. Eisenhower's first campaign did the presidential party fail to bring in both houses of Congress.

Events changed dramatically in the 1950s. Between 1954 and 1990 the president's party would control the Senate barely half the time and the House only a third of the time. Furthermore, party control meant less and less, as both John Kennedy and Jimmy Carter found to their chagrin. Despite majorities in both houses, neither president was able to enact major components of his program. Lyndon Johnson, the only other president of the period to have party control of both houses, was more successful at first, but his accomplishments owed much to the powerful emotions generated by Kennedy's assassination.

Officeholders who appealed to an increasingly nonpartisan electorate to gain victory, often achieving it without any significant reliance on the party for assistance, had no compelling reason to vote a party line. For them, as for voters, the parties were becoming irrelevant. A member of the Democratic party leadership in the House observed:

> Nobody in the United States Congress ever talks about the Democratic or Republican party. . . . I have never heard a member of the Congress refer to a colleague and urge a vote for him because he was in the same party. Most Democrats and Republicans could not recall three items on the platform of their party. . . . We have 435 parties in the House.[14]

The result of these developments was, as the 1980s began, that the parties were weaker than they had ever been. The candidate-centered campaigns had their most negative effect on the parties' organizational role, but they impinged on other party functions as well. Campaigns that presented candidates to the public as individuals rather than as partisans hastened the decline of party identification as a means of structuring voters' choice: "The voters did not decide all of a sudden that parties were bankrupt political institutions and mandate their decline. Rather, voters reacted gradually over the last quarter of a century *to the way in which politics was presented to them.*"[15]

Candidates for executive office—presidents and governors—appealed to the voters on the basis of leadership and competence, while legislators emphasized their service to their constituencies. Voters responded to these appeals as they heard them; they punished Jimmy Carter for the state of the nation and rewarded Ronald Reagan. At the same time they reelected the vast majority of legislators in both parties, in approval of the way incumbents fulfilled their stated roles and without regard to whether they shared either the partisanship or the policy preferences of successful or unsuccessful presidents.

Officeholders who were voted in as the result of candidate-centered campaigns emphasized electoral considerations in their decision-making calculus. Describing the culture of the House, a top staffer for the Democratic leadership distinguished between the "street-corner guys" and the "Atari guys." The former, a dying breed epitomized by former House Speaker Tip O'Neill and his Republican counterpart, minority leader Robert Michel, came to Congress originally through strong local party organizations. Their major career goal was to achieve seniority and thus important positions in the party leadership. Their orientation was hierarchical; when faced with a tough question, their response was to find out what the chairman or the leader thought about it.

In contrast, the Atari guys of the candidate-centered era arrived in Washington through their own efforts. Many represented areas that had been traditional strongholds of the other party. Many seemed supremely uninterested in their committee assignments; they sought rather to become national spokespersons for the "big issues" and were often notably nondeferential to the House establishment.[16] The same House staffer mused on the behavior of this new breed in their officeholding roles:

> They talk about issues, but little gets accomplished. They just talk. They don't care about bills or chairmen; they just care about sending messages. When they vote, they think, "What kind of ad can they run against me?" The biggest turnout at the caucus meetings is never for legislative discussions but to see the new party TV ads. They say, "Wow! This is great—I can save myself with this ad!"
>
> The only committees they care about getting on are Budget and Ways and Means so they can talk about the big macroeconomic issues, or Defense so they can talk about the big foreign policy issues, or Energy and Commerce so they can get PAC money. The Budget Committee is great because ... they don't have to make hard program choices, they can just debate the macroeconomic issues.
>
> What do they want? They want to be famous. For the old guys, friendships crossed party lines. For these new guys, it's message sending that crosses party lines.

California's Vic Fazio, a Democratic House member and exemplar of the Atari guys, confirmed this view: "People think you're important so they listen to you. The media want to hear from members of the Budget Committee." [17]

No wonder that through most of the 1970s party cohesion in both House and Senate, as measured by the number of votes on which a majority of legislators of one party opposed a majority in the other party, continued to decline.[18] Increasingly, executives and not parties set the legislative agenda; increasingly, legislators decided whether to support this agenda based largely on an electoral calculus.

Was the party's declining role in the electorate, as organization, and in government permanent and irreversible? So it seemed. In 1982 the American Political Science Association commissioned a set of papers to assess the state of the discipline. In the paper on political parties, Leon Epstein, a distinguished scholar of parties, asked his colleagues, "Are professional students of politics now champions of a lost cause, trying with words to roll back a tide of American antipartyism?" [19]

# The Parties Resurrected? Maybe

In the past few years some of the political scientists who exhibited the most pessimism about the future of the parties (and with it the broader American future) have seen signs of party renascence. One who argued in the 1970s that the weakened parties "may eventually bring the nation to a free floating politics in which prediction is hazardous, continuities are absent, and governmental responsibility is impossible to fix," [20] was more optimistic by the 1980s: "There is still hope and time available. The need for stronger parties is becoming evident." [21] Another student of party decline had second thoughts by 1984: "It is not inconceivable that the decline of political parties could begin to reverse in the near future." [22] The same year a third well-known scholar argued:

> The two parties show signs of strength as great, if not greater, than they have at any time in the past fifty years. It should be clear by now that the grab bag of assumptions, inferences, and half-truths which have fed the decline of party thesis is simply wrong.[23]

This substantial shift in tone was occasioned by a series of events, occurring mostly around and after the election of President Reagan in 1980, that apparently signaled the reversal of the decay of the party in all its major roles.

## Party in the Electorate

There was, first, the matter of party identification within the electorate. Although approximately a third of the voters stubbornly continued to call themselves independents, the proportion of Republicans crept upward, mainly at the expense of the Democrats—some indication that Reagan's admirers were extending their commitment beyond the titular leader of the party to the party itself. Between 1984 and 1988 in twenty-eight states that required party registration, Democrats lost 107,000 adherents, while the Republicans gained 2.1 million.[24]

There were other signs that Reagan's strong leadership polarized the electorate in a partisan way. Ticket splitting for House and Senate races dropped 7 percent between 1980 and 1982, and the percentage of survey respondents who could find no way to characterize the two parties, either positively or negatively, dropped eight points in the same period. The president himself polarized partisans in a truly dramatic fashion. Harris polls charting every president since Kennedy had found that Democrats and Republicans tended to disagree fairly modestly in their assessment of presidential performance in office. Most, for example, agreed that Jimmy Carter was not doing a very good job—only ten percentage points separated the assessments of the two groups of partisans. Richard Nixon held the previous record for polarization, with a twenty-seven-point difference between Democrats and Republicans. In October 1983, however, the partisan discrepancy in views of Reagan was a full thirty-four points, and a September 1984 CBS News/*New York Times* poll charted an unprecedented gulf of fifty-six points.[25] Thus there were modest signs that the electorate might finally be realigning toward the Republicans, a shift that had previously been "akin to waiting for the Second Coming—much discussion, not much happening." [26]

## Party as Organization

The strengthening of the party organizations at the national level continued apace. Both parties' congressional campaign committees engaged in extensive candidate recruitment and "nursing" activities. Fred Asbell of the National Republican Congressional Committee estimated that his organization was involved in a "major way" with sixty to sixty-five House candidates, or almost half of all NRCC-targeted districts in 1984. Martin Franks, director of the Democratic Congressional Campaign Committee, put the figure for his committee at thirty to thirty-five, "up from zero in 1980." [27]

There were signs that these efforts were bearing fruit. Analysts pointed to a sharp drop over time in the number of uncontested House seats; it began about 1960 but escalated in 1980 and 1982. They attributed this growing competition at least in part to the strengthened parties. [28] At lower levels there were reports of increasing state party activity in areas such as coordinated polling, media production, and mailings for legislative candidates. State party subsidies in many states extended to the level of county office. Thus at all levels there were new signs of life. The literature decrying the death of the parties was replaced by a new spate of books hailing their organizational revitalization. [29]

## Party and Governance

Finally, dramatic shifts were apparent in the legislative behavior of officeholders. We referred earlier to the falling levels of party voting in both the House and the Senate. The Reagan administration, however, seemed to polarize legislators in much the same way that it polarized voters. In 1987 a majority of House Democrats opposed a majority of Republicans on 64 percent of all recorded votes—an all-time high. [30] Additionally, there was a strong ideological cast to the partisan divisions, with the Republican members becoming more conservative across all major issue areas (social policy, foreign policy, and the economy) and the Democrats becoming more liberal.

The strength of these partisan divisions cut across all regions. Even though Republican legislators from the East were more liberal than the rest of their party, and southern Democrats were more conservative than other Democrats, no Republican regional group was more liberal than any Democratic group. As a group, eastern Republicans were still more conservative than southern Democrats. [31]

If "the ultimate test of party linkage is the behavior of the party member in government," [32] the signs seemed to indicate that in the 1980s officeholders were finally passing that test. Some analysts saw the increased party voting in the legislature as a direct consequence of the party's organizational activity. They speculated that the stepped-up party efforts that produced similar campaigns and similar issues across the country were responsible for the parties' more like-minded legislators. The campaign committees were seen as having a nationalizing and centralizing effect. [33]

The parties appeared to be regaining some of their lost effectiveness in all their roles. And if party meant more, it would follow that candidate-centered campaigns would mean less.

## The Parties Resurrected? Maybe Not _____

Although the evidence for revitalized parties seems impressive, the old saying "One swallow does not a summer make" applies powerfully in this case. Short-term changes do not always become long-term trends. Party identification among the electorate has been notably unstable throughout the 1980s. Identification with the Democrats ranged from an eighteen-point lead in the depths of the 1982 recession to a fourteen-point lead in the early fall of 1988 and, in the immediate afterglow of the 1988 presidential election, a seven-point lead. After the election of 1984, there was a virtual tie. [34] Two surveys that monitored party identification over twenty-two weeks during the 1984 campaign found frequent and substantial shifts during that election season. Analysts of these data concluded, "When we find that a campaign can move partisanship, we do not have proof that such changes will outlast that campaign." [35]

The effects of party organizational activity were also difficult to quantify. The Republicans' position in the states showed little overall improvement in the 1980s. Despite the massive efforts of the Republicans to elect candidates to Congress and to the state legislatures, George Bush entered the White House in 1989 as the twentieth-century president with the fewest fellow partisans in the House. [36]

Campaign committee staff members were at best tentative in agreeing with some academics that their work might influence the voting behavior of the legislators they supported. [37] They recognized that even grateful challengers, once elected, became incumbents able to command contributions from nonparty sources. A cautious political scientist noted, "Once in office, members of Congress may be invulnerable to party pressure based on past or prospective allocations of party campaign resources." Observing that the Republican party bureaucracy "has not developed substantial influence over policymaking by Republican officeholders," he went on to say, "Indeed, influence tends to run the other way."[38]

The party's influence on PAC contributions was also limited. A survey found that directors of PACs were most likely to seek information and take contribution cues from their largest and most influential colleagues. Corporate and trade associations looked for guidance more to the Business-Industry Political Action Committee (BIPAC), labor committees to the AFL-CIO's Committee on Political Education (COPE), and liberal ideological groups to the National Committee for an Effective Congress (NCEC) than any of them did to the political parties.[39]

Heavy contributions by business-oriented PACs to Democratic incumbents made Republican congressional leaders particularly irate. A contingent led by Senate minority leader Bob Dole called a Washington meeting of business PAC directors in September 1988 and threatened to support legislation limiting PAC activity. House minority leader Robert Michel and NRCC chairman Guy Vander Jagt followed up in October. In a letter to top corporate officials, they wrote that it was "disturbing to see so many contributions going to members who consistently oppose the interest you and other business leaders advocate."[40] PAC leaders were unimpressed. They were more interested in protecting their access to Democratic committee chairs and other incumbents, particularly after the failure of Republican challengers to gain seats in 1986 and 1988. The vice president of RPAC, the Realtors' committee, put it succinctly:

> Our members were demanding a lot more accountability. Gone were our free-spending days when we poured money down a black hole called "challenger candidates." Our marching orders on PAC contributions were very clear: Stop wasting money on losers. . . .
> We are a special interest group. Our interest is real estate and housing issues; it is not contra aid, it is not abortion, it is not minimum wage, it is not plant closings and it is not Japanese cars coming into this country.[41]

Finally, the effect of party activity on competition levels was erratic. Although the number of uncontested congressional seats had, as we have noted, dropped sharply after 1960, particularly in presidential years, it suddenly rose dramatically in 1984 to a level more than twice that of 1980. Of the fifty-three uncontested seats in 1984, forty-four were held by Democrats. Twenty-six of those were in the South, despite the resources the Republican party could offer challengers and its much improved southern performance. This pattern continued in 1988, when eighty House seats went uncontested by one of the major parties; sixty-one of those seats were held by Democrats.

It is also necessary to keep in perspective the high levels of party co-hesion in congressional voting. Although it is true that the Democrats were more unified in their opposition to the Republicans during the Reagan administration than at any time since 1908, it was also the first time they had found themselves on the defensive against an activist and ideological president. Their behavior was similar to the Republicans' reaction to Democratic activists John Kennedy and Lyndon Johnson in the 1960s. In Reagan's final year in office, party voting dropped back to the levels of 1979.[42]

Much of the time, even during the Reagan years, the percentage of party votes in which a majority (more than 50 percent) of Democrats opposed a majority of Republicans was less than half the total number of votes. In 1988 only 23 percent of House roll calls and 12 percent of those in the Senate resulted in as many as three-quarters of Democrats and Republicans opposing each other. True party-line votes, where at least 90 percent of those on opposite sides of the aisle were in disagreement, numbered only 7 percent of House votes and a mere 3 percent in the Senate. Thus on the majority of roll call votes, most legislators of both parties voted the same way, or partisans distributed themselves more randomly.[43]

Nonparty votes were often cast on the classic pork barrel issues that legislators point to when they run for reelection as constituency ombudsmen. If we use the loosest definition of party unity (that is, votes in which at least 50 percent of Democrats and Republicans oppose each other), legislation dealing with appropriations of funds comprised less than one-tenth of the 1988 party votes in both the House and the Senate. If we use the strict criterion of 90 percent of opposing partisans in disagreement, not a single appropriations vote could be characterized as a true party-line vote. For constituency-minded legislators, pork barrel issues loomed larger than their votes on national security and foreign policy matters, which were relatively speaking much more likely to have a strong partisan cast.[44] One congressional observer noted: "Rheto-ric is one thing, but when it comes down to who gets what, you pay at-tention to how they act, not how they talk. That's where partisanship falls apart."[45]

The overall note we sound in this section, therefore, is one of caution. Many of the trends of the last decade may be transitory; others are subject to the classic debate over whether a glass is half-empty or half-full. It appears to us that the political environment still contains many more forces that impel candidates away from parties and party discipline and toward the continuation of candidate-centered campaigns and what they imply for the behavior of voters and of candidates who become officeholders.

# Candidates and Parties: A Longer View _____

Whatever the American political landscape, one element has remained constant: The principal force driving most candidates for political office is the desire to win. The story of candidate and officeholder behavior in campaigns and afterward is always the story of what activities candidates believe will optimize their chances of winning. When the party organizations controlled nominations, directed campaigns, raised money, brokered policy, and cued voter decisions, candidates had no rational alternative to participation in this party system. They had to participate in it to achieve their goal—winning.

Developments in recent years have given candidates new means of winning. Voters who were less firmly bound psychologically to the parties were more open to nonpartisan appeals. New technologies provided candidates with alternatives to the party symbol and organization for communicating those appeals to voters. These changes are permanent fixtures of the political landscape. They argue for a continued diminution of the party role in setting candidates' fates and a continued increase in the ability of politicians to affect their own destinies. Parties thus can be only as important as candidates permit them to be. In the next section we elaborate on the most significant of the trends benefiting candidates—and thus candidate-centered campaigning—and consider the circumstances in which candidates might conceivably find strengthened parties to be advantageous to them.

## The Critical Role of Technology

Technology is the development most responsible for ending party primacy in campaigns. The parties had survived other massive social changes. Confronted by the Populist and Progressive threats to their hegemony, parties found ways to adapt to potentially devastating reforms such as the secret ballot and particularly the direct primary.

What made the advent of television and the computer unique was that they provided candidates everywhere with an effective alternative means of getting information about themselves to the voters. Newspapers, magazines, and radio paled in comparison with what television offered—a powerful combination of visual and aural messages. Candidates could enter voters' homes and give party organizations competition they had never had before.

If television provided the means for "wholesale" communication, the computer, with its ability to locate precisely the voters that candidates needed to reach and send a personalized message, furnished the means for "retail" communication. As Morris Fiorina has commented:

"Candidates would have little incentive to operate campaigns independently of parties if there were no means to apprise the citizenry of their independence. The media provide the means."[46]

There is no reason that the parties cannot also use these media. Their institutional advertising and direct mail efforts show that they are using them. But parties no longer have a monopoly on political communication. Once candidates learned that they could independently compete with party organizations and that they had the direct primary as the vehicle to do it, why should they give up their independence and control of their messages to the party organizations?

## The Matter of Money

One development that could compel candidates to rely more heavily on their party organizations is a campaign finance system controlled by the parties. If money has always been the mother's milk of politics, the enormous costs of the new campaign technology have made raising money, and lots of it, more imperative than ever. Giving parties a greater role in financing elections is always the first suggestion of reformers intent on strengthening the parties and ending candidate-centered politics. The American Political Science Association's Committee for Party Renewal has stated:

> No service to candidates is more important than the provision of money, and there should be few restraints on the ability of parties to raise and spend money in campaigns. . . . Parties themselves should be able to make unlimited contributions to the campaigns of their candidates for offices at all levels of government.[47]

Not unnaturally, party staff members endorse these views. A former director of the NRCC says, "If Congress and the Federal Election Commission are serious about wanting to help rebuild the parties, then they will have to look at us as something more than just super-PACs, and grant us major new authority and maneuvering room."[48]

This observation brings us to the crux of the matter. It is the officeholders in Congress who pass the legislation on campaign financing for candidates—in other words, for themselves. Their control of campaign money "buys freedom—freedom for candidates to run their own campaigns, freedom from the limitations of party, freedom to plot a future political career."[49] Any revision of the financing system will require broad consensus. A congressional staff member observes: "You're dealing with 535 experts. . . . They're not going to do anything that hurts their campaigns."[50]

It is precisely the lack of a consensus that has stalled change. As the 1980s progressed, many legislators became unhappy with the campaign finance system—but for diverse reasons. Some differences were attributable to the dissimilar situations facing House and Senate candidates, but the major conflicts stemmed from party-based dissension.

Fund raising, although a chore for all officeholders, was particularly wearisome for senators, who had to raise, on average, ten times as much for each contest as did House members. House incumbents, who needed less money and were less likely to run against strong challengers, tended to object to the system on philosophical grounds. Members of the upper house had more at stake personally.

A survey of officeholders found that twice as many senators as representatives spontaneously mentioned campaign finance reform as a needed change in congressional operations. Senators were twice as likely as representatives to believe that fund-raising demands cut into the time they should be spending on legislative work. One senator observed:

> I knew Congress well before I came here, but I did not know the amount of time consumed by fundraising and how that encroaches on your ability to work here. It devours one's time—you spend two or three years before your reelection fundraising. The other years, you're helping others.[51]

It was senators' unhappiness that led them to spend much of 1987 on the first major attempt at campaign finance reform since the early 1970s. David Boren, Democratic senator of Oklahoma, and Robert Byrd, then majority leader, led the reform efforts. Various versions of the Byrd-Boren proposals called for substantial public funding of Senate elections; limits on spending; a limit on PAC contributions, individually and in the aggregate; and discount rates for political advertising and direct mail. But longstanding partisan differences, both philosophical and political, prevented Senate passage of any campaign finance legislation in the 100th Congress of 1987-1988.

On philosophical grounds the great majority of Democrats favored public funding and limits on campaign contributions and spending. They argued that these measures would reduce the influence of money on politics generally and of wealthy special-interest groups specifically. They also held that doling out the same amount of public money to all candidates would create a "level playing field." In general, the Democrats believed their preferred reforms would make politics less biased toward the interests of the wealthy and would permit candidates with modest means to run for office.

But public financing and spending and contribution limits also appealed to the Democrats for political reasons. Democrats saw dangers in the current system. Wealthy individual contributors either to candidates or to party organizations were in shorter supply for Democrats than for Republicans. The Democrats also feared that if they lost control of their congressional majorities, pragmatic business PACs would act on their innate disposition to support Republicans more handsomely.

In addition, as long as there were more Democratic incumbents, more of them would profit from the benefits of incumbency. With the campaign finance reforms favored by Democrats, challengers could spend no more than incumbents and would not have electorally useful official resources such as the congressional frank and district offices.

Conversely, on philosophical grounds the Republicans opposed the new government spending and the enlarged bureaucracy that would be required by public financing. They saw spending ceilings on candidate communication as limiting the First Amendment right of free speech. To mitigate baneful effects of political money, Republicans proposed that much more of it be channeled to candidates through party organizations, releasing candidates from explicit or implied commitments to wealthy supporters. Although some Republicans were unhappy with the role of political action committees, most believed that PACs opened political participation to more players across the political spectrum.

The Republicans, like the Democrats, had less disinterested reasons for their preferred reforms. A system that gave more weight to individual donors and to large party contributions would, as we have noted, benefit them more than the Democrats. With a smaller base of strong partisans in the electorate, Republicans had to spend more to identify and persuade independents and weak Democrats to vote for them.

It was crucial that Republican challengers—particularly for House seats—should be able to match or exceed incumbent spending so that they could build recognition and make the case for voters to prefer them to incumbent Democrats. Otherwise, the Democratic hammerlock on the House of Representatives might continue indefinitely. It was sobering to Republicans that in 1988 their House leader, Robert Michel, had held his seat for thirty-two consecutive years but had never been in the majority party. The Republicans' inability to gain a majority for such a long period was a major stumbling block when they attempted to recruit ambitious and talented candidates for the House.

The GOP even had problems in keeping gifted officeholders from leaving their jobs. It was unthinkable that a Democratic heir apparent to an aging leader would quit the House to run for the Senate, but that was exactly what Mississippi Republican Trent Lott, second in line behind Robert Michel, chose to do in 1988.

When Congress returned after the 1988 elections, many members vowed to bring back campaign reform for another round. One change in the equation was the Republicans' newfound distaste, particularly among House members, for the PACs that, as we described earlier, ignored Republican appeals for more support. Still, most congressional observers believed that the partisan deadlock almost guaranteed that no major reform would take place. When asked about the probable outcome of a new reform effort, Democratic representative Al Swift of Washington State, a long-time participant in the campaign finance debate, responded: "If I tell you the truth, I'll be accused of declaring it dead before it starts. If I tell you otherwise, you'll think I'm a fool. It's going to be a very, very difficult process." [52]

As long as the major players have diametrically opposed views about the direction of revision in the campaign finance laws, change—if it comes at all—will probably be incremental at best, and it is extremely unlikely to give the parties a dominant role.[53]

## Ideology as a Vehicle for Party Coherence

If the party organizations are unlikely to get control over campaign money, is there some other function that parties could perform for candidates? A second possibility is that the party symbol could once again serve as a kind of shorthand cue to voters, signaling what the candidate's message is, in a way that would be to the advantage of the candidates. The message would be different and more powerful than in the past, because, thanks to technology, it would be a national message. If most candidates accepted the idea that the party symbol was of use to them personally and acted on that assumption by running as partisans, more policy content would be given to campaign debate and more coherence in government action would be produced on major issues, because candidates would see such a state of affairs as beneficial to their own electoral interests.

There are two circumstances in which candidates see the party symbol as a useful vehicle for their own campaigns and officeholding behavior. The first is when national debate over policy is phrased in terms of such sharply different alternatives that all politicians are virtually forced to choose between them. The second is when one party is such a clear favorite among voters that identification with it becomes a likely ticket to reelection. Let us look at the conditions that permit either of these circumstances to emerge and consider how likely either one is to produce a long-term tendency favoring stronger parties.

**Structured Policy Debate.**   Sea changes have regularly occurred in American politics about every forty years and have brought with them major realignments of party strength.[54] Jacksonian democracy, the Civil War and the Republican party's rise to power, the Industrial Revolution and McKinley's crushing of Bryan and the Democrats, and the Great Depression and Roosevelt's New Deal are the major landmarks. In each era the parties defined the terms of the national policy debate, and the one that won the debate emerged as the major party.

Two conditions were necessary for each of these realignments to occur. The first condition was a set of major issues on which there were two clear sides so that a meaningful debate could take place. The second was that there had to be a presidential candidate who would take a definite stand on one side of the debate and who had the vision and leadership qualities to make him the symbol of the debate. Andrew Jackson, Abraham Lincoln, and Franklin Roosevelt played major roles in winning the debate for their side; William Jennings Bryan played a major role in losing it for his.

In the 1960s another set of issues arose that could have produced a debate leading to another historical realignment. But the leaders were not there. Kennedy was assassinated. Johnson, with his call, "Come, let us reason together," preferred a consensus politics. Nixon gave up on converting Democrats, called for an "ideological majority" rather than leading his party, and was swept away by Watergate. Carter never decided between his instincts toward both fiscal conservatism and working-class populism. Then Ronald Reagan came to the presidency. Like Roosevelt, Reagan was elected primarily as a rejection of his predecessor, and he turned a negative mandate into a positive one.[55] His political dominance encouraged partisan ideological and policy coherence, as officeholders and their opponents measured whether it was to their electoral advantage to stand with him or against him.

**The Emergence of a New Republican Majority?**   The "Reagan effect," however, had only limited influence on the overall fortunes of the Republican party. Although the president remained very popular, even rebounding from the Iran-contra affair, his ability to extend his winning ways to his fellow partisans declined precipitously after the 1980 election. Reagan's 1984 coattails were extremely short, and, although Republican losses were held to a minimum in the 1982 midterm election, the party fared poorly, in historical context, in 1986 and 1988. George Bush's argument that he would carry on the Reagan legacy played some part in his being the first sitting vice president to ascend to the presidency in his own right since Martin Van Buren succeeded Andrew Jackson in 1836.[56] The public, however, did not choose to extend the mantle beyond the presidency.

Why did Reagan fail to consolidate a Republican majority in a potentially realigning era? The answer is that after the previous two realignments, in 1896 and 1932, nonpresidential candidates were dependent on the party symbol and organization. Lacking other ways to appeal to voters, candidates had to rely on the persuasiveness of the party's message—and hope it would carry them to victory. The majority party became a vast umbrella, a coat of many colors. The minority party became either a collection of "me toos," advocating little more than tinkering with the majority party agenda, or a reactionary remnant doomed to lose. Legislators were either insulated from presidential failures by the strongly partisan nature of their constituencies, or, if in the few marginal constituencies, they were at the mercy of the "surge and decline" of the president's fortunes.[57]

Unlike the politicians of 1896 and 1932, the politicians of today are not tied to their party or to its presidents in making their appeals. What President Reagan could accomplish in large measure was the elimination of the long-time Democratic advantage in partisan identifiers and a change in the issue agenda. When Democrats calculate how to fit in to this new state of affairs, though, they need have no worries about the symbolic baggage of their party affiliation. If Virginia voters could award a new Democratic senator 71 percent of the vote at the same time they were giving the Democratic presidential candidate 40 percent, or if North Dakotans could reelect a Democratic governor with 60 percent of the vote while giving his party's presidential candidate 43 percent, as both states did in 1988, the Democrats could win anywhere with convincing appeals. Unlike candidates in earlier realigning periods, candidates today can choose whether they wish to identify strongly with the party label and its presidential candidate. Strong candidates, not strong parties, produce the competitive political environment we now observe.

# The New American Political Party: The Party of Officeholders

The actors that comprise a political party vary depending upon which party role we look at. First, there are party identifiers, the voters who are disposed to favor candidates running with a particular party label. Then, there is the party organization, the men and women whose vocation or avocation is party work. Their job is to get candidates bearing their label nominated and elected to political office. Finally, there are the party's officeholders, whom we call the party in government. Most analyses of the political health of the American "parties," including our own to this point, define and appraise the parties in terms of the first two groups.

Looking at parties in terms of party identifiers and party organization, we find that the decline of the parties in the United States continues in many respects. But this view presents a puzzle well stated by one political scientist:

What then do we make of parties that win all the elections yet do not control their nominations, parties that take distinct policy positions yet whose leaders have little influence over their members, parties whose organizations have decomposed or atrophied, yet whose personnel and payrolls have blossomed, parties whose support by the electorate has declined yet which win more and more of the elections? [58]

To answer the question, we suggest a new and somewhat different look at the last element of the party triad, the party in government, or the party of officeholders and aspiring officeholders. Analysts of the party in government usually focus on its coherence as a *policymaking body*, looking at indices such as party unity on legislative votes. We propose to focus rather on the *electoral functions* of the party of officeholders. If the story of candidate behavior and officeholder behavior is always the story of what candidates believe will help them to win election, the question then is what resources do candidates find in the party in government that help them attain this end?

This is not to say that candidates have no goals but winning. They may seek power, influence, or policy ends, but as David Mayhew notes, winning election must be the "proximate," or immediate, goal.[59] None of the other goals can be pursued if the candidate is not elected. Since the government is organized as a partisan body and distributes more of the resources needed to obtain goals to the majority party, it is in the interest of all individual politicians that those carrying their party label win the majority of offices: "Enough must win . . . to enjoy the substantial status and enhanced opportunities to advance any shared policy preferences." [60] The party in government offers officeholders two principal electoral resources to enhance their individual and collaborative prospects: official resources and campaign money.

## Official Resources

In recent studies of officeholders, a dominant theme is the ability and propensity of incumbents to use official resources to advance their own careers and objectives. Richard Neustadt once observed that the president's greatest power is "the power to persuade." Newer studies focus on how contemporary presidents have augmented their official resources. With large White House staffs and more control over how the media present them, presidents have expanded their opportunities to be persuasive in setting the national agenda.[61] When incumbent presidents run for office, they typically use official resources in their campaigns, taking actions that benefit them electorally. The party's national committee becomes the presidential candidate's instrument, as George Bush demonstrated when he chose his campaign manager, Lee Atwater, to head the Republican National Committee in 1988. In earlier chapters we described how governors emulate these presidential behaviors.

Individual legislators are not as visible to the public as executive officeholders, so their use of official resources is less apparent. Politically aware citizens understand the electoral uses of the frank and the congressional district office, but students of the legislature are also interested in how the structure and substance of government have changed to accommodate the careers of political entrepreneurs. Legislative power traditionally belonged to a small group of senior members who held committee chairmanships and positions in the congressional leadership. But the advent of the entrepreneurial politician after the 1960s forced the party's congressional leadership to shift from a hierarchical style to a collaborative one. Not only did this shift enlarge the formal leadership, but it created informal opportunities for partisan colleagues to operate in ways that enhanced their electoral prospects.

**The Senate.** Between 1953 and 1972 the average number of senators who served on the four most prestigious or most powerful Senate committees was fifty. By 1984 the number had risen to seventy-nine—four out of five of the Senate's members. The leadership increased the number of seats on desirable panels and shrunk the number on less desirable ones or abolished them altogether. Junior senators, historically at a disadvantage in the biennial competition for good committee seats, were by the 1980s actually somewhat advantaged.[62] It was "the uncertain electoral environment of the 1970s" that "increased senators' incentives to take advantage of these opportunities."[63]

Even without relevant committee assignments, senators could use flexible parliamentary rules and rely on their access to the media to build a high profile on electorally useful issues. Texas's Phil Gramm, for example, was able to lead the effort to force Congress to reduce the federal budget deficit—a piece of legislation familiarly known as Gramm-Rudman—even though at the time he had never served on the Senate Budget Committee. A survey of the changing styles of senators concluded that the traditional restrained style was "not well suited to their reelection needs.... The increase in activism was the result."[64]

**The House.** Similar developments occurred in the House. Committees that dispensed tangible benefits to constituents grew larger between the late 1960s and the 1980s, while those that offered sparse benefits became smaller. During this period surveys that asked representatives to explain their committee preferences showed a strong upsurge in choices related to electoral concerns. So many subcommittee chairmanships were created in the 1970s that more than half the Democratic majority in the House came to hold some chairmanship.[65]

Opportunities for newly elected representatives to influence legislation after it left their committees were vastly enhanced, despite stricter parliamentary rules. In the 89th Congress of the mid-1960s, only 12 percent of the freshman members offered legislative amendments on the floor, and none succeeded in getting their changes included in the final bills. Not a single freshman was chosen to serve on the conference committees formed by representatives and senators to work out differences between the House and Senate versions of important legislation. Ten years later 86 percent of the freshmen offered at least one amendment on the House floor, and 68 percent had an amendment adopted. More than two-thirds served on conference committees.[66]

The formal partisan leadership in the House also expanded dramatically. In the 92d Congress of 1971-1972, there were 25 Democratic leadership positions in the House. By 1988 there were 114, occupied by ninety-eight different members. Most of the growth came from expanding the party whip organization (members responsible for ascertaining their colleagues' voting preferences on individual pieces of legislation). Congress's growing policy agenda and entrepreneurial members' independent voting stances made the larger whip organization necessary, but the many members who served in it also enhanced their opportunity to make their political and policy cases to the party's top House leaders—and to PACs, the media, and the public.[67]

Even the huge expansion of legislative and partisan leadership positions could not absorb all House members, but informal opportunities for influence and credit taking developed. To give members a chance to shape legislation and to claim credit for it, the parties organized partisan task forces to work on emerging issues such as arms control and international trade. Although the task forces were developed most fully by the majority Democrats, the Republican party's counterpart organizations gave Rep. Jack Kemp a platform to press for the landmark tax-reduction legislation known as Kemp-Roth. His plan became the centerpiece of the Reagan administration's early legislative triumphs, even though Kemp never served on the House's tax-writing committee. His stature rose to the point where he could become a serious presidential candidate in 1988. Although Kemp had never held a committee assignment that dealt with urban affairs, either, his novel ideas for improving housing and job creation led George Bush to name him secretary of Housing and Urban Development.

**Caucuses.** Enterprising legislators did not end their efforts to influence electorally useful policies through the formal and informal positions bestowed by the party leadership. Any group of members with shared interests could unite in informal caucuses. Many of these caucuses qualified as legislative service organizations (LSOs), which entitled them to staff and other official resources. When the 1960s began, there were only four such caucuses; by the 1980s there were almost a hundred.

Some of these caucuses represented intraparty factions. House members whose general policy orientation was to the left of the Democratic mainstream banded together in one of the first and most enduring of the caucuses, the Democratic Study Group. Moderate Republicans joined the Wednesday Group. Their more conservative opposite numbers could be found in the Conservative Democratic Forum and in the Republicans' Conservative Opportunity Society. Bipartisan and bicameral LSOs such as the Environmental and Energy Study Conference and the Arms Control and Foreign Policy Caucus permitted members from both parties and both congressional houses to explore major issues.

Other groups, including the Black Caucus, the Hispanic Caucus, and the Congressional Caucus for Women's Issues, reflected the policy concerns of important groups in the electorate. Regional problems gave rise to organizations such as the Northeast-Midwest Congressional Coalition. The interests of important constituents led members to join the Steel Caucus, the Footwear Caucus, the Travel and Tourism Caucus, and even the Mushroom Caucus. Most of the informal caucuses were established to influence the legislative agenda; coincidentally, they gave their leading members another base for influence and publicity.[68]

## Officeholders and Money

As we said earlier, until the last few decades state and local party organizations raised or brokered most campaign funds. Successful candidates now collect most of their campaign money from individuals and from political action committees, but the party in government provides three significant sources of campaign dollars: the congressional campaign committees, member PACs, and members' cash on hand.[69]

**Congressional Campaign Committees.** The largest amounts of money come from the oldest of these sources, the parties' House and Senate campaign committees, discussed in chapter 10. Studies of these committees often lump them together with the parties' national committees (the Democratic National Committee and the Republican National Committee), but they differ in a major way.

The RNC and the DNC are components of the parties' own, nongovernmental, organization. Although they are staffed by paid professionals, their top leadership is, at least nominally, selected by and responsible to the national committees' members—mostly nonoffice-holding citizens appointed by similar kinds of people on the state party committees. As we noted earlier in this chapter, the reality is that the president controls his party's national committee. Potential presidential candidates in the out-party jockey to elect a national party chair who is sympathetic to, or at least neutral toward, their presidential aspirations.

The congressional campaign committees, by contrast, have no members except legislative officeholders. The campaign committees' chairmen are chosen by legislators, from among themselves, in biennial elections that take place at the same time that officeholders choose their congressional party leaders. The leaders of the House campaign committees tend to be reelected year after year and to serve lengthy terms. Michigan representative Guy Vander Jagt has headed the National Republican Congressional Committee since 1975. California's Tony Coelho headed the Democratic Congressional Campaign Committee for six years before he was elected Democratic House whip after the 1986 elections. Arkansas's Beryl Anthony replaced Coelho and was reelected DCCC leader in 1988.

Campaign committee chairmen in the Senate serve for only one election cycle. In 1988 Sen. Don Nickles of Oklahoma replaced Minnesota's Rudy Boschwitz at the National Republican Senatorial Committee, and Louisiana's John Breaux succeeded George Mitchell of Maine at the Democratic Senatorial Campaign Committee. Each time the chairman changes at any of the four committees, substantial turnover occurs among the top staff. The new chairman has the prerogative to fill all major committee positions. In sum, unlike the parties' national committees, the congressional campaign committees are entirely creatures of the party in government.[70]

Before the 1970s the campaign committees raised insignificant amounts of money, compared to the state and local parties, and they usually contributed equal (and small) amounts to all incumbents. Rep. Michael Kirwan, for instance, who headed the DCCC during the 1960s, gave $500 to every Democratic House member up for reelection. When he died in 1970, he was replaced by Massachusetts representative Tip O'Neill. O'Neill was chairman in 1972, when many House Democrats feared being swept away in the Republican presidential landslide. His colleagues were grateful to O'Neill, who raised much more money than past committee chairmen. For the first time the campaign committee gave some money to promising challengers and provided modest campaign services such as limited polling. O'Neill was elected majority leader in 1972 and Speaker of the House in 1976. His service as DCCC chairman played some role in these successes, but when he became head of the campaign committee, he had already served nine terms in the

House. His ascension to Speaker of the House came primarily because he had followed the traditional route of seniority and had built a reputation as a skillful legislative craftsman.[71]

By the late 1970s, however, independent and entrepreneurial office-holders had taken over Congress. When officeholders chose their congressional leaders, seniority and legislative aptitude counted for less, and fund-raising abilities demonstrated at the campaign committees meant more, particularly on the Democratic side. In both houses of Congress, relatively junior members who had headed the campaign committees ran for important leadership posts and were able to defeat more senior members who were known not for fund raising but for the traditional legislative skills.

In 1986, when Democrats chose Tony Coelho as whip, he had served in Congress only eight years and had no legislative record to speak of. What he did have was six years of service as chairman of the DCCC. During this time he brought the House Democrats back from their 1980 debacle and turned the DCCC into an effective fund-raising and service machine. In his race for whip, Coelho easily defeated New York's Charles Rangel, who had twice as many years of service and was a senior member of the powerful House Ways and Means Committee. Rep. George Miller of California defended the Democrats' choice of the less legislatively distinguished Coelho as whip: "We gave him a charge.... He didn't have the opportunity to do policy. In fact, when he was here, we'd say 'Why aren't you in Omaha?' Or Albuquerque. Or wherever [raising money]. He wasn't supposed to be here." [72]

This pattern of giving more weight to fund-raising prowess than to legislative accomplishments in leadership races was repeated in 1988, when Democratic senators gathered after the election to choose a new majority leader. Their previous leader, West Virginia's Robert Byrd, had been chosen because of his legendary mastery of the Senate's compli-cated rules of procedure. One of the contestants, Daniel Inouye of Hawaii, was in the Byrd mold and was considered Byrd's heir apparent. Inouye was a senior member of the powerful Finance Committee, he had been in the Senate since 1962, and he was nationally known for his work on the special Senate panels that investigated both the Watergate and Iran-contra scandals. A second candidate, J. Bennett Johnston of Louisiana, was in his third Senate term and was acknowledged to be one of the Democrats' wiliest legislative strategists. The third candidate was Maine's George Mitchell. Although Mitchell also served on the Finance Committee, he did not enter the Senate until 1980. His main attributes for the leadership job were a pleasing television persona and the 1986 chairmanship of the DSCC, when he oversaw a record season of fund raising and the election of eleven new Democratic senators. With a strong base among the Democratic Senate class of 1986, Mitchell won on the first ballot.

**Member PACs.**   Most of the contestants for Democratic leadership positions also made liberal use of the second financial resource of the party in government, a personal PAC. Officeholders can establish nonconnected political action committees that can contribute to other candidates in the same way that interest groups do. All that is required of them is to find fifty contributors and to register the PAC with the Federal Election Commission.[73]

The first legislator to form a PAC was California representative Henry Waxman in 1978, when member PACs contributed the modest sum of $62,000 to their colleagues' campaigns. By October 1988 fifty PACs controlled by sitting members of Congress were registered with the Federal Election Commission. In the 1986 election cycle contributions from member PACs to candidates' campaigns reached almost $3.7 million, two-thirds of it flowing from Democratic officeholders to Democratic candidates. Almost all the contestants for the Democratic House whip and Senate majority leader positions in 1986 and 1988 established personal PACs and made sizable contributions from them. Before the whip race, Coelho's Valley Education Fund contributed $570,000 to 245 candidates during the 1986 cycle. Rangel reluctantly established a competitor PAC, but he managed to contribute less than half as much as Coelho to about half as many candidates.

Two of the majority leader contestants, Inouye and Johnston, formed PACs in 1987. By June 1988 the two PACs already had $376,000 to contribute, and both were expected to make the maximum allowable $5,000 contribution to each 1988 Democratic Senate candidate.[74] Most of the money collected by both PACs came from interests with legislative concerns that could be influenced by the senators through their committee chairmanships. Johnston had begun his fund-raising activities on behalf of his colleagues before the 1986 races, when he asked fifty business PACs for contributions to a dozen Democratic candidates, primarily challengers. He observed at the time: "They give the contributions to me and I give them to the other guys. It is very clear they are contributing to my leadership race."[75]

Although George Mitchell, who won the majority leadership contest, did not set up a PAC, he was equally effective in aiding his colleagues. To solicit donations for 1988 races, Mitchell continued to prevail on the contributors he had come to know during his DSCC chairmanship. He stopped raising money for his own 1988 Maine reelection contest in early 1987 and directed would-be financial supporters to his colleagues. Often he would receive the checks himself and send them to the grateful recipients.

The Republicans have had fewer leadership changes in recent years, but their 1984 contest for a new Senate majority leader was similar to that of the Democrats in 1988. The winner, Bob Dole, distributed more than $300,000 from his personal PAC, and his efforts were emulated by runner-up Ted Stevens. The third candidate, Richard Lugar, chaired the NRSC in that election cycle. Robert Michel, longtime Republican House leader, indicated after the 1988 election that personal PACs such as his would be used to supplement the cash and services provided by the NRCC.[76]

Almost all the other members of the leadership team in both parties who obtained their positions long ago or who had no contests also figure among the fifty members who have their own PACs. Most of the other legislators who control PACs either lost leadership contests (Rangel and Stevens), are prominent policy entrepreneurs (Henry Waxman), or use PACs as arms of legislative service organizations (Texas representative Charles Stenholm with his Conservative Democratic Forum PAC).

**Cash on Hand.** Disbursals from members' cash on hand are the final source of campaign money available from the party in government. We noted that California representative Henry Waxman created the first member PAC in 1978. The late representative Phillip Burton, who designed the Democrats' legendary gerrymander of California's congressional seats in 1980, innovated the use of cash on hand as a source of intramember contributions in congressional leadership races. Burton lost the majority leader contest to Jim Wright (now House Speaker) in 1976. Both Burton and Wright, along with another of the four chief contestants in the majority leader's race, made liberal use of cash-on-hand contributions to House Democrats that year.

Cash on hand, as we noted in chapter 4, has doubled as a source of federal campaign funds over the past decade, by 1986 amounting to more than a tenth of all congressional campaign expenditures. One reason that members with large amounts of cash on hand set up PACs is that the PAC permits them to make them larger contributions to individual candidates than they can disburse from cash on hand. (PACs permit a maximum contribution of $5,000 for each election, with no aggregate limit. From cash on hand the limit is a personal contribution of $1,000, with an aggregate limit of $25,000.)

# The Special Value of the Party in Government

What makes the resources of the party in government particularly valuable to officeholders is that there are only positive payoffs for those who dole out the resources and those who receive them. When candidates had to rely on the external party organizations to get them elected, they always feared that the state or local machine could "rotate" them out of office. Dependence on the patterns of party identification in a sometimes fickle electorate also bred insecurity.

But the partisan colleagues of officeholders in government, all of whom are seeking a partisan majority to advance their own ends, rarely betray them or withdraw their support. Nor do they reduce the legislative freedom of other officeholders in their party. Recipients of officeholders' resources are not required, or seldom even asked, to vote in a certain way on policy matters. They are asked only to win their own elections and so to contribute to the greater good of all the party's officeholders.[77]

Officeholders who control substantial resources have various personal goals. Some appear to be principally power seekers. A chief fund raiser for J. Bennett Johnston's PAC described its aims: "The goal is to make Bennett majority leader and not minority leader, and the way to do that is to elect Democrats." [78]

Others target their beneficence to those who also share their policy goals or who are positioned to advance them. Rep. Henry Waxman's PAC contributes particularly to other liberal Democrats; to fellow Democratic members of the Energy and Commerce Committee, which has jurisdiction over many of Waxman's special interests; and to California legislative candidates who can preserve the congressional district plan that keeps Waxman's hold on office secure (as well as the hold of several other representatives whose political careers he has mentored). Waxman describes his philosophy:

> One of the fundamental rules of my politics is there is no clear distinction between the political process and the legislative process. . . . It is important to get people into office to get things done I believe in. It's not enough just to make the most of the natural allies already there.[79]

The candidate-centered era has spawned a new electoral meaning of "party"—the party of officeholders and of office seekers. Presidents and governors control the national and state party committees. Legislators control the congressional and legislative campaign committees. A growing number of incumbents and aspirants for all these offices establish federal and state personal PACs and amass large amounts of cash on hand, which permits them to compete or cooperate as they individually prefer. For example, many North Carolina Republican congressional primaries have featured one candidate supported by the NRCC or NRSC and another supported by the Congressional Club, the personal PAC of Republican senator Jesse Helms.[80]

# Candidates, Parties, Campaigns, and American Democracy

Most analysts who have written about contemporary entrepreneurial politicians and their candidate-centered campaigns have not dealt with the role of the party in government as we have described it. Even those who have examined this other role still see only negative consequences in the decline of the political party as it is traditionally understood.

## Party Decline and Policy Dangers

The most widely accepted indictment of candidate-centered politics is that with the decline of the traditional parties, it is impossible for officeholders to make coherent policy or for voters to reward or punish those responsible for policy.[81] This argument asserts that entrepreneurially minded politicians may be locally "responsible" to their constituents when they fight for their share of government benefits, but they are nationally "irresponsible." The much-criticized federal budget deficit, for example, is attributed primarily to lawmakers' "easy" decisions to cut taxes and raise defense spending, while they are reluctant to make the "tough" decisions to cut federal domestic spending or raise taxes to pay for programs.

These politicians' lack of will is seen to stem from a concern about their careers. Without the protection of strong party identification among their constituents, officeholders' unpopular legislative votes can bring electoral defeat. Furthermore, the new campaign technology encourages candidates to make special-interest appeals. Candidates in close races have an incentive to promise something to every segment of their support coalitions—when computers can locate groups as narrow as middle-income black males, ages thirty to forty, who live in rental housing; when polls can discover what they want; and when direct mail and targeted media buys can reach them. And these candidates know that if they don't deliver on any promise, a challenger will probably remind voters the next time around.

Finally, proponents of this point of view argue that the fragmented power structure in Washington and in the state capitals also contributes to policy gridlock and immobilism. The fragmentation occurs on many levels. The individual officeholder has access to campaign resources and official resources; this independence enfeebles the authority of the party leadership and forces it to build new coalitions for each issue. In the House and Senate and in the state legislatures, presidents and governors are engaged in a constant and often losing battle to hold nominal partisan troops in line. In the federal and state capitals, leaders of the bicameral legislatures compete to be the primary shapers of important legislation, a kind of "cameralship" rather than partisanship.[82]

## Positive Aspects of Candidate-Centered Politics

These negative arguments have some merit. But there are also positive aspects to an individually centered system of campaigns and governance, and autonomous officeholders are developing strategies for governance appropriate to their new realities.

From an electoral point of view, the campaign funds dispensed by appendages of the party of officeholders are much more equitably distributed than those of their principal competitors—individual contributors and political action committees. The more PACs confine their contributions to incumbents, the more important are the legislative campaign committees as major sources of funds for challengers.

The incumbents most likely to pull in enormous sums from PACs—members of the leadership and of the prestige House and Senate committees—are increasingly recycling that money to challengers through their personal PACs and through disbursals of cash on hand.[83] This is another "everybody wins" strategy. Special-interest PACs improve their access to plead their cases. Incumbents help fellow partisans, who in turn can help advance the incumbents' own careers. Marginal incumbents and challengers have a new place to look to for assistance. Furthermore, challengers have no obligation to the special interests who originally contributed the money. State assembly majority leader Tom Loftus of Wisconsin, who heads a legislative campaign committee, colorfully describes the result of the new financing strategies: "A utility company gives a PAC check to a campaign committee consisting of me. I give it to someone who's in favor of socializing electricity." [84]

The negative effect that independent officeholders have on governance and policy coherence may be less clear than critics fear, and there may even be advantages to the current system. Those who look back on the "golden age," when strong state and local party organizations filled most political offices, often forget the dross of that era. Politics was a profession many entered because it provided a standard of living people could not achieve in private life. Some officeholders systematically looted public treasuries for their own enrichment or for that of their party organizations. Seniority protected powerful legislators who were so physically or mentally impaired that they were incapable of performing jobs they continued to hold. Many officeholders in one-party areas had no electoral competition, and they became lazy, arrogant, or corrupt. A "conservative coalition" of Republicans and southern Democrats torpedoed the policy objectives of many Democratic presidents.

In the contemporary era, on the other hand, the private economy offers many alternatives to public service, many of them with greater social status or financial reward. Those who are drawn to politics as a career more and more often are people with serious interests in public policy. Politicians have structured their environments in ways that advance their electoral prospects and also allow more of them to study policy alternatives seriously and to participate in policymaking. As Burdett Loomis said about these developments, "an institution that begins to work better for policy-oriented individuals may well work better for everyone." [85]

Officeholders also have less disinterested reasons to seek policies that are ultimately good for the public. With reelection more and more dependent on a personal vote rather than a partisan vote, the contemporary politician now sees each election as a job review by his employers. To perform their jobs well, public officeholders are dependent on many of their colleagues—including those across the aisle, across the street, and across town. Alan Ehrenhalt has described such legislative behavior: "On stage they are throwing things at each other and sword fights are going on. But behind the curtain there's basic cooperation going on. Otherwise there would be a huge embarrassment to all incumbents." [86]

Considering the extensive discussion of the awful policy consequences—immobilism, gridlock, stasis, particularistic legislation—that critics attribute to governance in a weak party era, it is instructive and perhaps surprising to look at the nation's public accomplishments since party decline became apparent in the 1960s. Since then the United States has withdrawn from a major war. Bipartisan congressional support has arisen for arms control and for foreign policy initiatives in Afghanistan, the Middle East, and southern Africa. The country survived the destruction of the traditional racial and sexual codes and achieved significant, if painful and incomplete, consensus on new ones. Congress accomplished landmark reforms of the tax and immigration laws. One political scientist therefore argues that still-gridlocked issues reflect a true lack of public consensus: "When reasonably broad agreement is reached on a course of action, the American system seems perfectly capable of coherent and expeditious responses, even on complex policy responses." [87] Another comments:

> Will policy . . . be less consistent or coherent than before? There is little reason to think so. . . . [The system] of the 1950s and 1960s, with its jurisdictional jealousies, awkward jurisdictional divisions and autonomous committee chairmen was hardly more capable of producing coherent policy. [88]

Perhaps without conscious design, American politicians have devised an ad hoc system of ways to take resolute policy action without encountering unacceptable electoral dangers. The common thread running through their activities is that all politicians can receive individual credit for actions the public is likely to favor and that blame cannot be attached to individual politicians when actions are necessary but likely to be controversial or unpopular.[89]

Examples abound in the 1980s. Democratic votes provided the margin of victory for President Reagan's popular tax cuts. The round of tax legislation that closed many loopholes and simplified rates was essentially a Democratic legislators' proposal, which Reagan embraced. The cosponsors of immigration reform were a Republican senator and a Democratic representative. The INF Treaty, which eliminated a whole class of nuclear missiles, received bipartisan support.

On the other hand, unpopular cuts in domestic programs were wrapped into omnibus budget reconciliation bills, continuing budget resolutions, and other complicated laws enabling politicians to avoid recorded votes on individual program cuts. Deficit-reduction legislation specified that if Congress could not reach agreement on the necessary cuts by a specified date, an anonymous government bureaucrat would do the job for them, automatically cutting most programs across the board. Federal legislators could even be absolved of perhaps their toughest vote—for raises in their own pay. An appointed commission made salary recommendations every four years; their recommendations could be rejected only by a special vote. If either house of Congress took no action, the pay raises would go through.

It is true that these actions were "irresponsible" in the sense that credit attached to all incumbents, while blame attached to none who could very easily be identified. In many cases, however, this anonymity enabled politicians to make some hard choices. The public seemed satisfied with the tradeoff, and voters reelected unprecedented numbers of incumbents.

At the close of the 1980s, Americans voted for another four years of divided government, as they had for most of the previous four decades. Their choice reflected an individualist, antiparty strain that runs deep in American culture. George Washington's farewell address warned against "the baneful effects of the spirit of party," which "distract the public councils and enfeeble the public administration." More than a century later, the Progressives put in place the chief instrument to destroy the party as an extragovernmental organization—the direct primary. Technological advances—television and the computer—completed the job.

When we look closely at candidate-centered politics, in which voters freely choose among individual candidates and in which individual officeholders must justify their records to voters, we find that its performance is not the nightmare critics paint. The direct communication between candidates and voters is only one aspect of a resurgence of direct democracy, in which voters do not see the need for parties as intermediaries.[90] If democracy is indeed "unthinkable save in terms of parties," the American parties of officeholders may be the most appropriate form for the current era.

# Notes

1. Quoted in *Congress Off the Record: The Candid Analyses of Seven Members*, ed. John F. Bibby (Washington, D.C.: American Enterprise Institute, 1983), 43.
2. James Bryce, *The American Commonwealth*, ed. Louis Hacker (1888; reprint, New York: Putnam, 1959), vol. 1, 119.
3. E. E. Schattschneider, *Party Government* (New York: Holt, Rinehart and Winston, 1942), 1.
4. Leon Epstein, "The Scholarly Commitment to Parties," in *Political Science: The State of the Discipline*, ed. Ada W. Finifter (Washington, D.C.: American Political Science Association, 1983), 128.
5. For representative discussions, see Samuel J. Eldersveld, *Political Parties in American Society* (New York: Basic Books, 1982), chapter 1; Martin P. Wattenberg, *The Decline of American Political Parties* (Cambridge, Mass.: Harvard University Press, 1984), 1-6.
6. Walter Dean Burnham, "Foreword," in Wattenberg, *Decline of American Political Parties*, xii.
7. Wattenberg, *Decline of American Political Parties*, 128. This argument is further discussed later in this chapter.
8. See Norman H. Nie, Sidney Verba, and John R. Petrocik, *The Changing American Voter* (Cambridge, Mass.: Harvard University Press, 1976).
9. Wattenberg, *Decline of American Political Parties*, 63; Larry J. Sabato, *The Party's Just Begun* (Glenview, Ill.: Scott, Foresman, 1988), 224, 225.
10. Larry J. Sabato, *PAC Power: Inside the World of the Political Action Committees* (New York: Norton, 1984), 163.
11. David E. Price, *Bringing Back the Parties* (Washington, D.C.: CQ Press, 1984), 25.
12. Epstein, "Scholarly Commitment to Parties," 142.
13. Sabato, *Party's Just Begun*, 207; Media General/Associated Press poll of 1,204 adults, April 29-May 8, 1988.
14. Democratic representative Thomas Foley, quoted in Austin Ranney, *The Referendum Device* (Washington, D.C.: American Enterprise Institute, 1981), 70.
15. Wattenberg, *Decline of American Political Parties*, 125. (Emphasis added.)
16. Burdett Loomis, *The New American Politician: Ambition, Entrepreneurship and the Changing Face of Political Life* (New York: Basic Books, 1988), is an extended study of the "new breed." An earlier important treatment is Robert Salisbury and Kenneth Shepsle, "U.S. Congressman and Enterprise," *Legislative Studies Quarterly* 6 (November 1981): 559-576.
17. *Congressional Quarterly Weekly Report*, September 13, 1986, 2135.
18. See the data on party cohesion in David W. Brady, Joseph Cooper, and Patricia A. Hurley, "The Decline of Party in the U.S. House of Represen-

tatives, 1887-1968," *Legislative Studies Quarterly* 4 (August 1979): 381-408; *Congressional Quarterly Weekly Report*, January 9, 1982, 61-64.

19. Epstein, "Scholarly Commitment to Parties," 147.
20. Gerald Pomper, "Impacts on the Political System," in *American Electoral Behavior*, ed. Samuel Kirkpatrick (Beverly Hills, Calif.: Sage, 1976), 137.
21. Gerald Pomper, *Party Renewal in America* (New York: Praeger, 1980), 15.
22. Wattenberg, *Decline of American Political Parties*, xvi.
23. Joseph Schlesinger, "The New American Political Party," *American Political Science Review* 79 (December 1985): 1152.
24. *National Journal*, December 3, 1988, 3097.
25. These data appear in Martin P. Wattenberg, "The Reagan Polarization Phenomenon and the Continued Downward Slide in Presidential Popularity," *American Politics Quarterly* 14 (July 1986): 219-246; Wattenberg, *Decline of American Political Parties*, xvii; John Kenneth White and Dwight L. Morris, "Shifting Coalitions in American Politics: The Changing Partisans," paper presented at the annual meeting of the American Political Science Association, Washington, D.C., August 30, 1984-September 3, 1984; the CBS News/*New York Times* polls of September 12-16 and November 8-14, 1984; and the ABC News/*Washington Post* poll of September 7-11, 1984.
26. White and Morris, "Shifting Coalitions," 5.
27. Transcribed remarks at the Roundtable on National Recruitment of Congressional Candidates: Trends and Consequences, annual meeting of the American Political Science Association, Washington, D.C., August 31, 1984.
28. Schlesinger, "New American Political Party," 1160.
29. For example, David E. Price, *Bringing Back the Parties;* Cornelius Cotter et al., *Party Organizations in American Politics* (New York: Praeger, 1984); Xandra Kayden and Eddie Mahe, *The Party Goes On* (New York: Basic Books, 1985); Paul S. Herrnson, *Party Campaigning in the 1980s* (Cambridge, Mass.: Harvard University Press, 1988).
30. *Congressional Quarterly Weekly Report*, November 19, 1988, 3334.
31. Calculated by *National Journal*, April 2, 1988, 873-899.
32. Schlesinger, "New American Political Party," 1168.
33. Gary C. Jacobson, "The Republican Advantage in Campaign Finance," in *The New Direction in American Politics*, ed. John Chubb and Paul Peterson (Washington, D.C.: Brookings Institution, 1985), 143-174; Sabato, *Party's Just Begun*, 99.
34. Carolyn Smith, ed., *The 84 Vote* (New York: ABC News, 1984), 43-44; George Gallop, Jr., "GOP Strength Declines," *Polling Report*, November 9, 1987, 2; George Gallup, Jr., and Alec Gallup, "Democratic Edge at 14 Points," *Polling Report*, August 22, 1988, 8; *New York Times*, November 10, 1988, B6.
35. Dee Allsop and Herbert F. Weisberg, "Measuring Change in Party Identification in an Election Campaign," *American Journal of Political Science* 32 (November 1988): 1014.
36. *Congressional Quarterly Weekly Report*, November 12, 1988, 3299, reviews state legislative results over the decade.
37. From transcribed remarks by Fred Asbell of the NRCC and Martin Franks of the DCCC at the Roundtable on National Recruitment of Congressional Candidates, August 31, 1984.
38. David Adamany, "Political Parties in the 1980s," in *Money and Politics in the United States*, ed. Michael J. Malbin (Chatham, N.J.: Chatham House, 1984), 111, 114.
39. Sabato, *PAC Power*, 46.

40. *Congressional Quarterly Weekly Report,* November 19, 1988, 3367.
41. *New York Times,* November 21, 1988, B17.
42. *Congressional Quarterly Weekly Report,* November 19, 1988, 3335.
43. "Universalistic" votes—those on which 90 percent of House members vote the same way—hovered at or above 30 percent of all roll calls between 1965 and 1980, a level unmatched in any prior congressional sessions since 1921. Melissa Collie, "Universalism and the Parties in the U.S. House of Representatives," *American Journal of Political Science* 32 (November 1988): 869.
44. *Congressional Quarterly Weekly Report,* November 19, 1988, 3335-3337.
45. *Congressional Quarterly Weekly Report,* January 16, 1988, 106.
46. Pomper, *Party Renewal in America,* 15-16.
47. "Principles of Strong Party Organization," position paper adopted by the Committee for Party Renewal, September 1, 1984; excerpts published in Committee for Party Renewal, "Policy Statement on the Role of State Parties," *P.S.* 21 (Summer 1988): 641-643, quote at 641.
48. Steven F. Stockmeyer, "Commentary," in *Parties, Interest Groups and Campaign Finance Laws,* ed. Michael J. Malbin (Washington, D.C.: American Enterprise Institute, 1980).
49. Frank J. Sorauf. *Money in American Elections* (Glenview, Ill.: Scott, Foresman, 1988), 334.
50. *Congressional Quarterly Weekly Report,* December 17, 1988, 3525.
51. Peter Lindstrom, *Congressional Operations: Congress Speaks—A Survey of the 100th Congress* (Washington, D.C.: Center for Responsive Politics, 1988), 80. The data in this paragraph come from this report, 13-20, 80-98.
52. *Congressional Quarterly Weekly Report,* December 17, 1988, 3529. A review of Byrd-Boren action and new proposals appears on 3525-3529.
53. For an extended discussion of this point and the further complications introduced by independent expenditures, unlimited personal spending by candidates, and constitutional issues, see Sabato, *PAC Power,* chapter 6.
54. Among the notable studies of realignment and realigning elections are James Sundquist, *Dynamics of the Party System,* rev. ed. (Washington, D.C.: Brookings Institution, 1983); V. O. Key, "A Theory of Critical Elections," *Journal of Politics* 17 (1955): 3-18; Walter Dean Burnham, *Critical Elections and the Mainsprings of American Politics* (New York: Norton, 1970); and Paul A. Beck, "A Socialization Theory of Partisan Realignment," in *The Politics of Future Citizens* (San Francisco: Jossey-Bass, 1974).
55. See the analysis in Gerald Pomper et al., *The Election of 1980* (Chatham, N.J.: Chatham House, 1981); Paul R. Abramson, John H. Aldrich, and David W. Rohde, *Change and Continuity in the 1980 Elections* (Washington, D.C.: CQ Press, 1982).
56. It should be noted that some vice presidents in earlier realigning eras ascended to the presidency upon the death of their predecessors and were then elected in their own right. They include William McKinley's vice president, Theodore Roosevelt, and Franklin Roosevelt's vice president, Harry Truman.
57. Angus Campbell, "Surge and Decline: A Study of Electoral Change," *Public Opinion Quarterly* 24 (1960): 397-418.
58. Joseph Schlesinger, "On the Theory of Party Organization," *Journal of Politics* 46 (May 1984): 371. In this article and in "The New American Political Party," 1152-1169, Schlesinger lays out a model of the American parties with some similarities to the model we present later in this chapter. The models differ critically, however, in their views of the party's organizational role.

For an extended discussion, see Barbara G. Salmore and Stephen A. Salmore, "Back to Basics: Party as Legislative Caucus," paper presented at the annual meeting of the Midwest Political Science Association, Chicago, Ill., April 9-12, 1987.

59. David Mayhew, *Congress: The Electoral Connection* (New Haven, Conn.: Yale University Press, 1974), 16.

60. Leon Epstein, *Political Parties in the American Mold* (Madison: University of Wisconsin Press, 1986), 6.

61. Richard E. Neustadt, *Presidential Power*, rev. ed. (New York: Wiley, 1980); Samuel Kernell, *Going Public: New Strategies of Presidential Leadership* (Washington, D.C.: CQ Press, 1986); Jeffrey Tulis, *The Rhetorical Presidency* (Princeton, N.J.: Princeton University Press, 1986); Barbara Hinckley, *The Symbolic Presidency: How Presidents Present Themselves to the Nation* (Chatham, N.J.: Chatham House, 1988).

62. These data appear in Barbara Sinclair, "The Distribution of Committee Positions in the U.S. Senate," *American Journal of Political Science* 32 (May 1988): 276-301.

63. Ibid., 298.

64. Barbara Sinclair, "Senate Styles and Senate Decision Making, 1955-1980," *Journal of Politics* 4 (November 1986): 903.

65. See Roger H. Davidson, "Congressional Committees as Moving Targets," *Legislative Studies Quarterly* 11 (February 1986): 19-33; Stephen S. Smith and Christopher J. Deering, "Changing Motives for Committee Preferences of New Members of the U.S. House," *Legislative Studies Quarterly* 8 (May 1983): 271-282.

66. Loomis, *New American Politician*, 40.

67. Ibid., 176.

68. This account of the development of the legislative service organizations draws heavily on Susan Webb Hammond et al., "Informal Congressional Caucuses and Agenda Setting," *Western Political Quarterly* 38 (December 1985): 583-605. See also Kernell, *Going Public*, 26-32.

69. This section concentrates on federal officeholders. See the account in chapter 10 of similar activities at the state level. Candidates' financial reliance on legislative campaign committees, the fund-raising prowess of the legislative leadership, and the need for leaders to be successful at fund raising to keep their positions has a longer history at the state level than in the federal capital. The Democratic assembly leadership in California, where extra-governmental party organizations were always weak, invented the idea of collaborative fund raising by the party in government in the early 1960s. Veterans of the California legislature later elected to the U.S. House first brought the practice to Washington.

70. See Herrnson, *Party Campaigning in the 1980s*, 40-44, for a discussion of the different perspectives of the party national committees and congressional committees.

71. See O'Neill's account of his career in Tip O'Neill with William Novak, *Man of the House: The Life and Political Times of Speaker Tip O'Neill* (New York: Random House, 1987).

72. Loomis, *New American Politician*, 220.

73. Much of the data on member PACs and their fund raising were collected by Ross K. Baker and appear in Baker, *The New Fat Cats: Members of Congress as Political Benefactors* (New York: Twentieth Century Fund, 1989).

74. *Congressional Quarterly Weekly Report*, October 8, 1988, 2775.

75. *New York Times,* August 12, 1986, A22.
76. Baker, *New Fat Cats,* chapter 2; Herrnson, *Party Campaigning in the 1980s,* 126-127; "Michel Has Designs on 1992," *National Journal,* December 17, 1988, 3194-3195.
77. Although there is the hope, of course, that beneficiaries will vote the "right way" in leadership contests, these internal congressional elections are by secret ballot, and many of those voting have received fund-raising help from more than one of the contestants.
78. *Congressional Quarterly Weekly Report,* October 8, 1988, 2779.
79. *Congressional Quarterly Weekly Report,* January 3, 1987, 18.
80. Michael Barone and Grant Ujifusa, *Almanac of American Politics 1988* (Washington, D.C.: National Journal, 1987), 874.
81. A growing literature on the left side of the political spectrum also argues that the traditional party organizations provided an important avenue, now missing and unreplaced, for the less wealthy to participate in politics and to influence the national agenda. This vacuum, they argue, is primarily responsible for lower voting turnout and feelings of political alienation. Representative works include Francis Fox Piven and Richard Cloward, *Why Americans Don't Vote* (New York: Pantheon, 1988); Thomas B. Edsall, *The New Politics of Inequality* (New York: Norton, 1984); Robert Kuttner, *The Life of the Party* (New York: Viking Penguin, 1987). However, careful empirical studies give, at best, very limited support to these arguments. See, for example, Raymond E. Wolfinger and Steven J. Greenstone, *Who Votes?* (New Haven, Conn.: Yale University Press, 1980); Ruy Teixeira, *Why Americans Don't Vote* (Westport, Conn.: Greenwood Press, 1987); Teixeira, "Will the Real Nonvoter Please Stand Up?" *Public Opinion* 11 (July-August, 1988): 41-44 ff.
82. Representative works making this argument include Bruce Cain et al., *The Personal Vote: Constituency Service and Electoral Independence* (Cambridge, Mass.: Harvard University Press, 1987); Gary Jacobson, *The Politics of Congressional Elections,* 2d ed. (Boston: Little, Brown, 1987); Sabato, *Party's Just Begun;* Alan Rosenthal, "If the Party's Over, Where's All that Noise Coming From?" *State Government* 57 (January 1984): 50-54.
83. See the data on member PAC donations to challengers in Baker, *New Fat Cats,* chapter 3; Clyde Wilcox, "Share the Wealth: Contributions by Congressional Incumbents to the Campaigns of Other Candidates," paper presented at the annual meeting of the American Political Science Association, Washington, D.C., September 1-4, 1988.
84. Quoted in Alan Rosenthal, ed., *The Governor and the Legislature: Eagleton's 1987 Symposium on the State of the States* (New Brunswick, N.J.: Eagleton Institute of Politics, 1988), 78-79.
85. Loomis, *New American Politician,* 227.
86. *Congressional Quarterly Weekly Report,* September 13, 1986.
87. Everett C. Ladd, "Party Reform and the Public Interest," in *Elections American Style,* ed. A. James Reichley (Washington, D.C.: Brookings Institution, 1987), 234.
88. Steven S. Smith, "New Patterns of Decision-Making in Congress," in *New Direction in American Politics,* ed. Chubb and Peterson, 233.
89. Paul Light makes a similar argument in his masterful account of the 1983 Social Security bailout, *Artful Work: The Politics of Social Security Reform* (New York: Random House, 1985).
90. The growing interest in direct democracy has produced several recent major publications. See, for example, David B. Magleby, *Direct Legislation: Voting on Ballot Propositions in the United States* (Baltimore: Johns Hopkins University

Press, 1984); Thomas E. Cronin, *Direct Democracy: The Politics of the Initiative, Referendum and Recall* (Cambridge, Mass.: Harvard University Press, 1989); Jeffrey F. Abramson et al., *The Electronic Commonwealth: The Impact of New Media Technologies upon Democratic Politics* (New York: Basic Books, 1988); Benjamin F. Barber, *Strong Democracy: Participatory Politics for a New Age* (Berkeley: University of California Press, 1984).

# Methodological Appendix

The data in this book come from three sources: the academic and popular literature, our own experiences as strategic participants or observers in a number of campaigns in several states, and structured personal interviews conducted by one or both of us. Most of the formal interviews were done when we were writing the first edition of this book. Although we interviewed or reinterviewed a number of people for the second edition (mostly for updating purposes), there were also, as we note in the preface, rich sources of published information to which we could turn that simply did not exist when we wrote the first edition.

These interviews ranged in length from one to four hours, and most have been preserved on tape. We requested that they be "on the record" and for attribution. In most but not all cases our subjects agreed. Our promise of confidentiality to some individuals or on some subjects has been preserved. Many respondents who are named have moved on to other positions; the job titles we attribute to them are those they held in the campaigns in question or at the time we interviewed them. All quotations in the text that are not footnoted come from our formal taped interviews. Aside from occasional minor editing to convert conversational English into intelligible written prose, the quotations come directly and without modification from transcriptions of the tapes.

We cannot count or formally list the many informal conversations with these interviewees and other participants or observers in campaigns with which we were centrally or peripherally involved, but these numerous encounters were also very significant in shaping our view of campaigns and in giving us the *verstehen* to write this book. In most of the campaigns we observed, including both Democratic and Republican ones, we were not neutral observers. Rather, in many cases, we were committed, paid participants. Because of our participant status, we had access to many aspects of a campaign that simply would not have been available to someone not completely trusted by the campaign.

We do not claim that our formal interviews constitute any sort of "scientific" sample of the campaigners' universe. Such a sample is probably impossible to construct in any case. As the text makes clear, however, the data are gathered from a broad spectrum. The positions our informants held varied enormously. The campaigns we describe and analyze include races for governorships, the state legislature, the House of Representatives, and the Senate. They include winners and losers, Democrats and Republicans, incumbents and challengers, and they span the country.

Generally, we saw our interviews as an opportunity to fill in gaps in our knowledge and sought out those who could do this. There seemed little point in asking busy people about things we already knew from the literature or from our own experience. The people we interviewed and the timing of the interviews were, of course, somewhat affected by events and "targets of opportunity." For the most part, however, they were connected to the stages of campaigns we describe in the book and to the corresponding stages of our research. Generally, campaign and party personnel were interviewed first, then polling and media consultants and reporters, and finally organizational personnel. As indicated, we went back a second time, and sometimes even more than that, to some very patient respondents who could advise us on multiple topics.

With this kind of research plan, there could not be a single formal questionnaire we could administer to everyone. We approached each interview with a list of questions, sometimes the same ones, and intensively instructed ourselves beforehand about the campaigns in which our respondents had participated. No one we approached declined to speak with us, although some were, at least in our judgment, more forthcoming than others. The interviews are almost exactly evenly divided between people we knew personally when we began and people we approached "cold" or with a recommendation from someone else we had interviewed. Whether we knew someone personally had almost no bearing on how "good" the interview turned out to be.

Our data also include confidential candidate polls, strategic memos, and similar materials supplied to us by their authors or their clients, generally with an assurance of confidentiality. Any scholar who has tried to obtain such material, even about a campaign long over, knows that there are few "state secrets" guarded so closely! We especially appreciate the trust respondents displayed in us by giving us access to these materials and permission to use them in some form. We are strongly convinced that our ability to obtain such material, and the almost uniformly high level of cooperation and friendly reception we received, stemmed from the respondents' knowledge that we have participated in campaigns—had "been there"—and were not merely students of them. The fact of that participation was much more important than which side we had supported in any given contest.

All the political advertising material we quote was broadcast. Some of it was supplied to us in the form of scripts or the original tape cassettes prepared for broadcast, and some of it was taped during air play. All of it is preserved in the original form in which we acquired it.

# Suggested Readings

## General

Agranoff, Robert. *The New Style in Election Campaigns*. rev. ed. Boston: Holbrook, 1976.

Greenfield, Jeff. *Running to Win*. New York: Simon and Schuster, 1980.

Hershey, Marjorie R. *The Making of Campaign Strategy*. Lexington, Mass.: Heath, 1974.

———. *Running for Office*. Chatham, N.J.: Chatham House, 1984.

Kelley, Stanley, Jr. *Professional Public Relations and Political Power*. Baltimore: Johns Hopkins University Press, 1956.

Kingdon, John W. *Candidates for Office: Beliefs and Strategies*. New York: Random House, 1968.

Leuthold, David A. *Electioneering in a Democracy*. New York: Wiley, 1968.

Mandel, Ruth B. *In the Running: The New Woman Candidate*. New York: Ticknor and Fields, 1981.

Nimmo, Dan, and Robert L. Savage. *Candidates and Their Images*. Santa Monica, Calif.: Goodyear, 1976.

## Voting Behavior

Burnham, Walter Dean. *Critical Elections and the Mainsprings of American Politics*. New York: Norton, 1970.

Campbell, Angus, Philip E. Converse, Warren E. Miller, and Donald E. Stokes. *The American Voter*. New York: Wiley, 1960.

Fiorina, Morris P. *Retrospective Voting in American National Elections*. New Haven, Conn.: Yale University Press, 1981.

Natchez, Peter B. *Images of Voting—Visions of Democracy*. New York: Basic Books, 1985.

Nie, Norman H., Sidney Verba, and John R. Petrocik. *The Changing American Voter*. Cambridge, Mass.: Harvard University Press, 1976.

Teixeira, Ruy. *Why Americans Don't Vote*. Westport, Conn.: Greenwood Press, 1987.

Wolfinger, Raymond E., and Steven J. Rosenstone. *Who Votes?* New Haven, Conn.: Yale University Press, 1980.

## Political Parties

Cotter, Cornelius P., James L. Gibson, John F. Bibby, and Robert Huckshorn. *Party Organizations in American Politics*. New York: Praeger, 1984.

Eldersveld, Samuel P. *Political Parties in American Society*. New York: Basic Books, 1982.

Epstein, Leon. *Political Parties in the American Mold*. Madison: University of Wisconsin Press, 1986.

Herrnson, Paul S. *Party Campaigning in the 1980s*. Cambridge, Mass.: Harvard University Press, 1988.

Kayden, Xandra, and Eddie Mahe, Jr. *The Party Goes On*. New York: Basic Books, 1985.

Ladd, Everett C., and Charles D. Hadley. *Transformations of the American Party System*. New York: Norton, 1975.

Mayhew, David. *Placing Parties in American Politics*. Princeton, N.J.: Princeton University Press, 1986.

Pomper, Gerald M., ed. *Party Renewal in America*. New York: Praeger, 1980.

Price, David E. *Bringing Back the Parties*. Washington, D.C.: CQ Press, 1984.

Sabato, Larry J. *The Party's Just Begun*. Glenview, Ill.: Scott, Foresman, 1988.

Sorauf, Frank J., and Paul Allen Beck. *Party Politics in America*. 6th ed. Glenview, Ill.: Scott, Foresman, 1988.

Sundquist, James L. *Dynamics of the Party System*. rev. ed. Washington, D.C.: Brookings Institution, 1983.

Wattenberg, Martin P. *The Decline of American Political Parties, 1952-1984*. Cambridge, Mass.: Harvard University Press, 1986.

## Presidential Campaigns

Asher, Herbert B. *Presidential Elections and American Voters*. 4th ed. Chicago: Dorsey, 1988.

Jamieson, Kathleen Hall. *Packaging the Presidency*. New York: Oxford University Press, 1984.

Kessel, John H. *Presidential Campaign Politics.* 3d ed. Chicago: Dorsey, 1988.

Polsby, Nelson R. *Consequences of Party Reform.* New York: Oxford University Press, 1983.

Ranney, Austin. *Curing the Mischiefs of Faction.* Berkeley: University of California Press, 1975.

Schramm, Martin. *The Great American Video Game: Presidential Politics in the Television Age.* New York: Morrow, 1987.

Wayne, Stephen J. *The Road to the White House.* 3d ed. New York: St. Martin's, 1988.

White, Theodore H. *America in Search of Itself: The Making of the President, 1956-1980.* New York: Harper and Row, 1982.

## Congressional Campaigns

Cain, Bruce E., John Ferejohn, and Morris P. Fiorina. *The Personal Vote: Constituency Service and Electoral Independence.* Cambridge, Mass.: Harvard University Press, 1987.

Clem, Alan L. *The Making of Congressmen: Seven Campaigns of 1974.* North Scituate, Mass.: Duxbury, 1976.

Fenno, Richard F., Jr. *Home Style: House Members in Their Districts.* Boston: Little, Brown, 1978.

_____. *The United States Senate: A Bicameral Perspective.* Washington, D.C.: American Enterprise Institute, 1982.

Fishel, Jeff. *Parties and Opposition: Congressional Challengers in American Politics.* New York: McKay, 1973.

Goldenberg, Edie N., and Michael W. Traugott. *Campaigning for Congress.* Washington, D.C.: CQ Press, 1984.

Jacobson, Gary C. *The Politics of Congressional Elections.* 2d ed. Boston: Little, Brown, 1987.

Jacobson, Gary C., and Samuel J. Kernell. *Strategy and Choice in Congressional Elections.* New Haven, Conn.: Yale University Press, 1981.

Loomis, Burdett. *The New American Politician.* New York: Basic Books, 1988.

Mann, Thomas E. *Unsafe at Any Margin: Interpreting Congressional Elections.* Washington, D.C.: American Enterprise Institute, 1982.

Mayhew, David R. *Congress: The Electoral Connection.* New Haven, Conn.: Yale University Press, 1974.

## State and Local Campaigns

Banfield, Edward C. *Big City Politics.* New York: Random House, 1966.

Gosnell, Harold F. *Machine Politics: Chicago Model.* 2d ed. Chicago:

University of Chicago Press, 1968.

Jewell, Malcolm E. *Parties and Primaries: Nominating State Governors*. New York: Praeger, 1984.

_____. *Representation in State Legislatures*. Lexington: University Press of Kentucky, 1982.

Jewell, Malcolm E., and David E. Olson. *Political Parties and Elections in the American States*. 3d ed. Chicago: Dorsey, 1988.

Rosenthal, Alan, and Maureen Moakley. *The Political Life of the American States*. New York: Praeger, 1984.

Smith, Thomas F. X. *The Poweriticians*. Secaucus, N.J.: Lyle Stuart, 1982.

Ware, Alan. *The Breakdown of Democratic Party Organization, 1940-1980*. Oxford: Clarendon Press, 1985.

Wilson, James Q. *The Amateur Democrat: Club Politics in Three Cities*. Chicago: University of Chicago Press, 1962.

## Campaign Management and Techniques

Asher, Herbert. *Polling and the Public*. Washington, D.C.: CQ Press, 1988.

Blumenthal, Sidney. *The Permanent Campaign: Inside the World of Elite Political Operatives*. Boston: Beacon Press, 1980.

Bruno, Jerry, and Jeff Greenfield. *The Advance Man*. New York: Morrow, 1971.

Godwin, Kenneth J. *One Billion Dollars of Influence: The Direct Marketing of Politics*. Chatham, N.J.: Chatham House, 1988.

Mauser, Gary A. *Political Marketing: An Approach to Campaign Strategy*. New York: Praeger, 1983.

Nimmo, Dan. *The Political Persuaders*. Englewood Cliffs, N.J.: Prentice-Hall, 1970.

Rosenbloom, David. *The Election Men*. New York: Quadrangle, 1973.

Sabato, Larry J. *The Rise of Political Consultants: New Ways of Winning Elections*. New York: Basic Books, 1981.

## Media

Broder, David. *Behind the Front Page*. New York: Simon and Schuster, 1987.

Clarke, Peter, and Susan H. Evans. *Covering Campaigns: Journalism in Congressional Elections*. Stanford, Calif.: Stanford University Press, 1983.

Diamond, Edwin, and Stephen Bates. *The Spot: The Rise of Political Advertising on Television*. Cambridge, Mass.: MIT Press, 1984.

Hess, Stephen. *The Ultimate Insiders*. Washington, D.C.: Brookings Institution, 1986.

Patterson, Thomas E. *The Mass Media Election: How Americans Choose Their President.* New York: Praeger, 1980.

Patterson, Thomas E., and Robert D. McClure. *The Unseeing Eye: The Myth of Television Power in National Elections.* New York: Putnam, 1976.

Press, Charles, and Kenneth Verburg. *American Politicians and Journalists.* Glenview, Ill.: Scott, Foresman, 1988.

Ranney, Austin. *Channels of Power: The Impact of Television on American Politics.* New York: Basic Books, 1983.

Vermeer, Jan Pons, ed. *Campaigns in the News: Mass Media and Congressional Elections.* Westport, Conn.: Greenwood Press, 1987.

## Campaign Finance

Alexander, Herbert E. *Financing Politics: Money, Elections and Political Reform.* 3d ed. Washington, D.C.: CQ Press, 1984.

Heard, Alexander. *The Costs of Democracy.* Chapel Hill: University of North Carolina Press, 1960.

Jackson, Brooks. *Honest Graft.* New York: Knopf, 1988.

Malbin, Michael J. *Money and Politics in the United States.* Chatham, N.J.: Chatham House, 1984.

_____. *Parties, Interest Groups and Campaign Finance Laws.* Washington, D.C.: American Enterprise Institute, 1980.

Overacker, Louise. *Money in Elections.* New York: Macmillan, 1932.

Sabato, Larry J. *PAC Power: Inside the World of the Political Action Committee.* New York: Norton, 1984.

Sorauf, Frank J. *Money in American Elections.* Glenview, Ill.: Scott, Foresman, 1988.

# Index